Critical Theory
and Educational Research

C.P. — Is there anything in this let
that challenges your
perceptions & experiences?

— What issues does it raise
for you?

— Is there anything you
disagree with?

— Can you relate CP to
anything you'd know
about CfE?

SUNY Series, Teacher Empowerment and School Reform

Peter L. McLaren and Henry A. Giroux, Editors

Critical Theory
and Educational Research

Edited by
Peter L. McLaren
and James M. Giarelli

State University of New York Press

The editors gratefully acknowledge the publishers of the *International Journal of Qualitative Studies in Education*, vol. 5, no. 1 (1992) for permission to reprint the Introduction and chapters 3, 6, 7, 10, 12, 13, and 15.

Published by
State University of New York Press, Albany

For information, address State University of New York Press,
State University Plaza, Albany, N.Y. 12246

Production by M. R. Mulholland
Marketing by Nancy Farrell

Library of Congress Cataloging-in-Publication Data

Critical theory and educational research / edited by Peter L. McLaren
and James M. Giarelli.
    p.   cm. — (SUNY series, teacher empowerment and school
reform)
    ISBN 0-7914-2367-0 (alk. paper). — ISBN 0-7914-2368-9 (pbk. :
alk. paper)
    1. Education—Research—Philosophy. 2. Critical theory.
I. McLaren, Peter, 1948-   . II. Giarelli, James M., 1950-
III. Series: Teacher empowerment and school reform.
LB1028C743 1995
370'.78—dc20   94-11201
                                                          CIP

10 9 8 7 6 5 4 3 2

Contents

Foreword

Sometimes a book serves as a "shot across the bow," a statement of some position that opens a line of debate, dialogue, and deliberation not entertained before. Other times, a book serves as the punctuation period, marking the culmination of a long debate with an integration and synthesis that stands as a definition for the immediate but indeterminate future. But still other times, books serve very different purposes than either the beginning or the end of an intellective sentence. Their purpose is the elaboration, enrichment, and refinement of a set of concepts, methods, skills, or streams of thought which have already been advanced. Critical Theory and Educational Research is just such a book.

Critical theory as a paradigm has been well accepted on the European continent for several decades, in part because of its historical roots in neo-Marxism. Neo-Marxism as a critical intellectual system never endured the political disfavor and ruin in Europe that it underwent in the United States during the McCarthy era. The continuity between neo-Marxism and the more critical poststructural and postmodern approaches and paradigms appears stronger in Europe than in the United States, and we are, after some decades, finally beginning to appreciate the strengths and contributions of criticalist theories (for there are several varieties) for educational research here.

Nevertheless, critical theories, unlike more conventional paradigms and models for research, are underexplored and only lightly elaborated, although the work of critical-theory scholars has virtually exploded in the past decades. The work of Gadamer, Habermas, the French poststructuralists and postmodernists, and the work of feminist scholars on this continent has lent weight and urgency to the our consideration of criticalist models. This book represents a further refinement of vital, pressing issues in the critical-theory arena.

By now the lexicon of critical language has become familiar to educational researchers. Lynda Stone, in Chapter 8, argues in fact that both the language, and by presumption, the positions of criticalist theorizers have been "coopted," so that a "theoretical conflation in the name of educational reform is rampant." Stone argues that "theory is indiscriminately appropriated and cited by theorists who are not themselves 'critical,' " intending to draw sharp distinctions between the criticalists and those who would simply borrow concepts in order to appear more theoretically advanced than they are. While there is no argument here that "reform" travels under many different passports, and that some of them represent the same systems which created the need for reform in the first place, it is, in my opinion, salutory that the language of the critical theorists is entering our discussions. Using the word "resistance" more often, for example, forces us to think about why and when and under what circumstances and more specifically how we might mount resistances to undemocratic practices in schooling. Prising terms like "oppression" and "historical structures" and "transformation" out of the closet and into mainstream language both legitimizes their consideration and at the same time, prompts their discussion in the arenas of research and teacher training as a matter of course. Terms like "difference" and "silence" and "voice" make us aware of differences and silences and voices our research has systematically ignored.

The cooptation that Stone decries may have negative consequences, but the positive effects of enlarging our vocabulary around issues of schooling, reform, and democracy seem to outweigh any disadvantages. It has been argued that one cannot "see" some phenomenon without a language to describe that thing. I would argue that the extension of our research lexicon permits us to engage a wider sphere of social dialogue and debate surrounding the forms and practices of education and by extension, educational research.

This book is a serious attempt to engage that debate, using serious, subtle, and enriching arguments to unpack our old assumptions: assumptions about the roles teachers play—and the roles that have been assigned to them—about the language we employ to enter the debate, about the ways in which we "name" and bracket "the other," about competing ideologies, about forms our research and texts might take, about our own roles as inquirers and ethnographers.

There is still much work to be done. Many issues remain incompletely explored. There is still no critical pedagogy in place, and we have only an unclear and inadequate idea of how to educate democratically. In higher education, we still do not know how to educate teachers for resistance and voice (especially since they themselves have come through systems of schooling that leave them unprepared for the exercise of constructive democracy, the dialectic of community involvement in the schools, or the leadership necessary for site-based management). We have only begun to uncover the forms and structures of oppression and violence that characterize American life, especially schooling. We have only imagined "communities of difference"; we don't yet know how to make them real entities, nor do we have much practice at living in them productively and with grace.

As a result, this book is a fertile "moment" in critical theory's history in this country. It is a comma between the beginning of a thought and its final form, the pause that permits possibilities to suggest themselves, that helps us think more richly and fully about what the end of the sentence might be, when critical theory's possibilities as a paradigm have been enfleshed and become mature. T.S. Eliot described this moment in "The Hollow Men" in 1925:

> Between the idea
> And the reality
> Between the motion
> And the act...
>
> Between the conception
> And the creation...

This book represents that "between" moment, the moment when all possibilities become potential realities, when the words are wrapped around ideas that can be made more than theory or potential. It deserves to be read because it moves us toward the dark and unexplored corners of our social processes, illuminating structures long hidden, forces unrecognized, and power struggles embedded in our discourses on schooling and democracy. It is a pause in the sentences of educational research well worth reflection; its meaning is a potentially new ending to the sentence itself.

Yvonna S. Lincoln
Texas A & M University

Foreword

I would like to speak to the contributions this anthology makes for our understanding of critical traditions of educational research. I initially focus on the importance of critical traditions as a visioning and revisioning of the relations of power in society. Then, I consider the broadening horizons that represent critical traditions within this book. The diverse representations are not viewed as an evolutionary development of disciplinary strategies. Rather, the distinctions among critical traditions embody fundamental battles about how power should be understood and political projects formed. I discuss these battles in a context where domination of Hegelian-Marxist conceptions of power and progress are being challenged. I also consider the different horizons to "critical" as responses to the conditions of modernity (or postmodernity) in which we live. Finally, the distinctions about critical traditions are viewed as existing within the markets and social spaces of intellectuals. The collection of essays in this book engages us in a reflexivity about these multiple layers of educational research.

The significance of this book lies in its oppositional stances toward the relation of state, power, and the knowledge of social science. Since the late ninettenth century in Europe and the United States, state's tactics of reform are heavily dependent on the social and later educational sciences (Wittrock, Wagner, and Wollmann 1991; Popkewitz 1991; esp. chap. 3 and 6). Expert-mediated knowledges were concerned with the "social question": how to bring about social amelioration through institutional formations and social policy. The invention of statistics, for example, was tied to the modern state's efforts to govern all aspects of the health, labor, and education of its citizens. Statistics, French for state arithmetics (in Britain, it was called political arithmetic), involved both qualitative and quantitative information.

The problem of governing in the social sciences involved two layers of social life. There were the tasks to promote social welfare through the reform of social institutions. Governing also was produced through the effects of the social sciences. Certain categories, differentiations, and distinctions were authorized whose effects were to normalize the relations of individuals to their social world. That is, a whole complex of institutions, procedures, analyses and reflections, and tactics emerged in the equations of power. These complexes inscribed certain dispositions toward the things in the world and the "self" as a productive element in that world. Foucault (1979) called the strategies of individualization that deployed power as a "governmentality."

Most training in social science posits a historical amnesia to the power relations inscribed in disciplinary knowledge. Sciences are made to seem a product of internal disciplinary developments of its methods and knowledge. Techniques of research are privileged as the demarcations of science. Graduate studies in statistics and field approaches are classified as research methods courses rather than as procedures that are given differential meanings within intellectual traditions or paradigms.

This book challenges that amnesia by enabling us to understand the complex relations that give structure to research procedures: how procedures receive meaning and coherence as they interrelate with the concepts, assumptions, and visions that underlie research. As Ladwig (1992) has argued, privileging techniques as either qualitative or qualitative are political strategies within the academy that have little to do with what is critical in research.

Critical traditions seek to reverse the historical amnesia by making the inscribed power relation as the problem of research. This occurs in two ways. One, there is a disciplined questioning of the subtle and indirect ways in which power works. The modes of inquiry are to understand how institutional patterns constrain and restrain the development of democratic conditions. Foci in contemporary critical social sciences give attention to how the marginization of people is constructed, the various forms in which power operates, and "of interrogating anew the evidence and the postulates, of shaking up habits, ways of acting and thinking, of dispelling commonplace beliefs, of taking a new measure of rules and institutions" (Foucault 1991, 11–12). Two, critical traditions are concerned with the implications of intellectual work to the formation of political projects.

But once we look more closely at the various meanings tied to critical traditions, we realize that there are few foundations on which to stand; the very constructions of critical research continually shift in the power relations in which they are reconstituted. From feminist studies to discursive examinations of working-class males and ideological critiques of pedagogical practices, this book provides a vivid understanding of the complex foci and discursive styles by which the patterns of social and self regulation occur. But these chapters are more than discussions of difference: they illustrate major challenges to the interpretative lenses and political projects that have guided left studies in the United States during the past few decades. The introduction of postmodern, (including poststructural, postcolonial, and feminist discourses) contest certain "foundations" of critical traditions inherited from nineteeth-century European forbearers. At the same time, the chapters provide examples of how this heritage, such as in current Marxist thought, has been transformed to maintain viability in changing conditions.

The relation of knowledge and power can be explored by focusing on certain continuities and discontinuities in current critical scholarship. The continuities can be considered in relation to Enlightenment commitments to social progress. The discontinuities among critical traditions can be explored through examining the assumptions about change and power. (I explore these distinctions more fully in Popkewitz, 1991). The distinctions can be located further through relating epistemological concerns of critical traditions to its particular historical conjuncture and the social space of critical research in the academy.

At a certain level, the different critical strategies in this book have certain continuities. The continuities reside, in part, with commitments to the Enlightenment project. One of the hallmarks of European and United States critical traditions has been a commitment to reason and rationality as providing for social betterment. The postmodern literatures, I believe, maintain the general commitments of the Enlightenment to working toward a better world, and share the concern of previous critical traditions with problems of power. But the postmodern practices entail repositioning the development of a normative basis for change and the reconstruction of political projects in which the critical researcher participates.

The discontinuities among critical traditions can be explored initially by focusing on questions about the epistemology of change. We can identify certain Marxist-Hegelian notions as dominating disciplinary debates about social change. Embedded in Western critical traditions is a nineteenth-century hope about progress: that intellectual work would provide the universal norms and direction to social change. This hope was carried into assumptions about contradictions and dialectics; that is, it was assumed that critical interrogations of social conditions will produce from identifying the contradictions a new synthesis. The synthesis identifies the strategies to overcome the repressive elements of society. The progress was global and redemptive. With some hesitations and some dissent, the Marxist-Hegelian position presupposed an evolutionary progress as critical researchers provided the normative boundaries to guide and direct change. The presupposition of progress in research is so deeply ingrained that it has been unquestioned.

Epistemologically, we can speak about the variations of post-modern literature as creating a rupture to the prevailing view of progress through at least three strategies. These are:

1. Change is viewed through examining ruptures and breaks in the epistemes; rules and standards of discursive practices that organize social life rather than through locating change in the sets of actors who rule or are ruled. This move has been called "the decentering of the subject" or the "linguistic turn" of social theory. Research focuses on how actors (and the subject) are linguistically con-structed *in* power relations and institutional formations. Language becomes part of the material practices in which subjectivity is formed.

    Without going too far from postmodern thought, we can liken the concern with ruptures to Thomas Kuhn's (1970) consideration of change in science as the break between normal and revolutionary science. Kuhn's approach to science is philosophically idealist but related to a long-standing European tradition in the history and philosophy of science to understand the problem of change (See, e.g., Tiles 1984). Postmodern literatures make this interest in breaks as a material interest through studies of power and social practices. Riley (1988), for example, draws this tradition into feminist literature through examining how the concept of woman varies historically. She argues that there is no "essential" concept of woman but one that is historically formed in power relations. She locates the different concepts of woman that are inscribed in social relations over time—and how the changing concepts construct the "subject" of woman in patterns of power that normalize gender relations.

    The notion of break or rupture brackets the *theoretical presuppositions* of progress in critical scholarship; but does not preclude moral/political considerations about possibility and moral issues, as I discuss later when considering the pragmatism of postmodernism. The revisioning of intellectual work relates to the formation of political projects as belonging in a democratic arena in which the intellectual has no authoritative position—rejecting the concept of the intellectual as what Pierre Bourdieu calls the modern "oracle." In Riley and Kuhn, for example, there is no teleology, no epistemological privileging of progress in research practices. The conception of rupture points to how power is inscribed in different conceptions of reason at different times; but intellectual work, being of the past and without teleologies, can make no a priori claim about the future.

2. Postmodern studies shift from a repressive concept of power to the deployments of power; that is, to the ways in which power works its way through the social body to produce social practices and identity. In general, we can understand previous critical traditions as interested in how groupings of actors limit or are limited by existing structuring patterns of society. Power is located in how particular classes in society establish their will as the will of the whole. The postmodern study of the deployment of power entails a revisioning of power through a Nietzschean conception of the will to know. For example, Spivak (1992) discusses the problem of translation as a political practice that entails multiple deployments of power. Focusing on the translations of women's texts from the Third World into English, Spivak argues that the specific actors who write these texts cannot be designated by their subject positions of gender or class. She explores how the discursive practices normalize and produce identities through a pervasive orientalism that obliterates Third World specificity and denies cultural citizenship. For Spivak, the concern is not to find the origin of repressive practices through a structural analysis that identifies class location; the concern is how sense is made to produce identities that inscribe power relations. Central to the study of power is how particular forms of reason about the "self" and a "common-sense" are inscribing; and thus providing conditions by which power relations can be ruptured as different possibilities from oppressive conditions are sought.

3. Earlier, I spoke of a Hegelian-Marxist tradition of a global and redemptive change. The normative boundaries to guide and direct change are defined a priori and through intellectual work. That tradition is spoken to in this book. At the same time, there are countertraditions which articulate a revitalized pragmatism in social theory. The relation of pragmatism to critical educational research has been best argued by Cherryholmes (1992). He maintains that there are certain "contiguent foundations" toward normative goals when seeking change, but that these goals are always contingently organized as people work toward findings solutions to their pressing problems. Political strategies are worked out through problem-solving techniques that echo Dewey's view that problems are not solved but merely give way to other ones; denaturalizing any immanent notion of progress. This pragmatism is found in the sociology of Pierre Bourdieu and the historical philosophy of Michel Foucault and Denise Riley.

I draw once more on Michel Foucault to illustrate a pragmatic notion of progress and agency that is different from previous critical traditions. In talking about his experiences in Tunisia during its revolution against colonialism, Foucault (1991) made the distinction between how "theories" (and theorists) can be progressive and how political practices can be progressive. The revolution was, he said, the result of the

> intolerable nature of certain conditions produced by capitalism, colonialism and neocolonialism. In struggle of this kind, the question of direct, existential, I should say physical commitment was implied immediately. Finally, the theoretical Marxist preparation offered to Tunisian students was not very indepth; nor was it developed very deeply. The real debate among them, on the choices of strategy and tactics, on what to do, did not involve a detailed analysis of the various Marxist ideological tendencies. It was something else entirely. And that led me to believe that without a doubt the role of political ideology, or of a political perception of the world, was indispensable to the goal of setting off the struggle; on the other hand, I could see that the precision of theory, its scientific character, was an entirely secondary question that functioned in the debates more as the means of deception than as truthful, correct, and proper criterion of conduct. (137)

In certain criticism of postmodernism/feminism arguments, the pragmatism is defined as relativistic. One can read the charges of relativism as having little to do with the lack of commitments or a normative-political position as the above statements would indicate. Rather, the concern of relativism is an attempts of critics to privilege their perspectives whose absence is defined as relativist and thereby worthless and not competent.[1]

A scaffolding occurs as we connect the different assumptions of postmodernism—change as ruptures, power as deployments, and a pragmatic conception of norms. These shifts in epistemological assumptions do not forsake the Enlightenment belief in reason, progress, and human agency; or in the importance of critique. Nor is there a denial of agency, that is, the ability of people to intervene in the world and struggle for better possibilities. But for certain of the postmodern writers, the inscribing of agency is in the pragmatic search for solutions in which norms of a just society are conditionally accepted and revised through the ongoing constructions of social practices; it is not by a prior theorizing of the subject and positing of practices as a precondition of progress itself.

At this point, we need to move from an epistemological discussion to the historical juncture in which the critical traditions are being reconstituted.[2] Intellectual traditions always exist within a dual space of disciplinary and moral/political fields (Bourdieu 1991). We can treat the struggles about critical research in this book as part of the conditions in which intellectuals practice their craft. With the challenges posed by postmodern literatures, we can also find important modifications in Marxist thought to respond to its social conditions, what Hall (1986) called Marxism "without guarantees." The various interpretations to critical research, then, are not only about what knowledge is to be valued; the stances toward research "tell" of the social relations and conditions of power in which critical traditions are formed.

In part, the differences can be understood through the political failures of the strategies of critical traditions from the 1960s through the 1980s. One can point to the aftermath of the 1968 crises in the United State, Europe, colonial revolutions in Africa, and more recently, the upheavals in Eastern Europe, as producing different strategies of political engagement as questions about democracy, possibility, and oppression were altered.

The differences in interpretative patterns are also part of trans-formations in the arenas of economy, culture, politics, and economics. In the past decades there have been shifts in the structural relations in which we act and locate our "selves" in those worlds (See, e.g., Boyer 1989, Giddens 1990). These shifts are signaled not only in intellectual life but in the larger political body. It is exemplified in the discussions about the transitions to a "post-fordist" economy, in changes in the arts and architecture, as well as the movement in the United States from the ideological politics of Bush that saw the world in unified oppositions to the pragmatic strategies for social change of Clinton.

The conjuncture of the different social moments involve a reconstitution of the patterns of social regulation and power that are not adequately accounted for through the previous forms of critical interpretation. There has been a tendency to undertheorize the productive relations of power/knowledge as well as to mistake structural logic for a logic of practice; for example, stipulating structural categories such as gender and class in an additive manner without explaining how these subjects are themselves constructed over time to produce power relations. As a response to various criticism, different strategies of interpretation and political practices have been generated. In light of current challenges, for example, we have witnessed an important rethinking of cultural Marxism (See, e.g., Hall 1986, among others). At the same time, the "identity politics" of certain feminist scholarship and anticolonial movements within the United States have refocused the notion of power to consider how the "self" is historically constructed, normalized, and disciplined. One can compare, for example, the differentiated implications for political practice that are embodied in the "identity politics" of postmodern feminisms from the structural priorities given as issues of class, race, gender are taken up in cultural Marxisms (see, e.g., Barrett 1992).

If the social conditions and political projects in contemporary life have changed, the different constructions of "critical" in this book are not "merely" descriptive differences about how to express realities but embody those power relations themselves. The various discursive practices that name critical research are different interpretative responses to grasp the phenomena *and*, at the same time, are a part of the social relations by which coherence, legitimacy, and possibility are constructed. Further, we can understand the arguments about postmodernisms, cultural Marxisms, feminisms, and other critical traditions as struggles among critical traditions about how to articulate and constitute the political projects of our social life.

Now, it would be easy if we could talk about intellectual work as being formed around purely analytic distinctions that demarcate different intellectual traditions, but the logic of arguments are often blurred and with multiple boundaries. As with the events of the world, intellectual distinctions and differentiations are pragmatically organized. The essays in this book interrelate Marxist discourses about reproduction/production of the past two decades with the current postmodern/feminist discussions about the role of discourse, the relation of power/knowledge and the construction of identity. Words like ideology, empowerment, discourse, power/knowledge, identity, marginality, and voice—words that draw from Marxist, feminist, and postmodernist discourses—coexist in an uneasy truce as various researchers align themselves with various political projects that are part of a mostly American discursive landscape. Conceptions of breaks in power relations are positioned with beliefs about emancipation and an evolutionary progress that relate to prior "modernist" commitments, which positions the expert as the oracle in service of the democratic ideal.

My final comment is related to the social space of academic community. When I read the general literature in social theory, it is morally charged about who "owns" the correct stances to "critical."

Underlying the moral charges are political strategies of academics. The politics are never articulated as such but cast in noble terms about who has the best paths toward salvation, although that salvation is through secular practices of research.

While the constructions of critical discourses are important in larger political struggles, these debates are also struggles about who has authority within markets of the academy and its social spaces. I refer to a notion of power that concerns the relative resources available as researchers construct visions and practices about "others," such as teachers. Here, I borrow from Pierre Bourdieu (1988) in thinking of educational research as a series of objective practices by which the problems and forms of argument in social science are institutionally located within social networks. The critical traditions exist within a social field of different groupings of academics who struggle to define the ordering principles that are to be considered as authoritative.

The political strategies of reactions and counterreactions are strong. From the "old" left are calls to reject postmodernism; in some instances as authoritative and totalitarian, and in other instances, as nihilistic and relativistic—arguments that make strong rhetorical claims but are contradictory in conclusions. John Clark (1991), a cultural Marxist from Britain, observed that when he read his first postmodern article, it produced "intense emotional reaction and an immense physical discomfort" (177)—not realizing that his statement itself draws attention to a major contribution of postmodern literature, namely on how power is inscribed in will, desire and the body.

"Postmodern" writers are not shy in their utterances about what are adequate epistemologies and political projects of intellectuals. They argue that changing social conditions of power require different sets of problems and epistemilogies. They also view much of the criticism directed toward postmodernism as a part of the tyranny of left structural intellectuals. Judith Butler (1992), a feminist philosopher, argues that structural categories of gender (and race and class) cannot be assumed as given, but are themselves categories that are historically constructed within power relations. (This stance, as can be inferred from the way in which I have pursued the argument about the different positions of critical research, is also close to mine.) The refusal of certain intellectual traditions to problematize their foundational categories, she continues, produces an authoritarianism that allows no political opposition to its intellectual position and "becomes an authoritarian ruse by which political conflict over the status of the subject is summarily silenced" (Butler 1992, 4).

The multiple layers of this book—its reflections on the epistemological, historical, and academic fields—constitute its most significant contribution. Its chapters enable us to grasp the battles about what knowledge is most important and who is to be authorized to speak about those visions and the revisioning of social life. It travels beyond the confines of an American discourse to consider an international range of arguments about critical research. As the "Quarrel between the Ancients and the Moderns" was a monument to both a rupture and continuity in the sixteenth century, so too, the debates about modernism, cultural Marxism, postmodernism, poststructuralism, and feminisms in this book can be read as a monument, in Foucault's sense, to changes in the historical and social relations of intellectual production.

The contribution of this book is that it enables us to understand those stakes. My interest here is not to claim that postmodernism supersedes modernism, an unusual claim that characterizes a period prior to its historical development. Rather, my purpose is to consider the intellectual struggles about what is "critical" as occurring within a social field whose constructions "tell" of the social relations in which critical thought is formed. The terrains staked out are not only linguistic; the struggles are about the different location of the work of intellectuals in the construction of the political.

Thomas S. Popkewitz

Notes

1. I appreciate Lynn Fendler's help in clarifying this rhetorical move in the debates about Marxist/postmodern scholarship.

2. I explore these conditions to understand the intellectual resurrection of Vygotsky and Dewey in U.S. educational psychology and studies of didactics (see Popkewitz, in press).

References

Barrett, M. 1992. "Words and Things: Materialism and Method in Contemporary Feminist Analysis." *Destabilizing Theory, contemporary Feminist Debates*, ed. M. Barrett and A. Phillips. Stanford: Stanford University Press. Pp. 201–219.

Bourdieu, P. 1988. *Homo Academicvs*. (Trans. P. Collier). Stanford: Stanford University Press.

———. 1991. *Language and Symbolic Power*. Ed. J. Thompson, trans. G. Raymond and M. Adamson. Cambridge: Harvard University Press.

Boyer, R. 1989. The Capital Labor Relations in OECD Countries: From the Fordist 'Golden Age' to Contrasted National Trajectories." in *Capital Labor Relations*, ed. J. Schor. In progress.

Butler, J. 1992. "Contingent Foundations: Feminism and the Question of 'Postmodernism' " in *Feminists theorize the political*, ed. Butler and J. Scott. New York: Routledge. Pp. 3–21.

Cherryholmes, Cleo H. 1992. "Notes on Pragmatism and Scientific Realism." *Educational Researcher* 21(6): 13–17

Clarke, J. 1991. *New Times and Old Enemies. Essays on Cultural Studies and America*. London: HarperCollins.

Foucault, M. 1977. Govermentality. *Ideology and Consciousness*, 6, 5–22

———. 1991. *Remarks on Marx: Conversations with Duccio Trombadori*. Trans. R. J. Goldstein and J. Cascaito. New York: Semiotext(e), Columbia University Press.

Giddens, A. 1990. *The Consequences of Modernity*. Stanford: Stanford University Press.

Hall, S. 1986. "The Problem of Ideology—Marxism without Guarantees." *Journal of Communication Inquiry* 10(2): 28–43.

Kuhn, T. 1970. *The Structure of Scientific Revolutions*. 2d ed. Chicago: University of Chicago Press.

Ladwig, J. 1992. "A Theory of Methodology for the Sociology of School Knowledge." Ph.D. diss., University of Wisconsin-Madison.

Popkewitz, T. 1991. *A Political Sociology of Educational Reform: Power/Knowledge in Teaching*, Teacher Education, and Research, New York: Teachers College Press.

———. In press. "Systems of Ideas in Social Spaces: Postmodernism Conditions, and Cultures/History in a Vygotskian Psychology." In *Cultural and Historical Theory of 1. Vygotsky: The Past, the Present, and the Future*, ed., V. Rubstov. Russian Academy of Educational Sciences.

Riley, D. 1988. *"Am I that Name?" Feminism and the Category of 'Women' in History*. Minneapolis: University of Minnesota Press.

Spivak, G. 1992. "The Politics of Translation." *Destabilizing Theory. Contemporary Feminist Debates*, ed. M. Barrett and A. Phillips. Stanford: Stanford University Press. Pp. 177–200.

Tiles, M. 1984. *Bachelard: Science and Objectivity.* Cambridge: Cambridge University Press.

Wittrock, B., P. Wagner, and H. Wollmann. 1991. "Social Science and the Modern State: Policy, Knowledge and Political Institutions in Western Europe and the United States." In *Social Sciences and Modern States: National Experiences and Theoretical Crossroads,* ed. B. Wittrock, P. Wagner, and H. Wollman. Cambridge: Cambridge University Press. Pp. 28–85.

Introduction:
Critical Theory and Educational Research*

The malaise of the Left is that the old is dying but the new cannot yet be born. We are searching for a new political language. We can imagine it resounding in our ears. But it is not yet on the tips of our tongues. Embarking on this search is risky. But it is inescapable.

> — Beatrice Campbell, et al., "Manifesto for New Times:
> Realignment of Politics" (1990)

As the history of Orientalist education demonstrates, a curriculum may incorporate the systems of learning of a subordinate population and still be an instrument of hegemonic activity....Until curriculum is studied less as a receptacle of texts than as activity, that is to say, as a vehicle of acquiring and exercising power, descriptions of curricular content in terms of their expression of universal values on the one hand, or pluralistic, secular identifies on the other are insufficient signifiers of their historical realities.

> — Gauri Viswanathan, *Masks of Conquest* (1989)

The promise and justification of science and social science have always been linked to their capacity to join theory and warranted knowledge to enlightenment and the liberation of the individual and society. The classical Enlightenment conception of scientific inquiry, though deeply flawed by historical biases, arose in direct opposition to certain moral and political ideas, such as dogmatism, authoritarianism, and centralized power, and in support of other moral and political ideas, such as rationality, freedom, and democracy. However, in the modern transmogrification of scientific inquiry into positivism, these latter ideals have been rendered officially meaningless and denied their validity by methodological prohibitions against evaluative statements in scientific inquiry. The consequence has been that positivistic science undermines its own origins in the Enlightenment ideal; thus positivism cannot fulfill its scientific or social purpose.

In recent years, many scholars in the humanities and social sciences have pursued alternative forms of research, truer in their fundamental epistemological, ontological, and ethical assumptions to the Enlightenment ideal, under the rubric of interpretive or qualitative inquiry. Although there is much to commend in the centrality this multiplicity of approaches gives to questions of meaning, intersubjectivity, and the social construction of knowledge, a nagging paradox persists. If interpretive research argues that it gives richer, thicker, more meaningful descriptions of the world than positivism, but cannot evaluate these descriptions, then it collides with the positivist separation of knowledge and value. If truth is interpretation and all interpretations are equally coherent within a given system, the capacity to make judgments about the relative merits of different systems becomes problematic. Richard Bernstein (1976) argues that when we talk about structures in the social world, we must attend to the fact that these structures reflect different interests and that these differences are not arbitrary, but rather are based on concrete social groupings that contain power to shape social structure, meaning, and typification differentially. The "pluralism" of the interpretive, qualitative researcher masks the fact that some versions of social reality are thought to be and are enforced as being more legitimate than others for reasons having nothing to do with their truth, beauty, or goodness. Thus, although the interpretive researcher may offer "new and improved" descriptions, or interpretations, of social reality, the methodological and ontological prohibitions against evaluating these interpretations results in a mimicry of positivism. As Bernstein writes, "It is not the business of philosophy to 'award prizes,' but it is indeed the business of philosophy and genuine theory to provide the basis for critical evaluation of the forms of life" (74).

Critical theory is, at its center, an effort to join empirical investigation, the task of interpretation, and a critique of this reality. Its purpose is to reassert the basic aim of the Enlightenment ideal of inquiry; to improve human existence by viewing knowledge for its emancipatory or repressive potential. In this way, a standard of judgment and value becomes possible. Like interpretivism, critical theory holds that knowledge is socially constructed, contextual, and dependent on interpretation. In contrast to interpretivists, critical theorists see a need and a basis for forming and understanding hierarchies of contexts and types of knowledge and evaluating them for their possibilities of contributing to progressive material and symbolic emancipation. Of course, this does not settle the debate. What kinds of knowledge best serve human emancipation? However, unlike positivism and interpretivism, mainstream quantitative and qualitative approaches, critical theory puts this problem at the core of inquiry.

The chapters of this book, though differing in many ways, all attempt to go beyond the qualitative and share an interest in examining the practical and theoretical problems related to the central aims of a critical theory of social inquiry. This collection has been assembled in order to further unpack contemporary debates within critical social theory and to tease out some of their implications for educational research and practice. As cultural workers currently residing in the United States, we find this a particularly pressing agenda, given the vitriolic character of the debates on education that have followed in the wake of what is currently being described as the crisis of schooling. Our primary concern in putting together this book has been to provide a conceptual and political ground from which to launch a politics of refusal against the concerted attacks by neoconservatives on what is perceived as the "political correctness" of the "leftist academy."

In the United States, educators who work in the public schools and the universities are currently witnessing a well-orchestrated frontal assault on efforts by progressive educators to make race, class, and gender issues central to educational research. That this is occurring at a time when race relations in the universities and throughout the larger society are in sharp decline, and racial incidents across the country are on the rise is particularly telling. The new left literacies that have been influenced by continental social theories, feminist social theories, and critical social theories in their many forms (e.g., postmodernist, postcolonialist, poststructuralist) are being attacked by conservative critics for being a subversion of the political neutrality and ideological disinterestedness that they claim the enterprise of education is all about. Of course, the real fear here is that the call among critical social theorists to rewrite the cultural, political, and social codes and privileging norms of the dominant society will threaten the linguistic, academic, and racial borders currently in place. There is also a concern among mainstream educators that the burgeoning interest in critical social theory may replace those Western forms of intellectual authority that are most in harmony with their own status as Mandarin metropolitan intellectuals. The recent debate over "political correctness" in the American academy is largely a reaction against the transdisciplinary character of much of what is occurring in recent literary theory and the social sciences and its capacity to reterritorialize the structures of academic discourse to the disadvantage of colonialist and neocolonialist species of intellectual labor. Interest in new forms of scholarship such as poststructuralism, feminist theory, deconstruction and postcolonialist criticism is being met by conservatives with the admonition that much of it translates pedagogically into forms of political indoctrination and leftist academic terrorism. This book challenges such an interpretation.

Another serious concern in putting together this book is to address what appears to be an increasing trend among leftist educators in the United States to retreat into the language of "plainspeak." There is growing evidence that a new species on anti-intellectualism is afoot that has affected both left and right curricular and pedagogical practice. As far as the leftist agenda is concerned, it appears to be transforming itself into a catch-all radicalism that dresses its dissent in the romantic anticapitalist-activist garb of the grassroots union organizer. Paulo Freire has referred to this as "basism." This is not to disparage the importance of community activism or direct political intervention at local, state, or federal levels; rather, it is to call attention to the current retreat from theory and the assault on educational ideas that do more than make simplistic appeals to common sense, union-style politics, and the supposedly self-evident truths of personal experience (Giroux and McLaren, 1992). Although it is certainly true, notes Larry Grossberg (1988), that the critical labor of intellectual life does not guarantee a progressive politics or form of political intervention, and that critical discourses are both constrained and empowered by their conditions and modes of production (i.e., access to specialized vocabularies, sites of intellectual production and distribution), this does not exclude the fact that intellectual life can have transformative social and political effects. Tony Bennett (1990) defends the production of an oppositional space within the educational system in a way that captures the dilemma we have attempted to sketch out above. He writes that

> Work in educational institutions, which involve extended populations for increasingly lengthy periods of their life cycles, is in no way to be downgraded or regarded as less vital politically than the attempt to produce new collective forms of cultural association with which criticism might engage. Politically committed teachers face enough discouragement without the added suggestion that the "real work" lies elsewhere. Before we all abandon the education system and set up camp in the counter-public sphere, a little head counting would do no harm. There is little doubt that, if the numbers reached by radical critical practices in the two spheres were weighed in the balance, the scales would tip decisively in favour of the former. Nor is there any doubt that, without the sustenance provided by the contradictory spaces within the educational system, the institutions comprising the counter-public sphere would have a hard

time of it: put simply, socialist and feminist publishing houses, radical theatre groups, and so on are massively dependent on the sales and audiences generated, in part, by the contradictory critical spaces that have been won within the education system. (239)

The project underlying this text can also be seen as a means of rethinking cultural assimilation and neo-colonialism—a conservative agenda in which differences are perceived as a threat to what is labeled as Western Culture and the significance of Greek and Roman antiquity. The concept of difference is crucial to educational practice, especially as it relates to recognizing how identity, subjectivity, and "otherness" are shaped. One important task is to acknowledge the historical and social situatedness of the discourses that frame and "colonize" our experiences and *locate* ourselves *in* our experiences. But schooling is also about forms of ethical address (Giroux 1992)—that is, about the relationships that we construct between ourselves and others (McLaren, in press). In other words, the process of becoming schooled is always already implicated in the borders that distinguish "us" from "them."

When we say that schooling constructs borders, we mean that it enables and/or constrains relations of power (both discursive and extradiscursive) and that these relations not only influence cognitive capacities but also speak to the way in which power is inscribed in the body, culture, space, and subjectivity. What does it mean to create a research practice and pedagogy as a language and practice of difference? First, it means rethinking research and pedagogical practices as the creation of multi-accentual meaning as distinct from a monolithic, totalizing, and premature closure on meaning. A language and practice of difference does not suggest that diversity in and of itself is necessarily progressive, but it does suggest that school curricula should be organized in ways that enable students to make judgments about difference, that is, about how society is historically and socially constructed both within and outside a politics of diversity and how existing social practices within the various public spheres are implicated in relations of equality and justice as well as how they structure inequalities around racism, sexism, homophobia, violence, exclusion and other forms of oppression. Second, it suggests that students need to cross over into different zones of cultural diversity in order to rethink the relationship of self and society, of self and other, and to deepen society's moral vision and political imagination. Further, a language and practice of difference raises the questions of how the categories of race, class and gender, sexual orientation, and other differences are shaped within the margins and center of society and how students can engage the relationships among history, culture, and language as a way of reclaiming power and identity (McLaren 1993).

The language and practice of difference to which we refer is built on the concept of border identity and the development of a politics of location as border-crossers (Giroux 1992). The politics of difference that undergirds this critical perspective examines how differences rearticulate and reshape identity such that identities are transformed and in some instances broken down, but are never lost. That is, they are identities immersed not in a centrist politics of consensus that leaves individuals to function as obeisant servants of the state, but rather in a politics of location that invites individuals to be reshapers of history. The diversity and difference we are describing is radically distinct from the liberal pluralism of consensus; it is more in keeping with Mikhail Bakhtin's conception of social and ethnic diversity. This distinction has been captured by Robert Stam (1991):

> In counterdistinction to a liberal discourse of tolerance, [Bakhtin] sees all utterance and discourse in relation to the deforming effects of social power. Second, Bakhtin does not preach a pseudo-equality of viewpoints; his sympathies, rather, go clearly to the nonofficial viewpoint, to the marginalized, the oppressed, the peripheralized. Third, whereas pluralism is grudgingly accretive—it benevolently allows another voice to add itself to the mainstream ("to those who have yet to share the benefits of the American dream" in the formulaic discourse of the politicians)—Bakhtin's view is polyphonic and celebratory. A Bakhtinian approach thinks "from the margins," seeing Native Americans, African Americans and Hispanics, for example, not as interest groups to be added on to a pre-existing pluralism, but rather as being at the very core of the American experience from the beginning, each offering an invaluable "dialogical angle" on the national experience. Fourth, a Bakhtinian approach recognizes an epistemological advantage on the part of those who are oppressed and therefore bicultural. The oppressed, because they are obliged by circumstances and the imperatives of survival to know both the dominant and marginal culture, are ideally placed to deconstruct the mystifications of the dominant group. Fifth, Bakhtinian dialogism is reciprocal, not unilateral; any act of verbal or cultural exchange leaves both interlocutors changed. (259–60)

Bakhtin's perspective on difference bears much in common with Chandra Mohanty's (1989–90) notion that difference cannot be formulated as simple negotiation among culturally diverse groups against a backdrop of presumed cultural homogeneity. Difference is the recognition that knowledges are forged in histories that are riven with differentially constituted relations of power; that is, knowledges, subjectivities, and social practices are forged within "asymmetrical and incommensurate cultural spheres" (181).

The perspectives of Bakhtin and Mohanty offer educators a common ground for challenging the categorical function of pedagogy and research as it is currently understood and practiced. This ground also can set the stage for overcoming the relentless and incorrigible despair that have been generated by current political realities and utopian possibilities. It is first and foremost a call for solidarity over consensus and for constructing a preferential option for the peripheralized and the dispossessed. It follows Slavoj Žižek's (1990) insight that when we negate the Other, we are also externalizing our autonegativity and self-hindrance. We therefore need to think of social and educational reform as a chain of equivalences that are *always open and incomplete*. As a practice that enables us to "refuse to narrativise our work in ways which reinscribe the absolute hierarchies of modernist epistemologies" (Grossberg 1988, 68), critical pedagogy stands in opposition to Habermas's ideal speech situation as a model for noncoercive communication (See McLaren herein). Žižek, for instance, has drawn attention to the fetishistic logic of Jürgen Habermas's position on the "ideal speech situation." He claims that it actually masks an acknowledgment of the limitations of the signifying field. For instance, he notes that "The way Habermas formulates the 'ideal speech situation' already betrays its status as fetish; 'ideal speech situation' is something which, as soon as we engage in communication, is 'simultaneously denied and laid claim to', i.e. we must presuppose the ideal of an unbroken communication to be already realized, even though we know simultaneously that this cannot be the case" (259).

The postmodern/postcolonial pedagogical and research practices that we envision reject an impartial universal absolutism or foundationalism in favor of an engaged and dialogical pluralism. However, we recognize Zygmunt Bauman's (1987) claim that a danger exists in moving from an impartial universal absolutism of foundationalism to a "multiple absolutism" within a pluralist worldview of local narratives (129). We agree that local, partial, and contingent discourses must prevent their localized character from becoming colonized by an incipient absolutism, but this need not lead to the abandonment of a search for community. The fact that we cannot rely on absolutist referents from the standpoint of either a modernist universalism or a local or "militant" particularism (the metalanguages of structuralism or poststructuralism) need not discourage educators from inventing themselves according to a provisional external ideal or from recognizing that there is no "truth about truth"; rather, inspiration can be drawn from the realization that identity need not be fixed in advance by internal necessity or as a function of race, class, or gender construction, but can be forged anew by exercising our sociological imagination and building new social spaces, an "arch of social dreaming," that will encourage students to contest the debilitating limitations of "mono-logical" thought.

The problem of binary thinking that informs logocentric discourse has been discussed at length by thinkers as diverse as Nietzsche, Benita Parry, and Michel Pêcheux and is worth summarizing. In his *Genealogy of Morals*, Nietzsche discusses the revolt of the slave against the master. His perspectivist account locates the discourse of the master in terms of the evaluative polarity of the existing antonymic pairs "good" and "bad" (Nietzsche 1967; Redding 1990). The noble is the measure of all that is "good," whereas his "other," the slave, is the measure of all that is "bad." But as Paul Redding (1990) notes, when the slave conceives of the master as "the evil enemy," he or she reactively inverts the evaluative polarity of the good/bad couplet, leaving the original pattern of indexicality intact. That is, the indexical "center" is still the way of life of the noble speaker. The slave's actions are determined from the perspective of the noble since the slave has no means of encoding any other way of life except from the perspective of the master and there is no opportunity to make "action-guiding" judgments of one's own. All that the slaves can do is reverse the evaluative polarity of the existing antonymic pairs. In this regard, Steven Connor (1989) notes that in its defense of the colonized and marginalized, critical theory must be "prepared to surrender its sense of its own territorial right to codify and manage the margins, determining the conditions under which speech from the margins is possible." This must be done in order to avoid what Connor calls the "romance of the marginal" that leads to "a Manichean universe of absolute opposites which is barely responsive to the actual complexities and overdeterminations of the situation under consideration" (236).

Michel Pêcheux has constructed a useful typology for understanding how discourses are engaged by various groups in contemporary social life. To *identify* with a discourse means that a group lies within the terms generated by the discourse; to *counter-identify* with a discourse means living within its governing structure of ideas but to reverse its terms; to *disidentify* with a discourse means going beyond the structure of oppositions and sanctioned negations that it supplies. Part of what we mean by a politics and pedagogy of difference is captured by Pêcheux's notion of disidentification. To disidentify means to deny the very frames of references that split off the marginalized from the dominators and to create, in pedagogical terms, new vocabularies of resistance that do not separate pedagogy from gender politics, values from aesthetics, pedagogy from power (see McLaren, 1993; Connor 1989).

In Benita Parry's terms (1987), a critical practice must do more than repossess "the signifying function appropriated by colonialist representation" or demystify or deform the rhetorical devices that "organize colonialism's discursive field." Rather, the founding concepts of colonialism's "received narratives" and the "monolithic figures and stereotypes of colonialist representations" must be refused. For Parry, resistance must include a critique of imperialism that does not treat race, class, ethnicity, gender, and sexuality as identical forms of oppression and that enables counterdiscourses to develop that are able to displace imperialism's dominant system of knowledge (28).

While the construction of disidentificatory discourses seems the most urgent option for critical educators, there is a danger in the possible abandonment of a universal application of the principles of freedom and justice in an attempt to get outside the metanarratives of value and morality. We need, in other words, to ground our theory of resistance (counterhegemony) as we struggle to negotiate among competing discourses and among multiple centers of identity. We court disaster unless we realize that totality and universality should not be rejected outright, but only when they are used unjustly and oppressively as global, all-encompassing, and all-embracing warrants for thought and action in order to secure an oppressive regime of truth. This is why the development of counterpublic spheres should not just occur in spaces outside and in opposition to the state (Bennett 1990), but also within the spaces of contradiction that exist in the larger social order. A politics of difference needs to sustain, develop, and exploit "the multiple contradictions generated within state bureaucracies" (239). In order to be able to appropriate the possibilities generated by these contradictions, we need to have a moral, ethical, and political ground— albeit a provisional one—from which to negotiate among multiple interests. Unless we have some provisional narrative of liberation, we can easily and unknowingly establish pedagogies and research practices that fall prey to the very error that critical educators seek to correct, that duplicate the original silencing of the Other, that replicate the concepts and systems of power they seek to revoke, that relegitimate the very terms they seek to reject.

That is, by repudiating domination without at the same time establishing some ethical bearings for a transcultural struggle for freedom, critical pedagogy and research practices could recover such domination in different forms. The pedagogies and research practices that both carry and are carried by this vision need not be so strategically pure that they checkmate mechanisms of oppression in every instance; rather they offer oppositional spaces for students to take up identificatory subject positions that speak to stategies and tactics of liberation and politically empowering forms of address and social practices. We need to ask these questions: Are our pedagogies and research practices built upon a normative backdrop that privileges Eurocentric and patriarchal representations and interests? Are our multicultural and feminist pedagogies and research practices mortgaged to theoretical formulations that, however deconstructed, still reaffirm the primacy of Western individualism, patriarchy, and class privilege?

As the work of Paulo Freire makes clear, a postcolonial pedagogy and politics of research must always be tied conceptually, politically, and ethically to a larger pedagogy of liberation (McLaren and Leonard, 1993; McLaren and Lankshear, 1994). In this context, resistance to domination and oppression must consist of more than a reactive transvaluation of dominant forms of knowledge and social practices— more than moral injunctions against dominant evaluative judgments and cultural forms. As long as resistance is reactive it positions itself as "other-centered" discourse (Redding 1990). Within a larger pedagogy of liberation, resistance must be an active, and not a reactive, transvaluation of dominant perspectives in order for it to constitute a project of possibility. It must be active if it is to generate new "action-guiding" perspectives that can allow cultural workers to escape the still invisible logic of domination that continues to underwrite many anticolonialist struggles and resistances.

In our attempts to understand the Other we do not need to take shelter in a universal citadel that houses Eurocentric, patriarchal, and colonialist narratives—one that stands above the messy terrain of textual, cultural, and geopolitical specificity or that removes us from the daily concrete struggles that characterize contemporary social life. However, as critical educators we do need to accept the responsibility that comes with giving the world meaning and for providing spaces for subjects to understand the literalness of the reality in which their subjectivities are inscribed, the contexts through which such a reality is articulated, and experiences which are imbricated in contradictory, complex, and changing vectors of power. We need oppositional pedagogical and research spaces for upsetting the grudging banality of mainstream educational encounters and for producing alternate subject positions informed by provisional and collective visions about what might constitute the public good.

We must be aware of the controlling cultural mode of our own research and pedagogies and the ways, often multifarious and unwitting, in which our students and our relationship to them become artifacts of the epistemes that shape the direction of our theorizing. We need to follow Edward Said (1983) in condemning the endless celebration of difference and otherness in a manner that smothers the connections between the construction and legitimation of discourses of the center and margins and the construction of empire. We must refuse, as well, textualism's failure to situate adequately discourses in relationships of power and hierarchies of domination. In addition, we need to eschew what Gayatri Spivak calls "reverse ethnocentrism" that, according to Robert Young (1990), evokes the nativist position "through a nostalgia for a lost or repressed culture [that idealizes] the possibility of that lost origin being recoverable in all its former plenitude without allowing for the fact that the figure of the lost origin, the 'other' that the colonizer has repressed, has itself been constructed in terms of the colonizer's own self-image" (168). With this perspective in mind, it is important that the postcolonial educator not fall into the trap, mentioned by Kwame Anthony Appiah (1991), of unwittingly joining a *comprador* intelligentsia of Western-trained intellectuals who "mediate the trade in cultural commodities of world capitalism at the periphery"—who posit unitary cultures of difference over against a monolithic West— that is, who essentialize and romanticize difference and simply recode the other in another story of neocolonialism (348). The latter amounts to little more than education as the seduction of the West.

Paulo Freire's experience of exile from his native Brasil—his "borrowed reality of exile," as he puts it—and his work in literacy campaigns throughout the world (Brazil prior to 1964, Chile, Nicaragua, Guinea-Bissau, São Tome, Cabo Verde, Principe, and Tanzania) has taught us something about the process of colonization. It has taught us that there are specific and distinctive reading practices for making sense of the world, and although these are not homogeneous, they possess a definite geopolitical and discursive locus. One such locus is the physical border that separates one nation from another and the discursive borders-within-borders that demarcate those privileged zones in which identities are differentially inscribed. Such dominant practices for reading the word and the world are to a large extent tied to the struggle for and the decline of empire—and to the ways in which the marginalized, the peripheralized, and the oppressed have attempted to resist reading practices that have been imposed by colonizer nations.

Perhaps the similarity that exists between European and American machineries of domination and structures of economic and political power—what Gilles Deleuze and Felix Guattari would call "forms of capture"—and the apparent freedoms enjoyed at the level of the popular can be accounted for by the fact that capitalism is essentially an axiomatic system based on the exchange and circulation of money. As a formal system that is immanent to social life in so far as it requires the routine exchange of equivalences rather than the adherence to any particular values, it can allow for multiple forms of desire and expression without fear or threat to its operation (Patton 1988, 92–93). Yet at the same time capitalism requires specific modes of yearning, specific structures of desire, specific sites of investment, and a specific politics of feeling in order to secure its goals—in order to make sure that individuals are reproduced as consuming subjects. It has additionally struck us that the attempt to impose a "new world order" by empires of the center is not necessarily tied to a coalition of armies, but can be secured, perhaps even more effectively, through the hyperreality of signs and images that are used by the mass-media empires of multinational corporations to market national identity and to assimilate differences under the guise of unity and solidarity. It is the nature and power of the various media apparatuses such as television that have largely effected the collapse between the local and the universal and created what Tony Fry (1988) calls "the drift to a convergence of a world order of economic systems and ecological abuse." Fry strikes a hyperreal chord of menace and resignation when he notes: "Coca-Cola says it all—'We are not a multinational but a multilocal' " (78).

Building an Arch of Social Dreaming

It is a historical irony that the 1980s marked the defeat of democracy by capitalism in the United States and the triumph of democracy over state communism in the Soviet Bloc countries.

—Douglas Keller, *Television and the Crisis of Democracy* (1990)

One purpose of this book is to construct the beginnings of a politics of solidarity that is respectful of identity politics but is more fundamentally concerned with establishing an ethics of commitment that precedes asking others to reveal or justify their own politics of location. This idea is present in the work of Richard Kearney and is worth summarizing. Kearney (1988) writes that "An other in need makes the ethical demand upon me—'where are you?' before I ask of the other the epistemological question—'who are you?' " Kearney follows this with the astute reading: "We are responsible for the suffering of the other before we know his or her credentials" (362). According to Kearney, this entails a correlative priority of praxis over and the primacy of questions dealing with the good and the just over those dealing with epistemology, ontology, or identity politics. Ethical action is, however, not uncritical action. In fact, it effectively demands acts of ethical discernment before making epistemological deductions.

Kearney writes that "When a naked face cries 'where are you?', we do not ask for identity papers. We reply, first and foremost, 'here I am.' " This is, Kearney emphasizes, not a return ticket to the humanism of yesterday. We do not, Kearney notes, need to go back to Sartre's cult of autonomous subjectivity in which the self is defined as an act of pure negation; rather we need to struggle to attain what Kearney refers to as an "ethical imagination." An ethical imagination is a fitting response to the postmodern condition because such an imagination entails deconstructive criticism but goes beyond it. It is "an imagination able to respond to *here I am*, even in the midst of the euphoric frissons of apocalyptic mirror play" (364). In other words, it poses a response to the signifying systems of play and parody, *différence* and dissemination, aporia and apocalypse, because the fact of the other will never let the ethical imagination rest. Perhaps it is a *neo-modern* rather than *post-modern*, response (see the chapter by McLaren, p. 278).

The face-to-face relation between self and other is not a ideological position but rather an ethical *disposition*. The "I" is disposed to speaking in solidarity with the other, not, we should emphasize, *as* the other. Kearney notes that the face-to-face is not a matter of two self-constituted subjects entering into a rapport of mutual presence, but rather "entails an ethical proximity of self to other which undercuts the comfortable notion of a co-presence" (452). It also "transcends the exclusiveness of 'I-Thou' intimacies" (452). It is always a contingent relation that "dispossesses me, decentres me, and by extension, disposes me to be an ethical subject-in-process (in Kristeva's sense)—a self always imbricated in a narrative temporality wherein its difference from itself, and the difference between itself and the other as *face*, is essential" (465). Kearney's phrase, "here I stand" always implicates a 'we' in the "I" and a 'there' in the "here." In this way, the ethical statement "I stand" surpasses the epistemological statement "I think" since the "I" derives from the call of the other ("where are you?") and can be understood to mean 'I stand up for and in for the other." As Kearney puts it, "We cannot subscribe to apocalyptic emptiness because we cannot renege on our responsibility to the other" (365).

This collection of essays is an attempt to pose some questions about the politics of schooling, educational research, and the construction of historical agency that can perhaps lay some groundwork for an arch of social dreaming—that can reintroduce the practices of the ethical imagination and a politics of solidarity and social transformation into what Hegel called our *Sittlichkeit*, our *shared social* customs and everyday cultural practices.

However, a postcolonial pedagogy and research practice avoids a collusion with the antinomies of essential oppositions such as self/other by refusing the Hegelian foundationalism of positing the self-identical ground of all difference. In this context, self-identity must always be understood as a situated practice and not as an inviolable, self-contained, and unified state as if there exists some uniform representationality or metaphysical edition of ourselves that can be won—as marketplace logic tells us—through hard work, perseverance, and self-sufficiency. The practice of critical pedagogy and critical theory have created an important crucible for reformulating and transforming both the meaning and direction of identity politics. In this time of momentous geopolitical transformation, we are witnessing a congruence of the space of subjectivity with a prefigured space of nationalist hegemonic unity. Within such a crucible, the vocabularies of the old left and new left brush vigorously against each other, sometimes merging into hybrid categories, more frequently clashing. Such a context also invites a postcolonial praxis to emerge that avoids the current politics of blame and guilt undergirding separatist attempts at critical pedagogy and research. The ideological-sensitive field of critical pedagogy must—in the domain of the academy and elsewhere—guard against its appropriation and reinscription by the discourses of liberal humanism. Trinh T. Minh-ha (1990) provides one example of such reinscription involving the notion of "interdisciplinary." Once a straight counterdiscourse, the term has now been co-opted in such a way that it has been emptied of its emancipatory possibilities. She writes:

> The notion is usually carried out in practice as the mere juxta-position of a number of different disciplines together. In such a politics of pluralist exchange and dialogue, the concept of "inter" (trans)formation and growth is typically reduced to a question of

proper accumulation and acquisition. The disciplines are simply added, put next to one another with their boundaries kept intact; the participants continued happily to speak within their expertise, from a position of authority. It is rare to see such a notion stretched to the limits so that the fences between disciplines are pulled down. Borderlines remain then strategic and contingent, as they constantly cancel themselves out. (4)

The borders between disciplines are often surreptitiously kept in place, even in so-called interdisciplinary programs that fall under the category of "cultural studies." A postcolonial pedagogy and research practice requires the dismantling of discursive borders and the opening up of what Homi Bhabha (1988) calls a space of translation that both accepts and regulates the moment of intervention in history. For Bhabha, the space of translation refers to the creation of a temporal space in which the act or event of theory "becomes the *negotiation* of contradictory and antagonistic instances" in which "hybrid sites and objectives of struggle" may be won. The hybrid moment of political change is a temporal space of rearticulation and translation "of elements that are *neither the One* (unitary working class) *nor the Other* (the politics of gender) *but something else besides* which contests the terms and territories of both" (13).

Bhabha notes that Western discourses of theoretical knowledge—even within various strands of critical theory—can serve as strategies of containing the Other, foreclosing on the Other, and turning the Other into a " 'fantasy' of a certain cultural space" (16) within a "closed circle of interpretation." In such instances:

> The "Other" loses its power to signify, to negate, to initiate its "desire," to split its "sign" of identity, to establish its own institutional and oppositional discourse. However impeccably the content of an "other" culture may be known, however anti-ethnocentrically it is represented, it is its *location* as the "closure" of grand theories, the demand that, in analytical terms, it be always the "good" object of knowledge, the docile body of difference, that reproduces a relation of domination and is the most serious indictment of the institutional powers of critical theory (16).

There is always a tension that exists within critical theory between its institutional containment and its revisionary force. One way out of this dilemma, suggests Bhabha, is to relocate the referential and institutional demands of such theoretical work not in the domain of cultural diversity but rather in the sphere of cultural difference. In order to maximize the emancipatory possibilities of postcolonial theory, we need another site for theory—the site of cultural difference. Whereas, Bhabha notes, cultural diversity places culture as an object of imperial knowledge, as "unsullied by the intertextuality of their historical locations," cultural difference "is the process of the *enunciation* of culture as 'knowledgeable,' authoritative, adequate to the construction of systems of cultural identification" (18). That is, it is a "process of signification through which statements *of* culture or *on* culture differentiate, discriminate, and authorize the production of fields of force, reference, applicability, and capacity" (18). This distinction is important.

Unlike cultural diversity, cultural difference calls into question the authority of culture as a knowledge of referential truth. The enunciation of cultural difference displaces cultural meaning into a time a cultural uncertainty and representational undecidability—a "zone of occult instability" and fecund hybridity where the subject of enunciation is split and where mimetic and transparent meaning and reference are ruptured and made relentlessly ambivalent. Cultural difference speaks to a necessary ambivalence in the act of interpreting cultural meaning. It also refers to a liminal zone of both translation and negotiation which ruptures the homogeneous, serial time of Western narrative structure with its imperialist forms of Othering and enables oppressed peoples to "negotiate and translate their cultural identities in a discontinuous intertextual temporality of cultural difference" (22) in order to rehistoricize and read anew the meaning of their lives within a praxis of emancipation. It is to the construction of liminal zones of translation and negotiation that a practice of postcolonial pedagogy and research aspires (McLaren, 1995).

Overview of the Essays

The essays in this book fall into no neat disciplinary divisions or categories of theory versus practice. The "border play" is a large part of their intent and engagement.

Henry Giroux's chapter, which introduces the rest, makes the Foucauldian point that discourse is not language seen as symbolic representation of reality. As David Jones and Stephen Ball write in their chapter, discourse does violence to things, it is an imposition. Giroux is concerned that the demands for commonsense clarity and unambiguous language, many from critical and progressive educational theorists, in the end accede to the power of the symbol to represent "reality" and ignore the fact that theory is *produced* and that in this production lies the possibilities for new expressions and norms of difference, negotiation, and resistance. Whose clarity? Whose ambiguity? In a fitting beginning for the essays to come, Giroux makes the production, texts, and practices of critical educational research themselves subjects of critical theory and educational research.

Like Giroux, much of contemporary critical theory is concerned with discourse, discursive practices, and power, and thus, many of the authors represented in this book make discourse a central problematic. David Jones and Stephen Ball focus specifically on one, though certainly not the only, perspective on discourse, that of Foucault. While wary of any simple-minded generation of "implications," Jones and Ball point to a number of Foucauldian concerns that might shape an educational research agenda.

Nick Burbules's treatment of ideology-critique, an important element in historical and contemporary varieties of critical theory, analyzes the many meanings of ideology and the implicit educational theories they assume. Burbules is ultimately interested in overcoming divisions between knowers, the process of knowing, the known, and the consequences of inquiry. He advocates a pedagogical view of ideology-critique that requires individuals to go beyond critique to the consideration of emancipatory ends.

Joe Kincheloe explores the borders between action research and postmodernism. For Kincheloe, action research is a logical educational extension of postmodern critical social theory. In stark contrast to "policy studies," whose aim is to provide "useful," expert knowledge for institutional planning, the core of critical action research involves its participatory and communally discursive structure and the cycle of action and reflection it initiates. The knowledge enabled through such reflexive and shared study leads not to bureaucratic directives, but, more important, to the possibility for emancipatory change, as Kincheloe puts it, "knowledge with the potential to wreak havoc."

Margaret LeCompte explores similar themes in her chapter on critical collaborative research. Moving deftly between an examination of the historical roots and traditions of action research and her own journey as a researcher, LeCompte faces head-on how issues of power, agenda, and voice distinguish and make more difficult the transition from action research to *critical, collaborative* research.

These issues are echoed in the next several chapters. Ron Sultana reminds us that the positivist and interpretivist emphasis on description fails to account for the "silences" in social reality, what cannot or does not get said in descriptive accounts. Sultana's essay explores the political implications behind the epistemology and ontology of ethnography and echoes Burbules's concern for a kind of research that occurs *with*, rather than *on*, others and is thus informed by a dialogue aimed at mutual understanding.

Kathleen Weiler also focuses on "silences" in texts. She examines the oral-history narratives of women and stresses the need to go beyond simple description through an analysis of the oppositions, gaps, and contradictions that emerge between our memories of the past and the material and symbolic contexts in which these memories are shaped.

Finally in this section, Lynda Stone's chapter on feminist educational research wrestles with the twin aims of critique and change central to the critical tradition. Although Stone recounts the multiple varieties of feminism and critical theory and the problematic history of their association, she also argues for an *"overt politics,* an endeavor to get beyond the skirmishes of the left. . .a proposal for educational alliance. . .that allows for significant and continuing theoretical differences yet allows for a praxiological 'coming together.' "

The normalization of poverty and violence in our cities and schools give us good reason to make such alliances. Yet to know what and how to make real, transformative change is itself opaque. David Jones's essay on the discourses of the urban school seeks to make problematic the assumption that "to know is to improve." In this Foucauldian view, Jones ably demonstrates how specific "school improvement" policies, practices, and texts in England and Wales can be read as species of contested discourses shaped by normative strategies of power, biopower, and archivized constraint.

Phil Carspecken offers an analysis at the school level of an experiment in progressive educational change. Carspecken's careful analysis of the pragmatics of speech from the perspective of someone who was at once a researcher, participant, and political actor is a fine example of research *as* education, ideology-critique *as* pedagogical participation.

Lois Weis's essay echoes concerns with voice, silencing, and listening in discourse. Her examination of how identity is constructed through the "discursive underground" of white, working-class, male practices in high school, while reminiscent of Paul Willis's work on the "lads," engages all typifications of the "Other."

Wendy Kohli and Carlos Alberto Torres give us examples of the possibilities and constraints on critical research and progressive educational change in concrete settings. Where Torres rightly describes the difficulties associated with doing a Freirean-based model of participatory action research and popular education from within the educational agencies of a capitalist state, Kohli's essay on critical educational research and reform in the Soviet Union reminds us that *all* forms of centralized power are hostile to emancipatory educational and social ends.

The interview between Paulo Freire and Moacir Gadotti, published here in English for the first time, is a model of honest dialogue between democratic educators. Reflective, humble, yet resilient and unflinching, Freire, as always, grounds the critical spirit in a pedagogy of hope.

Finally, Peter McLaren's article on critical ethnography demonstrates the shortcomings of mainstream qualitative and ethnographic inquiry, while echoing the need for critical educational researchers to enter into relations of cooperation, mutuality, and reciprocity with those whom we research, as well as one another. McLaren's sustained treatment of the body helps us break through one of the most persistent images of mainstream inquiry, "the talking head," and revision a form of embodied inquiry in which desire, particularity, solidarity, and hope are as important as truth.

These essays suggest, indeed insist, that we rediscover, even reinvent, our self-images as researchers, our practices of research, and our ideas of the aims of inquiry. They present models, ideas, examples, and theories to prod that reflexivity, but have no interest in offering the false solace of method. Where emancipation is the interest, all methods give way to dialogue. Our authors hope and believe that such dialogue is possible and invite your participation.

Peter L. McLaren and James M. Giarelli

Notes

* Slightly altered sections of this introduction will appear in Christine Sleeter and Peter McLaren, eds., *Multiculturalism and Critical Pedagogy* (Albany: State University of New York Press) and Peter McLaren, Rhonda Hammer, David Sholle, and Susan Reilly, *A Critical Pedagogy of Representation* (New York: Peter Lang Publishers). Some sections of this introduction have appeared in Peter McLaren, "Multiculturalism and the Postmodern Critique: Towards a Pedagogy of Resistance and Transformation," *Cultural Studies* 7, no. 1 (1993): 118–46 (which also appeared in Henry Giroux and Peter McLaren, eds., *Between Borders*, New York: Routledge); Peter McLaren, "Critical Pedagogy, Multiculturalism, and the

Politics of Risk and Resistance: A Response to Kelly and Portelli," *Journal of Education* 173 no. 3 (1991): 29–59 (which also appeared in Peter McLaren, *Life in Schools*, 2nd edition, White Plains, N.Y.: Longman, Inc. 1994; and James M. Giarelli, "Critical Theory and Educational Research: An Introduction," *Qualitative Studies in Education* 5, no. 1 (1992): 3–5.

References

Anzaldúa, Gloria, ed. 1990. *Making Face, Making Soul*. San Francisco: Aunt Lute Foundation.

Appiah, Kwame. 1991. "Is the post in postmodernism the post in postcolonial? *Critical Inquiry* 17, no. 2:336–57.

Ashcroft, Bill, Gareth Griffiths and Helen Tiffin. 1989. *The Empire Writes Back: Theory and Practice in Post-Colonial Literatures*. London: Routledge.

Baum, Gregory. 1991. "Goodbye to the Ecumenist." *The Ecumenist* 29, no. 2:1–3.

Bauman, Zygmunt. 1987. *Legislators and Interpreters*. Ithaca: Cornell University Press.

Bennett, Tony. 1990. *Outside Literature*. New York: Routledge.

Bernstein, Richard. 1976. *The Restructuring of Social and Political Theory*. Philadelphia: University of Pennsylvania Press.

Bhabha, Homi K. 1988. "The Commitment to Theory." *New Formations* 5:5–23.

Brydon, Diana. 1990. "The White Inuit Speaks: Contamination as Literacy Strategy." Pp. 191–203 in *Past the Last Post*, ed. Ian Adam and Helen Tiffin. Calgary, Alberta: University of Calgary Press.

Campbell, Beatrix, et. al. 1990. "Manifesto for New Times: Realignment of Politics." Pp. 448–53 in *New Times: The Changing Face of Politics in the 1990s*, ed. Stuart Hall and Martin Jacques. London: Verso.

Connor, Steven. 1989. *Postmodern Culture*. Oxford: Basil Blackwell.

Deleuze, Gilles, and Felix Guattari. 1975. *Kafka: pour une litterature mineure*. Paris: Editions de Minuit.

Eagleton, Terry. 1990. *The Ideology of the Aesthetic*. Oxford: Basil Blackwell.

Fry, Tony. 1988. "From (Sun)light to Sin." Pp. 72–82 in *It's a Sin*. Sydney: Power Publications.

Fry, Tony. 1989. *Old Worlds: New Visions*. Sydney: Hale & Iremonger.

Gates, Henry Louis. 1991. "Critical Fanonism." *Critical Inquiry,* 17:457–70.

Giroux, Henry, ed. 1991. *Postmodernism, Feminism, and Cultural Politics*. Albany: State University of New York Press.

———. 1992. *Border Crossings: Cultural Workers and the Politics of Education*. New York: Routledge.

Giroux, Henry, and Peter McLaren. 1992. "Introduction." In *Curriculum for Utopia: Social Reconstructionism and Critical Pedagogy in the Postmodern Era*: xi–xv. by William B. Stanley. Albany: State University of New York Press.

Grossberg, Larry. 1988. "Patrolling Frontiers: The Articulation of the Popular." Lawrence Grossberg, Tony Fry, Ann Curthays and Paul Patton. Pp. 35–71 in *It's a Sin*. Sydney: Power Publications.

Hutcheon, Linda. 1988. *A Poetics of Postmodernism*. New York: Routledge.

Jan Mohammed, Abdul. 1983. *Manichean Aesthetics: The Politics of Literature in Colonial Africa*. Amherst: University of Massachusetts Press.

Kearney, Richard. 1988. *The Wake of Imagination*. Minneapolis: University of Minnesota Press.

Kellner, Douglas. 1990. *Television and the Crisis of Democracy*. Boulder, Colo.: Westview Press.

McLaren, Peter (1995) *Critical Pedagogy and Predatory Culture*. London and New York: Routledge.

McLaren, Peter and Lankshear, Colin, Eds. (1994) *Politics of Liberation: Paths From Freire*. London and New York: Routledge.

McLaren, Peter (1993). "Border Disputes: Multicultural Narrative, Identity Formation, and Silenced Lives. Critical Pedagogy in Postmodern America." *Naming Silenced Lives*. Eds. Daniel McLaughlin and William G. Tierney. New York: Routledge. pp. 201–235.

McLaren, Peter and Leonard, Peter, Eds. (1993) *Paulo Freire: A Critical Encounter*. London and New York: Routledge.

Minh-ha, Trinh T. 1990. "Feminism, Film-making and Post-colonialism: An Interview with Trin T. Minh-ha." *Feminisms* 3 (September/October): 3–6.

Mohanty, Chandra Talpade. 1989/90. "On Race and Voice: Challenges for Liberal Education in the 1990s." *Cultural Critique* (Winter): 179–208.

Nietzsche, Friedrich. 1967. *On the Genealogy of Morals*. Trans. Kaufmann and Hollingdale. New York: Random House.

Parry, Benita. 1987. "Problems in Current Theories of Colonial Discourse." *The Oxford Literary Review* 9:27–58.

Patton, Paul. 1988. "Giving up the Ghost: Postmodernism and Anti-nihilism." Lawrence Grossberg, Tony Fry, Ann Curthoys and Paul Patton, Pp. 88–95 in *It's a Sin*. Sydney: Power Publications.

Redding, Paul. 1990. "Nietzschean Perspectivism and the Logic of Practical Reason." *Philosophical Forum* 22, no. 1:72–88.

Said, Edward. 1983. *The World, the Text, and the Critic*. Cambridge: Harvard University Press.

Slemon, Stephen. 1990. Unsettling the Empire: Resistance Theory for the Second World. *World Literature Written in English* 30, no. 2:30–41.

———. 1990a. "Modernism's Last Post." Pp. 1–12 in *Past the Last Post*, ed. Ian Adam and Helen Tifflin. Calgary, Alberta: University of Calgary Press.

Stam, Robert. 1991. "Bakhtin, Polyphony, and Ethnic/Racial Representation." Pp. 25–76 in *Unspeakable Images*, ed. Lester, D. Friedman. Urbana and Chicago: University of Illinois Press.

Viswanathan, Gauri. 1989. *Masks of Conquest: Literary Study and British Rule in India*. New York: Columbia University Press.

Young, Robert. 1990. *White Mythologies*. London: Routledge.

Žižek, Slavoj. 1990. "Beyond Discourse-Analysis." Appendix to *New Reflections on the Revolution of our Time* by Ernesto Laclau. London: Verso.

1

Language, Difference, and Curriculum Theory: Beyond the Politics of Clarity

Henry A. Giroux

Accessibility, which is a process, is often taken for a "natural," self-evident state of language. What is perpetuated in its name is a given form of intolerance and an unacknowledged practice of exclusion. Thus, as long as the complexity and difficulty of engaging with the diversely hybrid experiences of heterogeneous contemporary societies are denied and not dealt with, binary thinking continues to mark time while the creative interval is dangerously reduced to non-existence.

Trinh Minh-ha, *When the Moon Waxes Red* (1991)

Within the broader tradition of social criticism, especially as it is being developed in feminist theory, literary studies, art criticism, postcolonial analyses, and Afro-American cultural criticism, a new generation of critics has attempted to unsettle the status quo by refusing the traditional conventions, which call for writing in a language that is clear and unambiguous. In part, this approach to writing comes out of the recognition that new ideas often require new terms and that such writing can employ sometimes ambiguous, if not, on occasion, even clumsy formulations. This is more than a technical issue. Rather than suggesting that opaque writing is by default progressive and intellectual (Lowe and Kantor (1991), this argument is, in part, a response to a long tradition of anti-intellectualism in American life in which the call for clarity has been used to attack politically directed writing (Hofstadter 1963).

Moreover, it is a response to a legacy of commentary in which it is argued that such writing is "utopian" and therefore can be dismissed as impractical (Brosio 1990). Of course, a number of theorists have countered this response by arguing that United States education is supremely impractical from the point of view of its victims (Aronowitz & Giroux 1985; Giroux 1992; Hooks 1989).

Within the last decade, the attack on language has taken a new turn. A strange coalition of conservatives, liberals, and some Marxists have joined together to further argue that clarity is a paramount issue in privileging writing as a form of political and cultural expression. Writers such as Jacoby (1987) have warned "social critics against the danger of yielding to a new Latin, a new scholasticism insulated from the larger public" (236). Agger (1990) suggests that theory itself is to be dismissed because "it courts incomprehensibility" and' like much academic writing, "fails to invite dialogue, instead reporting itself as an objective account purged of authorial intentionality, perspective, passion" (35, 37). MacDonald (1990) believes that complicated discourses are the vehicle of what she calls vanguard theories and that such theories are incompatible with the latest findings in readability theories. To prove her point, she analyzes the sentence structure and use of terminology of a number of specific writers whose prose fails to pass her readability analysis.

This debate about language, clarity, and experience is increasingly being taken up by a number of educational theorists (Apple 1988a; Karp 1991). In what follows, I argue that attacks on critical educators for using a language that is allegedly "inaccessible" is structured in a binary opposition between clarity and complexity that both trivializes the debate around language while simultaneously contributing to a theory of language that is monolithic, unitary, and Eurocentric (Lowe and Kantor 1991; Miedeima 1987; Schrag 1988).[1] In part, I argue that the call for clarity suppresses difference and multiplicity, prevents curriculum theorists and other educators from deconstructing the basis of their own linguistic privilege, and reproduces a populist elitism that serves to deskill educators rather than empower them.

In opposition to this view, I argue for a theory of language that not only recognizes the importance of complexity and difference but also provides the conditions For educators to cross borders. where disparate linguistic, theoretical, and political realities meet as part of an ongoing attempt to engage in a "continual process of negotiation and translation between a series of individual and cultural positions" (Joselet 1989, 123). Finally, I argue that educators and other cultural workers need to take up the issue of language around a politics of difference, one that provides the conditions for teachers, students, and others to learn the knowledge and skills necessary to live in a manner in which they have the opportunity to govern and shape society rather than being consigned to its margins.

Language, Theory, and the Politics of Verification

The politics of clarity has become a central political issue in the debate over the relationship between theory and practice. In part, this position is built on the assumption that critical educators who write in a language that is considered complex perform the double mistake of removing themselves from the public debate about curriculum issues while simultaneously violating an alleged universal standard for linguistic clarity. The most well-known advocate of this position is Michael Apple (1983, 1988a). Not only is Apple continually quoted to legitimate this position, he has worked with a number of graduate students who have become strong advocates of the clarity and populist positions (Bromley 1989; Gore 1990; Liston, 1988).

But Apple's position is not limited to curriculum theorists working in higher education. The call to clarity is also exemplified in a growing number of critical academic and popular journals that appear to define their populist prose against, rather than in solidarity with, those journals and writers that use a more complex discourse (see, for example, *Radical Teacher* and *Rethinking Schools*).[2] The theoretical assumptions that inform the clarity position are stated succinctly in the following comment:

> Given the overt aim of democracy, the left has to be very careful not to mystify, not to make its claims in a manner that is nearly impossible to verify or clarify. For mystification has had a number of negative effects: It has led to a partial isolation of this work on the borders of scholarship and public debate, and its marginalization has grown because of the arcane quality that characterizes some of the language. . . . The nearly mystical quality of some critical work, its tendency not to take sufficient time to clarify its basic concepts or to write clearly, cannot help but limit its impact. (Apple 1988a, 4)

This argument serves to privilege language according to the degree that it is accessible to a general public and roughly corresponds to an objectively verifiable reality (Liston 1988). Within this context, empiricism and forms of Western rationalism constitute a strong alliance in the history of critical educational theorizing. Such theorizing is generally based on a reproductive model in which language is assigned the role of critically mediating between the determining force of the economy and the ideological interests capitalism produces and legitimates in different aspects of schooling.

Language in this context is privileged for its revealing function and for the ways in which it demystifies how meanings are mobilized in the interests of maintaining economic relations of domination (Bowles and Gintis 1976; West 1991). For example, this approach to schooling is often concerned with showing how the hidden curriculum of schooling reproduces the dominant relations of the workplace (Apple 1979; Bowles and Gintis 1976), how patriarchal relations articulate between the world of work and the organization of the school labor force, or how the production and circulation of textbooks is largely governed by the principles of political economy (Apple, 1988b).

Within this perspective, language provides a theoretical service in demystifying the means and processes by which capitalist relations organize and shape different aspects of school life. The task of the curriculum theorist in this model is not to question the reproduction thesis as a basic problematic but to show how such a model can be assessed empirically (Liston 1988). What is crucial to recognize here are the limits this position places on the very nature of the relationship between language and theory. Theory in this instance is so narrowly defined that it becomes nearly impossible to take it up as a form of writing produced within a language of negotiation and translation that allows an educator or any other theorist to rethink the role theory might play beyond the task of demystification.

In this case, what is lost is the active role language might play in both producing different theoretical discourses and creating specific social identities. More specifically, the advocates of clarity ignore how language might be used to generate theories that raise new questions and problems, and posit alternative territories of investigation. The shift in language from its revealing function to its more active role as a productive discourse is also useful in disclosing new forms of domination and in mobilizing new and diverse critical public cultures of resistance and political practice.

Proponents of the discourse of clarity assume that theoretical evidence corresponds to an objectively verifiable reality and the task of the theorist is to unmask such a correspondence. The central role of theory in this sense is generally one of demystification and explanation (Chrichlow 1991). This is not to imply that questions of validity, verifiability, and explanation should not be important concerns in educational research, but to suggest, as does McLaren (1992), that these concerns often mask the deeper ideological, partisan, and political interests behind positivist empiricism and its legitimating claims to scientific method, objectivity, and impartiality (Aronowitz 1990).

As a form of criticism, the discourse of clarity and empiricism fails on a number of counts. First, it is limited to a notion of theory that is confined to a single explanatory account of how schools work and teachers theorize. That is, it situates the process of schooling in a binary opposition between the processes of reproduction versus resistance and neglects many complex forms of negotiation and translation that transpire within school sites. Tied to the logic of a reactive model, it repeatedly oversimplifies the complexity of social and cultural life and, in doing so, runs the risk of being overly pessimistic and reductionistic.

Second, the assumption that theory only gains currency through its ability to either verify existing practices or empirically unmask how such practices reproduce relations of domination, undermines the role that theory might play in creating new spaces, practices, and values. Against the binarism in this position that comfortably pits theory against practice, I argue that both theory and practice are constructed in language and, hence, cannot be portrayed as causally related in which one merely is derivative of the other.

Theory and practice produce rather than reflect their object of reference and, as such, both must be analyzed as part of a complex politics of representation. There is never, in this case, a simple identity between theory and practice: both exist within a constant and shifting terrain of negotiation that calls into play the connection between the subject of theory and the object of practice (Bhabha 1988). Theoretical language in this sense is not defined exhaustively by the principles of verification and empiricism. It is also seen as a historical and social construction that actively organizes perception and communication. That is, in this context, theory becomes a form of writing "which does not translate a reality outside itself but, more precisely, allows the emergence of a new reality" (Minh-ha 1989, 22).

In effect, language as a theoretical discourse is neither wedded to a science of empiricism nor to banishing the multi-accentuality of signs as part of a broader attempt to create a singular approach to writing (Bakhtin 1981). Language is situated in an ongoing struggle over issues of inclusion and exclusion, meaning and interpretation, and such issues are inextricably related to questions of "power, history, and self-identity" (Mohanty 1989/90, 184). The struggle over language subordinates the issue of clarity and verification to the primacy of politics and ethics. I believe that a self-reflective notion of theory as resistance and struggle offers the possibility for addressing the complexity and engaging both the limits of existing theoretical languages and the emancipatory possibilities in inventing new discourses in order to analyze the relationship between school, culture, and politics. Laclau (1990) is worth quoting on this issue:

> The important epistemological breaks have not occurred when new solutions have been given to old problems, but when a radical change in the ground of the debate strips the old problems of their sense. This is what seems central to me today if one wishes to push forward the political debate.... It is necessary to construct a new language—and a new language means...new objects, new problems, new values, and the possibility of discursively constructing new antagonisms and forms of struggle. (1990, 162)

But the tendency to exhaust the meaning of theory in the demands of empirical verification does more than strip it of the opportunity to create new educational paradigms: it also generally ignores how theory is constructed out of those places and spaces we inherit and occupy, which frame our lives in very specific and concrete ways, which are as much a part of our psyches as they're a physical or geographical placement" (Borsa 1990, 36). What Borsa is emphasizing is the need for critical educators to turn theory back on itself, to use it to name our own location as educational theorists, "to politicize our space and to question where our particular experiences and practice fit within the articulations and representations that surround us" (Borsa 1990, 36).

Theory needs to do more than be stated in a clear language or "express" and verify "reality." It also needs to help educators understand how the politics of their own location carries privileges and secures particular forms of authority. More specifically, the discourse of clarity reveals a strong tendency to ignore questions about the partiality of one's own theoretical language, particularly with respect to the issue of who speaks, under what conditions, and for whom?

Reducing theory to issues of verification and empiricism does not do justice to the issue of the historical connectedness between the language of theory and how it frames its objects. Central to such a concern would be making problematic the significance of speaking from a particular place, such as the university or any other privileged institutional space, and how such a location serves to legitimize the grounds for certain inherited vocabularies (i.e., science, verification, empiricism) while excluding others (i.e., feminism, qualitative inquiry, Afro-American literature).

This issue is particularly relevant for intellectuals who are privileged by virtue of gender, race, and class. Such intellectuals reveal traces of colonialism in their emphasis on linguistic clarity without at the same time critically engaging how Eurocentrism privileges their own position as the guardians of universal linguistic norms, which in this instance serves to suppress rather than encourage a plurality of their theoretical discourses and forms of writing (Spivak 1990; Young 1990).

Clarity and the Suppression of Difference

The call for clarity by many curriculum theorists represents another side of the debate around language and theory that rests on a facile opposition between forms of writing that are complex or clear. This binarism is based on the presupposition that the simple invocation to clear language can by itself confer sense. This position also suggests that teachers should be able to engage theoretical treatises effortlessly. Ironically, this position places no burden of responsibility on the reader. Moreover, it also works within a correspondence view of truth that suggests that knowledge is external to language and that the most desirable theories are those that can most clearly "uncover" its secrets through a prose style that best serves as a clear spotlight on "reality."

The imperative to write in clear language redefines the relationship between language and power in largely strategic terms. It is argued that the tactical value of clear language in mobilizing large numbers of people warrants its use as a preferred element of political discourse and educational writing. Generally ignoring the question of who speaks, for whom, and under what conditions, the advocates of clarity have shifted their focus to the issue of who listens. Unfortunately, when structured around the binary opposition of clarity versus complexity, this particular focus on language not only ignores how multiple audiences read differently, it also subverts the very problem it claims to be addressing. It restricts the possibility for expanding public cultures of resistance by refusing to address the importance of developing multiple literacies that allow people to speak across and within cultural differences. Clarity in this case seems to me to do more to create intolerance than advance a receptivity to different discourses, languages, and theories.

I believe the call for curriculum theorists and critical educators to stick to a presumed standard of clarity suffers from a number of crucial flaws. The claim that some critical educators write in a language that is arcane and inaccessible reifies the question of clarity in presupposing rather than demonstrating a universal standard for measuring it. For example, do critics who invoke the issue of clarity have a specific standard in mind when they pass judgment on the literacy levels of

the various audiences that constitute the readers of theoretical books
on curriculum theory and practice? Is it the equivalent of a reading level
embodied in *Reader's Digest*? What is it about the defining characteristic
of their discourse that allows them to judge for all readers what is
accessible and what is not? Unfortunately, the discourse of clarity
appears to rest on a universal standard of literacy that presumably need
not be questioned.

This approach to language suppresses questions of context—Who
reads what under what conditions? More importantly, it strongly
suggests that language is a transparent medium merely expressing
existing facts that need only be laid out in an agreed-upon fashion
(Laclau 1990). Such a position runs the risk of fleeing the politics of
culture by situating language outside of history, power, and struggle.
While such an anti-theoretical stance may be comforting to some, it
provides no help in either understanding the complex relationship
between either theory and practice or between language and power.

The appeal to clarity often ignores how language is produced
within particular theoretical paradigms and taken up by diverse audiences across and within widely different cultural spheres. In doing so,
it fails to address the complex issue of how languages that challenge
traditional educational paradigms are obligated to create new categories
in order to reclaim new spaces for resistance, to establish new identities,
or to construct new knowledge/power relations.

The advocates of clarity need to be more reflective about the
ideologies that inform their own position on language and their
ideological construction of the category of "clarity." In this regard, one
must ask what makes these academics capable of reading certain
educational texts critically while simultaneously suggesting that most
educators are not intelligent enough understand them. For example,
in a review of McLaren's book, *Life In Schools*, Karp (1991) argues that
the theoretical portions of the book "are written in dense, academically-
inflated prose that makes for tedious reading" (33). This is a perplexing
assertion considering that McLaren's book is an introductory text in
social foundations that is written in an academic style very comparable
to introductory texts in sociology, cultural studies, political science, or
anthropology.

The "grass roots" elitism characteristic of Karp's position is not
difficult to recognize. What is important to note is that his elitism cannot
be viewed merely as a matter of personal taste, it is part and parcel
of a wider ideology in which teachers are called to serve as political
activists but are correspondingly viewed as too anti-intellectual and
"dumb" to reconstruct the experience of schooling in, and through, a

language that is critical, theoretical, and oppositional. Accordingly, this position suggests that activism and intellectual labor are mutually antithetical. Moreover, it legitimizes a position deeply implicated in one of the most powerful ideologies of the dominant culture, a position that invites teachers to deskill themselves while simultaneously placing them in positions of subordination.

But such arguments cannot be challenged merely around the hidden ideological constructions that hopelessly shape elitist appeals to the wisdom of clarity, or to attempts to legitimate the alleged self-revelations of classroom "practice" unhampered by the "intrusions" of theory. What seems to me to be the real issue in this discourse is the peculiar form of neo-colonial paranoia it exhibits, an implicit fear that the world as we know it is a social and historical construction, a world in which language is invented as part of an ongoing transformation of experience, a world that no longer lends itself to simple calls for clarity along with its complementary principles of universality and appeals to the final court of concrete experience (Kincheloe 1991).

In the age of post-colonialism, language has become a terrain of contestation and struggle. It can no longer suppress its complicity in particular forms of violence and oppression by either denying its structuring principles nor can it resist denying a space for historically silenced groups to rewrite their own histories and identities through a different language and set of experiences. The call for clarity incorporates a trace of colonialism in which the search for a unified single standard of writing is tied to the search for a unified identity, politics, and notion of truth. Of course, the problem of clarity is compounded when the universal reference that allegedly informs it is used to buttress a particular version of English. Clarity in this case methodologizes language and in doing so removes it from both a politics of representation and from history (Crowley 1989).

To argue against these concerns is not meant as a clever exercise intent on merely reversing the relevance of the categories so that theory is prioritized over practice, or abstract language over the language of popcorn imagery. Nor am I suggesting that critical educators mount an equally reductionist argument against the use of clear language or the importance of practice. At issue here is the need to both question and reject the reductionism and exclusions that characterize the binary oppositions that inform these overly pragmatic tendencies. In what follows, I suggest a much different theoretical and political approach to language, one that not only serves to situate my own work but speaks more broadly to the issue of educational criticism and its relationship to the pressing problems around language, knolwedge, and power.

Multiple Languages and Democratic Possibilities

> If we lived in a democratic state our language would have to hurtle, fly, curse, and sing, in all the...undeniable and representative and participating voices of everybody here....We would make our language conform to the truth of our many selves and we would make our langusge lead us into the equality of power that a democratic state must represent. (Jordan 1985, 30)

Implicit in Jordan's remarks is the necessity for educators to recognize how vital linguistic diversity is to cultural democracy. Fundamental to this position is the need not only to recognize how different voices, language, histories, and ways of viewing the world are made manifest in different languages and theoretical discourses, but also the need to recognize that some languages exhaust their ability to deal with some problems and issues. This suggests the need for new languages. Put differently, every new paradigm has to create its own language because the old paradigms often produce, through their use of language, particular forms of knowledge and social relations that serve to legitimate specific relations of power.

Oppositional paradigms provide new languages through which it becomes possible to deconstruct and challenge dominant relations of power and knowledge legitimated in traditional forms of discourse. At issue in these oppositional paradigms is the possibility for constructing educational discourses that provide the opportunity for educators to understand and engage differently the world of classroom experience as well as the larger social reality. This opposition often reflects major changes in thinking mediated and produced through related shifts in ways of speaking and writing. Oppositional languages are generally unfamiliar, provoking questions and pointing to social relations that will often appear alien and strange to many educators.

What is at stake here is not the issue of "bad" writing, as if writing that is difficult to grapple with has nothing important to say. Rather, the most important point to be addressed by educational theorists is not clarity but whether such writing offers a vision and practice for deepening the possible relations between the discourse of education and the imperatives of a radical, pluralized democracy. Hence, the defining principle for theoretical practice belongs to a "renewed interest in democracy, and...how a democratic culture might be fashioned" (Jay 1991, 266).

But there is another issue in the current debate about language that is often ignored by the advocates of clarity, particularly as it concerns the relationship between language and the notion of domination. It seems to me that those educators who make the call for clear writing synonymous with an attack on certain forms of theorizing have missed the role that the "language of clarity" plays in a dominant culture that cleverly and powerfully uses "clear" and "simplistic" language to systematically undermine and prevent those conditions necessary for a general public to engage at least in rudimentary forms of critical thinnking. In effect, what is missed in this analysis is that the homogenization and standardization of language in the mass media, the schools, and other cultural sites point to how language and power often combine to offer the general public and students knowledge and ideologies cleansed of complex discourses or oppositional insights. That critical educators have largely ignored this issue when taking up the question of language makes suspect not only their own claims to clarity but also the limits of their own political judgments.

A related issue needs to be addressed in this argument. Many educators often assume a notion of audience that is both theoretically simplistic and politically incorrect. It is theoretically simplistic because it assumes that there is one public sphere rather than a number of public spheres characterized by diverse levels of intelligibility and sophistication (Fraser 1990). Moreover, the suggestion that there is only one audience to whom critical educators speak provides no latitude for connecting diverse theoretical languages with audiences marked by difference with respect to histories, languages, cultures, or everyday experiences. Such a position flattens the relationship between language and audience and cancels out the necessity of the author/writer to take into consideration the historical, political, and cultural specificity of the audience or audiences that he or she attempts to address. Within this perspective, there is a tendency to perceive members of diverse public cultures as objects rather subjects, as socially constructed pawns rather than as complex and contradictory human agents who mediate, read, and write the world differently. The politics of such a position often either leads one into the exclusionary territories of Eurocentrism, eliticism, and colonialism, or into the political dead end of cynicism and despair (Hooks 1990).

I would argue that language is always constructed with respect to the specificity of the audience it addresses and should not be judged in purely pragmatic terms but also with regard to the viability of the theoretical and political project it articulates. It is not the complexity of language, in the most narrow sense, that is at stake but the viability of the theoretical framework the new language is attempting to constitute and promote. At one level, theorists need to ask questions regarding how language is disciplined, that is, they need to address "the ways in which discourse [is] controlled and delimited: [through]...systems of exclusions, the principles of classification, ordering and distribution, and the rules determining the conditions under which, and by whom, discourse could be deployed" (Crowley 1989, 1–2). Thus, the real debate over theory and language is about the specific ideological content of various theoretical discourses *and* how the latter promote specific forms of moral and social regulation as they are expressed in the organization of the school, classroom social relations, the production and distribution of knowledge, and in the relationship between the school and the larger community.

If the language of curriculum theory is to work in the interest of expanding a democratic curriculum and set of social relations, it is imperative that a theory of language expand the possibility for different ways of writing, reading, speaking, listening, and hearing. The appeal to clarity does not expand the democratic potential of language; on the contrary, educators need to acquire multiple literacies that acknowledge cultural and linguistic difference as the basis for a public philosophy that rejects totalizing theories—theories that view the other as a deficit, or attempt to take "the social and historical processes out of discourse in order to make a certain order of things appear natural and given" (Crowley 1989, 5).

What many educators forget is that the importance of language as theoretical practice is derived, in large part, from its critical and subversive possibilities. Hence, to judge curriculum theory next to the simple yardstick of clarity and "plainspeak" does not offer a serious enough challenge to educational discourses that often attempt to cover their ideological interests through an appeal to universality and the call for a single language. Nor does such a position recognize that support for a single theoretical language shares an ideological affinity with the current conservative demand for a common cultural identity based on forms of exclusion and hierarchy (Aronowitz and Giroux 1991). Moreover, the language of clarity does not provide the basis for understanding how language has become complicitous with an anti-intellectualism that undermines the ability of administrators and teachers to think in critical and oppositional terms.

I believe curriculum theory should be constructed around a number of critical discourses that constantly rewrite, problematize, and construct the nature of our everyday experiences and the objects of our inquiry. As a pedagogical practice, the language of curriculum should provide the ideological and institutional conditions for an ongoing dialogue between teachers, students, and other cultural workers as part of a broader attempt to link schooling with the imperatives of critical citizenship, social justice, and broader reform movements for reconstituting democratic public life (Giroux 1988). This suggests that any viable language of curriculum must be able to offer theoretical and pedagogical opportunities for educators to rupture and transform the crippling binary opposition between complexity and language, theory and practice.

Fortunately, there are a number of traditions in feminist theory, post-colonial discourse, literary theory, and in the growing traditions of critical and feminist pedagogy that have begun to create alternative projects in which language is being rewritten as part of an effort to redefine the relationship between politics, pedagogy, and collective struggle.[3] While such discourses and practices are always unfinished, they do offer new categories and hope for educators who believe that schools can still be changed and that their individual and collective actions can make a difference in deepening and extending democracy and social justice in the wider society (Giroux 1988).[4]

Notes

1. It is worth noting that some of the critics who rail against such language often do so in a prose that suggests their own identities are on trial in dealing with a discourse that is either complicated or points to an opposing theoretical position. For example. Lowe and Kantor (1991) write, "Much of the writing in this volume is so arcane that it suggests contempt for the reader" (124). Rather than engage seriously the issues raised in the book, Lowe and Kantor sidestep any serious analysis by impugning the motives of the writers. So much for the possibility of serious criticism.

2. See Karp's (1991) piece in *Radical Teacher*, which appears less as a review than as a policy statement. Also, see *Rethinking Schools'* October/November 1988 issue in which it provides an article on "Critical Pedagogy for Classroom Teachers: A Bibliography" (8). The list acknowledges the requisite gesture toward some of the work of Paulo Freire and then highlights a series of books that are decidedly more prescriptive than theoretical. Most importantly, outside of

Freire and Ira Shor, it excludes any major theoretical work in critical pedagogy published within the last decade.

3. I analyze these positions in detail in Giroux (1992).

4. My use of the terms democratic culture and democracy are linked to citizenship understood as a form of self-management constituted in all major economic, social, and cultural spheres of society. Democracy in this context takes up the issue of transferring power from elites and executive authorities, who control the economic and cultural apparatuses of society, to those producers who wield power at the local level. Democracy is made concrete through the organization and exercise of horizontal power in which knowledge must be widely shared through education and other technologies of culture.

At issue here is recognizing that democracy is not merely about the formality of voting but more substantively about having access to the technological and cultural resources necessary for individuals and social groups to be informed, make decisions, and exercise control over the material and ideological forces that govern their lives. I believe questions of democracy and citizenship occupy the center of an emancipatory project designed to educate administrators, teachers, students, and others to the expanding needs, rights, and obligations that are increasingly being promoted by new social groups and movements, including feminists, Black and ethnic movements, ecology activists, gay and lesbian groups, and vulnerable minorities such as children and the aged.

Democratic education in this instance would address the question of membership in a community—who does and does not belong. It would provide opportunities for students to not only learn the rights but also the responsibilities needed to sustain a democratic notion of public life. As such, it would not be enough to call for a closer link between the school curriculum and community; what is also needed is the opportunity for students to perform a public service that allows them (to take up the issue and practice of social reform as part of a broader attempt to identity and ameliorate through collective struggle forms of inequality and human suffering.

References

Agger, B. 1990. *The Decline of Discourse*. Bristol,, Penn.: Falmer Press.

Apple, M. 1979. *Ideology and Curriculum*. New York: Routledge.

———. 1983. *Education and Power*. New York: Routledge.

———. 1988a. Series editor's introduction. Pp. 1–6 in *Capitalist Schools*, ed. D. Liston. New York: Routledge.

———. 1988b. *Teachers and Texts: A Political Economy of Class and Gender Relations in Education*. New York: Routledge.

Aronowitz, S. 1990. *Science as Power: Discourse and Ideology in Modern Society.* Minneapolis: University of Minnesota Press.

Aronowitz, S. and H. Giroux. 1985. *Education under Siege.* New York: Bergin & Garvey.

Aronowitz, S. and H. Giroux. 1991. *Postmodern Education: Culture, Politics and Theory.* Minneapolis: University of Minnesota Press.

Bakhtin, M. M. 1981. *The Dialogic Imagination.* Austin: University of Texas Press.

Bhabha, H. 1988. "The Commitment to Theory." *New Formations* 5:5–52.

Borsa, J. 1990. "Towards a Politics of Location." *Canadian Woman Studies* 11 no. 1:36–39.

Bowles, S., and H. Gintis. 1976. *Schooling in Capitalist America.* New York: Basic Books.

Bromley, H. 1989. "On Not Taking Literacy Literally." *Journal of Education* 171:124–35.

Brosio, R. 1990. "Teaching and Learning for Democratic Empowerment: A Critical Evaluation." *Educational Theory* 40, no. 1:69–82.

Chrichlow, W. 1991. "School Daze." *Afterimage* 18 (May): 16–17.

"Critical Pedagogy for Classroom Teachers: A Bibliography." 1988. *Rethinking Schools* (October–November): 8.

Crowley, T. 1989. *Standard English and the Politics of Language.* Urbana: University of Illinois Press.

Fraser, N. 1990. "Rethinking the Public Sphere." *Social Text* 25/26:56–80.

Giroux, H. 1988. *Schooling and the Struggle for Public Life.* Minneapolis: University of Minnesota Press.

———. 1992. *Border Crossings: Cultural Workers and the Politics of Education.* New York: Routledge.

Gore, J. 1990. "What Can We Do for You! What Can 'We' Do for 'You'? Struggling over Empowerment in Critical and Feminist Pedagogy." *Educational Foundations* 4, no. 3:5–26.

Hofstadter, R. 1963. *Anti-intellectualism in American Life.* New York: Vantage Books.

hooks, b. 1989. *Talking Back.* Boston: South End Press.

———. 1990. *Yearnings.* Boston: South End Press.

Jacoby, R. 1987. *The Last Intellectuals: American Culture in the Age of Academe.* New York: Basic Rooks.

Jay, G. 1991. "The End of 'American' literature: Toward a Multicultural Practice." *College English* 53:264-81.

Jordan, J. 1985. *On Call*. Boston: South End Press.

Joselet, D. 1989. "Living on the Border." *Art in America* (December): 120-28.

Karp, S. 1991. "Critical Pedagogy." *Radical Teacher* Winter): 32-34.

Kincheloe, J. 1991. *Teachers as Researchers: Qualitative Inguiry as a Path to Empowerment*. Bristol, Pa.: Falmer Press.

Laclau, E. 1990. *New Reflections of the Revolution of Our Time*. London: Verso Press.

Liston, D. 1988. *Capitalist Schools*. New York: Routledge.

Lowe, R., and H. Kantor. 1991. Review of *Critical Pedagogy, the State, and Cultural Struggle*, by H. A. Giroux and P. McClaren, eds. *Educational Studies* 22, no. 1: 123-29.

MacDonald, S. P. 1990. "The Literary Argument and Its Discursive Connotations." Pp. 31-59 in *The Writing Scholar: Studies in Academic Discourse*, ed. W. Nash. Newbury Park, Calif.: Sage.

McLaren, P. 1992. "Collisions with Otherness: Traveling theory and the Politics of Ethnographic Practice." *International Journal of Qualitative Research in Education* 1, no. 2:1-15.

Miedema, S. 1987. "The Theory-Practice Relation in Critical Pedagogy." Phenomenology and Pedagogy 5, no. 3:221-29.

Minh-ha, Trinh. 1989. *Women, Native, Other*. Bloomington: Indiana University Press.

————. 1991. *When the Moon Waxes Red*. New York: Routledge.

Mohanty, C. 1989/90. "On Race and Voice: Challenges for Liberal Education in the 1990s." Cultural Critique 14 (Winter): 5-26.

Schrag, F. 1988. "Response to Giroux." *Educational Theory* 38:143-44.

Spivak, G. 1990. *The Post-Colonial Critic: Interviews, Strategies, Dialogues*. New York: Routledge.

West, C. 1991. "Theory, Pragmatism, and Politics." Pp. 22-38 in *Consequences of Theory*, ed. J. Arac and B. Johnson. Baltimore: Johns Hopkins University Press.

Young, R. 1990. *White Mythologies: Writing History and the West*. New York: Routledge.

2

Michael Foucault and the Discourse of Education

David M. Jones and Stephen J. Ball

> I wouldn't want what I may have said or written to be seen as laying any claims to totality. I don't try to universalize what I say; conversely what I don't say isn't meant to be thereby disqualified as being of no importance. My work takes place between unfinished abutments and anticipatory strings of dots. I like to open out a space of research, try it out, then if it doesn't work try again somewhere else. On many points—I am thinking especially of the relations between dialectics, genealogy and strategy—I am still working and don't yet know whether I am going to get anywhere. What I say ought to be taken as "propositions", "game openings" where those who may be interested are invited to join in; they are not meant as dogmatic assertions that have to be taken or left en bloc.

> Michael Foucault, "Questions of Method," in *The Foucault Effect* (1991)

In the spirit of this generous invitation we shall attempt to explore tentatively the implications of Michael Foucault's work for the science of education. In order to do this we shall examine initially Foucault's criticism of the "human sciences" and outline what we consider to be the lineaments of a Foucaldian methodology, bearing in mind of course Foucault's warning about the potential dogmatism involved in such a restitutive enterprise. Finally, we shall offer some observations about how a Foucauldian perspective might inform an understanding of both popular education and educational research.

As our opening quotation suggests, Foucault remained profoundly suspicious of the research enterprise in general and its claim to scientific validity. Foucault was clearly influenced by Georges Canghoulem's thesis that the norm of a specified project governed scientific practice and shaped the formulation of propositions that claimed the status of "truth." Canghoulems's history of biological science indicated that its project was scientific not directly through the actual truth content of its propositions, but through the manner in which they were arranged. This organization established a "veridical normativity" (Gordon 1980, pp. 37–39).

Foucault believed a similar process to be even more apparent in what he describes as the human sciences (particularly economics, sociology, psychology, and linguistics). In other words, the scientific claim of the human sciences cannot be taken for granted. This suspicion informs Foucault's own research and his stance toward the research endeavor. Truth, objectivity, and reason are reinscribed within the human, as well as the natural sciences, as what Foucault calls the effects of power. Consequently, his challenge to the groundwork of social scientific activity necessarily makes him a controversial figure.

As early as *Madness and Civilization* (1967) Foucault sought to stand outside established research traditions in order to demonstrate how epistemological development within the human sciences functions politically to neutralize social problems. Research, he contends, is intimately linked to the political management of social problems. A facade of objectivity obscures this process and empowers the research enterprise with the capacity to categorize, professionalize, and contain a specified social problem. The scientific method, moreover, constructs "a gaze" rendering a social object visible. Through methodical observation and careful measurement these human sciences can insert specified "objects of concern" into a network of ameliorative or therapeutic practices.

It further follows from the position that Foucault occupies that he entertains a healthy suspicion of any scientific claim to originality discovery or, more generally, of benefitting the human condition. Clearly, Foucault sought to detach the will to knowledge from the idea of progress and thereby refute the claim made by researchers in the human sciences that "to know thus to improve." There is a further consideration here. A normative endeavor to induce positive change informs the social scientific endeavor. It is no accident that "man" and "self" constitute the central objects of concern for social science and the project of modernity. Consequently, modernity, and the knowledge that constructs it, has been captured by a constant search for and elaboration of ethical prescriptions. These evolving *modes d'assujetissement* are made plausible by scientific authority.

Foucault viewed this essentialist project as ultimately political. "Knowledge of man", he contended, "unlike the sciences of nature, is always linked, even in its vaguest form to ethics and politics" (1970,

328). The quest for this knowledge combined with the idea of progress creates a contradictory legacy. Indeed, human science, as soon as it functions, "offends or reconciles, attracts or repels, breaks, dissociates, unites or reunites; it cannot help but liberate and enslave" (1970, 328) As David Hoy (1988) explains:

> Knowledge of man (though not necessarily of nature) is tied to politics, that is power, since knowledge is not only put to use, but the uses we have for gathering knowledge will themselves determine what sorts of knowledge we acquire. Knowledge is not gained independently of its uses, but the facts gathered will be functionally related to the uses to which they can be put. (19)

Significantly, in his inaugural lecture to the College de France, Foucault identified his own program research by opposing the notion that discovery or revelation was the purpose of the research endeavor or as he phrased it that "a great unsaid or a great unthought. . .runs through the world and interwines with all forms and all its events, and which we would have to articulate and think at last" (1971, 67). What then does this alternative Foucauldian perspective on research involve?

Of Discourse, Archaeology and Genealogy

In his endeavor to show "that things were not as necessary as all that," Foucault identified an interplay between "a code which rules ways of doing things. . .and a production of true discourses which serve to found, justify and provide reasons for these ways of doing things" (Foucault 1981, 8). Discourse in fact evinced how "men govern themselves and others by the production of truth." By truth, Foucault understood not the production of true utterance, but the formation of domains in which "the practice of true and false can be made pertinent" (1978, 8). He further maintained that his general theme was not society as such, but the "discourse of true and false, by which I mean the correlative formation of domains and objects and the verifiable and falsifiable objects that bear upon them" (8). Moreover, it was not merely the formation of domains of knowledge that intrigued Foucault but also "the effect in the real to which they are linked"!

Statements like these prompt us to wonder what precisely Foucault understood by discourse and its relationship to two related projects: a genealogy of power and an archaeology of knowledge. Discourse is in fact "a political commodity" whose "anonymous murmur" (Deleuze 1988, 55) emerges from a specific site such as in the case of education, the Department of Education and Science, the Inspectorate or the National Curriculum Council. Furthermore discourse involves two registers. In its relationship to knowledge, discourse exhibits "immanent principles of regularity." Basically, most research says little that is striking or interesting. New statements are rare and they are bound by regulations enforced through social practices or research methods and protocols (see Meloy 1992). Yet discourse is also deeply involved with programs designed to shape social reality.

Accordingly, discourse is a combination or "complex" of power and knowledge. Both the *Archaeology of Knowledge* (1972) and *The Order of Things* (1970) proposed the view that the human sciences proceeded according to the regime of the archive—the archaeological conditions of seeing and speaking, light and language, shape the formation of academic subject matter. Knowledge is, therefore, as Gilles Deleuze suggests in his illuminating study of Foucault, "stratified, archivized and endowed with a relatively rigid segmentarity" (Deleuze 1986, 73). By contrast power is geneolgical "It mobilizes non stratified matter and functions" (73). It unfolds flexibly, passing not through specific forms but through particular points, "which on each occasion mark the application of a force." Power transmits or distributes particular discursive features in the form of a diagram. In this view power, in the modern condition, does not derive from a unique centre of sovereignty like the government and is then applied to a passive or coerced population. It is instead, local, unstable and diffuse.

In this mobile and unstable domain strategies take shape. The strategies of power define a mobile, microphysical environment that cannot easily be reduced to knowledge. Nevertheless, knowledge seeks to permeate this microphysical space. Consequentiy, Foucault maintained, the sciences of man are "inseparable from the power relations which make them possible and provoke forms of knowledge (savoirs) which can more or less cross an epistemological threshold or create a practical knowledge (connaisance)" (Deleuze 1988, 74). Knowledge can never refer to a subject free in relation to a diagram of power, but neither can power be separated from the forces of knowledge that actualize it. Discourse then is "a complex of power and knowledge that ties together the diagram and the archive and articulates them on the basis of their difference in nature" (75). Or as Foucault explains it in *The History of Sexuality*: Between techniques of knowledge and strategies of power, there is no exteriority, even if they have their specific roles and are linked together on the basis of their difference" (1979, 130).

In spite of this mutual immanence Foucault sees no real confusion between the effective categories of power that incite and provoke discourse and the formal categories of knowledge such as education or punishment. The latter categories, however, necessarily have to be articulated and visualized in order to actualize power relations. By virtue of this displacement a discursive site, such as the school, the workshop, or the prison, has the capacity to integrate power relations by "constituting various forms of knowledge which actualize, modify and redistribute these relations" (Deleuze 1988, 77). It is the work of the statement, in Deleuze's view, by its rarity, repetition and regularity that achieves this integration and actualization. There are not many new statements about pedagogical methods for instance and they become discursively entrenched by continuous repetition (see Jones 1990). Regularity forms the curve or the rule that joins the individual points of power and facilitates the transmission of the diagram of power whether the schoolroom, the factory, or the prison.

Power, for Foucault, then is not simply violence or coercion. It is blind and mute, but precisely because of this, it incites speech and visibility. It works through the diagram. The diagram as the fixed form of a set of relations between forces never exhausts force. Force then always retains potentiality with respect to the diagram that contains it. It always affords the possibility of resistance. There are moreover different diagrams. As Colin Gordon has observed, "Our world does not follow a programme, but we live in a world of programmes, that is to say a world traversed by the effects of discourses whose object is the rendering rationalisable, transparent and programmeable of the real" (1991, 39).

In his key works *Discipline and Punish* (1977) and *The History of Sexuality* (1979) Foucault demonstrated a particular concern with the genealogy of power as it shaped an emerging modernity. Here Foucault identified two tendencies. In *Discipline and Punish* he elaborated the features of an anatomo-politics. This diagram involved the imposition of a particular taste or conduct on a multiplicity of different individuals. This microdisciplinary regime merely required a small number of subjects (the inmates of a prison or the pupils in a classroom) and a limited and confined space informed by a specified technology. In the case of the anatomo-political diagram, the Benthamite Panopticon (essentially a disciplinary arrangement that enabled guards to observe without the prisoners knowing when they were observed) constituted the apparatus of permanent observation applied to a specific body in a limited space. It came to form a polyvalent technology equally applicable to prisoners, the sick, the insane, factory hands or, for that matter, schoolchildren.

Alongside this disciplinary society, Foucault subsequently mapped in *The History of Sexuality* a biopolitical diagram of power. Different from, but not necessarily opposed to, the micropenal regime of the prison, bio-politics ordered and controlled life in a large population and in an open spare. Thus as Deleuze has once again observed, "The two pure functions in modern societies will be anatomo-politics and bio-politics and the two bare matters those of a particular body and a particular population" (1988, 72).In *The History of Sexuality* in particular Foucault attempted to show how a biopolitical game of "capture and seduction" came to inform the tutelary relationships of "parents and children, adults and adolescents, educators and students, doctors and patients, the psychiatrist with his hysterics and his perverts." Biopower seduces rather than coerces. Its attractions, evasions, and mutual incitement have "traced around bodies and sexes not boundaries not to be crossed, but perpetual spirals of power and pleasure" (Foucault 1977, 45).

Two further aspects of Foucault's thought should also be mentioned. Foucault's work often refers to the terms *technology* and *strategy*. By technologies he understands "coherent or contradictory forms of managing and activating a population." Like Bentham's panopticon they lend themselves to polyvalent tactical applications (Donzelot 1979, 77). By contrast, strategies "enable the implementation of a programme, (and) the generation of actions." Strategies offer a "practical objective for corrective intervention and governmental programmes or redirection" (77). Thus the technology of observation with its segmenting of a limited space to enable continual observation makes possible the application of specific strategies like the examination or the case study that reduces life to writing in a case file. There is then an interdependance between the technological and the strategic register.

However, it would be wrong to assume that discourse, its technologies, and strategies shapes the world unproblemmatically. The purpose of Foucault's genealogy is to reveal (if it reveals anything) not a correspondence between programs, practices, and effects, but "the manner in which they fail to correspond and the positive significance that can attach to such discrepancies" (Donzelot 1979, 77–78). Quite often the prescribed technology does not alter the social real in the way that the theory programmers envisage. This gap between technologies and strategic outcomes is not, Foucault maintains, one between "the purity of the ideal and the disorderly impurity of the real" (1979, 10). In fact, "there are in any social practice, whether education, medical care, or social work, usually "a series of strategies that are mutually opposed, composed, and superposed so as to produce solid effects that can perfectly well be read in terms of their rationality even though they do not conform to the initial programming" (Gordon 1991, 39). Discourse in consequence is not a medium for strategy but a resource.

Strategy then is indispensable for genealogy at the point where the noncorrespondence of discourses, practices, and effects create possibilities for operations whose sense is either unstated or unstable within any one discourse. Where the terrain of the strategy is social, like popular education for instance, there is always the further possibility that the competing or conflicting strategy programs will result in a new one. Technology by contrast acts as an independent principle for the multiplication, adaptation, and reorganization of effects. Yet as Gordon maintains, "a technology of normalisation always admits a certain freeplay" (1991, 38) and so facilitates a variety of strategic possibilities. The diffusion of techniques permits programs based on quite different normativities, such as political economy, social planning, or psychology to enter into permutations and exchanges. Indeed, as Foucault conclusively illustrates in *Discipline and Punish*, it is possible for a techno-logical apparatus like the prison to continue operating while adapting itself to a strategic role diametrically opposed to its initial program— not the elimination of criminality, but its exploitation.

Ultimately, Foucault's methodological concern is to elucidate the conditions that govern the rare and singular emergence of statements, whilst accepting that "ensembles of discourse proliferate" (Foucault 1978, 10). Such an approach enabled him to revive the Nietzchean enterprise of tracing the lines of transformation of moral technologies and write history in the present tense in order to show how subjects "govern themselves by the production of truth" – (Foucault 1981, 10). How we might ask could such a perspective inform our understanding of education and practice of educational science? It is to this that we shall finally turn.

Toward a Foucauldian Research Agenda

Interestingly, Foucault did not identify education as a human science or directly address its implications for a biopolitics. Nevertheless, in *Discipline and Punish* he does refer to the emergence of popular schooling within a disciplinary technology that sought through the architecture of the schoolroom, the gaze of the teacher, and the strategy of examination to normalize a population of students. Elsewhere in the *History of Sexuality*, Foucault drew attention to the confessional and tutelary relationship that exists between teacher and taught and the consequences this might have for pedagogy.

Medical science in particular has appropriated such confessional practices to facilitate the formation of technologies of the self framework of therapy and tutelage. From a Foucauldian perspective therefore social workers, children's clinics, and child guidance and school health services would constitute a network of advice that linked the child to the school and the school to the family. This tutelary complex and its capacity to reduce life to writing through the technique of the file would be of absorbing interest to a Foucauldian as it constitutes a technology for locating the urban family more precisely in a regime of power/knowledge. There are a number of other ways in which Foucault's postmodernism would volatize the epistemology of research in the human sciences. Against the development of totalizing theories, law-like regularities, and a desire for closure and rule-governed behavior, postmodernists generally pursue the singular, the discontinuous, the undecidable, and the catastrophic. Educational research from this perspective would seek not the closure of an explanation but the interpretation of the surface features of social life reading the school as a text. Moreover, the social texts can never be understood in terms of decisive, unifying structures. The postmodernist accepts instead that they are capable of multiple interpretations rather than subject to single truths. All of this rests upon a primary assumption of complexity rather than profundity as the object and purpose of research.

In some ways these lines of argument bode well for the ethnographer. The emphasis upon case study and context, the language of actors' meanings, complexity in action and in interpretation, and a commitment to understanding and description rather than explanation and cause would seem to contain at least echoes and resonances of a Foucauldian version of good research. However, there are two outstanding problems in reconciling ethnography with Foucault's epistemological relativism. First, there is Foucault's break with subjectivity, he displaces "man" as the source of knowledge and considers all human experience a product of discourse. Whereas by definition most ethnographers place the thinking subject as a primary source of knowledge. Second,- the break with subjectivity is linked to Foucault's argument in the *Order of Things* about the "death of man" in the modern period and his concomitant denial of the rational actor. Nonetheless, the diagram of a microphysics of power, which cannot be reduced to a single intention, would seem to be fertile ground for ethnographic as much as genealogical investigation. Here, however, Foucault has been criticized for failing to write into his calculus of power any role for agency, which appears to leave little conceptual space for forms of resistance (see Sawicki 1991).

There is an additional challenge to the ethnographer and to other kinds of educational research in Foucault's argument for the specificity of discourse. He will not allow us the convenient realist assumption that the world has its own expression. Discourse is not an approximation of nondiscursive reality. Discourse does violence to things. It is an imposition. This concern is clearly linked to Foucault's emphasis on surface and exteriority. Together they constitute a critique of those intellectual conventions that assume individual motives and intentions instantiate discourse. By contrast the strategy of exteriority involves an analysis of the "conditions of existence" of a discourse. This would entail identifying the range of possible statements that the discourse can generate, in other words, what is sayable and thinkable within a discursive formation, and exploring the social-historical conditions of discourse. Discourses accordingly empower and disempower, privilege and exclude. Such conditions are reproduced within discourse itself. Discourse is a central part of the relations of power within a society. It is an event that replaces the subject with a set of constitutive rules.

Consequently, whereas the archaeological endeavor is primarily concerned with an analysis in and of language, the genealogical project comes much closer to a sociology of discourse. Political and economic concerns feature and discourse entails practices that exist within and reproduce institutional contexts. Nevertheless, both in the clinic and the classroom it is the practice of the technologies themselves that form the object of Foucault's concern. He is encouraging us to look at things rather than for explanations.

Otherness and the Formation of Moral Subjects

In his history of insanity Foucault sets himself the task of writing a history of otherness. An attempt to speak for the unspeakable, to give madness both its own voice and its own history. For Foucault "otherness" is the historical a priori of Western culture. It comes in many forms: the alien, the strange, the criminal, the incomprehensible, the pathological, and most particularly the insane. The other is the exterior of both progress and history. Otherness is the antithesis of reason and epistemology seeks to subject it to reason. This subjection takes the form of scientific inquiry and diagnosis of the irrational subject, whether it be the criminal, the insane, the diseased, the child, or the woman. Psychiatry, anthropology, criminology, and sociology work to constitute otherness in discourse:

Once the other appeared in African and Asian dress, there began new so-called scientific inquiries that aimed at understanding and dominating these new objects. In this projection of reason underlying the formation of new disciplines, a rational knowledge was always juxtaposed to ignorance, humanity to inhumanity. (Harootunian 1988, 118)

The other becomes a moral subject. By contrast, Foucault attempts to explicate that which is conspicuous by its absence. Genealogies are insurrectionary knowledges, strategic interventions into the conditions of possibility of contemporary knowledge.

Let us give the term genealogy to the union of erudite knowledge and local memories which allow us to establish an historical knowledge of struggles and make use of that knowledge today. . . it entertains the claims to attention of local, discontinuous, disqualified, illegitimate knowledges, against the claim of a unitary body of theory which would filter, hierarchize and order them in the name of some true knowledge and some arbitrary idea of what constitutes a science as its objects. (Foucault 1980, 83–84)

Foucault's stance seeks to give voice to otherness and provide a form through which the universalizing prescriptions of the human sciences may be deconstructed. Thus, from a Foucauldian perspective we might see teachers as moral subjects that are appraised and managed. The contemporary image repertoire presents the teacher as an other—irrational, failed, requiring categorization and management (Ball 1990). School improvement and school effectiveness work to bring a normative gaze to bear not on pupils but increasingly upon teachers and measure and compare their performance in terms of outcomes. No longer to be trusted to speak they are effectively excluded from discourse, once marginalized they constitute an object of discursive concern. A Foucauldian might be tempted to wonder how such a situation had come about.

In posing such a question a research agenda might be provisionally delineated. It would initially interrogate the foundations of educational science and the conditions under which statements about popular education came to be made, achieved regularity, and established moral subjects. In exploring this emerging educational discourse the Foucauldian would explore the developing science of examination and its strategic effects upon a population whose management in depth and detail it facilitates (Hoskin 1990). This analysis would therefore draw attention initially to the archaelogy of popular education; to the way in which strategies of examination and classroom management have taken shape and become in turn objects of concern that offer further possibilities for discourse.

The Foucauldian would relish the irony that a scientific method for distinguishing between the normal and pathological population, like the examination, occasions new strategies that in turn evoke tactical resistances, failures, and consequent discursive reversals as well as new objects for discursive intervention. The continuing educational debate of the 1980s in England, for example, witnessed a shift from a discriminatory examination that marginalized large sections of the population, to a differentiatory examination technique, that sought to render the whole school population visible and available to a scientific gaze through continuous assessment and record of achievement, and comes ultimately to focus not on the failed pupil, but the failing teacher. The incoherences and reversals within the examinatory strategy would from a postmodernist perspective emerge within a genealogy of examination in which the possibility of what is examinable is regulated by an examinatory epistemology. Isomorphically the emerging concern, with Race, Gender, and Disability in educational discourse and the way in which they have volatized scientific objectivity in the school would constitute epistemological ruptures in educational discourse that offer opportunities for the invention of new strategies and further discourse. These mobile and polyvalent strategies that shape the urban school and penetrate the relationship between teacher and taught; the school and the family, and the school and the workplace would offer a micropolitical focus for the Foucauldian. Central to a reading of these ambivalent social texts would be Foucault's obsevation that the failure of a specific strategy is merely an opportunity and an incitement to discourse.

From a micropolitics of the school and the strategic force relationships that play across it, it would be possible to broaden the inquiry. This would entail an interrogation of the dialogue between educational sites and others constituted by politics, economics, and medicine, which together would form an assemblage or complex of power/knowledge. In this context we might trace the school's place in a eugenic technology that ordered the practice of the school in terms of physical fitness, the coding of gender, and the measurement of intelligence. The tracing of this diagram might reveal the ambiguous moral coding that has genealogically shaped the teacher and the taught. The manner in which the teacher occupied at different moments the role of moral exemplar, good father, nursing mother, health bringer, and moral technician would illustrate the extent to which educational science was profoundly caught up in *modes d'assujetissement* and the formation of an ethics of the body.

The ambiguous ethical role would illustrate the paradoxical manner in which a moral discourse has unfolded on the school site. It would also shed some light upon the problem we initially outlined. The trained teacher placed in the urban slum school to offer a regenerative example becomes in time herself the object of discursive concern and the opportunity of new discursive interventions. The emergence of the problematic teacher alongside the problem child in the problem family has become a notable feature of the current debate about the apparent decline in educational standards. A Foucauldian analysis of this decline and the culpability of the feckless and incompetent teacher would explore how the teacher has become paradoxically imbricated in the moral collapse she was strategically designed to address.

To conclude, Foucault and the work of subsequent poststructuralist thinkers like Gilles Deleuze and Jacques Donzelot offer challenging possibilities for educational research. Such an enterprise, however, would have to be informed by an awareness that "the interesting thing is to ascertain not what overall project presides over all these developments but how in terms of strategy the different pieces were set in place" (Foucault 1980, 62).

References

Ball, S.J. 1990. "Management as Moral Technology: A Luddite Analysis, pp. 153–66 in *Foucault and Education*, ed. S. J. Ball. London: Routledge.

Deleuze, G. 1988. *Foucault*. Minneapolis: University of Minnesota Press.

Donzelot, J. 1979. "The Power of Political Culture." *Ideology and Consciousness* 5 (Spring).

Foucault, M. 1970. *The Order of Things*, New York: Random House.

———. 1971. *L'ordre du discours*. Paris: Gallimard.

———. 1977. *Discipline and Punish*. London: Allen Lane.

———. 1979. *The History of Sexuality, Vol. 1*. London: Allen Lane.

———. 1980. *Power/Knowledge: Selected Interviews and Other Writings*, ed. C. Gordon. Brighton: Harvester Press.

———. 1981. "Questions of Method." *Ideology and Consciousness* 8 (Spring).

Gordon, C., P. Miller and G. Burchell. 1991. *The Foucault Effect: Studies in Governmentality*. Brighton: Harvester/Wheatsheaf.

Harootunian, H. D. 1988. "Foucault, Genealogy and History: The Pursuit of Otherness." Pp. 110–137. *After Foucault*, ed. J. Arac. New Brunswick: Rutgers University Press.

Hoskin, K. 1990. "Foucault under Examination: The Crypto-Educationalist Unmasked." Pp. 29–53 in Ball, *Foucault and Education*.

Hoy, D. 1988. "Foucault: Modern or Post-Modern." Pp. 12–41 in Arac, *After Foucault*.

Jones, D. M. 1990. "The Genealogy of the urban Schoolteacher." Pp. 57–77 in Ball, *Foucault and Education*.

Meloy, J. 1992. "Writing the Qualitative Dissertation: Voices of Experience." AERA Conference Paper, San Francisco, April.

Sawicki, J. 1991. *Disciplining Foucault: Feminism, Power, and the Body*. New York: Routledge.

3

Forms of Ideology-Critique: A Pedagogical Perspective

Nicholas C. Burbules

Ideology and Ideology-Critique

Ideology, suggests Michael Dale (1986), is a "conceptual chameleon." Indeed, the range of its meanings is so varied, and so colored by its theoretical surroundings, that its main value no longer may be as an explanatory category, but as a kind of Rorschach pattern, an indirect indicator through which we can read deep-seated beliefs and values about knowledge and politics held by those who employ the concept. In this essay I will review several different conceptions of ideology as they arise in contexts of ideology-critique. I will suggest, in fact, that the notion of ideology-critique is the more fundamental—that is, when one labels a position as "ideological," one *already* has made certain implicit decisions about how it is to be disclosed and criticized. These competing notions of ideology-critique assume competing epistemo- logical and political positions, as well as positions about how people change their beliefs; in other words, stances toward ideology-critique assume implicit educational theories. After presenting this point, I will conclude by recommending a *pedagogical* view of ideology-critique and will discuss some possible relations between ideology-critique and educational research.

Because many accounts of ideology focus on its effects, particularly its capacity to promote or suppress certain political interests, they have failed to address a more fundamental question: Why do people embrace ideologies? Clifford Geertz (1973, 202) suggests that the sociology of such accounts is too muscular and their psychology too weak. In his classic essay "Ideology as a Cultural System" Geertz helps us understand the appeal that ideologies hold for people and the real cognitive and affective demands they respond to. The significance of Geertz's account is in explaining the persistence of certain systems of belief and value, even when they have retrogressive or repressive effects: because they present plausible and relatively coherent explanations of the social world; because they encourage, reassure, and motivate people; and because they establish a basis for solidarity and a sense of one's position in the world. In short, ideologies represent a version of the world that helps people make sense of their circumstances. Any critical position that does not acknowledge such benefits regards persons as dupes, manipulated by ideologies foisted upon them, and locked into modes of thought whose consequences they do not understand.[1]

Offering a fully developed alternative conception of ideology is a project beyond the scope of this essay; here I simply want to suggest the importance of developing an understanding of ideologies that does justice to their plausibility and meaningfulness for those who embrace them. Many theories of ideology are limited in their ability to do this because they are more concerned with the effects of ideologies than with their genesis. Against this I would contrast a "poetics" of ideology: an accounting of its interpretability, its capacity to be read figuratively as well as literally, its strong emotional and spiritual connotations, and its flexibility and subtlety of appeal.[2] The sociological or political effects of ideologies, I would argue, need to be read through their psychological appeal, and vice versa. Certainly beliefs and values do motivate people to act, or not act, in various ways that need explaining. But many accounts of ideology link systems of belief and value to their macroscopic effects without examining the crucial intermediary processes of understanding, interpretation, and feeling through which ideologies actually are embraced by people and because of which they have their effects on action. Ideologies *reveal* as well as *conceal* aspects of social and political life; they are not simply deceptive or distorting (see Eagleton 1975, 89).

A related problem, also discussed by Geertz (1973, 193), is that the concept of ideology itself has become "ideologized." In other words, its typical uses are self-serving and pejorative ("I'm committed, but he's ideological"). Characterizing belief systems as ideologies is, in common usage, a handy way of attributing to them a host of implied failings—political contentiousness, manipulative uses of language, partisan ranting, sloppiness, inaccuracy, or downright falsehood—without bothering to substantiate such accusations. Thus, even identifying a system of belief as "ideological" implies that one already has criticisms of it, criticisms that frequently are left implied and are not articulated or defended. What makes such characterizations of ideology ideological is that by obscuring one's grounds for critique they come to be seen as undebatable. Rather, I will argue, the very characterization of something as an ideology entails an obligation to justify that characterization in terms of certain standards and judgments that one is prepared to spell out and defend.

An implicit commitment to such standards is true even of the position that avers that "everything is ideological." This point of view derives from theories in the sociology of knowledge that support relativistic positions on cross-cultural or cross-paradigmatic comparison and evaluation (for several classic statements of this position, see Kuhn 1970; Mannheim 1936, and Winch, 1958). Typically, theories of ideology are divided into "pejorative" and "nonpejorative" conceptions, the former implying a position of ideology-critique, the latter denying the possibility of such judgments. The latter view, however, is mistaken on at least three central points. First, the claim that every group possesses (some) ideological beliefs, which is probably true, does not support the conclusion that *all* beliefs are ideological. Similarly, simply because *some* beliefs are incommensurable or untranslatable into other frameworks— just as phrases in certain languages are—does not mean that the entire systems of belief are incommensurable or untranslatable. Second, as several philosophers have argued, the position of relativism often assumes the very basis for argumentation and generalization that it denies; and the more vehement and sweeping the assertions of relativism, the more ironic this inconsistency becomes. Relativism, to the extent that one espouses it as a justified position, is a belief based on certain standards of reasoned reflection; in short, no one can be a relativist through and through (see Siegel 1988). Third, and most pertinent for the purposes of this essay, even the position that claims that "everything is ideological" entails a conception of ideology-critique, although the standards behind it are more deeply buried and difficult to problematize.

Why do we use a term like "ideology" at all (especially if we think that "everything is ideological")? Even in the relativistic use of the term, it implies that any system of belief and value is partial, imperfect, and particularistic; indeed, the very significance of the relativistic position on ideology is that it claims that any one system of belief and value is limited and flawed. In this it undoubtedly is correct. But the problem is that this position—namely, that any system of belief and value is limited and flawed—assumes a vantage point from which systems can be *seen as* limited and flawed, which is a nonrelativistic claim. In other words, the very strength of the sociology of knowledge perspective is that it reveals the incompleteness of every system of belief and value, which is itself a position of ideology-critique, even if one extends it to all competing positions.

My point here is that the terms "ideology" and "critique" are an opposing pair. To be ideological is to be resistant to criticism: to insulate certain beliefs from the possibility of being questioned or to deflect questions as being illegitimate or irrelevant. To be critical is to acknowledge the existence of a basis for critique: to commit oneself to standards and norms that one is prepared to defend and against which one is prepared to allow one's own positions to be judged. Hence, "ideology-critique" never can be insulated from critique itself. Whatever one's stance (and I will discuss several possibilities), one is claiming in some sense an advantaged position. Yet there is a wide variety among different forms of ideology-critique in terms of their openness about what their standards are and their willingness to be judged in turn.

Five Forms of Ideology-Critique

The first, and most common, form of ideology-critique is scientific or rational critique. On this view, ideologies fall short of certain formal features of rational discourse: they ignore the facts, they argue fallaciously, they distort the truth, and so on. "Ideological ideas are like a dirty river, muddied and polluted by the impurities that have flooded into it....Thought determined by social fact is like a pure stream, crystal clear, transparent" (Stark 1958, 90–91). One version of this argument can be found in Harvey Siegel's *Educating Reason* (1988). Siegel says, " 'Enlightened rationalism,' i.e., the general view which takes rationality and critical thinking to be fundamental intellectual ideals, cannot be regarded as just another ideology....It alone sanctions the critical evaluation of all ideologies—including...itself" (75).

In quite a different context, this position is substantially the one favored by Karl Marx. In the *German Ideology*, he argued that an ideology was like a *camera obscura*, presenting an inverted picture of reality (Marx and Engels 1947, 47). At many points in his theory Marx contrasted ideology with a "scientific" account of history and society (particularly his own). For Marx, "Ideology [was] a belief system that makes pretentious and unjustified claims to scientificity....Ideology was failed science, not authentic science (Gouldner 1976, 9). Ironically, this position is fundamentally identical with that of conservative social scientists, such as Talcott Parsons (1959) who says, "The essential criteria of an ideology are deviations from social science objectivity. The criterion of distortion is that statements are made about society which, by social science methods, can be shown to be positively in error" (38).

In general, these sorts of views regard ideology as a subject of epistemic scrutiny and judge it against traditional measures of truth, clarity, and validity. The epistemological assumptions of such a position are fairly obvious: they assume that there is objective evidence against which purportedly "ideological" claims can be compared and found wanting. Less obviously, they assume that matters of social and political import can and should be resolved through persuasive arguments and through the application of objective social science or historical methods to the examination of the sources of problematic social situations and to the feasibility of prospective solutions to them. Finally, they also assume that presenting countervailing evidence, and formulating more logically valid arguments, usually will be sufficient to move persons away from the ideological positions they hold to more rational ones. Such assumptions are subject to question, of course. My purpose here is simply to point them out and to argue that they are frequently left unstated by those who use the label of "ideology" to characterize views they find "unscientific" or irrational.

A second kind of ideology-critique—*immanent critique*—was emphasized by the earlier critical theorists, particularly Max Horkheimer. From this standpoint, one challenges a belief system not by comparing it against a set of external standards but by showing that it does not measure up to its own (perhaps unstated) standards; it "proceeds, so to speak, 'from within,' and hopes to avoid, thereby, the charge that its concepts impose irrelevant criteria of evaluation on the object" (Held 1980, 106).

Because the Frankfurt theorists were concerned with the rise of fascism during the first part of the twentieth century and the central role that hegemonic culture plays in the survival of capitalism, they devoted central attention to the problem of identifying and criticizing ideologies. But because they also had deep skepticism about the objective status of social science knowledge,[3] they were unwilling to rely on concepts of research, evidence, or technical rationality as a basis for discrediting ideology. In this they moved beyond the traditional Marxist conceptions of ideology and ideology-critique. They opted, rather, for a stance that sought to disclose the hypocrisies, inconsistencies, and contradictions latent within modern Western culture, and in so doing to hold up a critical mirror that would reflect back upon the modern consciousness its own false consciousness.

Immanent critique arises on more personal levels, as well. We do this whenever we point out to friends or associates that they have contradicted themselves, or are failing to live up their own proclaimed values, or are failing to consider the true motivations of their actions.

In a sense, this is potentially a more fundamentally withering point of critique, since it alludes to criteria that the adherents of a system of belief or value themselves espouse.

Epistemologically, immanent critique withholds external evaluation of the system of beliefs or values being questioned, for it is directed more to internal coherence or consistency; but this also is an epistemic stance, since it does assume a more objective standard of clarity and consistency that ideological thought fails to meet. Socially and politically, this approach to ideology-critique values the raising of unstated or suppressed interests to open consideration and debate, ostensibly without judging a priori between them, but with the implicit assumption that when such interests are identified openly, only some will be able to withstand scrutiny. Hence, despite an initial appearance of tolerance, the critical theory approach does harbor substantive beliefs about better and worse ways to live. Educationally, this approach to ideology-critique assumes, as do the methods of Freudian psychotherapy, that diagnosing contradictions and leading persons to acknowledge their internal disjunctions is a necessary step in the process of transforming them. Hence, even when others do not share one's own assumptions and standards, there still is a basis for moving them to reconsider their views. One can say that critical theory seeks to apply this method at the level of culture and society.[4]

A third kind of ideology-critique is *deconstructionist*. As in immanent critique, here the critic does not argue for a position of epistemic superiority in challenging an ideology—indeed, most proponents of this approach deny the possibility of such a stance. Deconstructionist theorists explicitly reject notions of evidence, truth, or logical validity as granting any degree of objectivity in assessing beliefs and values. As Jean-François Lyotard (1984) and others have argued, such positivistic premises simply represent the grandiose self-assertions of just one other partial and particularistic way of understanding the world. The stance of the deconstructionist is one of ironic distance from all "metanarratives" that proclaim a universal method, perspective, or foundation.

On this view, then, ideology-critique cannot proceed from a position of epistemic privilege; nor can it, like immanent critique, invoke notions of internal consistency as a basis for evaluation, since for the more radical proponents of this view (Lyotard and Derrida in particular), even such apparently neutral criteria as clarity and consistency are no more than the remnants of an anachronistic search for intellectual order—remnants that must be abandoned in the pursuit of spontaneous and completely decentered interpretive freedom. Indeed, it is unclear initially whether such an intellectual stance even can support a notion of ideology-critique.

I think, however, that there is a notion of ideology-critique specific to the deconstructionist perspective, and its essence lies in this ironic, distanced gaze. Deconstructive criticism seeks to disclose mechanisms for constituting truth, meaning, and value as ultimately arbitrary and culturally particularistic; while certain claims may purport objectivity and universality, this too is simply part of their construction. The deconstructionist critic is like the heckler who sits in the front row of a magician's routine, shouting out for the audience every slight of hand, every palmed card, every feint, in the expectation that once the mechanisms of illusion are revealed, they will lose their capacity to captivate and deceive us. Ideology-critique proceeds, on this view, by weaning people away from their fond beliefs in metanarratives, to see the world as fractured, disordered, and irreconcilably plural. By seeking to demystify any particular system that claims to explain and organize the world, deconstructionism removes "arbitrary" constraints on our ability to shift perspectives or to construct ad hoc and idiosyncratic interpretations when they suit us. Politically, such an approach values freedom over consensus, plurality over community. Epistemologically, it is important to recognize that this view, like many other relativistic stances, seems to deny the possibility of any ground for epistemic authority, but in fact arrogates to itself a vastly privileged position, namely, the wise eye that sees all and is not deceived. Beneath its asserted claims of decentered authority, I believe, much of the deconstructive literature is actually remarkably authoritarian, broad, and conclusive in its pronouncements about the impossibility of justifying broad and conclusive pronouncements.

A fourth kind of ideology-critique, mentioned earlier, is an *argument from effects*. On this view, all systems of belief and value exist in a sociopolitical context and have consequences within the dynamics of that context. An alternative reading of Marx would emphasize this interpretation. Marx (Marx and Engels 1947, 64–66) says that it is because certain ideas are the *ruling* ideas that they are ideological; they are partisan in the class struggle. Louis Althusser (1972) stressed this aspect of Marx, for example, in analyzing how ideology functions as a "State Apparatus": "It is in the forms and under the forms of ideological subjection that provision is made for the reproduction of the skills of labour power" (246). For Althusser, in fact, ideology does not have only certain effects; it "has a material existence" manifested in relations, practices, and institutions (267–70).

This mode of critique differs from the first three in that its basis for judgment does not pertain to epistemic adequacy, reasonableness, consistency, and so on, but to the ways in which ideologies legitimate and support a social system that itself is judged. Some proponents of this view may not intend the term "ideology" pejoratively in every case. Rather, ideologies that support a social and political system that one judges favorably are, due to their effects, positive; ideologies that support social and political systems one judges harshly are, correspondingly, negative. Significantly, then, on this view, one cannot tell always from the features of a particular ideology whether or not it is problematic. One might need to know historical and contextual factors in order to judge if the ideology is having, or is likely to have, effects one desires.

An example of this analysis is offered by Douglas Kellner (1978), who argues that ideologies often have a "life cycle."[25] In an early phase (which he calls "ideology as ism"), an ideology may have progressive effects by motivating a spirit of social activism and reform, by establishing a sense of group solidarity, and by granting purpose and direction to a process of social change. Over time, however, as circumstances change—indeed, one might say, partly because of its success in promoting certain changes—the very same system of belief and value might become restrictive and even reactionary (Kellner calls this "ideology as hegemony"). The content of the ideology has not changed; the social and political circumstances have changed, and so have its effects. The basis for critique, then, is not content, but consequences.

This approach to ideology-critique is more politically hard-headed and pragmatic, although one might say it can lead to a certain opportunism and *realpolitik* orientation. My point is to show that such judgments assume that one has a substantive vision of what society ought to be like. If an ideology moves society in this direction, fine; if it does not, then one challenges it. Persuading persons of the (perniciously) ideological character of certain beliefs and values, then, requires a prior condition, namely, that they share, or can be brought to share, a commitment to the substantive goals for society that one favors.

A fifth, and related, kind of ideology-critique is even more instrumental, asserting that one can challenge an ideology only by confronting it with a counter-ideology. This stance is preferred especially by critics who espouse relativistic epistemologies, who do not believe that it is possible to apply criteria of comparison or assessment across systems of belief and value. According to this position, as discussed earlier, the merits of alternative belief systems cannot be adjudicated rationally; in the end, selections are made for nonepistemic reasons. Hence, if one finds a particular ideology repugnant, on this view, one only can proffer an alternative ideology and hope to attract others to it by whatever persuasive means necessary. Probably the best-known, and most effective, advocate of this view was V. I. Lenin.

However, this position, although relativistic on its face, does rely implicitly on nonrelativistic claims; for on whatever basis one is claiming the preferability of one's position over the other, one expects that claim to carry some weight with others—which means that some standards of truth or value are being applied across belief systems. Even if one believes that claims of truth or value cannot be demonstrated to be absolutely right and wrong, one certainly must believe they can be shown to be better and worse by some criteria.

This point can be put another way: To the extent that one adopts a position of ideology-*critique*, proclaiming the superiority of one way of thinking and acting over another, one patently is making claims about what is better and worse, not only for one's own preferences but for others' as well. Often proponents of this approach will purport not to be making universal or generalizable assertions; but in fact they are caught in what Karl-Otto Apel (1987; see also Habermas 1990) calls a "performative contradiction," belying in the very nature of their speech act what they claim to believe. Indeed, their relativistic metaclaims ring particularly hollow, given the absolutistic tone and sweeping manner with which they actually make pronouncements about the truth of relativism, as I mentioned previously.

This approach, I believe, also threatens to lead to the most cynical and manipulative approaches toward actually changing the views of others. By denying the possibility of bringing people to new social and political positions through reasoned discussion, this approach encourages the adoption of simple expediency. Such an approach to dealing with people makes an ironic bedfellow with the "liberating" and "empowering" ends it often purports to serve; but worse than this, it becomes a self-fulfilling activity. To the extent that one assumes that people are moved by ideologies, and so can be changed only by new ideologies, one perpetuates popular dependencies on simple answers, dogmatic beliefs in the justice of one's cause, exaggerated dichotomies between victims and persecuters, or between liberators and reactionaries—and the sort of naive utopianism that assumes we already know what the best kind of society is and that the only question is how to achieve it. This approach perpetuates, even exacerbates, a kind of political superficiality and, infantilism that can, I believe, be just as "oppressive" and restrictive of freedom as are the more visible external forms that oppression often takes.

A Pedagogical Perspective on Ideology-Critique

In sketching these forms of ideology-critique, I have tried to show how they differ in their assumptions about politics and knowledge: in claims about possessing a vision of the Good Society; and in methods and perspectives that grant special "nonideological" status to their own position, or, if their own position also is identified as ideological, a superiority grounded on some other basis. Much more needs to be said about how these beliefs about politics and knowledge are worked out in the context of each approach. Here my purpose is narrow and specific: I have tried to show (1) how assertions that a system of belief and value *is* ideological already presume a superior vantage point from which it can be disclosed and criticized (even if the superiority of this vantage point is implicit, unstated, and unjustified), and (2) how approaches to ideology-critique also assume educational notions about how people can be brought to change from belief in one ideological system to another nonideological or, if still ideological, *better* ideological system of belief and value.

Each of the five accounts I have discussed here has an educational point of view. From the standpoint of rational ideology-critique, change comes from presenting the weight of evidence and good arguments to those who simply are mistaken in their beliefs. The central metaphor here, one might say, is of opening a shuttered window through which holders of an ideology can glimpse the real world they have been missing. From the standpoint of immanent ideology-critique, change comes from pointing out to persons the inconsistencies and contradictions they themselves have fallen prey to, given their own (perhaps unrecognized) beliefs and desires. The central metaphor here is of holding up a mirror in which persons can see reflected back critically to them the prejudgments of their own beliefs and practices. From the standpoint of deconstructive ideology-critique, change comes from making explicit what is taken for granted, from showing the artificial nature of any attempt to assert an order of things that supercedes human attempts at interpretation and mimesis. The central metaphor here, mentioned earlier, is revealing the tricks of the magician so that they lose their capacity to captivate and mystify us. From the standpoint of ideology-critique based on effects, change comes from disclosing the effects of ideologies within a struggle over political power and privilege, in the expectation that once persons are made aware of these consequences, they will abandon or change beliefs that play a role in restricting their freedoms in favor of others that will enhance them. The central metaphor here is of drawing a map, of showing where certain roads lead to, in contrast to alternative routes. Assuming that people know (or can be shown) where society ought to be going socially and politically, they will judge these alternative routes accordingly. Finally, from the standpoint of ideology-critique as the promulgation of counter-ideologies, change comes from the popular appeal one can elicit for one system of belief and value rather than another; what this appeal happens to be based upon, in this view, is not the central issue. What matters is that, from the standpoint of the advocate of the ideology, it will change substantially and improve the prospects of those who come to embrace it and act upon it (whether they realize it or not). Here the central metaphor is of painting a picture; it does not matter what it represents or whether this representation is "accurate" (such a notion might not even make sense in this frame of reference); what matters simply is that people approve it and find it compelling.

It is important here to make several points. One is that my characterizations of these approaches to ideology-critique obviously are not the ones that proponents of these views would provide of themselves. Indeed, I have suggested at several points that advocates of one view or another are not always forthcoming about implicit judgments and assumptions they actually are making. Moreover, these approaches rarely exist in pure form; often theorists espouse elements of various approaches, mixing hybrid versions in which they embrace certain premises or assumptions but not others. Like any idealized typology, the one presented here only offers some broad categories for understanding the range of complex positions that persons actually hold. Obviously, I have greater sympathy for some of these approaches than others. Nevertheless, I do believe that this framework has merit in making more clear how assertions that a system of belief and value is "ideological," and that one sees this and knows how to challenge it, often are based on unstated assumptions which themselves are not always well-justified. If ideology and critique are opposing alternatives, as I have suggested, then the extent to which approaches to ideology-critique fail to subject their own presuppositions to critique they are subject to the same ideological status as the positions they claim to attack.

The most important of these assumptions, I have suggested here, are those that the approaches make about how people change their beliefs and acquire a "better," "truer," "more mature," or "less mystified" perspective. One way to frame this question is to ask, Why do we bother to criticize ideologies? The different versions of ideology-critique offer different answers to this question, ranging from trying to make people more rational to trying to create the perfect society. My point is that answers to the question "Why?" underlie choices about "How?" Critique itself is a practice, and how one conducts ideology-critique reveals deeper attitudes about knowledge and human freedom. Frequently, as I have shown, how critics engage in ideology-critique belies the aims they espouse. The relation of method to aims needs to be interrogated critically itself, or else one can be caught in the same ideological quagmire one means to escape.

A pedagogical perspective on ideology-critique requires us to think beyond critique to the emancipatory ends we mean to serve.[6] In fact, one might argue that the term "critique" implies an obligation to offer a positive reconstruction that the term "criticism" does not; if all that "critique" means is "criticism," why use the more pretentious French word?[7]

What habits of thought and action do we mean to promote by encouraging others to abandon certain ideological presuppositions, and how do our methods of ideology-critique relate to these? What authority do we claim as critics, and how is that authority established? Most important of all, are our own critical claims framed in ways that promote critical as opposed to ideological thought? A pedagogical perspective draws our attention to such questions and helps us to reconsider the process of ideology-critique (see Burbules 1988).

First of all, with whom are we speaking, and how do we engage them? Is our approach authoritative and assertive, or dialogical (see Freire, 1970 and 1985)? Do we credit persons with having embraced systems of belief and value for reasons, or do we regard them as dupes? I believe that a fundamental choice to be made in ideology-critique is to grant that people change themselves; that they have embraced most of the beliefs and values they have with their own purposes and needs in mind; and that if we mean to move them toward abandoning those beliefs and values or modifying them to accommodate alternatives, it must be for reasons they come to accept (see Fay 1977). Our aim is not to "refute" ideologies, but to provide persons with reasons that will induce them to change, and it is essential to see that these frequently are not the same thing. Speaking pedagogically, each of the five modes of ideology-critique discussed here has merit, yet each also has serious limitations.

Immanent critique, for example, has some advantages, since it consciously is directed at beginning with the beliefs and values that persons already hold as a starting point for change. Challenges or alternatives are posited primarily with the aim of promoting a degree of cognitive conflict within the belief systems others hold, thereby sparking them to reconsider and reformulate them. This approach is limited, however, by its exaggerated emphasis on the cognitive effects of ideologies and a neglect of the affective and aesthetic appeal they also hold; to disclose these latter elements a "poetics" of ideology is required.[8]

Pedagogically, we need to consider that systems of belief and value are complex; for *any* person, some positions will be more susceptible, and others more resistant, to change. If ideological beliefs are inflexible and restrictive, while beliefs subject to criticism are more flexible and responsive to arguments or evidence, then one must admit that we all hold certain degrees of each (which does *not* mean, therefore, that "everything is ideological"). More reasonable persons tend to be more willing to subject their positions to critical scrutiny and to admit they may be mistaken, and less reasonable persons are less so. This matter of degree along a continuum offers a more respectful and considerate way of thinking about reasonableness than bifurcating "rational" from "irrational" actors or relegating whole groups of people to the "ideological" domain simply because one fails to see the merit of their positions (at least from their own standpoint). A pedagogical perspective makes us see ideology-critique less as effecting a fundamental transformation in persons and more as encouraging their best qualities by respecting their positions as based on some process of ratiocination and reflection, even when we disagree with them.

Educational research can play a role in this pedagogical approach in at least two distinct ways. "Educational research" is an equivocal phrase: commonly it refers to research (quantitative, ethnographic, phenomenological, and so on) *about* education; less obviously, it also can describe research that *is* educational—research in any field whose problem definitions, methods, and styles of presentation are formulated with prospective audiences and contexts of use in mind. This latter kind of research is less interested in the "dissemination" of conclusions than with the shared edification of practice. Educational research in the first sense can play a role in ideology-critique by providing evidence (statistical, qualitative, personal, and so on) that may provide occasions for persons to reconsider and reformulate their positions in light of a broader range of information or perspectives (see, for example, Bredo and Feinberg 1982). Educational research in the second sense, however, goes to the heart of what I have called ideology-critique in the pedagogical mode: namely, engaging persons in a process that is directly responsive to their understandings and situation, directed toward the modification of systems of belief and value, but as a dialogue within which all parties can expect to be considered with respect and reciprocity.

Methods of condemnation, accusation, authoritative assertion, or the unilateral promulgation of counter-ideologies all are limited from this pedagogical perspective; they tend to foster the transferral of dependence, rather than liberation from it. They might be successful from the narrow standpoint of eliciting change; but as I have stressed repeatedly here, where the methods of ideology-critique are not consistent with the political and epistemic ends they purport to serve, they end up being self-defeating. A purely political and opportunistic standpoint makes the error of invoking norms that it is not in fact prepared to articulate and defend; if it deigns to do so, it then necessarily submits itself to a process of deliberation and critique that transcend the purely political and opportunistic realm. As Jürgen Habermas (1984) argues, when one makes assertions that one's position is more reasonable, or more right, than another, one undertakes an obligation to "redeem" that claim in critical (i.e., nonideological) discourse. In this exchange, certain privileges must be held equally: the privilege of questioning and disagreement, of proposing alternative characterizations of a position, of asking for clarification or justification, and so on. Obviously, this approach leaves open the question of who ultimately will be persuaded by whom; equally obviously, not all positions on ideology-critique accommodate this attitude of mutual consideration and respect.

This pedagogical perspective on ideology-critique avoids the dichotomous choice between the position that ideologies can be criticized only from the standpoint of a rational, scientific, objective stance, or the position that "everything is ideological," so that one can criticize a partial, incomplete system of belief and value only from the standpoint of another.[9] The pedagogical perspective claims that there are better and worse systems to choose from and that their respective merits can be assessed *reasonably*; that is, in light of a bounded, contextual process of mutual interchange that relies on standards that are not granted absolute status, but which nevertheless differentiate some methods of argumentation and persuasion as preferable to others (see Burbules 1991 and 1992). If ideology and critique are an opposed pair, then we need to endeavor, in the methods as well as the content of ideology-critique, to model the virtues of a fairer and more reasonable way of thinking, speaking, and influencing others.[10]

Notes

1. A similar account, based on a Foucauldian analysis, is offered by McLaren (1987, 305).

2. A rough version of this account is presented in Burbules (1983). Writing this essay has presented me with an opportunity to revisit these issues, and I hope to produce several essays updating and elaborating that project.

3. A skepticism evidenced by several essays in Adorno et al. (1976).

4. This position is set out in Jacoby (1975).

5. Kellner draws from and adapts the work of Gouldner (1976).

6. This point is made well by McLaren (1986).

7. I thank Ralph Page for pointing this out to me and for helpful comments throughout this paper.

8. A promissory note is hereby tendered that a project elaborating this "poetics" of ideology will be forthcoming.

9. Richard J. Bernstein (1983) challenges this same dichotomy.

10. The arguments in this essay have benefited enormously from the comments and suggestions of the Philosophy of Education discussion group at the University of Illinois: Bob Ennis, Zelia Gregoriou, Rohn Koester, Sally Pilcher, Bert Powers, Linda Ross, Philippe Ross, Pamela Salela, and Steve Tozer. Thanks also to Jim Giarelli for helpful comments on an earlier version of this essay.

References

Adomo, T., H. Albert, R. Dahrendorf, J. Habermas, H. Pilot, and K. Popper 1976. *The Positivist Dispute in German Sociology.* New York: Harper & Row.

Althusser, L. 1972. "Ideology and Ideological State Apparatuses." Pp. 267–70 in *Education: Structure and Society,* ed. B. R. Cosin. Middlesex, U.K.: Open University Press.

Apel, K-O. 1987. "The Problem of Philosophical Foundations in Light of a Transcendental Pragmatics of Language." Pp. 250–290 in K. Baynes, J. Bohman and T. McCarthy. *After Philosophy: End or Transformation?* Cambridge: MIT Press.

Bernstein, R. J. 1983. *Beyond Objectivism and Relativism: Science, Hermeneutics, and Praxis.* Philadelphia: University of Pennsylvania Press.

Bredo, E., and W. Feinberg. 1982. "The Critical Approach to Social and Educational Research." Pp. 271–421 in *Knowledge and Values in Social and Educational Research: Part III*, ed. E. Bredo and W. Feinberg. Philadelphia: Temple University Press.

Burbules, N. C. 1983. "Ideology and Radical Educational Research." Ph.D. diss., Stanford University.

———. 1988. "Ideology Critique and the Philosophy of Education." Pp. 47–58 in *Philosophy of Education 1987: Proceedings of the Forty-third Annual Meeting of the Philosophy of Education Society*, ed. B. Arnstine and D. Arnstine. Normal Il.

———. 1991. "Rationality and Reasonableness: A Discussion of Harvey Siegel's *Relativism Refuted* and *Educating Reason*." *Educational Theory* 41, no. 2: 235–252.

———. 1992. "The Virtues of Reasonableness." In *Philosophy of Education 1991: Proceedings of the Forty-seventh Annual Meeting of the Philosophy of Education Society*, ed. M. Buchmann and R. Floden. Normal, Il., Pp. 215–224.

Dale, M. 1986. "Stalking a Conceptual Charmeleon: Ideology in Recent Marxist Studies of Education." *Educational Theory* 36, no. 3:241–57.

Eagleton, T. 1975. *Criticism and Ideology*. London: Verso.

Fay, B. 1977. "How People Change Themselves: The Relationship Between Critical Theory and Its Audience." Pp. 200–233 in *Political Theory and Praxis*, Minneapolis: University of Minnesota Press.

Freire, P. 1970. *Pedagogy of the Oppressed*. New York: Seabury.

———. 1985. *The Politics of Education: Culture, Power and Liberation*. South Hadley, Mass.: Bergin & Garvey.

Geertz, C. 1973. *The Interpretation of Cultures*. New York: Basic Books.

Gouldner, A. 1976. *The Dialectic of Ideology and Technology*. New York: Seabury.

Habermas, J. 1984. *Theory of Communicative Action. Vol. 1, Reason and the Rationalization of Society*. Boston: Beacon.

———. 1990. *Moral Consciousness and Communicative Action*. Cambridge: MIT Press.

Held, D. 1980. *Introduction to Critical Theory*. Berkeley and Los Angeles: University of California Press.

Jacoby, R. 1975. *Social Amnesia*. Boston: Beacon.

Kellner, D. 1978. "Ideology, Marxism, and Advanced Capitalism." *Socialist Review* 42: 43–47.

Kuhn, T. S. 1970. *The Structure of Scientific Revolutions*. 2d ed. Chicago: University of Chicago Press.

Lyotard, J-F. 1984. *The Postmodern Condition: A Report on Knowledge*. Minneapolis: University of Minnesota Press.

Mannheim, K. 1936. *Ideology and Utopia*. New York: Harcourt, Brace & World.

Marx, K., and F. Engels. 1947. *The German Ideology*. New York: International Publishers.

McLaren, P. L. 1986. "Postmodernity and the Death of Politics: A Brazilian Reprieve." *Educational Theory 36*, no. 4:389–401.

———. 1987. "Ideology, Science, and the Politics of Marxian Orthodoxy: A Response to Michael Dale." *Educational Theory 37*, no. 3:301–26.

Parsons, T. 1961. "An Approach to the Sociology of Knowledge." Pp. 25–49 in *Transactions of the Fourth World Congress of Sociology*, no. 4, ed. K. H. Wolf.

Siegel, H. 1988. *Educating Reason: Rationality, Critical Thinking, and Education*. New York: Routledge.

Stark, W. 1958. *The Sociology of Knowledge*. Glencoe, Ill.: Free Press.

Winch, P. 1958. *The Meaning of a Social Science and Its Relation to Philosophy*. London: Routledge & Kegan Paul.

4

Meet Me behind the Curtain:
The Struggle for a Critical Postmodern Action Research

Joe Kincheloe

Teacher education's historical encounters with the domain of research has produced very few benefits. Assuming this failure, this chapter analyzes the action-research movement in a critical postmodern context, attempting in the process to theorize new ways of conceiving of teachers as researchers engaged in reflective and democratic practice. The research component of teacher education programs has typically involved a watered-down statistics course in master's curricula and nothing at all in pre-service programs. Action-research concepts such as the promotion of greater teacher self-understanding of his or her practices, conceptual change, and an appreciation of the social forces that shape the school are ignored in the traditional teacher research classes. Such classes with their circumscribed notions of research miss the specificity of the teaching act, the uniqueness of the teaching workplace, the ambiguity of practitioner ways of knowing. If we are serious about the production of critical, reflective practioners, then *democratic* action research cannot be separated from a single component of teacher education. The postmodern form of this democratic action research demands interrogation.

I will begin that questioning with an examination of the roots of this contemporary action-research movement in education. As early as the 1940s Kurt Lewin called for action research in social psychology. Taking their cue from Lewin, leaders in spheres as disparate as industry and American Indian affairs advocated action research. During the post-World War II era Stephen Corey at Teacher's College led the action-research movement in education. Corey argued that action research could help reform curriculum practice, as teachers applied the results of their own inquiry. There was considerable enthusiasm for the movement in the post-war period, but by the late 1950s action research became the target of serious criticism and started to decline. Analysts have posited that the decline was precipitated by the bifurcation of science and practice which resulted from the growth of the cult of the expert. As policymakers came to rely more and more on expert educational research and developmental laboratories, the development of curriculum and pedagogical practices was dictated from the top down. Thus, the production of research was separated from the ambiguous and complex would of the practitioner.

When action research was rediscovered in the United Kingdom in the 1970s, the motivation for its resuscitation involved the growing acceptance of the positivistic view of knowledge with its emphasis on specified, measurable learning outcomes and its degradation of the role of teacher as a self-directed professional. Educators were beginning to question the usefulness of positivism's abstract generalizations in the concrete and ambiguous situations in which they operated on a daily basis (McKernan 1988, 174–79; Elliott 1989a, 5). Still, however, teacher education continued to assume that the research dimension of professional studies involved the training of teachers in the use of quantitative methods. Research was defined as a positivistic form of data gathering and generalization production. So ingrained and unchallenged were such definitions of research that when action research advocates involved teachers in on-site teacher inquiry projects, the teachers reported that they did not consider themselves to have taken part in "real" research. Even those who felt that they had taken part in research maintained that it was a very low quality activity. Their college of education-generated definition of research as a controlled experimental design, replete with systematic statistical analysis, seemed to undermine their ability to reconceptualize what form research might take or how it might be connected to their lives as practitioners (Van Hesteran 1986, 217–18; Ross 1984, 114).

Fighting the image of research in the conventional wisdom, advocates of action research began to evoke new interest in the late 1970s. Aligning themselves with the attempt to redefine teacher professionalism, action researchers gained unprecedented respectability in the 1980s. In the midst of its success, action research found itself being molded and defined by many of the same people who had promoted the traditional forms of research in colleges of education. More critical teacher educators began to express concerns over the foundations of what often passed for teacher action research. Fearing a technocratic cooption of such inquiry, Patti Lather argued in 1986 that much of the action research conducted in schools was not critically grounded. Lather was correct then and now, as, unfortunately, much of the teacher research in the 1990s remains ahistorical and apolitical. As such, it lends itself to subversion by educational leaders who are tempted to employ a technical form of action research as a means of engineering practitioner "improvements" (Lather 1986, 263).

For example, many school projects have viewed teachers as researchers as implementors of theoretical strategies devised by researcher experts or administrators. In such situations teacher research involves testing how well particular strategies work through the analysis of particular techniques in their own classrooms. Promoted as teacher-friendly, these projects in the name of creating democratic workplaces actually promote a very restricted view of the role of teachers. Teachers are supporting actors incapable of playing leading roles, that is, in developing critical perspectives at the level of ideas (Connelly and Ben-Peretz 1980, 90–100) teachers in this context are still seen as mere executors. Advocates of teacher research who support this implementation orientation are quite naive when it comes to the realm of ideology. They do not realize that the act of administrators selecting problems for teacher to research is an ideological act, an act that trivializes the role of teacher. When administrators select problems for teacher researchers to explore, they negate the critical dimension of action research.

When the critical dimension of teacher research is negated the teacher-as-researcher movement can become quite a trivial enterprise. Uncritical educational action research seeks direct applications of information gleaned to specific situations—a cookbook style of technical thinking is encouraged, characterized by recipe-following teachers. Such thinking does not allow for complex reconceptualizations of knowledge and as a result fails to understand the ambiguities and the ideological structures of the classroom. Teachers, in this context, retreat to cause-effect analysis, failing to grasp the interactive intricacy of a classroom. The point that educational problems are better understood when considered in a relational way that transcends simple linearity is missed. Thus, teacher research becomes a reifying institutional function, as teachers, like their administrators and supervisors, fail to reveal the ways that the educational bureaucracy and the assumptions that support it constrain one's ability to devise new and more emancipatory understandings of how schools work (Orteza y Miranda 1988, 31).

Teacher research is coopted, its democratic edge is blunted. It becomes a popular grassroots movement that can be supported by the power hierarchy—it does not threaten, nor is it threatened. Asking trivial questions, the movement presents no radical challenges or offers no transformative vision of educational purpose, as it acts in ignorance of deep structures of schooling such as the positivistic view of educational knowledge. Teachers are assumed to be couriers, that is, information deliverers and are accorded a corresponding lack of status in the workplace (Ruddick 1989, 9; Ponzio 1985, 39–43). Uncritical educational action research fails to recognize that inquiry must always subject its findings to assessment and some form of critical analysis— and critical analysis is always dangerous in its unpredictability and transformative character.

What exactly is the difference between a coopted form of teacher research and critical form of teacher research? In both *Teachers as Researchers: Qualitative Inquiry as a Path to Empowerment* (1991) and *Toward a Critical Politics of Teacher Thinking: Mapping the Postmodern* (1993), I have attempted to delineate the requirements of critical action research: First, it rejects Cartesian-Newtonian notions of rationality, objectivity, and truth. Critical action research assumes that methods and issues of research are always political in character. Second, critical action researchers are aware of their own value commitments, the value commitments of others and the values promoted by the dominant culture. In other words, one of the main concerns of critical action research involves the exposure of the relationship between personal values and practice. Third, critical action researchers are aware of the social construction of professional consciousness. Fourth, critical action researchers attempt to uncover those aspects of the dominant social order which undermine our effort to pursue emancipatory goals. And, fifth, critical action research is always conceived in relation to practice— it exists to improve practice.

When conducted with these criteria in mind, critical action research is the consummate democratic act, as it allows teachers to help determine the conditions of their own work. Critical action research facilitates the attempt of teachers to organize themselves into communities of researchers dedicated to emancipatory experience for themselves and their students. When teachers unite with students and community members in the attempt to ask serious questions about what is taught, how it is taught, and what should constitute the goals of a school, not only is critical self-reflection promoted but group decision making becomes a reality (Carr and Kemmis 1986, 221–23; Aronowitz and Giroux 1985, 81).

Action research as defined here becomes the (logical) educational extension of a postmodern critical social theory. Since critical theory is grounded on a recognition of the existence of oppression, it stands to reason that the forces of this oppression have to be identified. Action research serves as a perfect vehicle for such a search. Without this critical recognition of domination and oppression, action researchers will simply consider the school site as value neutral and their role as disinterested, dispassionate observers. Change in this context is irrelevant—and according to Cartesian-Newtonian perspectives on research, this is the way it should be. Researchers are to maintain an uncommitted view toward the actions they encounter. In a world of oppression, critical theorists argue, ethical behavior demands that such dispassion must be confronted (Giroux and McLaren 1991, 70; Codd 1984, 10–11).

Whenever we dispense with values, political considerations, or historical context, our attempt to understand the situation we are researching is weakened. Our appreciation of an educational situation is contingent on the context within which we encountered it and the theoretical frames we brought with us to the observation. Cartesian-Newtonian modernism has told us that our research must serve no specific cause: but critical postmodernism has caused us to realize that every historical period produces rules that dictate what non-partisanship entails. In other words, different rules privilege different causes. Thus what we "see" as researchers is shaped by particular world views, values, political perspectives, conceptions of race, class, and gender relations, definitions of intelligence, and so on. Research, thus, can never be nonpartisan for we must choose the rules that guide us as researchers; critical theory's exposé of the hidden ideological assumptions within educational research marked the end of our innocence (Aronowitz 1983, 60; Elliott 1989b, 214).

To be critical is to assume that humans are active agents whose reflective self-analysis, whose knowledge of the world, leads to action. Action research is the logical extension of critical theory in that it provides the apparatus for the human species to look at itself. Critical action research that is aware of the postmodern perspectives on the production of subjectivity and the context of hyperreality can contribute to the sociocognitive emancipation of men and women. Such a socio-cognitive emancipation is the first step in our cognitive revolution; our post-formal effort to see the world and ourselves from new angles. Based on a democratic dialogue, an awareness of historical moment, and a passionate commitment to the voice of the oppressed, the postmodern insurrection redefines research, in the process producing a knowledge between the cracks, information previously swept under the rug.

In schools the firsthand, up-close perspectives of teachers previously relegated to a lesser significance are valued by action research as kinetic knowledge—that is, knowledge with the potential to wreak havoc. This information gained through action research's emphasis on observation and reflection promotes democratic change grounded on the understanding of participants. In the modernist discourse of science such an emphasis constitutes a radical change of approach (Codd 1984, 27–28; Young 1990, 149, 158). Action that reflective individuals take to correct the social and individual pathologies uncovered by teachers can be negotiated after the action-research process is completed. The critical core of critical action research involves its participatory and communally discursive structure and the cycle of action and reflection it initiates. Such a cycle does not produce a set of rules and precise regulations for the action it promotes. Critical postmodern action research provides a provisional framework of principles around which action can be discussed rather than a set of procedures. Teachers who engage in critical action research are never certain of the exact path of action they will take as a result of their inquiry (Young 1990, 158; Popkewitz 1981, 15–16).

A central part of this action involves the redefinition of knowledge. There are many dimensions to this redefining process, but one of the most important involves democratizing access to knowledge in schools and society. If knowledge is a form of cultural capital, then lack of access to it spells major problems for those on the margins of the culture of knowledge. Foucault has convinced us that knowledge is power: and though it is a hard pill for advocates of teacher empowerment to swallow, part of the reason that the teaching corps is delegated to the margins is that too many of them are ill-educated in colleges and teacher education programs. Teachers with weak academic, theoretical, and pedagogical backgrounds must defer to the judgments of educational leaders, the certified experts. The culture of technicist teacher education has tacitly instructed teachers across the generations to undervalue the domain of theory while avoiding questions of the ideological, psychological, and pedagogical assumptions underlying their practice. The power that comes from such understanding is a prerequisite for the critical attempt to redefine knowledge. Teachers must understand the social and political factors that contribute to knowledge production—indeed, the gaining of such an awareness should be a central concern of critical action research (May and Zimpher 1986, 94–95; Porter 1988, 508; Maeroff 1988, 508; Tripp 1988, 19; Giroux 1992, 98–99, 238).

Critical knowledge production begins when action researchers illuminate the taken-for-granted. Dewey focused our attention on such a process when he argued that teachers should operate on the basis of a reflective action that disembodies moral, ethical, and political issues from mundane thinking and practice. As action researchers maintain such a perspective in their everyday experience, they are able to explore the tacit forces that have encoded their own lives and their students' lives. In a sense, critical action researchers relearn the way they have come to view the world around them—indeed, they awaken from the modernist dream with its unexamined landscape of knowledge and unimaginative consciousness construction. Once awake, critical teachers as researchers begin to see schools as human creations with meanings and possibilities lurking beneath the surface appearances. Their task becomes the interpretation of schools, not just the chronicling of surface characteristics devoid of context (Hultgren 1987, 28; May and Zimpher 1986, 94; Lesko 1988, 147).

What do particular forms of teacher evaluation tell us about the purposes and values of my school, teacher researchers ask. Looking below the surface of standardized-test driven, behavioral assessment models of teacher evaluation, action researchers begin to uncover patterns of technicalization that erase teacher input into the determination of their own professional lives. Empowered with such knowledge, teachers gain the language to argue a case for their involvement in school policy. When principals and supervisors, for example, argue that teacher evaluation instruments necessitate particular forms of assessment, teachers will be able to point out the embedded within such instruments is an entire set of political, epistemological, cognitive, and pedagogical assumptions. Thus teachers will enter into a sophisticated, theoretically grounded negotiation with administrators about the terms of their evaluations, the terms of their professional lives.

Obviously, critical theory-based action research attempts not simply to understand or describe the world of practice but to change it. Proponents of such inquiry hope teacher education students will learn to use action research in a way that will empower them to shape schools in accordance with well-analyzed moral, ethical, and political principles. Teachers who enter schools with such an ability are ready to make a cognitive leap: indeed, the stage has been set for movement to the realm of a postmodern practitioner thinking. As critical action researchers endowed with a vision of what could be and a mechanism for uncovering what is, these teachers are able to see the sociopolitical contradictions of schools in a concrete and obvious manner. Such recognitions force teachers to think about their own thinking, as they begin to understand how these sociopolitical distortions had tacitly worked to shape their worldviews and their self-images. With a deeper appreciation of such processes, practitioners recognize the insidious ways power operates to create oppressive conditions for some groups and privilege for others. Thus critical teacher research opens net ways of knowing that transcend formal analysis (May and Zimpher 1986, 94–95; Hultgren 1987, 27–30).

Such teachers as researchers cannot help but turn to biographical and autobiographical analysis in their inquiry. Aware of past descriptions of higher-order thinking, such teachers in this situation become researchers of themselves, researchers of the formation of their own cognitive structures. Such inquiry produces a meta-awareness of an omnipresent feature of the role of critical postmodern teachers: they are always in the process of being changed and changing, of being analyzed and analyzing, of being constructed and constructing, of learning and teaching, of disembedding and connecting. The purpose of critical action research, thus, is not to produce data and better theories about education—it is to produce a metatheoretical understanding supported by reflection and grounded in sociohistorical context (Carr and Kemmis 1986, 39, 56, 123; May and Zimpher 1986, 94).

The metatheoretical and the self-reflective qualities of teacher research are forever intertwined with the process of sharing this practitioner research with others. One practitioner sharing his or her research with another is the best way know to foster a healthy questioning and a meaningful dialogue between practitioners. Successful dialogues will produce "felt responses" and further introspection, further revelations of ideological domination. Such interactions will move teachers to expose the sociopolitical values in their research and teaching, uncover the ideological assumptions that have directed their practices, and reveal the impact of their own race, class, gender, and religious affiliations on their everyday lives (Reinharz 1982, 182–83). This self-reflective quality of the teacher as researcher brings to center stage an extremely important dimension that uncritical teacher research misses. As the critical action researcher begins to reflect on his or her own consciousness, the realization begins to emerge that it has been shaped by a panoply of ideological forces—forces that often blind the teacher to an understanding of a multitude of important dimensions of classroom life.

If this is true of the practitioners themselves, then the same ideological forces must work to shape the everyday understanding, the self-perceptions of research subjects, namely, people in general. The very essence of critical teacher research involves the return to this realization—that subjects participating in social practices understand what is happening in their own lives, their own microcosms.

Of course, the way we teach or conduct research are products of these influences (Cherryholmes 1988, 111). If we are to ever operate as emancipated self-directed adults, we must confront the power of these forces. Indeed, in this confrontation we are obliged to deconstruct the power relations and the assumptions embedded in the term, emancipation. When post-structuralism confronts emancipation, some interesting things begin to happen. Action researchers should carefully watch the encounter. First, emancipation can no longer claim to be the "blessed redeemer" of educational and sociopolitical life once exposed to the provisionality of poststructuralism. Second, after a poststructuralist interrogation, emancipation's patriarchal foundations are revealed: as Gayatri Spivak (1987, 88–89) points out, no concept is free of the Nietzschean will to power. Third, informed by poststructuralist concerns, advocates of emancipation never again allow emancipation to escape questioning, to assume the position of a grand narrative. Fourth, humbled by poststructuralist deconstruction, emancipation is promoted as *one* way that an educational or a political situation could be improved, not as *the* way.

Despite this poststructuralist humility the problem remains—the goals of critical postmodern action research violate the neutrality, the nonpolitical claim of the dominant school culture's view of inquiry. Attempts of critical teacher researchers to examine and expose the forces that shape our consciousness and the assumptions of our research are viewed as efforts to politicize the research process. Again, poststructuralism forces us to question more deeply social and discursive assumptions. Rejecting a binary opposition between subjectivity and objectivity, we begin to uncover a modernist cult of objectivism. Devotees of the cult attempt to make invisible their own social beliefs and practices (the political domain) while concurrently pointing to the subjectivities and "bizarre" customs of the individuals they are studying (Roman and Apple, 1990, p. 40). They don't seem to realize that reality is tattooed by power, that the world's imprint on knowledge cannot be removed (McLaren 1992a, 83).

What mainstream empirical researchers cannot seem to understand is that meaning is a contested entity. What an event, an action, or a text means may depend on what question is asked about it or what is hidden from an observer. When operating from this perspective, analysts of research divert their attention from questions concerning the bias of the data to questions concerning the interests served by the bias—questions of whose meanings prevail. Such questions forsake the positivist search for a privileged reference point from which the truth of educational practice may be discerned. Thus what mainstream researchers once termed *human* predispositions, researchers informed by critical theory and postmodernism refer to as discursive imprints on subjectivity, namely, the consciousness construction that results from immersion in particular language games (McLaren 1992b, 321–322; Lather 1992, 14).

Opponents of critical postmodern attempts to problematize the constancy of meaning have trouble understanding that the definition of objectivity always involves a power struggle. In the late-twentieth-century struggle the guardians of orthodoxy (the progeny of Umberto Eco's blind monk in *The Name of the Rose*) guard the objective canon as the postmodern barbarians at the gate pose critical challenges to their sequestered elitism (Scott 1989, 688–90). Patti Lather describes this struggle for objectivity as a dinosaur culture fighting to maintain its dominance against the forces of chaos (Lather 1991, xvi). If the dinosaurs lose, the last pillars of Western civilization and the cult of objectivity will have been sabotaged. In no way should this critical postmodern challenge be interpreted to imply a lack of concern with empirical validity. Critical action research understands that even though objectivity is a social construction, data credibility can still be achieved by systematic approaches to reflective methods. Such methods involve interaction between researcher and researched. Such systematic inter-action lessens the possibility that action researchers will simply impose meanings on situations instead of construct meanings via a give and take with those they have studied (McLaren 1992a, 78; Lather 1991, 110).

Based on their negotiations with those they have researched, critical action researchers assess information on the basis of its ability to move its consumers and producers in an emancipatory and humanistic direction, namely, to help them achieve empowerment and self-direction through an understanding of the ideological forces that shape humans. For example, if action researchers are unaware of the unequal power relations in the school in which they are conducting their inquiry, how can they possibly grasp the importance and meaning of what they might perceive? When studying the school performances of a selected group of students, action researchers would be handicapped if they failed to account for the interaction between socio-economic class and a student's language usage. A student's usage of language, of course, seriously affects how well he or she does on a standardized test. Embodied in particular discursive fields students from specific backgrounds as well as the action researchers who analyze them will tend to perceive in the context of these fields (McLaren 1992a 79). If action research is to be praxiological, then such understandings are central and must be shared with those being researched. As students from cultures shaped by repressive forces of race, class, and gender begin to understand the power discourses that have molded them, appreciate the causes of powerlessness, and take such insights to form the basis of collective and individual actions to change repressive conditions, they are empowering themselves in the critical sense of the term (Shapiro 1989, 80–82; Lather 1991, 3–4).

Such considerations, however, are conceptual light-years away from the forms of action research approved for use in the school. Arguing from a different set of assumptions, noncritical advocates of action research maintain that the everyday knowledge of teachers is the most important form of educational knowledge we possess. While the everyday knowledge of teachers is more insightful than the positive knowledge of propositional language, it is not enough. It is not all that teachers need to know. Action research in education critically defined is not content to confine teachers as researchers to the task of collating what they and their colleagues already know. Even though the packaging of noncritical action research appears new and fresh, its flavor is the same. The theoretical assumptions are tailored to the cult of objectivity, which blinds participants to the complex of forces that move events in educational settings. The critical teacher researcher asks questions of deep structure of his or her school or classroom setting— in other words, he or she takes Habermas's notion of the emancipatory interest of knowledge seriously. Thus, critical teacher research will always aim to aid individuals in the attempt to take control of their lives, assuming that such autonomy is a moral right of human beings. This moral principle extends into the process of action research, as it demands that individuals who are studied have the right to participate in decisions that tend to produce knowledge about them. The concept of the dignity of those being researched is revered when power is shared in both the application and the production of knowledge about them. Such power sharing allows the researchers to gain new insights into the deep social structures that shape them, thus, enhancing the possibility of self-determination.

Bringing everyday practical knowledge to the forefront of our consciousness may be the first step in such a process but it is not the last—it must be supplemented by an awareness of the ideological construction of our consciousness and the educational and political results of such construction. Given such a purpose for critical postmodern action research, Patti Lather has proposed the notion of catalytic validity. Catalytic validity points to the degree to which research moves those it studies to understand the world and the way it is shaped in order for them to transform it. Noncritical action researchers who operate within an empiricist discursive community will find catalytic validity to be a strange concept. Action research that possesses catalytic validity will display not only the reality-altering impact of the inquiry process but it will also direct this impact so that those under study will gain self-understanding and self-direction (Altrichter and Posch 1989, 28; Van den Berg and Nicholson 1989, 16–18; Lather 1991, Kincheloe and Steinberg 1993, 303–304.

Teacher research that ignores the emancipatory interest ends up only ankle-deep in the school ocean, missing a kaleidoscope of undersea activity. Educational action research needs to move beyond exclusive concern with the individual and institutional levels of inquiry toward an understanding of the social and cultural structures that help shape the educational lives of individuals and help determine the consequences of schooling. When all three levels of inquiry are pursued by teacher researchers, a view of education far more sophisticated than the one produced by an uncritical attention to teacher practical knowledge emerges. It is more sophisticated in that it is multidimensional, genuinely practical, reflective, politically savvy, and emancipatory. This uncritical-action-research orientation is quite dangerous as it fosters severely limited views of teaching and the educational process in the name of innovation and democratic pedagogy. It covertly upholds the status quo, as it is unable to analyze the dominant forces that constrict teacher insight and school policy. As it ignores the wider social and political framework, it unwittingly reproduces extant ideology and denies teachers the privilege of questioning the authority of past educational practices (Ruddick 1989, 6–8).

As it denies teachers the right to self-direction, it also shuts its eyes to the values which appear throughout any effort to do research. It pretends that what counts as an educational improvement is obvious to all. If such a view is accepted, then research becomes simply a value-free, neutral technique used to measure how well we have reached consensual goals. What we call "improvement" is always problematic, always embedded with tacit epistemology, politics, views of human psychology, and ideology (Wallace 1987, 108–9). When researchers and educational leaders assert or even imply that there is consensus on educational goals, alarm bells should ring in the ideology-detection center staffed by critical teacher researchers.

Many of the pronouncements of advocates of uncritical action research illustrate an unawareness of our notion of social embeddedness, as they assume that everyday language is politically neutral and that value free. John Elliott, for example, has argued that everyday teacher concepts, expressed in everyday teacher language, should substitute for outsider perspectives. While Elliott makes a valuable point when he argues that teachers should protect themselves from the domination of the expert, he comes across as xenophobic when he maintains a "conceptual isolationism" for teachers. Concepts from social theory when presented with sensitivity for the unique role of the practitioner are necessary in the development of deeper understandings of the everyday life of the classroom and alternative perspectives on the goals and purposes of teaching. When it is not viewed as verified truth and not presented as a justification for top-down imposed goals for teachers, social theory can of course be very valuable. Elliott himself suffers from the effects of this conceptual isolationism, as he fails to comprehend the social construction of consciousness. Teacher language and concepts seem to him somehow miraculously free of ideological interference. Elliott takes his analysis to another level.

Focusing his attention on critical educational action research, Elliott calls it a dangerous conception of the teacher-as-researcher movement. Action researchers, he tells us, influenced by Habermas have perpetuated the false notion that the self-understandings teachers hold of their everyday activities make up ideologically distorted misrepresentations of the world. The purpose of critical theory, according to Elliott, is to provide teachers with modes of analysis which explain how this ideology distorts teachers' views of themselves and their teaching and works to justify hegemony. Since he rejects the possibility that a teacher's perspective on the world could be ideologically shaped, Elliott sees the intent of critical action research as mere politicization. The most important effect of critical action research, Elliott contends, is that it requires a dialogue between the critical theorist and the teacher. The critical theorist thus becomes merely the latest in a long line of experts who impose their opinions on teachers.

Elliott seems to forget that most people, teachers included, identify with or embrace ways of seeing that do not serve their best interests. Thus when teacher perceptions of the world of school are left unquestioned, the effects of power are left invisible. No matter what the way of seeing in question, critical deconstructive analysis points out the partiality of any perspective. As deconstruction alerts us to how our economic, gender, and racial positions shape our comprehension of various phenomena, we begin to understand that the questions generated in our action research reflect where we are standing in the web of reality. In light of such postmodern understandings, Elliott's tendency to unprovisionally celebrate the perspectives of teachers conducting action research is misguided. Whether the perspective be that of the critical academic, the educational leader, the student, or the teacher as researcher, the historical and cultural placement of the subject must be exposed and analyzed. Without question, the voice of the teacher must be respected, but respect does not imply a disinclination to question positionality (Lather 1991, 68, 145; McLaren 1992b, 333).

Elliott neglects another important point in his critique of critical action research: as opposed to other "outsiders," critical advocates of action research are not a part of a bureaucratic power structure that mandates teacher behavior. Whenever critical theorists would in the mode of positivism force their perspectives top-down on teachers, I would join Elliott in his condemnation of them. At present this is not happening. No room for outside opinion exists in Elliott's view of teaching and action research; in a critical action research context, he laments, "Teachers' self-understandings cannot alone serve as the basis for their emancipation from ideological control." Elliott's view of hegemony is quite unusual; while it excludes the identification of many of the forces which reproduce power in our consciousness, for example, media, traditional teacher education, gender relations, and so on, it includes all "outsiders" who analyze educational situations (Elliott 1989b, 50–53).

Elliott's perspectives have influenced other supporters of action research who also condemn critical teacher research for its desire to end open-minded inquiry. Jim McKernan writes in the spirit of Elliott that action research cannot be "held hostage" to the political ideology of the critical theorists. While he supports the effort to link critique and education in education, McKernan contends that this educational action should involve education and *not* politics—it should be an action that concentrates on issues of curriculum and instruction, not on political matters like social justice. In the name of educational improvement and political neutrality, positivism (in its modern postpositivist guise) pops up like a jack-in-the-box. McKernan's view is plausible only if we accept the positivist separation of facts and values and see the role of schools as politically neutral (McKernan 1988, 198–99). My reading of educational history tells a very different story—a tale of schools many times used for political purposes, schools undermined by unequal power distribution.

Such uncritical perspectives are not simply the province of traditional quantitative researchers or researchers who accept the tenets of positivism. The perspective is alive and well in, of course, the action-research movement and also within qualitative educational studies in general. The ability to make judgments is not viewed as a goal of qualitative research, many researchers argue. Of course, there is an element of truth in the pronouncement that we don't do qualitative research in order to judge how well a teacher is doing—but this is not the final word on judgment in a qualitative research content. We can refrain from making *personal* judgments while developing a set of criteria that allow us to judge the value of particular educational goals and outcomes—this is why it is so important for us to develop a provisional system of meaning. We need to ask and answer questions such as; Are these goals and outcomes just? are they respectful of human dignity? Whose interests do they serve? What are the epistemological assumptions embedded in these goals and outcomes? On what set of political beliefs are they grounded? This is judgment and indeed it *is* political. But to refrain from some form of judgment even in the name of neutrality is also political—critical awareness smokes us out of our pseudoneutral "high ground." We cannot avoid making political choices.

It seems obvious that any teacher's perspective unaided by different vantage points will guarantee that they remain unconscious of these tacit assumptions that direct their practice. They would be unaware, say, that they held sexist or racist viewpoints that affected their teaching or did not correspond to their authentically avowed principles. I do not doubt that those I refer to as the uncritical proponents of action research are genuinely concerned with granting teachers more insight into their professional practice, but such advocates fail to ask whether in the modern workplace teachers are free to initiate changes they consider necessary. Uncritical advocates of teacher research are uncomfortable with the so-called elitism of critical action researchers such as Wilfred Carr and Stephen Kemmis, who have focused on the theoretical and organizational structures that constrain the everyday practice of teachers. Can teachers make changes derived from their research and reflection, Carr and Kemmis ask. Often times the answer is no, given the self-perpetuating organization of schools and the ideological blindness of many school leaders. Uncritical action researchers, it seems, meet teachers only halfway—they throw one-half the length of the rope needed to pull them out of the water to safety. They speak the language of empowerment, and they concern themselves with the reflective power of teacher research, but they refuse to confront the structural conditions of schools and the larger society that preclude the translation of teacher reflection into emancipatory educational action (Wallace 1987, 108–9).

Uncritical advocates of teacher research are more and more using a critical vocabulary to describe their activities. Words such as "emancipation," "hegemony" and "domination" are heard and read quite often in the literature of action research. "Emancipation," for example is not employed in the same way by Elliott as it is by Giroux, McLaren, Carr and Kemmis, and myself. To Elliott (and many others) emancipation is a very specific situation—teachers freeing themselves from perspectives that emanate from outside the classroom; Giroux, McLaren, and Carr and Kemmis use the term to evoke the image of teachers freeing themselves from the hegemonizing influences of larger sociocultural forces. Elliott's concept of emancipation does not allow for a critical reconceptualization or decentering of dominant views of the purpose of teaching. Employing a language of critique in relation to particular teacher expectations, critical postmodern forms of questioning become from Elliott's perspective an unwelcomed political imposition from outside the school. Is it not possible to respect teachers and the sanctity of teacher knowledge and at the same time question particular interpretations and actions teachers derive from their reflection? (Elliott 1989, 2–3). Maybe an analogy outside an educational context would help. There is little doubt that a lawyer with thirty years of courtroom experience possesses a unique form of knowledge that could only be attained by this particular experience. This does not mean that we have no right to argue or disagree with his or her purposes for trying or not trying a case or for accepting one case and turning down another. Indeed, an outsider with a different set of experiences may provide valuable insight into particular aspects of the lawyer's work. Critical action researchers in education cannot allow their language to be coopted and stripped of its emancipatory meaning by analysts who don't understand the reality of power relations, the socially constructed nature of knowledge, and the suffering that comes out of the existence of domination in the social and educational world.

Lest I be misunderstood, I will close with a few reminders. In our attempt to preserve a role for advocates of critical postmodern action research in the conversation about teacher research, we are not attempting—as Elliott and McKernan would suggest—to argue that teachers should not become authorities on the discourse of schooling. Educational poststructuralists demand respect of teachers and teacher knowledge and seek to expose the insidious ways that outside experts can come to dominate teachers. This is not, however, the position of Elliott and McKernan, as they fail to discuss the discursive and power restrictions on understandings derived from teacher-conducted action research. Neither are we attempting to pose as outside experts ready to come in and "correct" the false consciousness or distorted perceptions of teachers. As poststructuralist critic Teresa Ebert maintains, we are interested in uncovering the ways that all of us, teachers included, are shaped by the ways lives are connected to dominant relations of power (Ebert 1988, 23). No one possesses a consciousness that situates him or her beyond history and political practices. None of us, as Peter McLaren contends, stands outside the policy structures of discourses. Our emotional investments shape our belief structures and our practices, what we "see" and what we look past (McLaren 1992a, 77). Action researchers can always profit from encounters with those who encourage them to uncover how their own inquiry reflects ways that they have been taught to "see." Without such understandings, teacher researchers will never get behind the curtain to see why the microcosm of education operates in the ways that it does.

References

Altrichter, H., and P. Posch. 1989. "Does the 'Grounded Theory' Approach Offer a Guiding Paradigm for Teacher Research?" *Cambridge Journal of Education*, 19 no. 1:21–31.

Aronowitz, S. 1983. "The Relativity of Theory." *The Village Voice*, December, p. 60.

Aronowitz, S., and H. Giroux. 1985. *Education Under Seige*. South Hadley, Mass.: Bergin & Garvey.

Carr, W., and S. Kemmis. 1986. *Becoming Critical*. Phildelphia: Falmer Press.

Cherryholmes, C. 1988. *Power and Criticism: Poststructural Investigations in Education*. New York: Teachers College Press.

Codd, J. 1984. "Introduction." In *Philosophy, Common Sense, and Action in Educational Administration*, ed. J. Codd. Victoria, Australia: Deakin University Press.

Connelly, F., and M. Ben-Peretz. 1980. "Teachers' Roles in the Using and Doing of Research and Curriculum development." *Journal of Curriculum Studies* 12, no. 2:95–107.

Ebert, T. 1988. "The Romance of Patriarchy: Ideology, Subjectivity, and Postmodern Feminist Cultural Theory." *Cultural Critique* 10:19–57.

Elliott, J. 1989a. "Studying the School Curriculum through Insider Research." Paper presented to the International Conference on School-Based Innovations: Looking Forward to the 1990s, Hong Kong.

———. 1989b. "Action-Research and the Emergence of Teacher Appraisal in the United Kingdom." Paper presented to the American Educational Research Association, San Francisco.

Giroux, H. 1992. *Border Crossings: Cultural Workers and the Politics of Education*. New York: Routledge.

Giroux, H., and P. McLaren. 1991. "Language, Schooling, and Subjectivity: Beyond a Pedagogy of Reproduction and Resistance." Pp. 61–83 in *Contemporary Issues in U.S. Education*, K. Borman, P. Swami, and L. Wagstaff. Norwood, N.J.: Ablex Publishing.

Hultgren, F. 1987. "Critical Thinking: Phenomenological and Critical Foundations." Pp. 27–45 in *Higher-order Thinking: Definition, Meaning and Instructional Approaches*, ed. Ruth G. Thomas. Washington, D.C.: Home Economics Education Association.

Kincheloe, J. 1991. *Teachers as Researchers: Qualitative Paths to Empowerment*. London: Falmer Press.

———. 1993. *Toward a Critical Politics of Teacher Thinking: Mapping the Postmodern*. Granby, Mass.

Kincheloe, J. and S. Steinberg. 1993. "A Tentative Description of Post-formal Thinking: The Critical Confrontation with Cognitive Theory." *Harvard Education Review*, 63:296–320.

Lather, P. 1991. *Getting Smart: Feminist Research and Pedagogy with/in the Classroom*. New York: Routledge.

———. 1986. "Research as Praxis." *Harvard Educational Review* 56:257–77.

Lesko, N. 1988. *Symbolizing Society: Stories, Rites, and Structure in a Catholic High School*. New York: Falmer Press.

Maeroff, G. 1988. "A Blueprint for Empowering Teachers." *Phi Delta Kappan* 69, no. 7:472–77.

May, W., and N. Zimpher. 1986. "An Examination of Three Theoretical Perspectives on Supervision: Perceptions of Preservice Field Supervision." *Journal of Curriculum and Supervision*, 1, no. 2:83–99.

McKernan, J. 1988. "Teacher as Researcher: Paradigm and Praxis." *Contemporary Education* 59, no. 3:154–58.

McLaren, P. 1992a. "Collisions with Otherness: Traveling Theory, Post-Colonial Criticism, and the Politics of Ethnographic Practice—The Mission of the Wounded Ethnographer." *Qualitative Studies in Education* 5, no. 1:77–92.

———. 1992b. "Literacy Research and the Postmodern Turn: Cautions from the Margins." Pp. 339–379 in *Multi-Disciplinary Perspectives on Literacy Research*, ed. R. Beach et al. Urbana, Ill.: National Council of Teachers of English.

Orteza Y Miranda, E. 1988. "Broadening the Focus of Research in Education." *Journal of Research and Development in Education* 22, no. 1:23–28.

Ponzio, R. 1985. "Can We Change Content without Changing Context?" *Teacher Education Quarterly* 12, no. 3:39–43.

Popkewitz, T. 1981. "The Study of Schooling: Paradigms and Field-based Methodologies in Education Research and Evaluation." Pp. – in *The Study of Schooling*, T. Popkewitz and B. Tabachnick. New York: Praeger Publishers.

Porter, A. 1988. "Indicators: Objective Data or Political Tool?" *Phi Delta Kappan* 69, no. 7:503–8.

Ross, D. 1984. "A Practical Model for Conducting Action Research in Public School Settings." *Contemporary Education* 55, no. 2:113–17.

Ruddick, J. 1989. "Critical Thinking and Practitioner Research: Have They a Place in Initial Teacher Training?" Paper presented to the American Educational Research Association, San Francisco.

Scott, J. 1989. "History in Crisis: The Others' Side of the Story." *The American Historical Review* 94, no. 3:680–92.

Shapiro, S. 1989. "Towards a Language of Educational Politics: The Struggles for a Critical Public Discourse of Education." *Educational Foundations* 3, no. 3:79–100.

Spivak, G. 1987. *In Other Worlds: Essays in Cultural Politics*. New York: Methuen.

Tripp, D. 1988. "Teacher Journals in Collaborative Classroom Research." Paper presented to the American Educational Research Association, New Orleans.

Van den Berg, O., and S. Nicholson. 1989. "Teacher Transformation in the South African Context: An Action Research Approach." Paper presented to the International Conference on School-based Innovations: Looking Forward to the 1990s, Hong Kong.

Van Hesteran, F. 1986. "Counselling Research in a Different Key: The Promise of Human Science Perspective." *Canadian Journal of Counselling* 20, no. 4:200–234.

Wallace, M. 1987. "A Historical Review of Action Research: Some Implications for the Education of Teachers in Their Managerial Role." *Journal of Education for Teaching* 13, no. 2:97–115.

Young, R. 1990. *A Critical Theory of Education: Habermas and our Children's Future*. New York: Teachers College Press.

5

Some Notes on Power, Agenda, and Voice:
A Researcher's Personal Evolution
toward Critical Collaborative Research[1]

Margaret D. LeCompte

This chapter traces the role changes I have undergone during my professional life as an action researcher. Drawing on my past experiences in applied, collaborative, and critical research in a variety of settings, this chapter culminates with a focus on my current fieldwork, a critical and collaborative research project in a school district on the Navajo Reservation.

Collaborative research has changed a great deal since my first experience with it, in what started as a job during graduate school and ended up as research for my master's thesis. I was a member of the research and evaluation team for the first federally funded experiment in school decentralization, located on the south side of Chicago. The project was a joint effort among strange and historically hostile bedfellows—the University of Chicago, the Chicago Public School system, and two militant community organizations—the Welfare Rights Organization (WRO) and The Woodlawn Organization (TWO), which had been initiated by Saul Alinsky. The Woodlawn Experimental School Project (WESP), which was my first real field research, was a genuine baptism of fire. The research team was part of the management team, and the management team was the most convenient target for ire of TWO and WRO when things went wrong—which was often. Gang activity in the vicinity of the school meant I ran through hails of bullets to get to the school and was under verbal fire in every meeting. White members of the staff were frequently accused of racism and condescension. I felt I finally had become acceptable to my WESP colleagues on the night Martin Luther King Jr., was assassinated. As I cowered in my apartment under a curfew and the west side of Chicago burned down, tanks from the National Guard rumbled down my street. Suddenly my telephone rang. A leader of the WRO, a woman who had accused me the day before of being a racist spy for the University, called to make sure I was safe and to warn me not to come into the community until she phoned to say the streets were clear.

After graduating, I participated in other, less dramatic, collaborative research projects. In North Dakota I served as a university-based researcher for a social impact study of strip mining which the state legislature commissioned. In this project, interdisciplinary and inter-institutional collaborative links had to be established between the two universities and four departments doing the research, the legislative committees that needed our results, and the innumerable community organizations whose opinions, workloads, budgets, and histories we had to probe. Though the task was complex and the linkages delicate, the issues were less explosive; my only life-threatening experiences involved weathering blizzards in western North Dakota and drinking too much beer with informants in local bars.

Later I acquired a different role: as director of Research and Evaluation for a large urban school district in Texas, I became an internal, rather than an external, evaluator. I was an insider in the sense that I worked for the school district, but at the same time, I remained an outsider with regard to the programs and staff I and my office had to evaluate. Sometimes the superintendent used us as a kind of SWAT team. We were invited to meetings to stand around, much like members of the Secret Service, whenever the superintendent wanted to stress the seriousness of the topic under consideration. At other times, we were required to investigate more traditional issues of concern to the administrative staff, principals, and teachers. How well I did my job was determined by how well I could convince the school people that (1) I was not really out to get them—despite my occasional SWAT-like functions; and (2) that what I was doing would help them do their job better. Complicating the task of persuasion were the agendas of interested constituencies or stakeholders whose concerns had to be considered: In addition to the politics of the school district constituencies themselves, which seldom involved getting physically shot at but at times were just as exciting, my staff and I had to collaborate with the teachers' unions, the business community, the Office of Civil Rights and the Justice Department, cultural arts councils, social service agencies, and a whole variety of voluntary associations, parental organizations, and watchdog groups concerned with safeguarding the moral and intellectual fiber of youth.

My most current work is a long-term project on school reform. I have been asked to help a public school district in the Navajo Nation to restructure and with its efforts to reduce dropout rates. In this project, with which I have been involved for over four years, I am trying to put into practice everything I have learned in the last twenty-three years of doing applied, action, or collaborative research; I also am trying to integrate concerns of postmodern thinking in the way I interact in the research site, interpret the results, and disseminate the findings. Part of this effort involves trying to redefine what collaborative research means, which involves untangling a virtual morass of influences on this particular kind of research. It also involves developing new models for how it might be carried out. In the pages that follow, I will provide a brief history of the origins of collaborative research in anthropology, sociology, and activist applied research, as I understand them. I then will discuss how I have adapted and extended those models to conform to the roles and challenges I face in the research site I call Pinnacle Unified School District.

The Tangled Influences on Collaborative Investigation

Collaborative research as it currently is practiced—or attempted—in education derives from two traditions that initially had little to do with each other. The first tradition is that of applied research and evaluation in anthropology, sociology, or organizational psychology. This tradition has been practiced by contract or in-house evaluators or by more-or-less applied funded researchers, who define collaborative research as follows:

1. It is done in interaction with the subjects of the research.
2. It is done at their request.
3. It is done on topics which the subjects have identified to be of concern to them.
4. It is done with the purpose of being useful to or of improving conditions of life of the subjects of the research.

Viewed in this light, collaborative research has no fundamental concern with power, agenda, and voice—factors that have radically changed contemporary collaborative efforts. I was well within this tradition in the WESP, and in the Texas school district; I also was within this tradition in North Dakota.

The other tradition comes from university-based academic researchers, whose forays into the real world often are limited to voluntary projects, short-term evaluations, or, in recent years, have been bootlegged under the aegis of funded teacher training, inservice, and school reform projects. The first group of such researchers comes from a critical, Marxist, feminist or postmodern background that is disenchanted with the epistemological and ontological constraints of positivism. Its concern has been to develop a research style that is less detached from the experience of the people being studied and more engaged in reducing oppression. Much of the work of these researchers, whom I call architects of a critical academic tradition in education, remains at the level of theory and exhortation, rather than being rooted in social practice outside a university setting.

The second group consists of teacher educators, whose work is informed not by critical social theory, but by psychology, curricular practice, and artistry (LeCompte and Bennett DeMarrais 1992). This work focuses on student empowerment and is found largely in the fields of literacy, or the teaching of reading and writing. Teacher-student collaboration in journals and creative writing projects is used to improve student achievement in the language arts generally, to improve student self-esteem, and to empower students.

A third group focuses on teachers. It uses simple research skills to help teachers become more reflective and self-critical about their instructional practice and curricular philosophies, and in so doing, equates self-critique with the initial stages of empowerment. My current work in the Navajo Nation seems to draw on both the applied and the critical academic traditions.

The Applied Research and Evaluation Tradition

The applied research and evaluation tradition is the older. It is concerned with practice rather than theory and its primary theorists are evaluators, usually from a quantitative and experimental background who, like House (1979) and Stake (1978), began to discover the utility of hands-on qualitative research in the late 1970s; and applied anthropologists and field sociologists, who had begun a tradition of qualitative evaluation some years earlier (see, for example, McCall and Simmons 1969, Becker 1958). Collaboration for these researchers served not as a path to change or as an end in itself, but as a cure for some of their most difficult investigatory problems. One is that of *knowledge utilization and dissemination* (Huberman 1991), a concern which finds voice in the frequent lament: "*Why* don't or won't my clients listen to me?" Another is the problem of getting people to give researchers the information they need.

Collaboration as an Aid to Research Utilization

Issues of knowledge utilization most often have been viewed by researchers as a problem of salesmanship: Researchers simply have to be persuasive enough to convince people (clients) to buy the product (research results). Without such persuasion, researchers have found that reports will be folded, filed, and forgotten even before the research team folds its tents and steals away. Huberman (1991) describes the problem of lack of knowledge utilization as the "two communities" problem; he views it as a function of the differences in norms, rewards, and sensibilities between the community or culture of researchers and the community of school people. When research is not used, it is because the recipients fail to view it as the researchers intended, often because researchers failed to establish shared understandings about research goals or educate recipients in how they should make use of the research results.

Huberman characterized the relationships that impede knowledge utilization between research and client communities or cultures as *hello-goodbye*: in which "researchers and practitioners met, danced briefly, and wandered off in different directions," *two planets*: in which interaction is between two cultures—research and educational practice—neither of which has much knowledge of, interest in, respect for or contact with the other; and *stand-off*: in which disagreement over domains exists. Stand-offs produce no agreement on who has the right to be on whose turf, and little attempt to negotiate toward consensus. The clients feel that the researchers have no business meddling in their affairs. The two groups are like "two porcelain dogs, snarling at one another on the doorstep." They interact administratively not because they want to or feel each other's inputs to be useful, but because, on an organizational chart, they were set up to do so.

One way to enhance the persuasive powers of the evaluator has been to involve research subjects as participants, or *collaborators*, in the research process. This means more than just presenting the original plan to the clients before work begins, and then hiring a few local people as research assistants—or defining collaboration of clients in terms of their role as providers of information. Huberman suggests that "for a study to have a strong conceptual influence on practitioners, face-to-face interaction between researchers and practitioners must occur not only at the completion of the study (the "hello-goodbye" approach) but also during, and ideally, before conduct of the study. Such contacts include getting interim feedback on study findings; establishing "personal" contacts with researchers; having several people in the unit involved early on with the study; having substantive exchanges with researchers prior to dissemination; overcoming initial "suspiciousness" about social science researchers or research; and maintaining contacts during the study between supervisors/directors of the program and the research team (Huberman 1990, 382). These procedures enable researchers to get a better understanding of the concerns and characteristics of people likely to be the ultimate users of their research; give practitioners a better idea of the potential value of the study; serve to "keep the conversation going, and allow both sides to see where, and in what form, the findings are likely to be meaningful" (Huberman 1990, 365).

All of these suggestions soften the positivistic structure of the "hello-goodbye" approach of standard external evaluations, where pre- and post-test designs are used and the objectivity required of researchers mandates minimal contact with the people being evaluated. Implementing these suggestions constituted some of the first steps toward newer models of action research.

Clients as Collaborators and Stakeholders

Researchers also have used collaboration to increase their ease of access to information. Jean and Stephen Schensul, a team of applied anthropologists, have long called for making practitioners equal partners in the process of decision-making, detailing their efforts in several review articles (1981, 1992). As an example, Gibson's (1985) two year project in "Valleyside," California, illustrates some of the issues which arise in collaborative applied research. Gibson's project was designed first, to investigate whether or not John Ogbu's (1978, 1988) analysis of impediments to the achievement of minority students held true for a Punjabi Sikh community, and second, to determine ways to improve the levels of educational achievement in the community. The project was funded by the National Institute of Education, and was initiated by the local school district, supported by powerful members of the Sikh community, including the local Sikh temple, and staffed by individuals from both the university community and the local minority community.

Gibson's operational problems arose in determining *when* and *with which components of the participating institution* researchers should initiate collaborative efforts. Gibson's co-investigator was a prominent local Sikh, a Ph.D. who initially seemed to have wide support among various factions in the community, but who later proved to be the leader of one rather vocal subgroup.

The program had many crises, most of which Gibson believes derived from the failure to achieve consensus and adequate collaboration. Gibson states early on that the project was not designed as a change effort and that she was not a change agent. However, problems arose because participants wanted to co-opt the research project to facilitate changes they hoped the project would effect. The Sikh community wanted the research results to show that major changes were needed to eliminate racism and prejudice on the part of the school district; the school district wanted the results to show a need for different kinds of curricula, and denied the charges of racism altogether. These competing agendas made execution of clear objectives for the study problematic.

Gibson did involve the community in the handling of research funds, and this caused many headaches. She failed to include in her budget indirect costs to the local fiduciary agency to pay its staff for administering the grant. As a consequence the staff of the agency became overtaxed, which led to charges that the project funds were only benefiting certain segments of the community. To address the kinds of communications Huberman advocates, she also tried to involve community members in the process of research itself, which created even more problems. Most collaborators—teachers and community members—were not trained in research, and those who were, were not trained in the discipline informing the study. She says "It would have been easier to do the fieldwork on my own than to 'beat my brains out trying to instruct others in how to do research' " (1985, 147). The need to achieve consensus on operations often conflicted with the need to press ahead with research tasks. Interviewers from the Sikh community had problems interviewing community members because their respondents felt no incentive to provide information they felt already had to be known by the interviewer. Because of the competing agendas and objectives described earlier, the co-investigator and Gibson could not agree on a final interpretation of data. They "compromised" by writing two reports, which neither the district nor the funding agency would accept. One segment of the community demanded that the co-investigator be fired. The other felt the report was a cover-up by the school district.

Conflict over Consensus in Models for Collaboration

In much of the evaluation literature, problems such as these have been described politely as differences between stakeholders. Seldom do "knock-down, drag out", or bloody words like "conflict," "politics," or "power" ever enter the literature. In fact, the aim among many educational evaluators who advocate collaborative approaches has been to smooth over conflict. They attempt to achieve consensus among stakeholders (Guba and Lincoln 1988; Lincoln and Guba, 1985), rather than focusing on the activities of warring camps or irreconcilable life-or-death propositions.

My experience has been that the consensual model is difficult to maintain in the face of conflict in the field. Part of this is because, as I have indicated, the structural-functional and positivistic flavor of earlier evaluation models also makes understanding of such drama difficult. The Woodlawn Experimental School Project was one long battle between nonnegotiable demands. Meetings were screamers. Lost battles meant lost status, power, and position, even lost jobs. Winning meant personal, political, and economic survival. Living through those experiences was like living in a war zone. I have some of the same kinds of memories from the school district; while participants would agree to disagree from time to time, the rule of thumb was "keep your back to the wall" forever after if you really exposed wrongdoing or incompetence. Since evaluators lived and worked with the people under scrutiny, they needed to fight long, hard, carefully, and strategically for their agendas, counting enemies and watching where they were as carefully as poker players count cards.

I have found the second tradition, or the critical academic tradition, to be a better explanation for the complexity of conflict in field research. It adds two important dimensions to collaborative research. First, it asserts that collaborative research is designed to be "emancipatory," in that it makes those studied aware of the conditions which oppress them, and it helps them to design ways to resist oppression. Second, it makes research subjects and investigators *co-equals* in the "telling of the story," or the analysis and interpretation of results. I would like now to discuss the origins of this tradition.

The Critical Academic Tradition

The critical academic tradition has been spearheaded by researchers with a postmodern and critical distaste for traditional science. They reject positivism with its emphasis on neutrality, especially with its mandated detachment of the researcher. They complain that positivistic science objectifies the people studied, and stamps out or obliterates any vestiges of researcher involvement...for people who desperately *want*, because of their Marxist, feminist, or generally activist persuasions, to *be* involved, and to make a difference. In a recent article, Patti Lather (1990) quotes from Edward Said (1989) in a telling way: "Is it possible for [social science] to be different, that is, to forget and become something else, or must it remain a partner in domination and hegemony?" (315). The "difference" Lather seeks is a form of inquiry that rejects the notion of science as value-free, and states instead that it is value-constitutive or value-producing. That is, science itself constitutes a set of biases (see also Keller 1983; Keller and Grontkowski 1983; Nielsen 1990). It also places the researcher squarely at the center of the project, as director, conceptualist, orchestrator, and arbitrator. By contrast, critical collaborative research de-centers the researcher, making him or her a participant in and subject of the investigative process, rather than simply the disembodied Other who directs and documents it. Critical collaborative research thus rejects as arrogance what Mishler (1986) has called the inherent asymmetry of relationships between the researcher and the researched. Such asymmetry exists because it is the researcher who poses the questions, selects the informants, and then processes, gives form to, and interprets their answers.

Critical collaborative research also questions the possibility that universal truths exist and the utility of reason and logic as means to truth by reframing them in Foucault's (1980) terms to be "effects of power." Like objectivity, truth, logic, and reason can no longer be construed as givens with no independently innocent existence. Rather, they owe their being to their connection— or lack of it—to power and positionality, which weigh very heavily in the determination of what counts as legitimate knowledge. In other terms, the person who can pay the piper calls the tune, even in terms of what constitutes truth.

Critical collaborative researchers assert that the investigators' task is to encourage their subjects to think about life beyond the horizons of current experience (Lather 1990, 332). Their central concerns have been to give voices to their subjects, and to bring together scholarship and advocacy in ways that generate new ways of knowing, capable of interrupting (existing) power imbalances. These scholars make clear the connections among education, pedagogy, and social action: "The line between emancipatory inquiry and pedagogy blurs as critical [or applied] researchers focus on developing interactive approaches to research" (Lather 1990, 325).

The Issues of Power, Agenda, and Voice

Much of what these scholars do has been done before, by applied anthropologists and community organizers like Myles Horton (Adams 1980), Paolo Freire (1973), and Saul Alinsky (1972), who used inquiry, fact-finding, and taxonomic categorization) to impart a disciplined and transformative focus to community problems. However, most critical theorists in education have been housed in the Academy, not in oppressed communities. Lacking activist field experience, they have had to discover anew what I call issues of power, agenda, and voice. In doing so, however, they have begun to redirect relationships between universities and educational practitioners, generating what only can be called a new kind of collaborative research.

The concept of voice involves the realization that reality is constructed of the perceptions of the many participants in any social setting, including research settings. Especially in research settings, there are multiple voices and cross-cutting discourses. What were once called stakeholders now become part of the polyvocality of the setting; their interests constitute stories which, for them, create a definition of the situation or of the reality in which they live. It is the sense of this reality which makes the conflicts among stakeholders more than mere differences of opinion; they are, in fact, conflicts over who has the right to define truth. The passion and even violence of interaction among stakeholders is a function of how important it is for each to have their version of truth—or reality—legitimized.

Multiple realities create for ethnographers the issue of polyvocality, because multiple realities require ethnographers to tell multiple stories. To do so they have experimented with models from literary criticism, novels, poetry, oral history, and biographical narrative. The issue of how to narrate a story, or how best to get an honest story honestly told, has been jazzed up and "disguised as an epistemological issue, a matter of how to present subjective views separate from coloring objective facts" (Geertz 1989) or a matter of how to deal with different ways of knowing.

The Difficulty of Speaking for the Other

Current anthropologists have great difficulty with the authenticity or legitimacy of speaking for other people or appropriating their voices—especially people who differ from them in race, class, ethnicity, gender, or status. The self-reflective, relativistic stance of anthropology as a discipline is conducive to this kind of guilt. For example, Geertz (1989) treats ethnography as a kind of "disease or addiction: 'dishonest...pernicious and self-serving,'...an extension of the 'Western societal project'—imperialistic, intrusive, and disruptive."

Geertz suggests that "where once we wanted to save the savage from himself, now we want to save him from us. [But both kinds of salvation] have little to do with the savage" (1989, 25). Such a position may seem a bit far-fetched with regard to the relatively familiar "savages" whom educational researchers study. However, it is important to remember, as Mishler (1986) points out, that all research is asymmetrical, simply because the researcher is the person who frames the questions and in telling the story, has the last word.

Awareness of these issues is in some ways a post-modern phenomenon. As Geertz puts it (1989, 72), "The discomfort of asymmetry...the loss of confidence and the crisis of ethnographic writing that goes with it, is a contemporary phenomenon and due to contemporary developments....It is not how [things] stood for Sir Edward Evan Evans-Pritchard."

At one level, postmodernism derives from the critical tradition; it is, in fact, a rejection of old authority, including the authority of scholars who give *voice* to the authoritative canon. For example, the rejection of positivism can be viewed as a postmodern rejection of the authoritative canons of traditional science and traditional epistemology. In rejecting the old, postmodernism seeks to give voice to voices never heard before, give legitimacy to ideas that had been denied, and to make possible the upending of all standards, conventions, and rules. It is the postmodern perspective that says that there is no reality or truth, that there are, in fact, only multiple realities and truths, each held in the mind of the perceiver or believer. Postmodernism as a conceptual (or nonconceptual) frame has incorporated the methods of social constructivism and symbolic interactionism. It encourages scholars to view reality as a situational, negotiated, and constructed phenomenon.[2] It also has encouraged Marxist, critical, and feminist scholars to engage in a disciplined search for the effect of contradictions on perceptions of reality. This view has begun to shift the locus of power in research, especially in collaborative or applied research, since the Other being studied is so intimate, so close, that it cannot easily be objectified. Anthropologists (see Marcus and Fischer 1986; Clifford and Marcus 1986) in particular have struggled with how to portray this new reality, but this struggle has profoundly affected educational research, especially collaborative research which also purports to be empowering.

The Issue of Power

If earlier, more traditional, applied researchers struggled with knowledge utilization and how and where to collaborate, contemporary educational researchers are finally learning that they must struggle with issues of power. These in turn, have to do with structural and constructed asymmetries in the research setting. Some have to do with differences of race, class, status, gender, and position—including that of the researcher. Many researchers still view these factors as irrelevant to individual, discrete research projects, but they do so at their peril. Trying to get around issues of power simply by being objective, "aware of one's own biases, and honest about how one's views, beliefs, and biases affect the research process" will not help the researcher escape.

Neither will careful monitoring of one's "subjectivities" (Peshkin 1988), though doing so is a useful strategy by which to begin confronting them. Trying to portray all the multiple voices, or multiple and multilayered discourses, also fails to absolve the researcher. Doing so ignores the fact that some voices are more powerful than others and can "speak for" the community by hiding or altering data, rewriting or refusing to release the report, blackmailing or firing the researcher, or any number of other equally effective strategies.

The Issue of Agenda

I define the term "agenda" in terms of vested interests. Part of the issue of power in research is that inquiry—or investigation—*is* a political process, informed by multiple subjectivities, possessed of multiple entrenched interests, and framed in multiple agendas. One of these agendas involves what questions, exactly, will be asked by researchers. Another is who will participate in the answering of the questions. Yet another is how and by whom the research results will be used—a question that involves more than abstract discussion of researcher ethics. Still another involves the constraints of the research paradigm itself. Often, research is correctly perceived by those studied as a way to justify or preserve the status quo, if informed by structural-functional analyses, or to upset the apple cart, if oriented to critical or conflict perspectives. Researchers who ignore agendas often find themselves caught in the sort of bind described by Gibson (1985).

Some Examples of Collaborative Research
(And What's Wrong with Them)

Having described what I think collaborative research is and has been, I now analyze some examples of collaborative research by several pioneers in this genre. The efforts of these researchers were designed to be both collaborative and empowering or emancipatory.

Petra Munro (1991) was interested in the self-conscious career development of teachers. She did ongoing interviews with a group of recently retired schoolteachers, carrying on a dialogue with them about the twists and turns of both her own and their professional lives.

Andrew Gitlin (Gitlin and Smyth 1989) has developed a peer-evaluation project in which he and the teachers whom he teaches mutually observe and criticize each other's pedagogy.

Elizabeth Ellsworth (1989) taught a seminar on "Media and Anti-Racist Pedagogy" in response an uproar on her campus over institutional racism. Its function was not to see *if* racist practices existed, but to document *how* it operated. The class was to culminate in a public campus intervention based upon racist practices the students identified. It was shaped around a syllabus drafted jointly by Ellsworth and the students.

Patti Lather (1991) also developed a specifically liberative curriculum in a class for undergraduates in a women's studies program. Its intent was to organize a collective struggle within the classroom that would enable students to recognize and change the systemic conditions of oppression which affect their lives.

Joe McPherson (a pseudonym) and a group of Native American teachers tried to increase the number of highly trained minority teachers. A course which he taught at their school on the reservation was designed to help the teachers enter a master's degree program.

Henry Giroux calls for teachers to "redefine and change the nature of the conditions under which they work; . . . to shape the ways in which time space and knowledge organize everyday life in schools." He calls for teachers to create the ideology and structural conditions necessary for [teachers] to write, research, and work with each other in producing curricula and instructional power (Giroux 1988, 193–95).

What's Wrong With This Picture?

Now I would like to tell my stories in a slightly different way. Regardless of researcher intent, critical collaborative research is difficult, both for researchers and participants, and even the best planned and executed projects can lead to unintended problems.

Petra Munro's attempts to achieve collaboration with her teacher-informants were rebuffed. The retired teachers rejected every attempt she made to interject her own story into the narrative. Their job, they said, was to tell their story, not to listen to hers—the trials of a much, much younger woman.

The individuals with whom Gitlin and Lather worked are students in their classes. The topics they work on are assignments for classes, not independently chosen, and students are graded on their peer evaluations. As Roman (1992) points out, "Given the power relations involved in carrying out a professor's research agenda while taking her course, or functioning in other senses as her student subordinate," it is difficult to see how such research can be called empowering, collaborative, or participatory in an egalitarian sense. Nor is it easy to see what issues of informed consent mean in the context of being graded (Roman 1992, 301).

Liz Ellsworth discovered that the very structure of asymmetry which she was trying to explore was reproduced in her classroom. The voices she was trying to hear were silenced, and the old assumptions dominated the discourse.

Joe McPherson's teachers had not been told he was doing research on them, nor had he asked their permission to publish the stories they told in class. They only knew that his class was designed to get them ready for graduate work.

Henry Giroux's discourse is so complex teachers often can understand little of it. Some of his suggestions increase the sense of powerlessness teachers have by requiring them to do things they feel are impossible and unrealistic, given the exigencies of their everyday lives as teachers.

The critical, collaborative, and activist tradition, of which Munro, Lather, Gitlin, Ellsworth, Giroux, and McPherson are a part, constitutes a very small minority of all educational researchers. Their work has been done on the margins of educational research, and often in the context of considerable disapproval and disesteem. As such, the continued efforts of these researchers to expand and extend their models is to be applauded. My own work has been informed by their successes. However, I also have learned from the imperfections of their early work.

The concerns these projects raise include the following: Each was generated by the researcher, not initiated by the participants. They reflected the needs of researchers and tended not to incorporate the feelings, wants, and desires of research participants. Several of the researchers seemed to be unaware of many structural constraints and realities operating in their participants' lives.

None of these projects resolved the problem of differences in status and power—or asymmetry—between the researcher and the researched. These included asymmetries between teacher and student; researcher and practitioner; old and young. In many of these projects, the researcher's agenda was not clear to the research subjects from the beginning, and operated independently from whatever agendas research subjects might have had. Many of these projects defined the research participants as in need of empowerment, whether or not they understood the concept or wanted to be empowered. All of these projects, except for the resolution implied in Ellsworth's work, define emancipation or empowerment in terms deriving from a Eurocentric, Enlightenment perspective on individualism. They all assume that the act of doing research, by itself, is empowering.

Each of these projects represents an uneasy transition from traditional positivism to early critical collaborative models. As such, they are pioneering efforts. However, while attempting to give voice to participants, each still speaks with the voice of the researcher and is framed in accordance with the agenda of the researcher, who retains power to define the results of the research. The researchers define themselves as collaborators, but do not address how they might actually have silenced their participation. Collaboration is treated as a cure for the problem of participant agendas, and the issue of power is tiptoed past with the tacit, if mistaken, assumption that naming participants as collaborators makes them as co-equals.

In summary, all these projects reflect a naiveté about issues of power, agenda, and voice in fieldwork, which I feel characterizes much critical collaborative work in education.

The Problem of Innocence and Ignorance

Fieldwork naiveté derives from the innocence that belief in objectivity and detachment made possible. It is a post-positivistic hangover, often fostered by lack of prior field experience in non-university-centered settings. Neither professional scholars nor students are very well prepared for the political realities of life in the field. Fieldwork courses prepare novices for dirt, mosquitoes, boredom, people who do not want to talk to them, and even funny food. Fieldwork courses, however, do not prepare researchers for threatened, power-hungry participants or open hatred, much less for people who will stop at little or nothing to kill a project or bury research results. They do not prepare investigators to realize that the research project and its staff are just one of the vested interests in a setting, and a new kid on the block at that. If the voice of the researcher carols an uncongenial tune, powerful people will have no compunctions about silencing the singer (see McDade, 1987).

Even for those whose training included a "total immersion" in exotic cultures, time-honored research procedures that distance the researcher from the researched and disassociate research experience from our personal experience make it possible to avoid responsibility for consequences of researcher behavior in the field.

Methodological Disassociation

Among the common practices that facilitate disassociation and avoidance of responsibility is failure to spell out methods—how the data were selected, collected, and analyzed—under the guise of engaging in intuitive, interpretive, and holistic approaches to data analysis. Another is ignoring the experiences of the ancestors. Rosalie Wax (1971),

Gerald Berreman (1962), M. N. Srinivas (1976), William Foote Whyte (1984), Robert Kiste (1981), and Hortense Powdermaker (1967)—to name only a few of the most accessible—all have written eloquently about the interpersonal dimension of fieldwork long before issues of researcher role, subjectivity, and voice became of such concern in educational research. Our students would be well served were they familiar with this literature.

Disassociation occurs when researchers avoid conflict by focusing on narrowly program- or case-specific objectives or narrow, context-free analysis of topics like curriculum offerings or teacher-pupil interaction. These can be structured in a way that avoids altogether the incorporation of racial, class, gender, and status issues. The psychological paradigm that dominates educational thinking in the United States makes this methodological cop-out easier in educational ethnography. Psychological thinking encourages researchers to view race, class, gender and other such "variables" as noise to be "controlled" in the research design. Because the unit of analysis is the decontextualized individual, exploration of social structural and political contexts becomes irrelevant.

Disassociation is encouraged by researcher anxiety. Scholars often fail to share both research-in-progress and final results with participants, on the grounds that they couldn't, shouldn't, or wouldn't understand what was written. Too often, these concerns hide researcher fear that if participants knew what the researcher were writing, they would ask the researcher to leave the research site. Too often, concerns over disclosure focus on danger to the researcher's project, not to the subjects of the study. As a consequence, disclosure comes at the end of a study, if at all, when the risks are less. The consequence often is that researchers cease to take any risks—at least insofar as facing up to their subjects with the issues and facts they have uncovered is concerned.

Finally, disassociation also is facilitated by the traditional use in much research of the timeless and static "ethnogranhic present." This eschews a consideration of change, deifies the past, and renders conflict an aberration, rather than a natural component of human social life.

Summary

Issues of power, agenda, and voice are givens. They must be integrated into the research design and made at least potentially central to the analysis and explanation. If this is not done, researchers are left in the clutches of experienced and politically savvy members of vested interest groups. Because researchers don't expect their work to be like a street fight, they may, at the very least, end up defending themselves or apologizing to clients or research participants for flawed analyses that could not avoid these issues. In addition, the structural realities of participants' lives are givens. Often they cannot be overcome simply by participating in conscious-raising activities, even if these are focused on "empowerment," nor can they be reduced in the mere process of being a member of an ethnographic or "voice-giving" research project (LeCompte and DeMarrais 1992).

A Critical Collaborative Approach to Fieldwork

In my work in the Pinnacle School District, I have attempted to fuse both the applied and the critical traditions. In so doing, I have encountered—and been unable to resolve satisfactorily—some of the same problems as did the researchers whose work I have described earlier. However, my work differs from theirs in that it is not expressly directed toward empowerment or emancipation of participants. It cannot be called emancipatory research, despite its collaborative nature. It has involved "studying up"; the focus is administrators. As a consequence, while I have not actively sought to eliminate oppression of "lower participants" in the district, I have instituted interactive models for my work, and I have adopted a number of strategies to facilitate the reform efforts desired by teachers and administrators. First and most important, I have made a long-term commitment to the work. I have been involved for four-and-a-half years in this project and see no imminent closure. I have tried to remain a welcome guest by anticipating district needs and providing services to fulfill them. These have included teaching extension classes, consulting with individual teachers, writing grant proposals, instituting data collection projects, and serving as a troubleshooter or liaison among warring factions in the administration (see LeCompte 1992, 1994). I also have steadily engaged in a dialogue that questions assumptions behind or discourse framing educational practices and administrative processes that seem to me oppressive.

I was fortunate in being invited by the district to participate as a consultant in their reform efforts; now I am attempting to maintain my relationship with the district as one-among-equals; to investigate research problems which the district identifies even as I sometimes reframe them in scholarly terms (which I hope they will come to use); to set aside my own agendas from time to time and to adopt the frameworks of the district participants; to integrate my telling or version of the story with theirs; and to give the district people as much public opportunity to tell that story as I have.

In making it clear that I want to be helpful to the district, also have made clear my personal agenda which includes that I must publish so as not to perish professionally. As a consequence, district administrators know that I use the data I collect for them in the stories I write about them. However, I ask the participants involved for feedback on drafts of any paper before I present or publish it. The feedback has always altered the story told. Many of these stories also have been told collaboratively in public forums such as symposia at professional associations in which I and my Pinnacle colleagues have been participants. Thus, in publishing, their ideas and mine are presented, and often the result is a synthesis. District personnel all believe that what they are doing is important for Navajo children; they see our joint efforts as a way of achieving much-needed and deserved visibility.

The process of achieving synthesis has, however, meant that I have had to give up on some of the cherished projects I would like to study, and to write grant proposals for programs *the district* wants funded. It has meant being mentored—and humbled—by Anglos. It also has meant being mentored and criticized by Navajos in ways which, at first, my own culture did not prepare me to recognize. Failure to recognize feedback has been embarrassing.

In integrating the postmodern notion of voice in my work, I have had to contend with the multiple voices and multiple realities that participants in the research setting construct (LeCompte 1992). I also have had to give up some of my own analytic categories in the process of getting people to write down what they think and how they define their terms. This practice created a truly Bakhtinian dilemma when I tried to "give voice to" my district colleagues by using participant terms in my own writing. Suddenly I found myself censored by a professional association, whose agenda included changing the discourse of education.

In 1991, I organized a symposium on our collaborative efforts for one of my own professional associations. The theme of the session emphasized the multiple and changing roles we all have assumed over the last several years, and the participants included district administrators, a former teacher, consultants for the district, and myself. After much struggle over a title, we came up with "Collaboration in the Trenches." The symposium was accepted by the Program Chair, but only on the condition that we change the title to eliminate the phrase "in the trenches." The Program Chair felt that that phrase—or any other "war-like metaphors," for that matter—was inappropriate and used too frequently in education. His wish to change the metaphoric discourse of education was countered by my protest that to do so silenced the participants in our project. After some negotiation, the issue of participant voice prevailed, and we remained "in the trenches" on the program. The incident did, however, make quite clear just how salient power, agenda, and voice are in educational research, and how alert critical collaborative researchers must be for their silencing and confounding presence—even when trying very hard to "do things right."

Notes

1. A debt of gratitude is owed to Donna Deyhle, University of Utah, Audrey Kleinsasser, University of Wyoming, and Phil Carspecken, University of Houston, for their comments on earlier versions of this chapter.

2. In borrowing this notion of reality, however, it has not also simultaneously retained the theoretical underpinnings of sociology. As a consequence, it risks a descent into relativism or nihilism (LeCompte 1992, 1993).

References

Adams, Frank (with Myles Horton). 1980. *Unearthing Seeds of Fire: The Idea of Highlander*. Winston-Salem, N.C.: John C. Blair.

Alinsky, Saul D. 1972. *Rules for Radicals: A Pragmatic Primer for Realistic Radicals*. New York: Vintage Books.

Berreman, Gerald D. 1962. *Behind Many Masks: Ethnography and Impression Management in a Himalayan Village*. Monographs of the Society for Applied Anthropology, No. 4. Society for Applied Anthropology.

Clifford, James, and George Marcus. 1986. *Writing Culture*. Berkeley and Los Angeles: University of California Press.

Ellsworth, Elizabeth. 1989. "Why Doesn't This Feel Empowering? Working Through the Repressive Myths of Critical Pedagogy." *Harvard Educational Review* 59:297–324.

Foucault, Michel. 1980. *Power/Knowledge*. New York: Pantheon Books.

Freire, Paolo. 1973. *Education for Critical Consciousness*. New York: Seabury.

Geertz, Clifford. 1989. *Works and Lives: The Anthropologist as Author*. Stanford: Stanford University Press.

Gibson, Margaret A. 1985. "Collaborative Educational Ethnography: Problems and Profits." *Anthropology and Educational Quarterly* 16, no. 2:124–49.

Giroux, Henry A. 1988. "Critical Theory and the Politics of Culture and Voice: Rethinking the Discourse of Educational Research." Pp. 190–211 in *Qualitative Research in Education: Focus and Methods,* ed. Rodman Webb and Robert Sherman. Philadelphia, Pa. Falmer Press.

Gitlin, Andrew, and John Smyth. 1989. *Teacher Evaluation: Educative Alternatives.* Philadelphia, Pa: Falmer Press.

Guba, Egon, and Yvonne Lincoln. 1988. *Fourth Generation Evaluation.* Newbury Park, Calif.: Sage Publications.

House, Ernest R. 1979. "The Objectivity, Fairness and Justice of Federal Evaluation Policy as Reflected in the Follow-Through Evaluation." *Educational Evaluation and Policy Analysis* 1, no. 1:28–42.

Huberman, Michael. 1991. "Linkage Between Researchers and Practitioners: A Qualitative Study." *American Educational Research Journal* 27 (Summer):363–93.

Keller, Evelyn. 1983. "Gender and Science." Pp. 187–207 in *Discovering Reality,* ed. S. Harding and M. Hintikka. *Discovering Reality.* Boston: D. Reidel Publishing.

Keller, Evelyn, and Christine Grontkowski. 1983. "The Mind's Eye." Pp. 207–25 in *Discovering Reality,* ed. S. Harding and M. Hintikka. Boston: D. Reidel Publishing.

Kiste, Robert C. 1981. "The People of Enewetak Atoll versus the U.S. Department of Defense." In *Ethics and Anthropology: Dilemma in Fieldwork,* ed. R. Rynkiewicz and J. Spradley. Reprint. Malabar, Fl.: Robert E. Krieger Publishing.

Lather, Patti A. 1990. "Reinscribing Otherwise: The Play of Values in the Practices of the Human Sciences." Pp. 315–33 in *The Paradigm Dialog,* ed. Egon G. Guba. Newbury Park, Calif.: Sage Publications.

———. 1991. *Getting Smart: Feminist Research within the Postmodern.* New York Routledge.

LeCompte, Margaret. 1994. "Defining Reality: Applying Double Description and Chaos Theory to the Practice of Practice." *Educational Theory,* Vol. 44, no. 3 (Summer), pp. 277–298.

———. 1993. "Frameworks for Hearing Silence: What Does Telling Stories Mean When We Are Supposed to Be Doing Science?" In *Naming Silenced Lives,* ed. D. McLaughlin and W. Tierney. New York: Routledge. Pp. 9–29.

LeCompte, Margaret and Kathleen Bennett DeMarrais. 1992. "The Disempowering of Empowerment: Out of the Revolution and into the Classroom." In *Educational Foundations,* no. 3, Summer: 5–23.

Lincoln, Yvonna, and Egon Guba. 1985. *Naturalistic Inquiry*. Newbury Park, Calif.: Sage Publications.

Marcus, George, and Michael Fischer. 1986. *Anthropology as Cultural Critique*. Chicago: University of Chicago Press.

McCall, George J. and J. L. Simmons. 1969. *Issues in Participant Observation: A Text and Reader*. New York: Random House.

McDade, Laurie. 1987. "Telling Them What They Do Not Want To Hear: A Dilemma in Ethnographic Evaluation." Paper presented at the Annual Meeting of the American Anthropological Association, Chicago.

Mishler, Elliot G. 1986. *Research Interviewing: Context and Narrative*. Cambridge: Harvard University Press.

Munro, Petra. 1991. "Multiple 'I's': Dilemmas of Life History Research." Paper presented at the American Educational Research Association, 3–7 April 1991, Chicago.

Neilson, Joyce McCarl. 1990. Introduction. Pp. 1–41 in *Feminist Research Methods*, ed. J. M. Nielson. Boulder, Colo.: Westview Press.

Ogbu, John U. 1978. *The Next Generation*. New York: Academic Press.

———. 1988. *Minority Education and Caste*. New York: Academic Press.

Peshkin, Alan. 1988. "In Search of Subjectivity: One's Own." *Educational Researcher*, October, 17–21.

Powdermaker, Hortense. 1967. *Stranger and Friend: The Way of an Anthropologist*. London: Secker & Warburg.

Roman, Leslie G. 1992. "Whose Voices Speak with Whom?" *Historical Studies in Education/Revue d'histoire de l'education* 4, no. 2:295–305.

Said, Edward. 1989. "Representing the Colonized: Anthropology's Interlocutors." *Critical Theory* 15:205–25.

Schensul, Jean J., Stephen L. Schensul, Maria Gonzales, and Eugene Caro. 1981. "Community-Based Research and Approaches to Social Changes: The Case of the Hispanic Health Council." *The Generator* 12, no. 2:13–26.

Schensul, Jean J. and Stephen L. Schensul. 1992. "Collaborative Research: Methods of Inquiry." Pp. 161–201 in *The Handbook of Qualitative Research in Education*, ed. M. LeCompte, W. L. Millroy, and J. Preissle. San Diego, Calif.: Academic Press.

Srinivas, M. N. 1976. *The Remembered Village*. Berkeley and Los Angeles: University of California Press.

Stake, Robert E. 1978. "The Case Study Method in Social Inquiry." *Educational Researcher* 7:5–8.

Wax, Rosalie H. 1971. *Doing Fieldwork: Warnings and Advice*. Chicago: University of Chicago Press.

Whyte, William Foot. 1984. *Learning from the Field: A Guide from Experience*. Beverly Hills, Calif.: Sage Publications.

6

Ethnography and the Politics of Absence

Ronald G. Sultana

By speech, silence becomes the centre and principle of expression, its vanishing point. Speech eventually has nothing more to tell us: we investigate the silence, for it is the silence that is doing the speaking.

Pierre Macherey, *A Theory of Literary Production* (1978)

Introduction

This article is about the silences that often are registered but not so often highlighted and analyzed with the anthropological tools of the ethnographer, referring as these do to the empirical world that can be captured. While there is abundant literature that helps the ethnographer refine the technical aspects of the writing of the narrative, it has been only recently that the political implications behind the epistemology and ontology of ethnography as a research strategy have been addressed in any depth.

Rather than, therefore, looking at ways of improving the collection of data, this paper will consider an aspect that hitherto has been largely ignored in ethnography. The focus will be on what the ethnographic text leaves unsaid. A number of silences will be identified with reference to the process, content, and political effectiveness of ethnographic narratives, although it will be argued that these silences or gaps are not all of the same kind, and that some rather than others are more promising in the construction of radical educational theory and practice.

Qualitative research, in itself, seems little concerned with the absences that frame (or are at the heart) of the narrative it weaves—the "reality" it claims to reflect—or the process through which the phenomena are represented. The roots of ethnography are to be found deeply embedded in a regime of realism, inasmuch as it sets out to represent the empirical world that "is." There is, indeed, a danger that the ethnographic narrative entraps the writer and reader in this nominal positivist world: details of what happened, who spoke, what was said. It is the dictatorship of data, from which concepts and generalizations arise, "faithfully" representing the particulars from which they have been abstracted. In these positivistic moments that govern ethnographic representation, silence has little value and can only be regarded negatively—an empty absence that, in a matter of time, could and should become full of words.

Not so for the radical ethnographer who approaches phenomena in the spirit of Nietzsche or Marx or the critical theorists: as dangerous illusions, where the "what is not" is infinitely more important than the "what is." The nonpositivist accords silences, gaps, and absences a special and prestigious place in his/her theoretical engagement with the world and looks to them for clues that will lead not only to reflexivity but to praxis. The "real" is subjected to problematization, for it is "historically produced in the course of conflicts and struggles or collective life. Realism stabilizes and naturalizes the object and apparatuses of perception and knowledge" (Wexler 1987, 85). In purporting to tell us "what happened," realistic ethnography presents itself as a complete narrative. But the sum of the details of the ethnographic text never can be complete and are riven with contradictions and absences, for they too, in Lukacs's (1971) words, have to be understood "as aspects of a totality, i.e., as the aspects of a total social situation caught up in the process of historical change" (162).

How, then, to deal with the incompleteness of a text? This question does not imply that ethnographies somehow should be "complete texts" that "tell all there is to tell." As Tyler (1986) argues, "Every attempt will always be incomplete, insufficient, lacking in some way, but this is not a defect since it is the means that enables transcendence. Transcendence comes from imperfection, not from perfection" (136). But incompleteness does pose a challenge to the critic whose task is similar to that of a therapist, that is, "not to cure or complete [the text]; but to explain why it is at it is" (Eagleton 1976, 92). The problem with this kind of exercise, however, is that the silences and absences easily can become the repository for all that the critic projects.

So do we commit ourselves to nihilism when we privilege silence? Quite the contrary—it is to discover, if not the grand narratives, at least the master narratives (Giroux 1988) that shape detail. It is to delicately balance the more emancipatory moments of postmodernist thought with that tradition that allows not only critique but also utopian dreaming. To privilege silence is to realize that text is ideology inasmuch as it attempts to reflect the world in a coherent and totalizing manner. It is to admit, in the spirit of modern philosophy, the limits of reason and thus to open the way for the valuing of silence, unknown and unrespected by idealist and positivist philosophy alike. The privileging of silence is a strategy for recognizing the status of the ethnographic text as a construct, and hence to render it immediately a candidate for deconstruction.

In order to accept this interpretation of silence, however, it also is necessary to presuppose the existence of some form of master narrative that weaves the tale into some version of a totalizing vision—a point well made by McLaren (1988) when he argues in favor of an "arch of social dreaming...the conquest of a vision of what the total trans- formation of society might mean" (74). But this would seem to imply that silence and gaps always are ideological, which would mean in practice that simply by having the master narrative at hand, and using it as a template on the presenting narrative, will quickly show up the ideologically significant silences, now identifiable in confrontation with the "whole story," as it were. It is therefore important at this point to construct a grammar of silence, to have some guidelines to mark a path through the impossibly difficult task of finding our way through the maze of silence. As Macherey (1978)—the Althusserian theorist of the "absent center" in literary texts—argues, we need to ask if the silence denotes

a true absence, or is it the extension of a half-presence?...Will it be the pillar of an explanation or the pretext for an interpreta- tion?...Can we say that this silence is hidden? What is it? A condition of existence—point of departure, methodological beginning—essential foundation—ideal culmination—absolute origin which lends meaning to the endeavour? Means or form of connection? Can we make this silence speak? What is the unspoken saying? What does it mean? To what extent is dissimu- lation a way of speaking? Can something that has hidden itself be recalled to our presence? Silence as the source of expression. Is what I am really saying what I am not saying? Hence the main risk run by those who would say everything. After all, perhaps the work is not hiding what it does not say; this is simply missing. (82, 85–86)

How, then, are we to distinguish between what an ethnographic narrative cannot say, refuses to say, and simply does not say? And do we develop an inverted ethnographic method by measuring silences, whether acknowledged or unacknowledged? One way of working toward the resolution of these questions is to consider the various types of silences that can be attributed to ethnography. I will do this in the next section of this paper, referring critically to an ethnographic study that I carried out in 1986 (Sultana 1987) in order to contextualize and illustrate the points that I make.

Ethnography and the Semiotics of Silence

In the identification of some of the more important silences within ethnographic texts, it would be useful to classify the absences and gaps along certain criteria. I use two guidelines in developing this classificatory system, the first being organizational, and the second political. While the concern of the former is to systematize the presentation of ideas, the latter interest is the political re-ciphering of these silences in favor of transformative action in the world. In the interest of systematic presentation and clarity, I will number the variety of absences I identify, while in no way claiming that there are no gaps within the very text that I myself produce. These absences will refer to (1) process, (2) content, and (3) political ontology of ethnographic texts. The concluding section of the paper will deal with the politics of silence, pointing toward new ways of making that silence speak in favour of a more just and humane world.

Ethnographic Process and Silence

The doing of ethnography, the very choice of qualitative research as a tool, itself can be framed by a number of silences. Tyler (1985) and Clifford and Marcus (1986) argue that since ethnography inscribes culture in discourse rather than merely describes it, it is the end of description, for the very act of writing binds politics and poetics. The choice of ethnography, in this sense, needs to be justified as much as what one does with—and how one writes—ethnography. Many, including Gitlin, Siegel, and Boru (1989), have highlighted the need to expose the formative influence behind the silence of the researcher, the "author-as-author" who often constitutes herself/himself as "author-as-fieldworker," inviting the reader into the realm of narrative realism where everything there is to tell is narrated in a neutral fashion. It is because the researcher edits himself/herself out of the text that we often get so little information on such details as the researcher's expectations and presuppositions, or the surprises that were encountered in the field.

Not that the researcher can, in any real manner, suspend the biases that are at work. Rather, as in Gadamer's (1979) discussion of modern hermeneutics, research should be characterized by a reflexivity that enables us to understand the possibility of a multiplicity of viewpoints and "to respond to opposing arguments by a reflection which deliberately places us in the perspective of the other." (110). But, as Gitlin et al. (1989) argue, "It is impossible for the researcher to understand the 'subject' unless she/he enters into a dialogue with the 'subject' aimed at mutual understanding" (243). They go on to point out the contradiction by those researchers who claim to be "concerned with emancipatory change" and who therefore are "interested in contesting relations of domination," but who in fact "use a method which reproduces the type of relations they so despise" (249).

Hence, in considering the silences and absences in the process of ethnographic research, it is precisely this possibility of gaining insight from others that often is precluded, for the emphasis, as McLaren (1990) points out, is on doing research *on*, not with, others. It is this kind of approach that stresses, for instance, the need to keep the researcher's opinions and perspectives privy from those being "researched." In carrying out my ethnographic study of three school communities in New Zealand, where the focus was the gauging of the school-to-work messages given by the form, content and process of the schools and the kinds of reception that the students afforded these messages, I often was caught in a frustrating and ideologically contradictory position. Students, for instance, would tell me of sexist or racist attitudes and comments of teachers, but I would feel reluctant to confront the school communities with these criticisms, afraid that such early feedback somehow would change the nature of the schools, and that I would go against the ultimately positivist principle of introducing extraneous "variables" into the research (laboratory?) field.

The attempt not to jeopardize the research by trying hard not to change the situation by acting upon it led, of course, to a number of problems. The maintenance of an "objective front" with teachers, for instance, certainly reinforced the subordinate positions of teachers as "researched." The attempt at withholding also creates some insincerities which I found difficult to deal with, both at the ethical and the political level. For how can one possibly be effective in challenging teachers to regard their practice critically if, in our own work as researchers, we resort to underhanded ways in order to satisfy our appetite for yet more detail?

It is perhaps for this reason that the point of view of those researched too often is not heard within the ethnographic report. Critics on the left, such as Reynolds (1980–81, 84), have in fact taken inter-actionist ethnographic accounts to task for canonizing the perspectives of the social members in the explanation of social phenomena, to the exclusion of the arbitration of the intellectual or social scientific class. But radical researchers too often have gone to the other extreme and have been too ready to ignore, for instance, the cultural constraints under which teachers labor, leading to "teacher-bashing" accounts that effectively jeopardize any interaction between researchers (who "know it all") and workers in schools. While it does make sense to criticize ethnographies that are influenced exclusively by phenomenological and ethnomethodological traditions, it needs to be accepted that the sense-making practices that individuals utilize to interpret their world are to be given importance and that, for epistemological and practical political reasons, these should be "triangulated" with other possible accounts, including those of the ethnographer who positions herself/himself within a particular ideological discourse.

Another silence that structures the creation of ethnographic texts is the rather politically naive view that these "anatomies of detail" (Wexler 1987, 85) somehow will be used automatically *in favor* of those with whom the researcher has political sympathies. Few researchers have outlined the danger that their ethnographies will become yet another of the panoptic erections in service of the governing episteme of our times to surveil, discipline, and punish. The consideration of this became real for me when, in the course of feedback to staff in the school communities I had researched, I produced vivid descriptions of the resistant strategies developed by Maori students, with the intention to encourage a debate on the need for cross-cultural schooling. My hope that this would lead schools and teachers to become more sensitive to the realities that groups of students experience in their daily lives often was co-opted, however, and the data reinterpreted in terms of another goal, that is, that of better controlling what was often considered to be pathological behavior. There always is a risk, therefore, that the progressive agendas of ethnographers are hijacked and their labor appropriated for conservative, if not oppressive ends.

Content, Silence, and the Selective tradition

Ethnography as realist text seeks to reflect the empirical world that it focuses upon, and in its more emancipatory moments it does so in a critical manner. While for some time the tradition has been to give pride of place to "thick description," the real promise of ethnography as a transformative tool is fulfilled when it becomes theoretically embedded and when it, therefore, tries to recover the silenced context, the conditions and the relations in the light of which phenomena need to be apprehended. As West (1984) has argued so well, it has become possible to situate particular ethnographies within wider structural accounts, and this synthesis of phenomenon and form is possible not only at the epistemological level but, as we shall see in the next section, also can be articulated at the political level (Sharp 1982).

Such a synthesis is particularly promising in order to make sense of the gaps in narratives that are to be found within institutions such as schools. Gramsci's notion of "hegemony"—as well as Williams's (1977) related insight that one of the key ways through which control is maintained is through the "selective tradition"—are particularly useful theoretical tools in our attempt at analyzing what can be referred to as the "logic of non-events." As Eagleton (1976) has argued, "Ideology is present in the text in the form of its eloquent silences" (89). In other words, hegemony is possible because silence is privileged in a reactionary manner, and ethnography attains its radical promise when, rather than dancing to the music it hears, it listens intently to that silence, making that silence speak volumes in favor of the powerless and oppressed.

There is an important kind of silence with which a radical ethnography should engage. This is the silence of the context in which the text is framed, what Bisseret (1979) calls "the referent." Silence thus constitutes part of the metaphysics of presence and, in contrast to the more anarchic moments of postmodernism, depends on "something being outside and anchoring the symbolic relations of the text" (Wexler 1987, 135). The referent functions by attributing lack or absence to those who do not possess the qualities attributed to others holding dominant positions. In the case of my own study, the hidden referent nearly always was the capitalist world of work as it is, and to which the students constantly and unproblematically were asked—coerced even— to refer to in their preparation for transition to "the" world of work (Sultana 1988, 1989, 1990). This is why my own ethnography is replete with references to that which was *not* said, and while, on the surface, such writing seems to contradict the nature of ethnographic writing, any radical researcher working within this mode constantly has to appeal to that which is not there. Indeed, what I prefer to call "inverted ethnography" is the only way that one can subvert the positivistic regime of realism that still lingers on in this research strategy. Those who do not read the silences in a text "read from the same ideological framework, share the same repressions, and take for granted the same silence. . . . It is still only by distancing ourselves from the familiar modes of representation that we can expect to identify the areas on which ideology is silent" (Belsey 1980, 137).

The selective tradition needs to be exposed and explored in any ethnography that claims for itself radical and transformative intentions. For the curriculum narrative revels in common sense ideas that express and encapsulate the requirements of the dominant class. In my own study, a curriculum that purported to teach about the world of work prepared students to accept that world uncritically, often failing to problematize key issues such as wealth, power, oppression and exploitation, the wage relationship, class, gender, and race relations on the workforce, and collective struggle on the part of workers through trade unions. In such instances, silence is a key element in the discourse made available to students, having an ideological function inasmuch as it conceals the power relations that structure the content and process of the educational encounter.

Not all silences in the content of the text are ideological in the sense developed above. There are meso (institutional) and micro (classroom) as well as macro contexts that explain why some things are left unsaid (McNeil 1987), though, this having been said, the point still can be made that the resulting silence can function in favor of the reproduction of the wider social formation. In my study, the silence of teachers on trade union matters did have an ideological function, but the context of the absence of messages on workers' movements often was motivated by a fear of conflict in the classroom. Anxiety that different opinions about unions might lead to classroom conflict led many teachers to adopt "survival strategies" to ensure their own comfort rather than educational ends (Hargreaves and Woods 1984).

But this is not in itself a sufficient explanation of the "microdynamics" of silence. Remaining with the example of messages about trade unions, it becomes clear that classroom dynamics can interrelate with ideological and macro reasons for the privileging of one silence over another. Those teachers who were afraid of conflict also were those whose ideological positions were most obviously bourgeois, who would, for example, become hostile if someone suggested to them that they belonged to a "teachers' trade union" rather than a "professional association." On the other hand, those who did break the silence on trade unions were those who, like technical teachers, had participated at some stage in productive work and who had experienced firsthand capitalist relations of production and therefore had become politicized in favor of collective struggle and change.

The Political Ontology of Ethnography

The problem that needs to be addressed here is the silence that reigns over the effectiveness of ethnographic research strategies in bringing about change in school communities and in educational policymaking, if not, as sometimes is claimed even more ambitiously, in the wider social sphere. Some researchers and methodologists have given this issue some attention, and Pollard (1984), for instance, has argued that it is perhaps realistic to expect ethnography to have more impact at the micro level because of the nature of ethnographic work, for it enhances the possibility that actors in schools can make the movement from unexamined "practical consciousness" to the more critical self and system awareness of "discursive consciousness" (Giddens 1976).

All this is acceptable, except that there have been few ethnographic studies that have told the readers much about the effectiveness of their study in bringing about change in any progressive direction. We often are presented with richly detailed descriptions, but once the narrative ends, the implicit assumption is that the readers (presumably the teachers and administrators of the school communities researched would be among them) somehow will improve their practice just by reflecting on it. Change will follow, it is implied, after consciousness has been raised. But does change follow? This question applies equally to the institutional and classroom levels as it does to the macro societal level. For ethnography often has been justified on the grounds of its political effectiveness. Shipman (1984) for instance, in a paper on ethnography and public policy, describes policymakers as "hungry for evidence," and he regards ethnographic work as having a clear potential role by virtue of the inadequacies of previous quantitative work. Sharp (1982) has claimed that theoretically embedded ethnography has a political rationale, since "a scientific political practice requires knowledge of the fissures, ruptures, and contradictions in capitalism's mode of appearance which guide political and pedagogical work. Ethnography can offer insight concerning the points at which politicization is possible, feasible, and productive of greater awareness and concerning the processes through which this could be achieved" (60). But while such political aspirations speak with a "language of possibility" about establishing more equitable and democratic social arrangements within and outside school, ethnographers on the left have to be more specific about their effectiveness in bringing about such progressive change. There have been too many ethnographies that conclude with a rousing

appeal about the resistances and contestations, as well as the contradictions and systemic fissures identified by the ethnographer, while one
is left almost entirely in the dark about whether these spaces, these
cracks in the structure, actually do modify, if not radically transform,
the world in favor of progressive ends.

In my study, there were varied responses by teachers and school
principals, as well as boards of governors, to feedback sessions about
my ethnographic narrative. At one level these responses were quite
positive: it was gratifying to see teachers acknowledge the damaging
effects of structures, curricula, and pedagogies that they promoted
unproblematically in schools and to engage with them in an attempt
to come up with alternative, more transformative modes of practice.
However, seven years following that research, I really wonder whether
it has made any real difference in the structures and practices of those
schools. But there is, in the tradition of educational ethnographic
research, hardly any mention of the frustration such as I felt when,
after spending so much time, money, and effort in carrying out research
in those schools, I receive letters from friends who tell me that things
have not really changed at all. Assuming for a moment that as a
researcher I had all the technical details right (in terms of using the
available tools effectively), then the problems that need to be confronted
are whether we still have to develop a theory of how an audience
changes itself (i.e., does consciousness-raising work?) or if the tool, that
is, ethnography itself, is inadequate.

That the latter is probable emerges in Burbules's (1986) echoing
some of the concerns raised above, when he points to the need to move
from description and analysis to active involvement within school
communities. In the light of the issues raised throughout this paper,
therefore, radical educational researchers should move away from
merely describing school life to promoting specific versions of it,
versions that have been identified as being more equitable and democratic than the ones currently being engendered. In other words, the
radical researcher would be involved in a sort of Freirian pedagogy—
often advocated for teachers by radical researchers—where she or he
highlights various democratic and emancipatory voices, introducing
new themes that heighten the chances for a truly critical education to
occur. As Burbules (1986) notes, this is a crucial theoretical and political
shift because it supplants the attempt to study and understand,
somewhat dispassionately, the prospects for school reform in favor of
advocating such reform, insisting upon its possibility and becoming
actively involved in making the possible probable.

Conclusion

There is, of course, great skill in the ethnographer's depiction of life. The point of this paper has been that the real genius of the radical researcher will be to transform that life to come closer to a democratic vision. This is no easy task, for a number of reasons, some of which are very practical. It is doubtful whether the bureaucracies we call schools will allow any person to function inside the institution who has the explicit aim of bringing about change. The whole point of bureaucracies is system-preservation.

But it is incorrect to pursue a strategy, such as descriptive ethnography, which, while satisfying, indeed gratifying, our "need" to know, is largely ineffective in promoting transformation. The method favored in this paper—what is referred to as "inverted ethnography"— privileges silences because of the contention that the more substantial is to be found in that absence. We thus (actually or figuratively) develop a sign to highlight certain ideological silences, much as during the Renaissance mathematicians developed the zero as a sign about signs, "a meta-sign whose meaning is to indicate, via a syntax which arrives with it, the absence of certain other signs" (Rotman 1987, 1). Since "ideology exists because there are some things which must not be said" (Eagleton 1976, 90), "inverted ethnography" can do very little that is more radical than actually to dare to voice the unsaid. Thus, radical ethnography can shed its subservience to the regimes of realism in order to become a meditative and reflexive vehicle "because we come to it neither as to a map of knowledge nor as a guide to action, nor even for entertainment. We come to it as the start of a different kind of journey" (Tyler 1986, 140).

Note

This article began as an attempt to answer a challenge that Michael Apple addressed to me in 1987, that is, to think through the implications of ethnography trying to document "non-events." Mary Darmanin and Peter Serracino Inglott helped by referring me to relevant sources in the sociology of literature and the philosophical dimensions of "silence."

References

Belsey, C. 1980. *Critical Practice*. London: Methuen.

Bisseret, N. 1979. *Education, Class Language and Ideology*. London: Routledge & Kegan Paul.

Burbules, N. C. 1986. "Education under Siege: A Review." *Educational Theory* 36:301–13.

Clifford, J. and G. Marcus eds. 1986. *Writing Culture: The Poetics and Politics of Ethnography*. Berkeley and Los Angeles: University of California Press.

Eagleton, T. 1976. *Criticism and Ideology*. London: New Left Books (Verso edition).

Gadamer, H. G. 1979. "The Problem of Historical Consciousness." Pp. 103–60 in *Interpretive Social Science: A Reader*, ed. P. Rabinow and W. M. Sullivan. Berkeley and Los Angeles: University of California Press.

Giddens, A. 1976. *New Rules of Sociological Method*. London: Hutchinson.

Giroux, H. A. 1988. "Postmodern and the Discourse of Educational Criticism." *Journal of Education* 170, no. 3:5–30.

Gitlin, A., M. Siegel, and K. Boru 1989. "The Politics of Method: From Leftist Ethnography to Educational Research." *International Journal of Qualitative Studies in Education* 2, no. 3:237–53.

Hargreaves, A. and P. Woods, eds. 1984. *Classrooms and Staffrooms*. Milton Keynes, U.K.: Open University Press.

Lukacs, G. 1971. *History and Class Consciousness*. Cambridge: MIT Press.

Macherey, P. 1978. *A Theory of Literary Production*. London: Routledge & Kegan Paul.

McLaren, P. 1988. "Schooling the Postmodern Body: Critical Pedagogy and the Politics of Enfleshment. *Boston Journal of Education* 170, no. 3:53–83.

———. 1990. "Field Relations and the Discourse of the Other: Collaboration in Our Own Ruin." Pp. 149–63 in *Experiencing Fieldwork: An Inside View of Qualitative Research*, ed. W. B. Shaffir and R. A. Stebbins. Newbury Park, Calif.: Sage Publications.

McNeil, L. M. 1987. *Contradictions of Control*. London: Routledge & Kegan Paul.

Pollard, A. 1984. "Ethnography and Social Policy for Classroom Practice." Pp. 171–99 in *The Social Crisis and Educational Research*, ed. L. Barton and S. Walker. London: Croom Helm.

Reynolds, D. 1980–81. "The Naturalistic Method of Educational and Social Research—A Marxist Critique." *Interchange* 11, no. 4:77–89.

Rotman, B. 1987. *Signifying Nothing: The Semiotics of Zero*. London: Macmillan.

Sharp, R. 1982. "Self-Contained Ethnography or a Science of Phenomenal Forms and Inner Relations." *Boston Journal of Education* 164, no. 1:48–63.

Shipman, M. 1984. "Ethnography and Policy." Pp. 273–82 in *Field Methods in the Study of Education,* ed. R. Burgess. Lewes, U.K.: Falmer.

Sultana, R. G. 1987. "Schooling for Work in New Zealand." Ph.D. Diss., University of Waikato, Hamilton, New Zealand.

———. 1988. "Schooling Tomorrow's Worker: Trade Union Education in Secondary Schools." *New Zealand Journal of Industrial Relations* 13:3–20.

———. 1989. "Transition Education, Student Contestation and the Production of Meaning." *British Journal of Sociology of Education* 10, no. 3:287–310.

———. 1990. "Gender, Schooling and Transformation." *New Zealand Journal of Educational Studies* 25, no. 1:5–25.

Tyler, S. 1985. "Ethnography, Intertextuality and the End of Description." *American Journal of Semiotics* 3, no. 4:83–98.

———. 1987. "Post-Modern Ethnography: From Document of the Occult to Occult Document." Pp. 122–140 in *Writing Culture,* ed. J. Clifford and G. E. Marcus. Berkeley and Los Angeles: University of California Press.

West, G. W. 1984. "Phenomenon and Form in Interactionist and neo-Marsist Qualitative Educational Research." Pp. 256–85 in *The Social Crisis and Educational Research,* ed. L. Barton and S. Walker. London: Croom Helm.

Wexler, P. 1987. *Social Analysis of Education: After the New Sociology.* London: Routledge & Kegan Paul.

Williams, R. 1976. *Marxism and Literature.* New York: Oxford University Press.

7

Remembering and Representing Life Choices: A Critical Perspective on Teachers' Oral History Narratives

Kathleen Weiler

We wanted to break down the opposition between the imaginary and the real, and to show for personal life narratives as for anywhere else, that no statement that is made about one's past individually, is in any way innocent of ideology or of imaginative complexes. We wanted to break down the differences between the public and the private, and the personal and the political, by showing that the same kinds of imaginative paradigms which structure ideology and which structure politics, also structure the ways in which people understand their own lives.

R. Samuel, "Myth and History, A First Reading" (1988)

Focusing on the construction of subjectivity, especially the contradictions individuals are unable or unwilling to repress, feminists have used the "bad fit" of imposed social roles as an impetus for social transformation.

S. Frieden, "Transformative Subjectivity in the Writings of Christa Wolf" (1989)

Critical and feminist research in education has taken some unexpected turns in the late 1980s and early 1990s, raising questions and suggesting theoretical new directions for research in a number of fields (see Britzman 1991, Lather 1991). In this paper I will examine critical and feminist approaches in the history of education, specifically by looking at oral history, an approach that lies at the intersection of life history, biography, and narrative studies. A feminist history of women in education is still being explored and developed from a number of perspectives. Local histories and the quantitative analysis of census and school records have provided a much more detailed picture of women students and teachers, and the questions raised by postmodernist feminisms have challenged traditional narrative histories. The debate over the term *woman* itself, for example, has led feminist historians to consider how subjectivities are constructed through both discourse and practices. The influence of recent feminist literary analysis has led to an interest in discourse and to a consciousness of the construction of historical texts as narratives open to interpretation and analysis, rather than simple reflections of a "true past."

In this paper, I present one reading of oral history narratives—retired teachers' own presentation of their life choices to become teachers. I focus on two issues in these accounts: first, the contradiction or "bad fit" between the teachers' memories of their own "free" decisions and the restrictions and limitations on women's roles and work revealed through other historical sources and even in their own accounts; second, the challenge, in their presentations of themselves, to accepted hegemonic and authoritative definitions of what it means to be a teacher or what it means to be a woman. By focusing on these contradictions and challenges to hegemonic definitions, I explore what Samuel (1988) identifies as the ways in which "the same kinds of imaginative paradigms which structure ideology and which structure politics, also structure the ways in which people understand their own lives" (15). In terms of the history of women teachers, an examination of the contradictions and silences in the memories of retired teachers suggests the structuring paradigms and processes that shape both individual consciousness and collective understanding of experience. A reading of these memories thus may uncover both the forces that shaped individual lives of teachers and call into question the dominant views of women teachers as historical actors. My reading of these memories challenges the idea of an essential womanly nature and instead suggests that gender is an unstable and constantly shifting construct always being recreated through the process and language through which we understand and define ourselves. I want to suggest as well that the unacknowledged and unreconciled contradictions in these narratives present both obstacles and possibilities for feminist political intervention and social change.

In considering these narratives, I do not intend to claim a final and authoritative reading. I have been influenced in my analysis by a number of approaches to personal narratives—the work of the Popular Memory Group of the Centre for Contemporary Cultural Studies at the University of Birmingham; Luisa Passerini's study of the Turin working class; and by the ongoing feminist analysis of women's personal narratives and memories in a number of fields (Butler 1990, Haug 1987,

Personal Narratives Group 1989, Popular Memory Group 1982). All of these approaches are concerned with what might be called a history of consciousness. This approach is in some sense similar to Foucault's (1972) archeology of knowledge, but unlike Foucault, approaches like those of Passerini and the Popular Memory Group are concerned with analyzing oral history narratives as fragments of ordinary lives as revealed through memory; their methodology is that of oral history. While this approach opposes an empiricist view of the past as something unchangeable and "there" to be discovered, it does not reject the idea that the past existed and exists and thus can in some ways be known. That is, it does not imply a denial of material reality, but instead recognizes the constructed quality of memory itself. Thus the reading of popular memory can suggest ways of conceptualizing the relationship of ideology, consciousness, and material life. Popular memory reveals the past not as a set of facts uncovered through the interrogation of eye witnesses, but as a social construct expressing power conflicts and competing meanings. This approach to popular memory emphasizes that ordinary people's memories are deeply affected by how the past is presented in hegemonic apparatuses—the dominant memory. This dominant memory recalls Bakhtin's (1981) formulation of an "authoritative discourse" that offers (or imposes) a language in which to frame our past and present selves. But it emphasizes as well the heteroglossic instability of memory, the ways in which memories can be subversive, can suggest what Gramsci (1971) conceived as "good sense" or what Bakhtin proposed as "internally persuasive discourse."

Reading oral history narratives critically calls into question the obviousness of these tests as evidence and makes self-conscious the act of reading or interpreting them as narratives. The Popular Memory Group (1982) suggests two approaches to analyzing oral accounts: what they call reading for structure and reading for culture. In reading for structure, the researcher examines how popular memory recalls the "experience" of the material world and how it can reveal the workings of that world—for example, the organization of work, the solution to material needs such as food, housing, clothing, or child care. In reading for culture, the researcher examines how memory is organized to make sense of the events and experiences. This kind of reading recognizes that oral accounts are constructed by each individual within specific cultural and social contexts and that they can be read and in a sense decoded to reveal underlying structuring processes. As the Popular Memory Group puts it, "It is plain, reading such accounts, that they are the products of thought, artifice, verbal and literary skills, always involving authorship in this sense, having (like all 'sources') an active presence in the world...so information about the past comes completely with evaluations, explanations and theories which often constitute a principal value of the account and are intrinsic to its representations of reality" (228.) Thus both structural and cultural readings of these accounts rest on a conceptualization of what the Popular Memory Group refers to as "social individuals" who "speak out of particular positions in the complex of social relations characteristic of particular societies at particular historical times" (234).

The concern with the use of oral sources to uncover the organizing principles and processes that structure memory and consciousness as a collective process is a major focus of Passerini's (1987) study of the memories of fascism of workers in Turin. In her work, Passerini reads both for structure and for culture. Thus she argues that oral accounts can be sources for "the history of the events of everyday life," but at the same time argues for the analysis of the structuring processes of memory. Passerini, like the Popular Memory Group (1982), is not concerned primarily with attempts to uncover a fixed truth or "what really happened" from oral accounts, but rather sees oral accounts as evidence of mental reconstructions and symbolic ordering of experience. As Passerini puts it, "Interpretation should be able to recognize the various levels of expression and eventually find through other sources, as well, the historical contexts wherein they make sense. The guiding principle could be that all autobiographical memory is true; it is up to the interpreter to discover in which sense, where, and for which purpose" (197). She emphasizes the ways in which individuals call upon structuring devices of narrative to make sense of life experience. For Passerini, what is of greatest interest is to try to understand the processes of memory, not just as a matter of individual psychology, but as representative and constitutive of class identity. She thus looks at these accounts as narratives reflecting collective conventions open to formal and structural analysis.

Passerini (1987) emphasizes that oral accounts are not simply shaped by the questions of the interviewer (although she does not discount the importance of considering this effect), but she argues that even when asked by an interviewer in a more or less artificial situation "When someone is asked for his life-story, his memory draws on preexisting story-lines and ways of telling stories, even if these are in part modified by the circumstances" (28). These narrative forms and story lines, she argues, employ a cacophony of discourses, the authoritative discourse of hegemonic meanings as well as collective systems of meaning, what Gramsci (1971) would call common sense. Passerini's emphasis on recurrent narrative forms begins to uncover how people reconcile contradictions, how they create meaning from their lives and a coherent sense of themselves through available forms of discourse. At the same time, she is concerned with the "bad fit" or "gap" between "preexisting story lines" and individual constructions of the self through memory. As individuals construct their past, they leave unresolved contradictions at precisely those points at which authoritative discourse conflicts with collective cultural meanings or an internal oppositional discourse of critique.

The analysis of gaps and contradictions is a major concern of feminist scholars in a number of disciplines who are exploring women's narratives. These scholars are concerned with "exploring the social construction of the self, the genesis of collective identities, and the oppositional elements in narratives that challenge dominant ideologies of genders" (Osterud 1990, 83). These studies are concerned particularly with how women present and interpret their own life experiences within a society and culture defined by male dominance. Simone deBeauvoir wrote in *The Second Sex* that "one is not born a woman, but rather *becomes* one" (301). This comment is a useful starting point to begin to view identity or subjectivity as unfinished, ongoing, and contested, particularly in the context of the kind of feminist analysis I am proposing. This conception of subjectivity suggests that not only are our contemporary lived experiences of our essential natures of men and women historically and socially constructed, that is, that they are lived within imaginative paradigms, but that even as we live within these constructed categories, our identities or subject positions *man* and *woman* have to be constantly recreated. What often results from this work of creating ourselves is a kind of dissonance or incomplete and unreconciled subject.

This leads back to the narratives of oral history. A number of historians and feminist theorists have argued that oral history narratives can be read to reveal this process of the construction and constant struggle to create gendered selves. One of the most interesting of recent feminist work on personal narratives is the collection of essays by the Personal Narratives Group (1989) from the University of Minnesota, *Interpreting Women's Lives*. This collection examines many of the same concerns as those addressed by the Popular Memory Group (1982) and by Passerini (1987) and her group in Turin. Central to the essays in *Interpreting Women's Lives* is the concept of hegemony, in this case patriarchal hegemony through which an unequal gender structure is taken to be in some sense "true." As the Personal Narratives Group points out in their introduction to this collection, "Women's personal narratives...are especially helpful in understanding androcentric hegemony because they document a variety of responses to it" (7). They thus consider some narratives as counternarratives to a hegemonic vision in that they defy the rules defining social relationships or present alternatives to accepted views of what is appropriate or true. Some narratives discussed in *Interpreting Women's Lives* are framed by an acceptance of patriarchal norms and reveal how those norms are reproduced by women themselves. Still others present a negotiation and construction of self in contradictory ways. But as the Personal Narratives Group very usefully points out, whether framed as resistance or acquiescence, women's narratives are framed within or against a system of domination.

This focus on examining the process through which women present themselves in memory is the focus of other projects, for example, the work of Haug (1987) and her group in Germany. In this project, a group of women collectively shared and analyzed their memories of their own sexuality. Through the collective analysis of these memories, the social and collective quality of the individual construction of identity was illuminated. Once again, the focus here is on memory as a process, and one deeply shaped by hegemonic authoritative discourse as well as by subversive or oppositional narratives. As Haug puts it,

> The day-to-day struggle over the hearts and minds of human subjects is located not only within social structures, the pre-given forms into which individuals work themselves, but also in the *process* whereby they perceive any given situation, approve or validate it, assess its goals as proper and worthy, repugnant or reprehensible. What emerged in our analysis as a particular way of processing the social world, as its appropriation by individuals, has to be seen as a field of conflict between dominant cultural values and oppositional attempts to wrest cultural meaning and pleasure from life. (41)

The work of Haug (1987) and her group and the essays collected by the Personal Narrative Group (1989) emphasize the constant construction and reconstruction of the self, what feminist theorists such as Flax (1987) refer to as the "unstable self." In this process of engagement with the world, one not only constructs a coherent self, but also in a sense rewrites the narrative of a personal past history. As feminist historians argue, men and women seem to view their past differently; men tend to view themselves as the subjects of their own lives, whereas women often speak of the lives of others, with themselves as observers.

Women's placing themselves at the periphery or as the objects of events mirrors both patriarchal hegemony and the structure of dominant cultural myths and stereotypes. As Haug puts it, "The way our culture represents the reproductive role of women—for example in literature or folktales—turns them into mere objects. It is for this reason that women in particular have only fragments from which to piece together their own past memories. . . .The fact of not being included in history as active participants encourages women ultimately to accept themselves as 'pieces of nature'—which leaves them at the mercy of the dominant culture (49). While many women's narratives present themselves as shaped by forces outside of their control, counternarratives of women as rebels also exist, such as those provided by Passerini (1987), for example. Thus in constructing their life stories, women seem to have available to them different discourses, but in all of them the dominant is revealed—either by being incorporated or by being resisted.

In the following discussion, I want to build upon these theoretical concerns—particularly Samuel's (1988) concept of "imaginative paradigms" and Frieden's (1989) suggestion that we focus on the "bad fit" or contradictions in women's presentation of themselves as a source for social transformation—to explore retired women's presentation of their decision to become a teacher. In my examination of these teachers' presentation of their choice to become teachers, I raise questions about the essential nature of women, about how identity is "constructed and regulated," as Butler (1990, 5) puts it, and explore how underlying assumptions and imaginative paradigms organize and shape our understanding of the world and actions in it. In this discussion, I examine two examples of contradiction raised in these narratives: first, the contradiction or "bad fit" between the teachers' memories of their own "free" decision to become teachers and, in the same accounts, the restrictions and constraints on women's roles and work. The second, and I think related, example is the challenge in their presentations of themselves, to accepted hegemonic definitions of what it means to be a teacher. I will focus here on women who describe themselves as having been tomboys when they were children, but who fail to name this as dissonant or challenging to accepted views of what it meant to be a woman or later to be a teacher. In both cases, teachers present themselves and their life choices in ways that challenge hegemonic definitions of women teachers and women as mothering, self-sacrificing, and passive. But in both examples, contradictions and a kind of dissonance to accepted conceptions of society and gender are left unacknowledged. These contradictions and challenges suggest what Samuel refers to as the "imaginative paradigms which structure ideology and politics," and that also "structure the ways in which people understand their own lives" (15). These memories are open to readings that begin to name the forces that shaped individual lives of teachers and to call into question the accepted views of women teachers as teachers and as "women."

The narratives I discuss are from interviews of white Protestant retired teachers who were born between 1899 and 1913 and who taught in the schools of Tulare County, California, from the 1920s through the 1950s.[1] Fifteen retired teachers were selected in three ways: they responded to a query I placed in the county retired teachers association newsletter, their names were suggested to me by other teachers in the course of interviews, or their names appeared in newspaper accounts or on membership lists of retired teachers organizations. They thus represent a very small, arbitrary, and random sample of the retired teachers in the county. It is striking, though, that the occupation of their fathers (twelve of the fifteen were ranchers or farmers) follows the occupational data of the 1900 census for Tulare County.[2] While the women I interviewed differed to some extent in terms of economic class, in most respects they were very similar in social background. Economic need for them to work varied, but in every case they said that the idea that they would gain post-secondary education and work as teachers was either expected or approved by their parents.

Respondents differed in class background and education. Five of the teachers attended private universities or the University of California. Four of these five teachers were daughters of businessmen or professionals. The fifth received her bachelor's degree from Stanford by studying during the summers in a special program for teachers. Expectations of the four women from business or professional families seemed to be that they would attend college. Polly O., for example, recalls that her parents had talked of her going to college as a matter of course: "They had always talked from the time I was a little kid; they talked about my going to college. I always took it as a matter of course that I would." Polly O.'s father was a Methodist minister, and although her mother did not go beyond high school, as Polly O. remembers it, "she was always reading." For other women, the question of college was taken as natural and accepted by parents. What is striking in all four of these accounts is the ways in which the gender structure of jobs limited and shaped choices, but was not directly mentioned by these respondents. This structuring of occupation was seen as natural and is unquestioned. What is equally striking, though, is the assumption that they would work if they were not married. Both the limitations in terms of occupational choice and the need to work are accepted as natural in these accounts, without obvious objection or resentment. The same acceptance of both the limitations of employment for women and the expectation that they would work until they married is expressed in the accounts of the eight teachers, all daughters of ranchers or farmers, who attended Fresno State College, the nearest teacher training college, or who took the county teachers' examination.

Five of the six teachers who attended Fresno State were born between 1904 and 1910 and attended Fresno State in the mid and late 1920s. The sixth began teaching with an emergency certificate after working in the county superintendent's office for several years. She completed her bachelor's degree at Fresno State in 1950. In the late 1920s, Fresno State was the only four-year college in the San Joaquin Valley and provided the least expensive teacher education available to the residents of Tulare County. For the six teachers who attended Fresno State, the economic need to work was central. But economic necessity was not offered immediately as a reason for their choice by the teachers. Ellen A., who was given to her uncle and aunt to be raised after her parents' divorce, provided contradictory reasons for teaching. Her father, who came to visit her only "five times in [her] life," paid her way through Fresno State.

K.W.:   When did you decide to go to college and become a teacher?
Ellen A.: I can't remember a time I didn't think I was going to. It was always there that I was going. My father put me through school.
K.W.:   Where do you think you got the idea to become a teacher?
Ellen A.: I have no idea. Just that I wanted to be a teacher. There were no other jobs open. You either became a telephone girl or you could work in a packing house—There were no girls working in banks—that was it.

In this sequence, Ellen A. begins by saying she has "no idea" why she made her choice, she "just wanted to be a teacher." In this statement she presents this choice as a free decision. But immediately she describes a situation in which there were very few options for women, not even working in banks. Thus in this short passage she both asserts her free choice that matches the hegemonic vision of isolated individuals acting on their own volition and then immediately presents the common sense reality of the restrictions that she faced as a woman. She thus constructs her past through the authoritative and hegemonic discourse of free choice, but the limits of a patriarchal society break through her narrative to create unreconciled contradictions.

The need to work also appears in the account of Hannah A., who passed the county teachers' examination when she was twenty-three as a married woman with a small child. In this account as well, the role of economic need is downplayed.

K.W.:   When did you decide you wanted to be a teacher?
Hannah A.:   Well, I went four years to high school. I started going
               with my husband when I was a junior. By the time I
               was through high school, we decided to get married.
               So, I graduated in May and we were married in October.
               About a year and half later, we had a son. After we'd
               been married about five years, I decided that I wanted
               to go back and I wanted to teach school. So, I went over
               to Visalia. My sister was living over there then and I
               stayed a week with her, took the county examinations,
               and passed.
K.W.:   What did your husband think of this?
Hannah A.:   He didn't think much of it, but then...
K.W.:   You mean, he didn't approve of it, or...
Hannah A.:   Not exactly, but...
K.W.:   Did you need the money?
Hannah A.:   We needed the money. He was driving a school bus at
               that time. Up until that time, he worked with his father
               in the cattle business. Of course, you may think the cattle
               business is something wonderful, but there's not, unless
               you have a big operation, there's not much profit. I
               wanted our son to have an education and I couldn't see
               him getting it any other way unless I did something
               about it. So that's how come I did what I did.

In this account, both the economic need to work and the tensions with her husband around her decision to become a teacher are evident but only emerge when I continue to ask questions about the reasons for her decision. Her claim that she became a teacher in order to give her son an education seems very much like a later elaboration. She was contradicting local custom in teaching as a married woman with a small child (many schools in the county would not even hire married women at this time), and none of my other respondents mentioned the need to save to send children to college or to provide for their education. It seems more likely to me that a combination of immediate economic need and personal need for autonomy underlay Hannah A.'s decision to take the teachers exam and become a teacher. Markedly absent from her account is any rationale of loving children or imagining herself as a teacher in terms of hegemonic definitions. But again like other respondents, she presents her decision as a matter of personal choice without challenging accepted views or limitations.

In all of these accounts of the decision to become teachers, respondents present themselves as free agents who chose teaching as work; in this they speak through the authoritative discourse of the United States as a society composed of individuals free to make the choices that shape their lives without impediment. While economic need and the limitations of other opportunities are present throughout these accounts, they are not named or included in the narratives of freedom of choice. What does this presentation of free choice mean for the ways in which these women have constructed themselves in memory? On the one hand, this depiction of themselves as free agents does not challenge the gender segregation and patriarchal privilege of the world in which they lived. These women do not challenge, for example, hegemonic assumptions that teaching is "naturally," women's work. On the other hand, the reasons they put forth for becoming teachers are not presented in terms of the dominant set of images and assumptions about women teachers—that they are nurturing, self-sacrificing, only seeking a transition between father and husband. Instead, they present themselves as free individuals who make choices; when they are asked to elaborate this choice, they make clear their need to support themselves through work. Thus their narratives present common sense rationales for their choice to work that challenge hegemonic views of women teachers. But because they directly and consciously fail to challenge those assumptions or call into question the patriarchal structure in which they made choices, they leave contradictions unreconciled.

The second example of contradictions between remembered experience and hegemonic definitions can be seen in the case of women who remember themselves as tomboys as children. The tomboy was an accepted role in the strongly patriarchal world of the early twentieth century when these women were growing up. Both Evelyn B. and Beatrice H. described themselves as tomboys when they were children. I asked these women what exactly tomboy meant.

K.W.:   What did it mean to be a tomboy?
Evelyn B.: You played with the boys, and I guess if anybody dared you to do something, you just went ahead and did it. You know, I'd walk on the top of the ridge pole on the barn, and I was the fastest runner in school over here except for the man principal.

K.W.:   Did you play sports?

Evelyn B.:   Oh yes. I was on the boy's baseball team. Third base.

When asked if there was a contradiction between having been a tomboy
as a child and becoming a teacher, a tmditional woman's job, Evelyn
B. simply replied, "I didn't think about it."

K.W.:   You didn't think about it?

Evelyn B.:   No, I was not about to work out in the fields, packing
              grapes and picking figs, and I was not about to do that
              all my life. And I wanted to help my parents. Here I was,
              the oldest one in the family now because my sister was
              married. So, when I did graduate, I went to the bank and
              borrowed fifty dollars—one of the first things I did when
              I graduated from Fresno State, because I had a contract,
              and they would give you money on a contract. So, I
              borrowed fifty dollars and got my mother a washing
              machine. Oh boy! If you don't think that helped out!

     Evelyn B. does not see, or at least does not acknowledge, any
contradiction between being a tomboy, seen as daring, competitive and
capable, and being a teacher, the traditional woman's role. It may be
that Evelyn B. wants to sidestep any contradiction here. But another
possible reading is that she does not see teaching as stereotypical
"woman's work," calling forth traditional qualities of nurturance and
motherliness. Instead, she describes the appeal of teaching in terms
of its better working conditions and pay and in terms of its material
advantages, in this case, the washing machine for her mother and
family. In choosing to work as a teacher, Evelyn B., in fact, built upon
the capability and strength she identified as characteristics of a tomboy.
The contradictions between tomboy and teacher were not lived by her—
they exist at the level of hegemonic definitions of what it means to be
a tomboy and what it means to be a teacher, but not in the internal
discourse of Evelyn B., who uses the possibilities of teaching to meet
her own needs and to express the qualities that she had earlier lived
as a tomboy.

K.W.:   When most people went to Fresno State, then, if you went
              there, the idea was that you were going to be a teacher.
              Is that right?

Evelyn B.:   Yes, unless you decided to be a librarian or a file, you could
              learn how to file things.... But what I went for was to be
              a teacher. I didn't know about all these other things.

For Evelyn B., then, like many of the other teachers, did not describe the intrinsic appeal of teaching, but needed to work and saw only limited options. Her failure to name this situation as constraining is similar to her statement that she "didn't think about" the decision to become a teacher immediately followed by her statement that she didn't want to pack grapes or pick figs.

For Beatrice H. being a tomboy was remembered as a more conscious choice. She did not have brothers, and her father encouraged her to do and be whatever she liked. When she was about nine years old she overheard girls at school talking about boys' advantages.

Beatrice H.:   These girls were angry because the boys got the best of everything and boys were top class citizens and girls were shoved behind and the people would rather have boys when they had new babies. . . .I took this all in. Something like this never occurred to me up until then.

After hearing this, Beatrice H. wanted the advantages of being a boy. The handyman on the ranch told her that if she kissed her elbow she would become a boy, but, try as she might, she couldn't manage to kiss her elbow. When her father came home, she told the story to him.

Beatrice H.:   After I told him all my troubles he patted me on the head and he said, "You just don't worry a thing about it. You're my boy and we won't care what other people say." And from that time forward he would whenever he introduced me to people, he'd say, "This is my boy." . . . He taught me to hunt and ride and whatever he was doing, working on the cars or anything, I always had my nose stuck in everything. I remember going with the neighbors for raccoon hunting at night, we'd take our dogs and go raccoon hunting around through the swamps. . . . Back in those days, of course, it wasn't settled like it is now. Out around the rivers and all the swampy land and open country, we'd go hunting and they'd take me along. Along with the men and the boys. So I just grew up that way. He always, he stuck to his word and he always just treated me like he would a boy.

After that Beatrice H. no longer wanted to *be* a boy; instead, she dressed and acted like a boy, "much to [her] mother's disgust," but

supported by her father. For Beatrice H., as well, there was no contradiction between being a tomboy as a child and becoming a teacher.

K.W.:   Why did you become a teacher?
Beatrice H.:   I always liked children. When we moved over into
                 town. . .there I started babysitting for people around the
                 neighborhood. I went on into high school and I babysat
                 all the time. I enjoyed small children. I recall I guess my
                 junior year teachers would help us decide what we
                 wanted to do. I remember my counselor, talking to her
                 and she'd ask me various questions, and I said I thought
                 I would like to work with small children. And she said,
                 "I think you're right. I think you'd make a good
                 kindergarten or primary teacher." Back in those days you
                 could go to Fresno, I could go three years and get a
                 credential for kindergarten or primary in just three years
                 time. So that's what I did.

    Being a tomboy as a child, dressing like a boy, hunting raccoons,
and being addressed by her father as "my boy" did not contradict a
liking for children and her adolescent vision of herself as a kindergarten
or elementary school teacher. Beatrice H. does not tie her assumption
of boys' clothes and her movement in the male sphere of hunting and
cars to sexuality, but her account is a sharp challenge to heterosexual
views of what it means to be a girl. And yet the seeming contradiction
between the tomboy and the school teacher are left unreconciled in her
narrative. Like Evelyn B., Beatrice H. saw teaching as a way to earn
a living and to express her own abilities. She later became a teacher
of blind children, member of the school board, and a well-known
spokesperson for education in her town. For her, it was a natural
progression from being an adventurous tomboy to being a capable
teacher. The clash between the subversive tomboy and a hegemonic
view of teacher is not named here. Instead, both Evelyn B. and Beatrice
H. put forward a way of "being a teacher" that builds upon the strength
of "being a tomboy." In their narratives they speak as capable and "free"
people who make a choice to act in the world as teachers. But they do
not name or acknowledge the dissonance between this internally persuasive discourse and the authoritative discourse of what it means to
"be a teacher." As tomboys, Evelyn B. and Beatrice H. were both rebels
against conventional roles for girls, but neither of them moved from
their remembered strengths as unconventional rebels against traditional
girls' roles to a critique of patriarchal assumptions about teaching as

women's work or of the social limitations available to them when they came to choose work. The contradictions simply are left unaddressed and unintegrated.

What do these narrative accounts contribute to our understanding of teaching as women's work? First of all they raise for us the question of what it means to be a girl, a boy, a man, a woman. Hegemonic views of women teachers as nurturing and self sacrificing are clearly called into question by these narratives. These women's presentation of their decision to become teachers challenges accepted notions of teaching as a means of expressing essential womanly natures. In this respect, these narratives call into question essentialist views of what it means to be a woman as well as what it means to be a woman teacher. Butler (1990), arguing against essentialist binary conceptions of gender writes,

> The deconstruction of identity is not the deconstruction of politics; rather, it establishes as political the very terms through which identity is articulated. This kind of critique brings into question the foundationalist frame in which feminism as an identity politics has been articulated. The internal paradox of this foundationalism is that it presumes, fixes, and constrains the very "subjects" that it hopes to represent and liberate. The task here is not to celebrate each and every new possibility, but to redescribe those possibilities that *already* exist, but which exist within cultural domains designated as culturally unintelligible and impossible. (148–49)

Following Butler, I want to suggest that the challenge to essentialist and binary conceptions of gender implied in these narratives can lead us to see possibilities that already existed and exist. We are asked to consider how gender constructs have shaped assumptions of who is the teacher, who is the principal, who has the authority to speak or to define the world. But these assumptions about gendered subjectivities and the organization of work are not obvious. They must be revealed, articulated, and challenged.

While cultural possibilities are revealed in these narratives, the narratives at the same time fail to acknowledge contradictions or constraints. Much is implied in these narratives about limits, both in terms of patriarchal power and material constraints. But in their accounts, these women do not directly challenge patriarchal structures or power arrangements. The teachers accept the world in which they move as natural and present their decisions as a matter of free choice. Thus, the limited number of job choices for women are not limits, the rebel tomboy is not rebelling, the way the world is arranged is natural and inevitable, what was done does not contradict the dominant view of what should have been done. As we read these accounts "for structure," the material conditions in which these women lived and worked and the economic and personal reasons for their decisions to become teachers becomes clearer. When we read "for culture," the complexity of the "imaginative paradigms" that organize their memories is suggested; as Bakhtin (1981) commented, they speak a language "overpopulated with the intentions of others" (293). Thus these accounts reveal how memories can contain unreconciled contradictions to accepted assumptions and at the same time fail to challenge hegemonic definitions precisely because things are not raised to the level of consciousness. But at the same time these accounts provide examples of the possibilities that already exist in Butler's (1990) terms, and that need to be made culturally intelligible and possible. I hope this reading of the contradictions and strengths in these narratives will contribute to a revisioning of the history of women teachers and to the creation of a future when girls will no longer try to kiss their elbows to become boys, but will simply feel free to ride through the open country, whoever they are.

Notes

1. These are from a series of twenty-four interviews I conducted between 1987 and 1989. I have identified these teachers by pseudonyms to protect their privacy.

2. In 1900, 81 percent of the women teachers in the county listed in the census (66 of 81) were unmarried and lived with their parents or relatives. Of those, sixty lived on ranches or farms.

References

Bakhtin, M. 1981. *The Dialogical Imagination*. Austin: University of Texas Press.

Beauvoir, S. de. 1972. *The Second Sex*. London: Penguin.

Britzman, D. 1991. *Practice Makes Practice*. New York: State University of New York Press.

Butler, J. 1990. *Gender Trouble*. New York: Routledge.

Flax, J. 1987. "Postmodernism and Gender Relations in Feminist Theory." *Signs* 12:621–43.

Foucault, M. 1972. *The Archeology of Knowledge*. New York: Pantheon.

Friedan, S. 1989. "Transformative Subjectivity in the Writings of Christa Wolf." Pp. 172–88 in *Interpreting Women's Lives*, ed. Personal Narratives Group. Bloomington: Indiana University Press.

Gransci, A. 1971. *Selections from the Prison Notebooks*. New York: International.

Haug, F. 1987. *Female Sexualization: A Collective Work of Memory*. London: Verso.

Lather, P. 1991. *Getting Smart. Feminist Research and Pedagogy with/in the Postmodern*. New York: Routledge.

Osterud, N. 1990. "American Autobiographies." *Gender and History* 2, no. 1:80–85.

Passerini, L. 1987. *Fascism in Popular Memory: The Cultural Experience of the Turin Working Class*. Cambridge University Press.

Personal Narratives Group. 1989. *Interpreting Women's Lives*. Bloomington: Indiana University Press.

Popular Memory Group. 1982. "Popular Memory:Theory, Politics, Method." Pp. 218–42 in *Making histories*, ed. R. Johnson, G. McLennon, B. Swartz, and D. Sutton. Minneapolis: University of Minnesota Press.

Samuel, R. 1988. "Myth and History, A First Reading." *Oral History* 16, no. 1: 10–17.

8

Feminist Educational Research and the Issue of Critical Sufficiency

Lynda Stone

Introduction

One morning in the fall semester 1993, I am shaken out of the reverie of marking a set of philosophy papers by the shrill ringing of the telephone in my office cubicle.[1] Calling from the mainland is the (courageous) director of a major educational philanthropic organization. She has been looking at the collection of papers of feminism in professional education that I have edited, and she has some money for me. At my disposal is a sizeable grant to use to bring a blue-ribbon group (say fifty people) to an all-expenses paid institute in "paradise." Our task (only generally conceived at this point) is to develop a working plan to undertake a research project in feminist critical education targeted for high schools in North America. A first step for me, in addition to budget layout, is to write a prospectus for the institute. After shakily saying thank you and goodby (and giving a yelp), I begin to conceptualize this document. Starting questions are such as these: How shall the project be defined and bounded? Who will be invited? For the last question, I begin a list of admired colleagues and friends; for the first question, I write down "feminist researchers" and "critical theorists." I pause, something much more is surely needed.

What follows is the position paper that I develop to clarify the issues for the institute prospectus.[2] Its sections first consider the set of implicit questions raised above: the question of rationale, the question of definition, the question of critical sufficiency. Second, as a general but "sufficient" answer, a section overviews a series of enabling conditions. Last is a concluding return to my office.

The Question of Rationale

A rationale for the institute must be established in a nexus of present times, states of affairs in the west generally and in education in particular, in research and its theory, and in research from the left. A project for feminist critical research makes no sense unless it is backgrounded by present historic conditions. In these nineties, in spite of fairly recent U.S. presidential politics,[3] a relatively conservative agenda addresses problems of a postmodern world. This is the era of "postisms" that no one seems to understand and to work out—as if a working out in some preconceived way were possible. There seem to be no ends to crises (R. Young 1990)[4] of postindustrial capitalism and its postliberal politics (Bowers 1987). A eurocentric domination (past its prime) has indeed led to worldwide economic recession, massive ecological distruction, and venal interethnic strife. Moreover, this domination is challenged by a postcolonial "third world" that no longer "knows its place."

Not surprisingly, the education institution manifests the same crisis state. As Thomas Popkewitz puts this, "as a primary institution . . . schooling ties polity, culture, economy, and the modern state to the cognitive and motivating patterns of the individual. . . . [Relative] are historically formed patterns of knowledge, . . . power, and institutions" (1991, 13). Nationally in the United States, the general state of affairs is "translated" into localized problems of school governance and finance, of "low test scores,"[5] of unprepared teachers and unruly students. All of these, of course, as "education politicians" assert, are due to the errors of those "on the other side"; fingers of blame are pointed and repointed at all levels of governance. And, generally speaking, "reform" is "best conceptualized" by those of the center and right. The radical left, with calls for structural and systemic change, receives scant attention outside its continual chirping from within the academy.

Given its own power to mask and mystify current conditions and to legitimate itself, educational research is diverse but restrained. While small squabbles erupt now and then, a seeming rapproachment exists between quantitative and qualitative researchers, between psychology and its more sociological counterpart (say in research on teaching). As long as the extremes are silenced, business in the education academy proceeds, and both the practice of education and its theory are caught up in the prevailing discourse of "reform" (Popkewitz 1991).[6]

This situation produces a response from left theorists who in common see the need for, sometimes pine for, a more radically motivated politics with "collective" focus. Most know that the Marxist-sixties are long gone but they cannot seem to agree on what to do. Indeed, what has occurred is this: a penchant for critique has itself become individuated and has fractured a left unity. If squabbles sometimes occur among researchers in the center, stronger disagreements—often personal ones—take place among members of the left (see Wexler, 1987).

However, at times when politics is put aside and wholesome theoretical disagreement is explored, a healthy pluralism has resulted. Better said, self-criticism has tendered significant scholarly benefit. The pertinent example comes from feminist theorizing, in which Sandra Lee Bartky (1992) writes, there are "critical differences." Seen as vital and rigorous rather than "intellectually irresponsible," feminism is *feminisms* in which alliance rather than consensus is the political aim (see also Fraser and Nicholson 1990, 33). Here is Bartky:

> [There are] eco-feminists, anarchist feminists, Marxist feminists, socialist-feminists, lesbian feminists, lesbian separatists, lesbian vanguardists, existenialist feminists, pychoanalytic feminists, (be they Freudian, Jungian, Kleinian, Lacanian, or object-relations oriented mothering theorists), matriachialists, cultural feminists, gynocentric feminists, post-modern feminists who follow Derrida, postmodern feminists who follow Foucault, French-oriented feminists who follow Krestiva, Irigaray, Wittig, Cixous, etc. (57).

Unnamed by her are allies of significance, "womanists" and other feminists of color, post-colonial varieties, and holdovers from liberal feminism. Clearly not all academic feminists are leftist and radical, however, most applaud the theoretical viability of their differences, even as these differences are used against them by attackers from the right. They unite against what has been conceptualized as "ten years of blurring the distinction between scholarship and politics" (Yates 1992).[7]

By implication, several important points for a problem of definition emerge from this example. One is that no label or definition suffices today to bound left theory and research. A second is that pluralism rather than monism is appropriate. A third is that critique and out of it occasional conflict are both "natural" and valued. A fourth is that politics and scholarship are inseparable. What these points imply for the proposed institute and its educational project is returned to in relation to subsequent conditions of sufficiency.

A Problem of Definition

One more significant aspect of the situating of this prospectus and its institute in present times needs mention, this because it leads directly to the problem of definition: In precollegiate and much of professional education—seemingly anywhere outside the traditional research academy—the influence of the left is largely in disarray. That it is in disarray, first of all, is not recognized by everyone on the left. Some theorists do reside in institutions with large liberal/radical reputations and followings. Some believe that feminism is alive and well and that critical theory has made a substantial mark. Some others (I among them) am astounded at this belief—surely where they live and work is decidedly different. Where I live and work feminism remains "still invisibilized" and critical theory is co-opted.

The invisibility of feminism in education institutions takes several forms, in denying its need, marginalizing its adherents, and downgrading its research agenda. In the first case, a principal attitude toward feminism is not that it is "doing just fine," but rather that it is "out of date." No longer, so the belief goes, is there a need for feminism. This is because either there no longer are any problems for women in education, or if there are problems, they are being solved.[8] In the second case, those who are feminist researchers are still singled out and not taken seriously. The belief is that her and his ideology clouds the course content and the research agenda. In the third case, a feminist research agenda is defined as supplementary. The belief is that a researcher ought not to specialize as a feminist and that any work in this arena is extra— something just not necessary in times of general educational crisis. Added to these beliefs is the one from above that "those feminists cannot get their own act together" so they can have little of substance to say.

While feminism is virtually nonexistent—or lacks much substantive influence in practical professional education—the situation for critical theory is somewhat different. Its influence is co-opted in several ways, in tokenism, in the conflation of all left projects, and in subsumption under a manufactured consensus or eclecticism. In the first case, critical theory impacts professional education to the extent that having a token "critical theorist" on faculty is de rigueur, especially if there is already someone who does "regular" curriculum theory, sociology, anthropology, or philosophy. In the second case, by others not enmeshed in left theorizing, everyone is understood to do the "same" work; thus a feminist, a critical theorist, a poststructuralist, and so on are all the same. Addition of the need for racial and ethnic representation (assumed as alternative and reformist) complicates this further.

The third case, of theoretical consensus and eclecticism, is of such seriousness that it requires elaboration. The point is that critical theory is indiscriminately appropriated and cited by theorists who either are not themselves "critical" or who have not sufficiently interrogated their own position in comparison to those not only on the left but located there in particular theoretical ways. Virtually every educational researcher, especially those doing qualitative research, understands the roles of history and context and theory-ladenness—at least as influences to be "reckoned with".[9] Almost all the research from within the American mainstream (that I read today) accepts the "hidden curriculum,"cites Willis' study, refers to Bourdieu's "cultural capital," and supports Freirean pedagogy (allied with the writings of Dewey). Moreover, it is undertaken by "transformative intellectuals" who implicitly advocate a relatively simple marriage of feminism and critical theory. Everyone accepts the partnership—"knows" Gilligan, Lyons, and their colleagues; sees connections to Apple, Giroux, and their fellows; and believes that Lincoln and Guba do the same work as others who are "critical." A theoretical conflation in the name of educational reform is rampant.[10]

Others recognize aspects of this present situation. For instance, Ladd Holt and Frank Margonis (1992) name both the tendency of some critical theory to foster "conservative" ends as well as the process of cooption (232).[11] Likewise, Michael Apple (1992) points out the faddishness of much of critical theorizing itself (130) in what might be termed consensual processes of "political correctness." In this regard, he writes, "We have tended to move too quickly away from traditions that continue to be filled with vitality and provide. . .[insights into domination in curriculum and pedagogy]"(129). Although his point is slightly different, Apple names as faddish much of the bandwagon of postmodernism. Given its own conservative stream, this fits both a general point from Holt and Margonis and the more pervasive third case just described.

Definition, that is, agreeing on some common ground, is a starting place for addressing the problematic situations of feminism and critical theory, in educational research—and in educational practice. Agreement, writes Iris Marion Young (1990), is commitment to a politics of difference." Strategically, it seems (to me) initial steps are to recognize and to ally members of the critical left against forces of cooption, while welcoming fellow travelers within a range of authentically critical perspectives. This means to cease making enemies of one another.[12] Finally, this means to engage in careful theoretical work, that is, to maintain significant scholarly differences. Young summarizes, "Radical politics. . .must develop discourse and institutions for bringing differently identified groups together without supressing or subsuming the differences" (320). Theoretically plausible are two steps in the current development of critical discourse practices. The first is to recover "collective memory" (Apple 1992, 130), and the second is to create a language of collective translation. The latter is attended to in the next section; the former concludes this one.

A common memory for feminists looks something like this: continued attention to opposing sexist oppression and upholding sisterhood, continued legitimation of the personal and self-conscious, continued valuing of critique out of diversity, continued development of an evolving theoretical base, continued recognition of central "historical" concerns—issues of body and voice, of public life and equality, of processes of collective understanding and action. Out of this, asserts bell hooks (1989; cited in Giroux 1991), is a possible solidarity arrived at through "struggle with one another" (Giroux 1991, 35).

A common memory for critical theorists looks something like this: continued attention to opposing hierarchial domination based on class (race and gender), continued remembrance of structural roots and of centrality of history and ideology, continued understanding of a dialectical tradition, continued utilization of languages of critique and possibility, continued recognition of central conceptions—of work and production, of contradiction and contestation, of social movements. Today, given "the plethora of competing jargons and systems. . .[and] antisystems" (Adams 1986, 1), what results is an expanded definition of "criticism."[13]

And finally, for initial purposes of definition, feminism and critical theory across all formulations do share some ideas that need not be essentializing of their particularities and their differences. These are a set of political agreements. Both are committed to emancipation and empowerment of persons. Both recognize the centrality of ideologies of power and change. Both are self-consciously oppositional to dominant traditions in theory and research. Both contextualize research in social and normative terms. Both are cognizant of the importance of education as a site of liberatory struggle. Both see their work, their theorizing and their politics, as praxis. Significantly, Patti Lather (1991) writes: this means that the " 'reciprocally' educative process. . .[between researchers and researched] is more important than product. . .[in contributing] to consciousness-raising and transformative social action" (72).

The Problem of Critical Sufficiency

Recovering, in Apple's term, a collective memory, is well and good and should be done. However, this act does not seem sufficient to resolve ever-present political problems for left research: their internecine warfare and their failure to influence substantive educational change. Somehow they (we) must "get their act together" in order to be educationally praxiological, to "radicalize" students, teachers, and schools. The thesis of this chapter is that "the act" is comprised of a rapproachment between feminist and critical researchers and their theories. Within the pluralisms that characterize both strands of research, several attempts have already been proposed. To some degree these are evolutionary and overlap, yet there remain important distinctions. Along with the conceptual commonality described in the preceding section, each names itself "feminist" and "critical theorist," but with slightly differing formulations.

Here is an overview of these attempts: The most historical group sought "marriage" between Marxism and feminism in writings dating from the early eighties. Theoretical vows were exchanged that centered on the Marxist ideas of masculinist production and work, to which were added conceptions respectively of feminist reproduction and sexuality—as unifications of class and gender (Benhabib and Cornell 1987, 2–3). In a classic statement, Catherine MacKinnon (1983) summarizes women's location in sexual work: "Heterosexuality is its structure, gender and family its congealed forms, sex roles its qualities generalized to social persona, reproduction a consequence, and control its issue" (228). Writers today who call themselves "critical feminists" and "socialist feminists" continue this tradition, and others particularly in the "postmodern" genre are historically evolved and sympathetic to an updated union.[14]

Utilizing the work of the critical, socialist and increasingly of postmodern and poststructural feminists are three overlapping formulations in educational research.[15] In what she names as "postpositivist feminist empirical practice," Lather (1991) is engaged in a process that in places she names a conjunction. Her aim, as I take it, is to sort through "this unprecedented cross-disciplinary fertilization of ideas that opens up possibilities. . .in a diffusion of legitimacy and authority" (7). Along with similar others, she argues for the centrality of pedagogy in processes of transformation (15). Also committed to pedagogical change is Henry Giroux (1991) who most recently employs the term "postmodern feminism." Its fruitfulness lies in a dialectical opposition to modernism "in favor of a broader theoretical attempt to situate both discourses (modernism and postmodernism) critically within a feminist political project" (31). Among feminists influencing his views are bel hooks and Teresa de Lauretis; and from Chantal Mouffe comes inspiration for his notion of "border pedagogy" (247).[16] Lastly, challenging what they believe is still a patriarchial dominance within the critical pedagogy movement is a group of "poststructural feminists." Assuming this temporary label, they reject all attempts to subsume trajectories of difference under a generalized other (Luke and Gore 1992, 5) and for this reason question the theorizing of postmoderns like Giroux. They are united in efforts to "go beyond the deconstruction of the normative masculine subject valorized as the benchmark against which all others are measured...[to challenge incorporation and marginalization]...[by writing from within] the feminist project of standpoint—standing firm on a politics of location and identity" (Luke and Gore 1992, 6-7). Compiled is an important collection of papers that highlights this feminist critical project and that includes contributions from Elizabeth Ellsworth, Valerie Walkerdine, and Lather.

There is much to learn and continue to learn from efforts by theorists just identified, those most closely linked to feminism and critical theory. In what remains of this essay, an alternative tack is suggested in the notion of "critical sufficiency." This alternative is an overt *politics*, an endeavor to get beyond the internal skirmishes of the left—a proposal for educational alliance. It is an alliance that allows for significant and continuing theoretical differences yet allows for a praxiological "coming together" if only for a brief time. It continues Apple's (1992) project from above, and picks up the feminist spirit of Young's (1990) "politics of difference" and of bel hook's (1989) call for solidarity. As reason enough to pursue this alternative, hooks asserts, "If we cannot engage dialectically in a committed, rigorous, humanizing manner, we cannot hope to change the world" (25).

Roots for critical sufficiency are several. A first set comes from writing cited above. Holt and Margonis (1992) mention the idea that theorizations seemingly from the left may not be "sufficiently critical" (232). Their approach is to critique inappropriate conceptions of history and structure that advocate following a "middle road" between neoconservatism and "the old left" (citing Young 1990). Rather than the late modernist critique of Holt and Margonis, Lather's (1991) conjunctive approach posits a turn to postmodernism; however, she begins with "given enabling conditions" of every woman's experience— "the disjunctures in her own life and the means necessary for change" (xviii). In spite of a tug, a trace of essentialism and structuralism, Lather names her own conjunction of feminism and critical theory—and her own positionings and perspectives—as plural and fluid.[17] The concept of sufficiently enabling conditions soon described acknowledges a debt to these theorists.

A second set of sources are from the traditional/late-modern philosophy of science and language. The first of these is an intriguing idea from Thomas Kuhn (1970)—this is translation. Suggesting by analogy to leftist disagreement, a communication breakdown among different scientific communities, Kuhn writes, that "what the participants can do. . .is recognize each other as members of different language communities. . .and then. . .attempt to discover the terms and locutions that. . .are foci of trouble for inter-group discussions" (202, see also 198).[18] This attempt at discovery not only determines areas of disagreement but also of agreement as it begins a process of communication.

Founding this process are certain shared assumptions: For participants in translation, communication is and need only be partial; difficulties are not merely linguistic but incorporate other aspects of their experiences and theorizings: working together (in this case for an educational praxis) necessitates efforts to "experience vicariously something of the merits and defects of each other's points of view (202). Above, suggested starting points are a common ground of definition and a common "collective memory." Particularly pertinent is the body of political agreements already described, and as well, a general commitment to critical research.

Three aspects of "translation" are especially fruitful. The first is the maintenance of theoretical difference as well as basic agreements, among them of an initial working agenda. The second, as Kuhn relates, is that "persuasion need not succeed, and if it does, it need not be accompanied. . .by conversion" (202–3). In the present case, this means that no hierarchy need be established among contesting critical theorists and no creation of adverse feelings of powerlessness and inferiority. Moreover, a third is that the left need not act in ways that are antithetical to the content of its own critique: criticial theorists do not reinscribe superordinate and subordinate power relations that are ethically and educationally harmful.[19]

Thus far, sources for critical sufficiency indicate relevance for some degree of "criticalness," some set of experiential conditions, and some communicative process for enactment. Related to Kuhn, the final source also concerns philosophy of language, in this case the traditional theory of causality. The point, to begin, is that this theory is transformed for a social-critical agenda.

The issue of sufficiency, taken up as a matter of degree, refers back to the ordinary usage of 'sufficiently critical' by Holt and Margonis. This is understood as part of the logic of necessary and sufficient conditions. A bit of background is in order: The concept of sufficiency is part of a tradition of philosophic interest in cause and effect in which over time, strong notions of universality and uniformity of causes—and in the form of laws—were given up (Taylor 1967). This theoretical change, one notes, is part of the evolution of the modern search for certainty. Most recent attention to causal attributes of language was found in the writings of the logical positivists in the early part of the twentieth century. The "giving up" of strict causal laws by philosophers such as Hart, Honore, Ayer, and Collingwood incorporated a turn to conditions.

Taken primarily from earlier writings of John Stuart Mill, the general idea is that for any event to occur (such as, for example, communication by critical theorists) one or more conditions "necessarily" must also occur. Among possible conditions, the theory relates, are those necessary, sufficient, and both. Recognized *subsequent* to the event, necessary conditions were those "which are such that, had any of them not occurred, the change in question (the event) would not have occurred either" (Taylor 1967, 62). Sufficient conditions were the totality of necessary conditions; and following from these definitions, one and only one condition was both necessary and sufficient. In moving away from strong causation, significant discussions of conditions focus both on human agency and on novelty.

A further turning away from positivism effects the concept of conditions. In his writings, Cleo Cherryholmes (1988) sets the stage for sufficiently enabling conditions of feminist critical research. He asserts, "We choose and act...without the benefit of positivist victories. Our choices and actions, in their totality, are pragmatic responses to the situations in which we and others find ourselves. They are based upon *visions* of what is beautiful, good, and true instead of fixed, structured, moral, or objective certainties" (151). In adopting what Cherryholmes calls a "critical pragmatic strategy", the present idea of sufficiency is understood as embedded in situated discourse practices whose meanings are continually reconstructed, dispersed, and deferred. Entailed are deconstructive notions of silences and gaps, of traces and sedimentation, of ambiguities and contradictions (152, 160). (As I take it), what is desired is the broadest range of "authentic" and sufficient criticalness that maintains a recognition of an now-contingent basis for language in human interaction and understanding.[20]

Cherryholmes's conditions are poststructural, located at the far end of a range of those sufficiently critical. This is his own theorization, strategically developed for particular purposes, a particularization that itself is fluid and changing—for him and for all others. Because of the range of conditions, formulations of critical sufficiency need not be either poststructural or postmodern.

Sufficiently Enabling Conditions

Critical sufficiency is a concept of praxis. In the case of the proposed research institute and its aims, it allows for a practical leftist politics. It allows for agreement to work together—a shared ideology it might be said—in spite of theoretical disagreement. Such an agreement is constituted of a set of enabling conditions. As just indicated, these occupy a range of fluid meanings and interpretations that, most appropriately, are continually recreated and renegotiated in each moment of politics.[21] Here follows a brief statement of the elements of agreement, elements that are based in a broadly defined late modern/postmodern social theory. Its minimal basis is a giving up of "modernist" certainty. A note: each statement that follows has a well-delineated basis in theory; each researcher working within a feminist critical praxis is obligated to work through, and to adopt, adapt, or construct theoretical particularities.

Epochal tension. Whatever one's present epochal alignment, critical sufficiency entails recognition of a set of world conditions different from those of the past, and a minimal acknowlegment of a tension of changing senses of the world. Perhaps at present, the most strategic political posture is to define modernism ard post-modernism as interrelated and dependent on each other. If conditions are recognized, their names may not matter.

Historical non-necessity. Critical sufficiency entails recognition of changed conditions of necessity, of the strong notions of cause and effect discussed above. Minimal acknowledgment incorporates agreement on the centrality of history, of historical sensitivity in the construction of theories and explanations. An acceptable range includes a strongly historicist belief that history itself is particular and contingent—whether one calls it historicist or post-historicist.

Anti-essentialism. Just as historical necessity is given up, so is a metaphysic of essentialism in other modernist theoretical formulations. The latter is any expression of totality, singularity, sameness, or oneness.[22] Minimal is acknowledgment of the giving up of essentials as objectivism and foundationalism, of static theoretical frameworks and starting points. At the very least, other essentials such as social structures and functions as well as cultural universals are understood as changing.

Contextualization. Conditions of criticalness are sufficient if there is acknowledgment of two aspects of contextualization, of the place of language in a world that is "socially constructed." Both acknowledge materiality but as itself theoretically non-essential. A contextual range is acceptable, from weak to strong contextualization. The former takes context as influencing, as opening possibility; the latter takes context as limiting possibility—given present societal conditions.[23]

Theory-ladenness. A critical recognition of the role of theory entails its presence in life and in life as language. Language is thought; thought is never neutral, given the social construction accepted above. Herein aspects of the social world impinge upon understanding of the physical world: minimally, perception is theory-laden, what is seen is culturally influenced. Maximally, theories are themselves theory-laden: What is asked and answered, in what ways, and by whom are all societally contingent.

Identities. Given the noncertainty of previous categories, the privileging of self, and especially of an essential human rationality, gives way in two respects. The first is to recognize the limitation of all experience because it is partial of and momentary to others' experiences; the second is to acknowledge experience as tied to societal location. These steps are minimal; maximal is to accept the multiplicities of all singular persons—a significant aspect of poststructural "selves."

Ethicality. Underlying what above are primarily epistemological conditions is a "social turn" in their understanding and, concomitantly, an ethical commitment to their enactment. If the world is socially constructed, *we* do this together, in a condition of situated relations. The point: a feminist critical project is not sufficient unless there is agreement to work together for the eradication of human cruelty and evil. This is a strong effort—against pain, separation, and helplessness.[24]

Reconceptualizations of power. Implicit in the above categories are relationships of power, now changing and altered. Power becomes antipower, in which tradition, convention, societal privilege, as well as history and language take on new dimensions. Modernist contradictions are acknowledged; some are lived with and some are transformed. Consider various dimensions of antipower: first as temporality-that is, as momentariness, ambiguity, dispersion, fluidity; second as plurality, that is, as multiplicity, multivocality, multiculturalism; third as re-creation, that is, as reconstruction, recursion, reconstitution; and fourth as otherness, that is, as difference, playfulness, irony, and contradiction itself. A notion of antipower encapsulates the central critical element of the *politics* of a changed lived world.

Conclusion

Days later I am suddenly aware of the warm Hawaii morning outside my window and the completed text on my office desk. Writing this "position paper" has been both difficult and exhilarating, difficult from wanting to state my beliefs and ideas carefully, exhilarating because of its completion. As I sit, I am thoughtful about the politics of the paper and, clearly, of the proposed institute. I know that the paper may be ignored, or it may be misunderstood. Moreover, it may cause conflict—some of it precisely of the non-praxiological kinds that are critiqued in the paper itself.

So what of feminist educational research? And what of the issue of critical sufficiency? The thesis has been that feminist critical research is possible—and productive—by a range of theorists. Their productivity, by implication, is a politics of alliance. This alliance, it is important to remember, works for structural and systemic educational change—changes that are surely merited by present states of affairs. Practically, these states are ones of much inequality, domination, and near chaos; theoretically, these states are ones of much, unnecessary internecine battling. Neither need exist in worlds that are socially constructed and ethically grounded.

Understanding the present states of feminisn and critical theory in professional education is a first definitional step toward alliance. Herein the assertion has been that feminisn is still largely invisibilized and critical theory largely coopted. A second step is recognizing that the feminist and critical left "must get its act together," initially by recalling both separate and conjunctive common memories. A third step is to study, critique, and indeed modify the concept of critical sufficiency: to try it out perhaps (at particular moments and over time) to gauge its praxiological utility. At the last, this means to work with and through the proposed set (or another similar set) of critically sufficient enabling conditions. This, I conclude, is not a facile task, nor is it essentializing of differences given the character of the conditions themselves. However, it is a task necessary for the survival of left, critical influence in education. It is a task that requires *our* ethical commitment because it, or something like it, may be the only possibility before us—the only hope we have.[25]

Notes

1. A long tradition of creating thought experiments exists in philosophy. There is no basis in fact for this story except for Hawaii residence and my own

editing of a book of feminist theory readings. For examples of such experiments, see Rorty 1979 and Noddings 1992; also see Stone 1994.

2. In keeping with developments in feminist theorizing, I need to position myself in this writing. I am female, white, middle-aged, an unmarried heterosexual, presently an untenured professor. I write only for myself and in no way pose essentialist views in the name of others. See also Miller 1991.

3. I am writing this chapter just prior to the 1992 U.S. presidential elections.

4. See Robert Young's 1990 work on Habermas and the latter's use of "crisis."

5. A bold black and red headline "bigger than Pearl Harbor" reads "Test Scores Plunge," *Honolulu Advertiser,* 2, October 1992 (Ralph Stueber, personal commuication).

6. As Popkewitz (1991) stipulates, the meaning of "reform" changes over time and presently is constituted of both ideologies of individualism and professionalism (14).

7. Right theorists maintain the neutrality and objectivity of theory as nonpolitical.

8. This is in spite of research like the most recent from Gilligan and her colleagues (Brown and Gilligan 1992), and in spite of nationwide surveys that indicate the inequality of girls' and boys' school achievement (AAUW 1992).

9. These terms carry different meanings, depending on whether they are being used in traditional or critical research.

10. Many researchers in curriculum and teaching trace their theory of eclecticism from Joseph Schwab, introduced in the first of three essays on "the practical." See Schwab 1978, 295.

11. While I disagree somewhat with their critique of Robert Young, the general point made by Holt and Margonis (1992) is important.

12. Thanks to Chet Bowers for discussion of the significance of the friend-enemy distinction.

13. Criticism and textual discourses name most postmodern formulations of theory across the disciplines. A cooption results in retaining narrow views of art or literary criticism or in essentializing the meaning of this theoretical term.

14. See Nicholson 1990 for an recent reformulation, and especially (I think) Bartky 1990.

15. These writings in no way exhaust the vital field of critical education. Three other strands that deserve mention are those allied around the British

sociologists of knowledge, those conducting empirical studies of gender biases in schooling, and those connecting specific elements from Continental social theory to matters other than pedagogy.

16. See hooks 1989; de Lauretis 1986; and Mouffe 1988.

17. This is a tension shared by most "critical" feminists who fear "giving" up the category of gender in poststructuralist theorizing.

18. Kuhn cites Willard Quine for his source on "translation." See Quine 1960.

19. Kuhn makes two additional comments about translation: (1) that most people fear the process as foreign to them; and (2) that engaging in translation potentially leads to seeing the world in new ways from a kind of gestalt assumption of new languages. (203–4). Rorty (1989) writes similarly.

20. Authenticity has been mentioned a couple of times. By this I mean that any adherent, and not just members of the professional academy, demonstrate thoughtful study of the collective memory.

21. Lather's experiential conditions are transformed here into theoretical ones. For both of us, praxis is practical/theoretical politics is practical/theoretical.

22. See Stone 1992.

23. A critical language of possibility is transforming of these societal conditions (lest there be cooption again).

24. My ethical thinking and my own commitments owe much to Nel Noddings; see here Noddings 1989.

25. Thanks to Louise Bogart, Cleo Cherryholmes, Barbara Klemm, Sharon Rowe, and Trule Thacker for assistance. Special thanks to Priscilla Ross and to Peter McLaren and James Giarelli for their invitation and their faith in the work.

References

Adams, H. 1986. Introduction. Pp. 1–22 in *Critical Theory since 1965*, ed. H. Adams and L. Searle. Tallahassee: Florida State University Press.

American Association of University Women Educational Foundation. 1992. *Executive Summary: How Schools Shortchange Girls?* Washington, D. C.: National Educational Summit on Girls, 12, February 1992.

Apple, M. 1992. "Education, Culture, and Class Power: Basil Bernstein and the neo-Marxist Sociology of Education." *Educational Theory* 42, no. 2:127–45.

Bartky, S. 1990. *Feminity and Domination: Studies in the Phenomenology of Oppression*. New York: Routledge.

———. 1992. "Letters to the Editor." *APA Proceedings and Addresses* 65, no. 7:55–58.

Benhabib, S., and D. Cornell eds. 1987. *Feminism as Critique: On the Politics of Gender*. Minneapolis: University of Minnesota Press.

Bowers, C. 1987. *Elements of a Post-Liberal Theory of Education*. New York: Teachers College Press.

Brown, L., and C. Gilligan. 1992. *Meeting at the Crossroads: Women's Psychology and Girl's Development*. Cambridge: Harvard University Press.

Cherryholmes, C. 1988. *Power and Criticism: Poststructural Investigations in Education*. New York: Teachers College Press.

de Lauretis, T. 1986. "Feminist Studies/Critical Studies: Issues, Terms, Contexts." Pp. 1–19 in *Feminist Studies/Critical Studies*. Bloomington: Indiana University Press.

Ellsworth, E. 1992. "Why Doesn't This Feel Empowering? Working Through the Repressive Myths of Critical Pedagogy." Pp. 90–119 in *Feminisms and Critical Pedagogy*, ed. C. Luke and J. Gore. New York: Routledge.

Fraser, N., and L. Nicholson. 1990. "Social Criticism without Philosophy: An encounter between Feminism and Postmodernism." Pp. 19–38 in *Feminism/Postmodernism*, ed. L. Nicholson. New York: Routledge.

Giroux, H. 1991;. "Introduction: Modernism, Postmodernism and Feminism: Rethinking the Boundaries of Educational Discourse." Pp. 1–59 in *Postmodernism, Feminism, and Cultural Politics*, ed. H. Giroux. Albany: State University of New York Press.

Holt, L., and F. Margonis. 1992. "Critical Theory of a Conservative Stamp." *Educational Theory* 42, no. 2:231–50.

hooks, b. 1989. *Talking Back*. Boston: South End Press.

Kuhn, T. 1970. *The Structure of Scientific Revolutions*. 2 ed. Chicago: University of Chicago Press.

Lather, P. 1991. Getting Smart: Feminist Research and Pedagogy With/in the Postmodern. New York: Routledge.

Luke, C., and J. Gore, eds. 1992. *Feminisms and Critical Pedagogy*. New York: Routledge.

MacKinnon, C. 1983. "Feminism, Marxism, Method and the State: An Agenda for Theory." Pp. 227–56 in *The Signs Reader: Women, Gender & Scholarship*, ed. E. Abel and E. Abel. Chicago: University of Chicago Press.

Miller, N. 1991. *Getting Personal: Feminist Occasions and other Autobiographical Acts*. New York: Routledge.

Mouffe, C. 1988. "Radical Democracy: Modern or Postmodern?" Pp. 31–45 in *Universal Abandon: The Politics of Postmodernism*, ed. A. Ross, Minneapolis: University of Minnesota Press.

Nicholson, L. 1987. "Feminism and Marx: Integrating Kinship with the Economic." Pp. 16–30 in *Feminism as Critique*, ed. S. Benhabib and D. Cornell. Minneapolis: University of Minnesota Press.

Noddings, N. 1989. *Women and Evil*. Berkeley and Los Angeles: University of California Press.

———. 1992. *The Challenge to Care in Schools: An Alternative Approach to Education*. New York: Teachers College Press.

Popkewitz, T. 1991. A Political Sociology of Educational Reform: Power/Knowledge in Teaching, Teacher Education, and Research. New York: Teachers College Press.

Quine, W. 1960. *Word and Object* Cambridge: MIT Press.

Rorty, R. 1979. *Philosophy and the Mirror of Nature*. Princeton: Princeton University Press.

———. 1989. *Contingency, Irony, and Solidarity*. Cambridge: Cambridge University Press.

Schwab, J. 1978. "The Practical: A Language for Curriculum." Pp. 287–321 in *Joseph Schwab, Science, Curriculum and Liberal Education: Selected Essays*, ed. I. Westbury and N. Wilkof. Chicago: University of Chicago Press.

Stone, L. 1992. *The Essentialist Tension in Reflective Teacher Education*. Pp. 198–211 in *Reflective Teacher Education: Cases and Critiques*, ed. L. Valli. Albany: State University of New York Press.

Stone, L., ed. 1994. *The Education Feminism Reader*. New York: Routledge.

Taylor, R. 1967. "Causation." Pp. 56–66 in *The Encyclopedia of Philosophy*, ed. P. Edwards. New York: The Free Press.

Walkerdine, V. 1992. "Progressive Pedagogy and Political Struggle." Pp. 15–24 in *Feminisms and Critical Pedagogy*, ed. C. Luke and J. Gore. New York: Routledge.

Wexler, P. 1987. *Social Analysis of Education: After the New Sociology*. New York: Routledge.

Yates, S. 1992. "Letters to the Editor." *APA Proceedings and Addresses* 65, no. 7:74–76.

Young, I. 1990. "The Ideal of Community and the Politics of Difference." Pp. 300–323 in *Feminism/Postmodernism*, ed. L. Nicholson. New York: Routledge.

Young, R. 1990. *A Critical Theory of Education: Habermas and our Children's Future.* New York: Teachers College Press.

9

The Discourse of the Urban School
and the Formation of a Therapeutic Complex

David M. Jones

Capture and seduction, confrontation and mutual reinforcement: parents and children, adults and adolescents, educators and students, doctors and patients, the psychiatrist with his hysteric and his perverts, all have played this game continually since the nineteenth century. These attractions, these evasions, these circular incitements have traced around bodies and sexes, not boundaries not to be crossed, but perpetual spirals of power and pleasure.

—Michel Foucault, *History of Sexuality, Vol. 1* (1976)

In the genealogical endeavor to trace the lines of transformation of moral technologies, Michel Foucault has shed a disconcerting light upon the role played by an apparatus like the school and academic disciplines like sociology, psychology, and education in the construction of a biopower. Foucault's attempt in *The History of Sexuality* and *Discipline and Punish* to write history in the present tense in order to show how objects "govern themselves by the production of truth," has important resonances for the contemporary deployment of discourses concerning the production of positive self-imagery through educational technique; the function and form of examinations; and the formation of categories of special need.

However, there has been no significant effort to apply Foucault's "fragmentary philosophical insights" (Foucault 1981), to deconstruct the play of force relationships in contemporary objects of educational concern. The modest purpose of this paper is to present a diagram of biopower and suggest ways in which it might illuminate current educational discourse in England and Wales.

1

In the *History of Sexuality* 1978 and *Discipline and Punish* 1977
Foucault identified a series of force relationships in the human sciences
that established the individual as both a subject and object for
power/knowledge. Foucault noted the emergence of disciplinary
technology in the nineteenth century that transformed the manner in
which power was deployed. Traditionally, Foucault contends, a juridico-
political order presented power in terms of law, sovereignty, and
obligation. In this "classical" view sovereignty consisted in the "power
of life and death" exercised over subjects. Constrastingly, there developed alongside this view of power, in the course of the nineteenth
century, a governmental concern with the ordering of life.

This new power over life evolved in two basic forms, or more
specifically constituted "two poles of development" (Foucault 1978, 135).
One pole centered on the body as a machine characterized by the
development of disciplines, "an anatamo-politics of the human body"
(139). The second pole focused on the species body, the population in
general, whose supervision "was effected through an entire series of
interventions and regulatory controls" (140). A biopower began to
operate initially in eleemosynary schemes of public health, public
education and public housing. Indeed, Foucault maintains, there was
"an explosion of numerous and diverse techniques for achieving the
subjugation of bodies and the control of populations marking the
beginning of an era of biopower" (140).

Crucially, biopower required the deployment of sexuality. Situated
at the juncture "of the body and the population, sex became a crucial
target of a power organized around the management of life rather than
the menace of death" (147). An assemblage of disciplinary mechanisms
like the school, the hospital, and the housing trust articulated and
ordered biopower. This biotechnology employed tactics whose
"operation is not ensured by right, but by technique, not by law but
by normalization, not by punishment but by control, methods that are
controlled on all levels and in forms that go beyond the state and its
apparatuses" (89). The nineteenth century, therefore, witnessed a
transformation in the codification of powers. How we may inquire does
this recodification and its anatomo-political deployment affect popular
schooling?

It was, Foucault argues, through the descriptive and regulating
power of the human sciences (medicine, pedagogy, economics, and
demography) that the social body came to place itself under the
normalizing and calculating gaze of surveillance. This science in particular

took the moral conduct of the population both as its object of analysis and its target of intervention (Foucault in Rabinow 1984, 351-52). To achieve this, it had to develop techniques that would render the individual calculable and describable. In particular, Foucault contends, disciplinary science transformed the religious technique of confession and recoded it in terms of the scientific rule of the normal and pathological rather than the clerical rule of conscience and sin. The formation of this normalizing gaze of the human sciences further necessitated the development of regulatory mechanisms in order to qualify, measure, appraise, and hierarchize.

This gaze and its associated technology focused upon the family. A series of regulatory and corrective mechanisms immured the family and while ostensibly seeking to modify the intensity of its demands, actually penetrated it in an increasingly detailed manner. Caught between the traditional demand for the family to function as a socio-economic unit and the blandishments of a biotechnology, its members had little alternative but to "broadcast the long complaint of its sexual suffering," to the new practitioners of bioskills—the doctors, teachers, and, in time, social workers, psychologists, and psychiatrists, whose expertise lay in the confessional skills of listening, observing, advising, and assessing (Foucault 1978, 110).

In *The Policing of Families* (1979) Jacques Donzelot has traced the impact of this advisory or tutelary complex upon the family and in particular the urban working-class family. Donzelot believes that the operation of this normalizing/pathologizing process had the effect of reformulating family life in the urban space. The wife and mother became the special target for the biodiscourses of education, health, saving, and domestic economy: "The woman was chosen by the medical and teaching professions to work in partnership with them in order to disseminate their principles, to win adherence to the new norms within the home" (Deleuze, in Donzelot 1977, xxi). The bioprocess isolated the urban family and turned it inward. In fact, it was "forged on the basis of a turning back of each of its members onto the other in a circular relation of vigilance against the temptation from outside—from the city and the street. . . being isolated it was now exposed to the surveillance of its deviation from the norm" (xxi).

In Foucault's notion of a biopower and its subsequent elaboration by Donzelot, the popular school plays a critical role. The urban elementary school opens the inadequately differentiated classes of the urban slum to an evaluating and encoding eye. In the nineteenth century the school functioned both as a moral machinery to transform "street arabs" into ethical subjects and a "laboratory for the observation of anti-social tendencies" (Foucault 1977, 176). To form subjects permeable by a biopower the "scholar" had to be isolated, analyzed, and disciplined. It did this through the elaboration of two techniques: the case study and the examination.

The documentary technique of the ease study transformed real lives into writing. The accumulation of documentation, moreover, by correlating performance and behavior over time lowered the threshold of describability. The case study made possible the era of the calculable man (Foucault 1977, 184–94). The technique of examination clarified or objectified this process. The examination, central to the notion of educational science, made "each individual a case" (191).

Examination and writing opened a field of anatomo-political possibility. It could establish the individual as an analyzable object within a competitive system that permitted a classificatory arrangement of similar objects. The apparatus of the classroom and the classificatory techniques of examination formed an exclusive domain of "normalizing judgments" that in turn permitted the tracing of the limit that defined difference "in relation to all other differences, the external frontier of the abnormal" (143).

By the early twentieth century, the school functioned as a normalizing apparatus within a wider technology of advice and insurance. The school, the hospital, the multivalent agencies of social welfare, all provided institutional sites for a constellation of counselors and technicians to practice the strategies of a biopower on a receptive population. Strategies that might have the apparent objectives of "saying no to all wayward or unproductive sexualities," but in fact "function as mechanisms with a double impetus: and power" (Foucault 1976, 45). A biopower, in fact, that "questions, monitors watches, spies, searches out, palpates, brings to light." By the late twentieth century, these tutelary strategies had saturated the urban family with medical, psychological, and pedagogic norms. How we may wonder does this constellation of technicians and the biotechniques they practice function in the current educational "crisis" characterized as it is by a volatilization of pedagogic norms?

We can broadly trace three discourses that have shaped urban education in the twentieth century. These often contradictory discourses have formed a common object of concern—the teacher's function in the dispersal of a biopower. It is to this discursive formation that we next turn.

2

The first discourse whose regularity intrudes upon the practices of the classroom may be traced to 1944. Its' object of concern is "secondary education for all" and its aim is the creation of equal educational opportunity. This discourse is progressive. It attempts contradictorily to make education comprehensive, but describes this endeavor in 1968 as providing elitist "grammar schools for all." Accordingly, the comprehensive discourse promised a vision of an egalitarian, meritocratic democracy.

Counterposed to this discourse is one coterminous with the development of popular education itself. This discourse emphasizes standards, examination, and accountability and may be traced to 1861. More recently, it has opposed the seductive collectivism that bureaucratically imposes equality with the morality of free choice and the bracing spirit of competition. These competing visions of education in a mass democracy haunt the debate over educational standards and the Education Act of 1989.

Since 1976, however, and the national launch in the United Kingdom of a "great" educational debate, they have been remobilized and redeployed in curious configurations that elude reading in terms of political distinctions between an egalitarian left and an elitist right. The emerging discursive arrangement has in fact reversed earlier discourse. Thus the record of achievement, at one moment a radical deconstruction of traditional modes of examination, has now become an orthodoxy among conservative, manpower trainers and adherents of vocational education. Indeed, conservative local authority education officers like Donald Naismith enthusiastically endorse a radical restructuring of schooling that might once have been dismissed as the utopian speculation of deschooling extremists like Ivan Illich. Elsewhere, antiracist and antisexist educators advocate separate schooling for girls and black children; twenty years ago such advocacy would have been the prerogative of intransigent reactionaries.

This fissured discourse has been made even more volatile by growing governmental and media concern with popular education. Media fascination with educational issues and the subsequent development of television and radio programs and newspaper columns devoted to the latest educational research has transformed education into simulation (Baudrillard 1988). In this implosive condition, the survey functions as the mechanism for the circulation of more and more information that increasingly induces or simulates the effects it purports to investigate.

Between 1985 and 1988 the educational media reported research that variously proved that standards of literacy were improving; that educational standards were falling; that comprehensive schools were successful with the average student; that comprehensive schools and mixed-ability teaching had failed the average child; that teachers needed to encourage pupils to be more assertive; that teachers neeed to set clear behavioral standards; that the comprehensive school neglected the child in special need; that special-needs legislation would integrate children into the mainstream; that special-needs legislation had kept students out of the mainstream; that comprehensives spent too much time on pastoral care and devoted too little attention (at various times) to the curriculum; the management of the classroom; antiracist education; and antisexist education. At the same time research also evinced that teachers expected too little from students; teachers set unrealistic targets; and finally the proposed national system of testing would differentiate but not discriminate between examinees and that any meaningful examination has to discriminate.

This "ecstasy of description" intensifies the educational object so much so that educational discourse becomes increasingly incoherent (Meaghan Morris 1984, 92). What impact does this volatile spiral of information have upon the object of educational concern, the school, and its capacity to deliver an effective education?

Foucault never failed to point out that discourse was a "resource for strategy" (Foucault 1981, 8). The crucial strategic implication of the escalating concern about state schooling is the implicit and increasingly explicit failure of the school and a fortiori the schoolteacher in delivering an adequate education.

In its ealier phase the tutelary gaze of a biopower focused upon the pathogenic family and the bad parent. The advice profferred by a network of biotechnicians would either normalize or isolate the urban problem family.

By a tactical reversal the tutelary agencies in successfully engendering need and dependence upon their counseling techiques, have themselves been seduced into a biotechnology that monitors them. The teacher, like the social worker, has become implicated in the concern ascribed to the object of his or her intervention. Thus although the problem child, in the problem family, in the problem area, remains the primary target for pedagogic/medical/social normalization, yet, by a pathogenic social osmosis, the tutelary agencies themselves have become additional objects of concern.

In education, this process has been exacerbated by the Great Debate and the discourse of teacher failure. The figure of the urban schoolteacher has been captured as an object of discourse. Fascination with the teacher in turn excites discourse and demands further intervention.

In this discourse of failure we can trace the emergence of three broadly therapeutic strategies intended to reverse the "decline" in standards, but whose real effect has been to open the school to further surveillance and examination. These strategies share a common discursive concern about the manner in which the teacher establishes normative judgments on the school site. They locate teachers in a network of power relationships that render them both increasingly visible and potentially pathological. The first strategy relates to the educational management of those in special need; the second refers to the pedagogic development of antiracist and antisexist strategies; and the third to the deployment of new monitoring and examining techniques.

3

The first strategic development that volatilized the operation of normative judgment in the urban secondary school was the Education Special Need Act (1981). The act created new categories of special need and new procedures for monitoring them. The aim of the 1981 legislation was to integrate wherever possible pupils who suffered any form of learning disability into mainstream education. Isomorphic with this aim went a challenge to the inflexible and stigmatizing labels employed by schools and their tutelary associates to pathologize and exclude those deemed ineducable in mainstream settings.

The new rhetoric of special educational need significantly borrowed many of its themes from the "new" sociology of education pioneered in the course of the seventies. This critical sociology laid the epistemological basis for challenging the labeling processes central to the way in which the urban school established norms of behavior. Exposure of the school's hidden structure for managing abnormality permeates the critical literature of the seventies (see Lloyd-Smith 1984, Swann 1981) and constitutes the mise-en-scène to the integrative strategies proposed in the successive reports of Warnock (1978), Hargreaves (1984), and Fish (1985).

At the practical level of the school site, this integrative strategy created a new vocabulary of special need and a new machinery to monitor its implementation. The school special needs department now assesses the school's effectiveness in integrating pupils with difficulties, but it is the school's educational psychologist that occupies the crucial tutelary role. The 1981 legislation transformed the school's educational psychology service (EPS) into a paradigm for the delivery of paratherapies. In theory the EPS would both assess the effectiveness of integration and act as the diagnostic gatekeeper for the distribution of statements of special need and additional therapies. Through the deployment of its special knowledge the machinery of special need would make the whole school population available to a scientific gaze that would modify and eventually re-mediate the school's propensity to pathologize.

Warnock contended that at one time or another up to 20 percent of the school population might fall into a category of special need (Brennan 1982, 57). The legislation of 1981 envisaged a gradual but uniform move to a pattern of integrated provision for those diagnosed to suffer from learning difficulty. The implementation of the act since 1983, however, has been characterized by heterogenaity and in certain areas increased segregation (Swann 1986). Indeed, we learn from recent research (Wills 1988) that the statement of special need, the specific technique designed to draw the child with a learning difficulty, the parent, and the school into a caring and mutually supportive relationship, has had a completely different outcome at the level of the school. Local Education Authorities (LEAs) in fact tactically deploy the statement in order to exclude those diagnosed as requiring special provision from mainstream schooling. Paradoxically, the integrative vision has succeeded in formulating a new and multivalent technology for assessing the school population that more efficiently establishes the external limit of the normal.

Even more confusingly, the school that develops a particular expertise in dealing with those pupils who "may for short periods of time" fall into a category of special need can easily be the victim of its apparent success. A school that achieves too much success in integrating students, especially students with emotional and behavioral difficulties, may paradoxically cease to function as a mainsteam educational setting. To illustrate this we can point to the example of a secondary comprehensive in an area of educational priority in Willesden, North West London. In 1986, the adviser for special education for the borough described it as a model for dealing with, and counseling students with emotional and behavioral difficulties. The head of the special needs department at the school emphasized the "care and counseling" that both her department and the staff of the school put into their difficult student population, many of whom had been excluded from other schools in the borough. She contended that the school "deals with kids who have in some cases been very hurt by school. . . .We have a whole school policy on special need, because we are a small school (with a declining role) we can put a lot of emphasis into pastoral support." The school in fact had clearly embraced and attempted to implement the notion that "every teacher is a teacher of special needs" (Booth & Statham 1985). Yet as the school had acquired a local reputation for integrating students with specific learning difficulties, it nevertheless suffered because of its poor reputation in terms of public examinations.

In 1987, Her Majesty's Inspectorate (HMI) published a highly critical assessment of the school's curriculum and its delivery. Subsequently, the educational correspondent of *The Sun* pondered rhetorically whether it might not be "the worst school in Britain?" (*The Sun*, 4 September 1988).

This extreme case illustrates the curious and contradictory implications that the practice of special need can have upon the school site. The emerging discourse has strategic effects at a number of different levels. The integrationist ideal established a new flexible machinery of assessment characterized by a technology of case conferences and regular reviews that challenged the rigid and segregative practices traditionally applied by schools to their marginal population. Implicitly, it challenged the school's autonomy. It required the urban school teacher to establish new modes of assessing students. All teachers were now teachers of special need, consequently they were drawn ineluctably into a therapeutic relationship both with parents and pupils and other tutelary agencies. In practice, this machinery of counseling, overseen at the level of the local authority by a therapeutic bureaucracy of advisers, social workers, and psychologists, sought to expose, not the special need of the student, but the school and the teacher to a new and flexible mode of assessment.

The second discursive strategy to penetrate the increasingly beleagured urban school offers a yet more radical problematization of the school and the teacher in terms of race and gender. It seeks to correct the school's inequitable treatment of its students by introducing a therapeutic machinery of equal opportunity at the level of the local authority. In this discourse the LEA becomes the site that disperses strategies of antiracism and antisexism. Accordingly the LEA is deeply preoccupied with the relationships that the school and the teacher establishes with the nascent self-image of the student through its curriculum and the student through its curriculum and "ethos." The LEA, therefore, interrogates and challenges the unquestioned and unconscious practices of the urban school in order to enable disadvantaged or oppressed students to acquire self-esteem and "positive self-images." The school has to enhance self-esteem and "positive self-images." The school thus has to be rendered continually accountable to a notional community whose representatives constitute a therapeutic or "cool" bureaucracy that constantly assess the school's attempt to modify its inherent racism and sexism.

The discursive reversal of pedagogic imagery that equal opportunity proposes is far more extreme than that suggested by special need. Whereas the discourse of special need questioned only the practices through which the school sought to establish its limit by excluding specific abnormal students, the discourse of equal opportunity questions the total practice of the school the traditional relationship established between the school and the urban community.

Insuch a reading, then, not only the student and his family, but the school, the teacher, and the pastoral agencies of the school are increasingly opened to a machinery of surveillance. By reversing the relationship between the school and the community, antiracist and antisexist rhetoric established an insistence at the level of the local authority for the creation of additional agencies to monitor the urban school and its practices. Such a strategy sought to supplement the school's attempt to monitor the norm, with a further examination of the school's particular failure to enhance equally the educational opportunities of black and female students.

This shift in the tutelary network has, it will be argued, created a new bureaucracy that through a proliferation of units monitoring the school attempts to disperse a series of therapeutic technologies at the micropolitical level of the classroom. This phenomenon has been little explored. Here we propose the outline of a cartography that traces the emergence of a discourse about race, gender, and education and its application and implications for one outer London Local Education Authority.

After 1968, there appeared, from a variety of educational and political sites, statements that formed the female, the black, the gay, and the disabled bodies as their objects of concern. This discursive insistence had by the mid-seventies extended its scope to an examination of the urban school and its role in perpetuating racist and sexist practices. This critique reached a threshold of scientificity when educational research gave credibility to the notion of the school as a site for the manufacture of educational alienation and the marginalization of black and female children. The achievement of this threshold facilitated the deployment of the report, that favored technique of governmental inquiry, to establish the "truth" of the school's failure to deal equally with all its pupils. In this burgeoning attempt to locate and correct inegalitarian practices may be traced a genealogy that passes from Rampton (1981) through the Swann report (1985) to more specific micropolitical investigations into local authority practices like the Eggleston (1983) and Barrow (1984) reports. It is the strategic implications of the Barrow report, which evaluated the delivery of education in one local authority (Brent, North West London), that we shall next consider.

The Barrow report, commissioned in 1981 and completed in 1984, established the dimensions of the problem of racism in Brent schools. On the strength of its finding, the LEA developed a specific technology to correct the inequality in its schools. Central to the Barrow report's identification of an all-pervasive racism in Brent's schools was a curious definition of what actually constituted racism. Thus the report contended that what was in fact at stake in relationships between teacher and pupil, and school and community, was "ethnicism," a "refined form of racism that is in the ideological air we breathe." The report described ethnicism as "in all the relations of all people, the practices of all institutions and the consciousness of at least all Europeanised societies. . .those societies who had a colonial, imperial past as well as those which have been built on the basis of the extermination of indigenous people" (74). Equipped with such an all-embracing formula, the Barrow report proceeded to discover that racism is "a structural, cultural and ideological form and set of relations, processes and practices, in terms of a race and ethnic relations structure in which the inequalities and differentiation interest in the wider social structure are related to physical and cultural criteria of an ascriptive kind and are rationalised in terms of deterministic belief systems, which tend to make reference to biological and anthropological science" (Barrow 1984: 74) (74).

A crucial consequence of such a definition was that all schools and a fortiori teachers who did not constantly interrogate their classroom practice must necessarily be racist. Accordingly, the report cast suspicion upon the motivation of teachers and the structure of the schools and argued that Brent school had to be exposed to an autonomous apparatus to monitor and correct the school's racism. The object of this new machinery would be to reverse the norms that the teacher enforced. Consequently, it formed not the problem child and his or her family, but the problem teacher and his or her concealed racism as objects of concern. Significantly, the report codes positively the deviant acts that the school attempts either to modify or to sanction. Thus, black youths who misbehave in terms of the norms of the classroom in fact articulated "the inert perceptions of white working-class school students" (46). The report went on to cite approvingly the view of the Brent Curriculum Development Support Unit that "teachers cannot compromise with racism in any form and retain any credibility as educators. They should examine very carefully what is called normal education because it is that which is the problem. It is indeed the beliefs of educators about who and what is normal and equal which are the problems" (124).

The problem of the urban school and the black child, therefore, was not primarily educational, but moral. The Barrow report called for a new awareness on the part of educators of the "moral and political truths" of antiracism. In order to give shape to these new truths, the report called for new strategies that would "challenge and defeat racism" though a "fundamental change in self as well as in relations, practices and structures" (133).

The Barrow report's criticisms sought to reverse the manner in which the school functioned as an anatomo-political mechanism. The report demanded strategies that would liberate the teacher, the school, and the community from the unexamined consequences of the school's normalizing function. It questioned traditional practices in pastoral care, special need, instruction, and examination (133) in order to create a new awareness—an antiracist consciousness. Paradoxically, the report required the LEA to form additional agencies to monitor and galvanize the experiences and values of those previously marginalized by the process of education. Indeed, the process of liberation required a new and transformative bureaucracy nominally accountable to an oppressed community.

In the light of the Barrow report's discovery of proliferating racism and (less dramatically) sexism (46), the local authority introduced a series of initiatives to control and examine more precisely the relationship between Brent secondary schools and the population they had failed. In 1985, the borough implemented a code of Equal Opportunity in its employment practices. This code subsequently formed the foundation for a proliferation of agencies that surveyed and transformed the sexist practices in the borough's distribution of social, educational, and health services. A "cool" or therapeutic bureaucracy emerged in Brent after 1985 to transform the false consciousness of the traditional machinery of tutelage in education and the social services.

From 1985 Brent's education committee created new units to instrumentalize the strategy at the level of the school site. These equal-opportunity units effectively offered new training courses. A new order of technologists emerged to deploy techniques to correct and transform teacher consciousness.

The most far-reaching exemplification of this strategy was Brent's Development Programme for Race and Equality (DPRE). Introduced in 1987 by the education committee at the height of the McGoldrick case,[1] the DPRE constituted a supplementary educational bureaucracy. The education committee gave it autonomous power to investigate all aspects of the school, its teachers, curricula, and pastoral care regimes and to devise new curricular initiatives.

This new apparatus, then, constituted the borough's response to the problem of continued racism and sexism on the school site. The DPRE sought to instrumentalize at the level of the school site a strategy designed to alter the specific *mode d'assujettisement* and *rapport a soi* that existed between the teacher and his or her teaching and the pupil with him- or herself (Foucault in Rabinow 1984, 352). DPRE curricular initiatives emphasized positive gender and ethnic self-images. The curriculum must henceforth liberate and not alienate the student. Simultaneously, teachers must constantly examine themselves for perpetuating a racism and sexism so deeply rooted in their parapraxes and somatic performances that they are virtually unaware of it, but which fellow teachers and students must detect and ruthlessly expose (Foucault, in Martin 1988, 42).

The strategies devised by the DPRE intended to transform the ethical practice on the school site by transforming the earlier tutelary relationship between the school and the family. Central to the problem of the urban school's failure, in this reading, was the fact that it privileged false values and imposed them on oppressed communities. Existing values in the classroom must therefore be transvalued. A healthy or true ethical climate could only be realized, however, if the teacher through programs of training achieved a new self-consciousness.

Interestingly, the techniques deployed on equal-opportunity training courses for teachers in Brent schools were scientified and therapeutized versions of the Christian confessional tradition. Training programs attempted to exact a new pedagogical relationship with the self—a new awareness—through the specific device of testifying to personal experience. The training on such courses tried to reveal the concealed prejudices of teachers and how they communicated them to students (*Brent Equal Opportunity Training* 1986).

The new technology of the self deployed in such training emerged from a therapeutic blend of the human sciences and an evangelical technique of testament. A salvationist technique was translated from a teleological context and applied as pedagogic therapy. It is in fact a secularized version of a technique of the self that Foucault indentified as "exomologesis" (Martin 1988, 42)—a mode of appeasing one's judges by a confession of faults.

The exomologetic therapies of antiracism, antisexism, and positive self-imagery extracted a secularized version of an originally religious penance in order to induce new ethical conditions. "Penance," Foucault notes, "is the affect of change, of rupture with past and world.... It in fact serves to mark the refusal of self, the breaking away from self"

(Martin 1988, 44). Ostentatious gestures of testament and reformation by both trainers and trainees have the function of showing the truth of the state of being of the sinner, or more precisely, in their therapeutic educational setting, the racist or sexist teacher. Self-revaluation was at the same time destruction of the racist self. By this "new" technology the "penitent" teacher superimposed truth about the self through a violent rupture and dissociation.

The training programme constituted than a symbolic, theatrical and ritualistic hermeneutics. Its genealogy may be traced from the testifying of evangelical black churches (so evident in Brent educational politics), through secularization by the human sciences, notably psychology, into therapeutic practices that instrumentalize an egalitarian and antiracist reality in the staff rooms and classrooms of Brent comprehensives.

Discourse is, however, a strategic resource and its instrumentalization often has outcomes different from those envisaged by theory programmers. At the micropolitical level tactics developed that contested or reversed the new technologies. At the level of the staff room in a number of Brent secondary schools teachers viewed the attempt to impose a new consciousness intrusive. Teachers interviewed felt they had to watch what they said and to whom they said it. Significantly in one school with a particularly active DPRE teacher the staff room ceased to be a focus of interaction. Teacher tactics on the school site sought to undermine local authority strategy by evasion and simulation. An example in Foucauldian terms, of the pleasure that comes from evading a power that questions, monitors and searches out (Foucault 1978, 46). In this case, however, the pleasure of evasion belonged not to the problem family or the problem child but to the problem teacher.

Yet it is most notably in the school's relationship with the disaffected student that the conflict between the different strategies of antiracism and the conventional pastoral machinery of the school is most apparent. According to the established tutelary practice of advice and counseling that dominates the pastoral structures of inner-city schools, the school tries to "cope" with the problem student. Once the school has "tried everything," however, and the staff have reached "an intolerable level of stress," the school "reluctantly," after a "series of incidents," excludes the child (Lloyd-Smith 1984, 115). This tutelary mode established the school's limit through a machinery of case conferences and professional advice that eventually placed the emotionally difficult children in an environment more appropriate to their needs.

Antiracism explicitly confronted this technology of school management. In the antiracist perspective, by contrast, the child's or, more precisely, the black student's, resistance to the school's tutelary practice exposed the school's implicit racism.

The conflict between these two strategies had substantive implications for secondary education in the borough. Between 1985 and 1989, the borough closed all special provision for secondary-age disaffected students. On a number of occasions the LEA subcommittees on suspensions and exclusions refused to support a school's decision to suspend and exclude a disruptive student. Even more problematically, the special needs subcommittee refused to endorse statements of special need for black students put forward by the school's psychological service. Nevertheless, a number of school-age students were referred for guidance or effectively excluded from school without the LEA admitting the veracity of the grounds for refusal or exclusion. As a consequence there developed an irresoluble conflict between the norms applied by Brent schools and the values embraced by the LEA that effectively resulted in many students seeking education outside the borough or not receiving education at all.

The discussion of equal opportunity and its educational effect at the level of the school in our North London LEA "committed to positive educational initiatives" (DPRE bulletin no. 1) curiously shared discursive resonances with a wider governmental concern with national educational standards. This similarity is at first surprising when one considers the very different educational aspirations of the London Borough of Brent's education committee, the Centre for Policy Studies, and the Manpower Services Commission.

Yet on closer examination a number of common features begin to emerge. The discourse of the failure of the urban school is in fact a mobile and multivalent one. The failure of the teacher in terms of the standards set by a radical LEA and the failure of the teacher at the level of a national debate about standards share a common theme— the failure of popular education.

It is about the standard or norm that must be achieved, however, that the object of concern becomes elusive. This elusivity invites a spectacle of fascination and seduction. Thus a growing number of institutional sites pursue the pleasures of identifying the falling standards in state schools. Genealogically, statements about standards and examination results emerge from university research departments from the early seventies identifying problems in curriculum delivery. By 1976 the growing concern about the urban school initiates a Great Debate on educational standards. Growing media fascination demands

more and more educational information. By the late eighties the failings
of state education forms part of a wide-ranging discourse about moral
decline, crime, and urban decay. Political parties, and pressure groups
of various hues (Hillgate, the Confederation of British Industry, the
Trades Union Congress, the Adam Smith Institute, the Manpower
Services Commission, the National Society for the Prevention of Cruelty
to Children) feel free to comment upon the inadeqdacies of school
teachers, while television, the national press, and magazines ranging
from *Women's own* to *City Limits* offer revelations and suggest nostrums
for the problem teacher, the problem child, and the problem school.
The *Sun's* headline of November 1987 "Lazy Old Sir" captured the
essence of that fascination that exposes the teacher to a mobile and
multivalent gaze. The insistent pursuit of a measure by which the
inadequacy of the teacher may be assessed has generated, we shall
argue, a new image of teaching in a panopticon of permanent
examinability.

Central to the discursive concern about teaching standards is the
examination. Improvement in standards, it is contended, may only be
improved by yet more sophisticated assessment and examination.

However, a further consideration is implicit in the desire for
standards. It also wishes to extend the community of the examinable.
Although much current educational debate is posed in terms of
"excellence," the population identified as problematic is the 40 percent
of pupils who underachieve and leave school without marketable skills.
The discourse of standards identifies the efficiency of the school as an
object of concern and prescribes a series of strategic responses to deal
with it.

Initially, this strategy assumed the school could be rendered
efficient if the teacher is accountable not to a head or a local authority,
but to a national curriculum. This strategy curtailed teacher autonomy
by placing her in a curricular machinery in which the teacher, the child,
and the school are revealed to an examinatory technology. At the same
time a further strategic development trained students to deploy themselves successfully in the marketplace.

This apparently modern drive to efficiency has in fact revealed,
not a recent problem of schooling, but the displaced archaeological
sediment of generations of popular education. The contemporary
concern about techniques of assessment, efficient teaching, and useful
education has always been central to the development of compulsory
education. The GCSE[2] and the new National Curriculum constitute the
apotheosis of this development. The GCSE's flexibility encoded a
technique of permanent assessment applicable to all but the most
irremediable or elusive of sixteen-year-olds.

The disturbance of the archaeology of popular schooling that the current concern signifies, reveals significantly utilitarian features. The national curriculum, in fact, anticipates a return to the *Chrestomathia*. In 1809, Jeremy Bentham had devised a school that was a laboratory of "permanent examinability," which induced in the subject habits of calculation. Subsequent proponents of the examining school controlled by a Benthamite inspectorate also averred that the only method of inducing efficient teaching was through independent examination. Thus John Stuart Mill in *On Liberty* contended: "An age might be fixed at which every child might be examined, to ascertain if he (or she) is able to read. . . . Once in every year the examination should be renewed with a gradually extending range of subjects, so as to make the universal acquisition, and what is more retention, of a certain minimum of general knowledge virtually compulsory. Beyond that minimum there should be voluntary examinations on all subjects, at which all who came up to a certain standard of proficiency might claim a certificate" (Mill in Warnock 1970, 240).

In the current debate, however, the utilitarian view of the examination has been supplemented by a less threatening therapeutized mode of examination. In the guidelines produced for the GCSE between 1987 and 1988, examining boards like the MEG, NEA and LEAG emphasize the "positive" grading of assignments. The examination boards and their representatives assert that the new technique of examination "differentiates but does not discriminate."

This shift in examining strategy can only be read in terms of the culture of care and concern that the tutelary therapies have engendered. In this culture of narcissism, educational consumption demands the "user-friendly" examination. Yet at the same time as the new examination technology is nonthreatening, nonsexist, and antiracist, it remains nonetheless both diagnostic and scientific. It still measures. Thus we are informed by Peter Wilby in the *Independent* of 21 April 1988 that "it is Monday morning at Rainsford Comprehensive. . .and the top third-year maths class is sitting an examination. But the children start by moving tables and chairs so that they can sit close to their friends. . . . Clearly this is no ordinary examination and no ordinary maths curriculum either. It is part of the graded assessment in mathematics scheme (GAIM) (as opposed to GASP or GAMLL)." Underlying the new examinatory technology, Wilby shows, is the view that "classroom teaching and assessment should go hand in hand, children's achievement throughout schooling should be recorded." Consequently, Mathew Portal, head of graded assessment at the LEAG observed, "everybody knows the state of play, a child can say 'this is the progress I have made in this lesson or this week.' "

The new machinery of assessment, however, renders the student absolutely visible to the gaze of a permanently examining biopower. The new machinery Wilby contends will end the "terror of the one off examination." But in its stead we learn that henceforth "every lesson, every piece of homework—even children's casual comments. . .can count to achieving a new level."

The brave new world of positive examination, moreover, volatilizes conventional notions of success and failure. Wilby maintains that "a GCSE grade G no longer represents a failure to achieve a higher grade; it can represent the first step on a climb towards a grade A." Significantly, even the "attainments" of the slowest children are rewarded by a "statement of achievement." Unsurprisingly, Wilby embraces the fact that "examining is no longer a mysterious process," because "everything is new, in the open." Through seducing the student into the process of examination, therapy has finally achieved the Benthamite vision of a completely visible society realized through absolute examinability.

In the course of the *Independent*'s education editor's glowing assessment of implementing the new examining technology at Rainsford, only Andy Ruck the colorfully named head of CDT intimates a note of hesitation. Ruck argued that "staff have to be careful that they don't turn it (assessment) into a continual 'I'm writing a report on you thing. . .' you also have to be careful not to turn it into a race. . . .The children have to realize that the only competition is against themselves."

It is the way the technology seduces the student into a condition of continuous self-examination that invokes a society of permanent examination. It is this technology, moreover, that links the strategy outlined in the national curriculum of diagnostic testing to the strategy of skilling outlined in programs of vocational education like TVEI (Technical and Vocational Education Initiative) and CPVE (Certificate in Pre-Vocational Education). This discourse of vocationalism, designed for those beyond the grasp of mainstream examination, also depends for its implementation on the technology of the self contained in the confessional discourse of the record of achievement.

The new technology, therefore, is polyvalent and without limit. In the opinion of the Further Education Curriculum Review and Development Unit's report on *Profiles* (1982) there is a "continuum" between education and training. Schools, consequently, operate as "knowledge brokers" in an "inter-agency context." Critical to the creation of the student both as educational consumer and consumed is the profile or record of achievement that literally "opens up" students to themselves and to their "assessors." In *The Knowledge Revolution* (1981) Norman Evans contended that profiles were about "helping individuals to develop by recording in a supportive way the knowledge, skills and experience they individually pssess." Elsewhere, Derek Rowntree has referred to the "humanizing" function of the profile which (like the GCSE) "differentiates, but does not classify or rank in an order or preferability" (FEU 1985, 9). Indeed, Rowntree averred, "The thrust is from the nomethetic to the ideographic, dividing the students up from one another like the opening out of a fan" (10). An image that illustrates that "the recipient of the report is put into a new and more human relationship with the assessors." Such evocative imagery and the technique of "criterion based assessment" that it discloses invests the student with a positive and flexible self-image through a personal record (a life reduced to writing) that illustrates the student's achievement (10).

In evaluating a pilot CPVE project in Luton, the FEU assessed the manner in which the students internalized the mechanisms of self-assessment through the therapeutic technique of negotiating with the trainer/confessor and the writing of the self-report. A technology so mobile that it equally privileged the skill of answering a telephone call or the ability to wash and clothe oneself carefully (FEU 1985, 25).

In effect, the technology of recording achievement and criterion-based referencing through a mixture of therapy and self examination internalizes the Panopticon. The supplementing of the norm by a plethora of assessment techniques inscribes a flexible persona capable of infinite aceptability. Such a persona fits well with a society that simulates rather than creates and which consumes "lifestyle" rather than produces artifacts. A cool bureaucracy dispersing a gulag of non-threatening therapy induces a culture of narcissism (Lasch 1985, chap 6). A culture that through a process of scientific and tutelary monitoring achieves a therapeutically mediated condition of both "equality" and "excellence".

4

The application of discourse analysis to the contemporary education debate exposes features that demonstrate both continuity and dislocation. The promotion of schooling as a biopolitical strategy apparently founders upon the ambivalent figure of the schoolteacher.

It has been the intent of this paper to show how the discourse of the failure of the teacher that has emerged since 1976 has agitated and reversed a complex of relations that obtain on the school site and the manner in which these relations have been established and assessed. In order to extend more completely an examinatory technology, the figure of the teacher had to be interrogated and exposed. In *Discipline and Punish* Foucault argued that failure and success are inadequate criteria for measuring the social. Indeed, the failure of the teacher that emerged in the aftermath of the 1976 debate offered only the opportunity for new strategies of schooling and assessment.

The inexorable consequence of finding the teacher to be a fragile and dubious social figure permitted the development of a range therapeutic and examining techniques and new bureaucracies to monitor them. Thus seemingly quite discrete strategies for monitoring and assessing the success of urban education became clearly linked by the fact that they put the figure of the teacher under erasure and sought instead to mobilize strategies of assessment tied seductively to techniques of self-imagery that play across the school site.

The first moves in this direction were conducted under the sign of special educational need after 1981. This initial attempt to reverse or criticize teacher perception of the classroom space was perhaps least dramatic and most easily assimilated into the tutelary complex of the urban comprehensive. It nevertheless made possible in a number of urban LEAs a much more contentious disturbance of the image repertoire of schoolteachers and their relationship to their problematic social construction of race and gender.

The discovery of racist and sexist teachers produced the demand for more effective teacher control. This in turn provoked the formation of a series of monitoring units that demanded greater self-awareness on the part of teachers and the development of positive self-imagery on the part of students. At the same time, from an entirely different perspective the Department of Education demanded that teachers interrogate the material they teach and the way in which they facilitated the extension of the community of the examinable through new techniques of assessment. These techniques too placed the teacher in a therapeutic relationship with students who in turn reformed themselves through their positive self-imagery, coursework, and records of achievement.

Finally, we should observe that the discursive interventions so far considered can have tactical outcomes quite different from their strategic intentions. Thus the discourse on special needs does not necessarily integrate more effectively the child who possesses a statement of that need. The discourse of equal opportunity does not eradicate race and gender issues but perhaps exacerbates them. The search for new methods of assessment does not end the traditional examination, it radically extends the community of the examinable. These pedagogic strategies have in fact achieved a supplementation of the norm. Moreover, through biopolitical therapies new technologies of the self extend the machinery of surveillance and examination into the consciousness both of the teacher and the taught, or more accurately in terms of its own vocabulary, the trainer and the trained. A polyvalent technology that insists the subject speak its own failure, and confess its racism, genderism, oppression, disability, and unexaminability. In this therapeutic pleasure of confession a postmodern gulag disperses a micropenality through the mediating therapeutics of the tutelary complex.

Notes

1. The McGoldrick case concerned the dismissal of a Brent Head teacher for an alleged racist remark.

2. GCSE—Ceneral Certificate of Secondary Examination.

References

Barrow, J. et al. 1984 *The Two Kingdoms: Standards and Concerns Parents and Schools Independent Investigation into Brent Secondary Schools.* London: London Borough of Brent Education Committee.

Brent Education Committee. 1983 *Education for a Multicultural Democracy* London: London Borough of Brent Education Committee.

Brent Education Committee. 1988 *Brent Equal Opportunity Training.* London: London Borough of Brent Education Committee.

Baudrillard, J. 1983 *Simulations* New York: Semiotexte.

Baudrillard, J. 1988 *The Ecstasy of Communication* New York: Scmiotexte.

Booth, T. & Statham, J. ed. 1985 *The Nature of Special Education* Milton Keynes: Open University Press.

Brennan, W. 1982 *Changing Special Education* Brighton: Falmer Press.

Development Programme for Racial Equalaity (DPRE) 1988 *Why DPRE?* London: London Borough of Brent Education Committee.

Donzelot, J. 1979 *The Policing of Families* London: Hutchinson.

———. 1979 "The poverty of political culture" *Ideology & Consciousness* no. 5 London: I&C publications.

Eggleston, J. 1983 *Racism in Secondary Schools* Birmingham: Birmingham Education Committee.

Evans, N. (1981) *The Knowledge Revolution* London: Grant Macintyre.

Further Education Unit 1981 *Profiles* London: FEU.

Further Education Unit. 1985 *Project Report: Converting Working into Learning* London: FEU.

Foucault M. 1977 *Discipline and Punish* London: Peregrine.

————. 1978 *History of Sexuality* Vol 1. London: Peregrine.

————. 1979 "On governmentality" in *Ideology & Consciouness* no. 5. London: I&C publications.

————. 1981 "Questions of method" in *Ideology & Consciousness* no 8. London: I&C publications.

Fish, J. 1985 *Educational Opportunities for All ILEA* Consultation Document. London: Inner London Education Authority.

Hargreaves, D. 1984 *Improving Secondary Schools: Report of the Committee on the Curriculum and Organizing of Secondary Schools*London: Inner London Education Authority.

Lasch, C. 1985 *The Culture of Narcissism* New York: Abacus.

Lloyd-Smith, M. ed. 1984 *Disruptive Schooling: The Growth of the Special Unit.* London: John Murray.

Martin, L. ed. 1988. *Technologies of the Self* London: Tavistock Publications.

Mill, J.S. in Warnock, M. ed. 1970 *Utilitariansim.* London: Fontana.

Morris, M. in Frankovits, A. ed. 1984 *Seduced and Abandoned the Baudrillard Scene* Sidney (Glebe): Stone Moss Press.

Rabinow, P. ed. 1984 *The Foucault Reader* London: Peregrine.

Rampton, A. *West Indian Children in our schools* 1981. London: HMSO.

Swann, W. ed. 1981 *The Practice of Special Education.* Milton Keynes: Open University Press.

Swann, M. ed. 1985 *Education for all the Report of the Committee of Inquiry into the education of children from ethnic minority groups.* Cmd 9453. London: HMSO.

Warnock, M. 1978 *Special Educational Needs Report of the Committee of Inquiry into the education of handicapped children and young people.* Cmd 7212 London: HMSO.

Wills, J. *The 1981 Education Act: Policy and Provision for Special Educational Needs* Brighton: Falmer Press.

10

Pragmatic Binary Oppositions and Intersubjectivity in an Illegally Occupied School

Phil Carspecken

Abstract

This paper analyzes ethnographic data collected on a school that was illegally occupied and run by a militant working-class community. The study focuses on the pragmatic infrastructures through which communicative acts were constructed between the participants. The infrastructures display a structure of binary identity oppositions that were linked across settings in relations of homology. In addition, assumptions and beliefs the activists held about the nature of schooling and politics are reconstructed and found to display a structure of logical implication between terms. This reconstruction focuses on the way in which the pragmatic infrastructures that make communication possible implicate tacit "ideas" that may be articulated into a discourse resting on implicit assumptions that mediate pragmatic binary oppositions as their third terms. In this way, a "use" or "act" theory of meaning is related to existential identity claims accompanying social acts.

Semantic versus Pragmatic Models of Social Texts

Both structuralist and poststructuralist studies of society have drawn attention to the way in which the meanings of words, sentences, and concepts depend upon a system of relations between other words, sentences, or concepts. One of the most frequent structures discovered in this type of analysis is that of binary oppositions in homologous strings. Thus, within a particular culture, "right" may be opposed to "left" in a way that is homologous to an opposition between "vertical" and "horizontal," an opposition between "dark" and "light," and so on.

An understanding of any particular term in the structure presupposes an understanding not only of its binary opposite but also of the entire homologous string of oppositions (Levi-Strauss 1967; Maybury-Lewis and Almagor 1989).

Binary structures have been found to characterize syntactics (e.g., subject-predicate), semantics (e.g., actor-acted upon), and narrative form (hero-villain). However, so far there has been little exploration of binary oppositions in pragmatics. This paper explores the possibilities of a structuralist approach to pragmatics and uncovers two types of pragmatic structure at work in a school that was illegally occupied and run for a year by working-class parents in Liverpool, England. A primary structure of "identities" (which I shall argue are pragmatic rather than semantic phenomena) existing in binary oppositions and homologous strings is displayed in relation to a secondary structure of intersubjective terms linked through logical implication.

The importance of applying pragmatic models in contrast to semantic and/or narrative models to the study of social interaction cannot be exaggerated. Most structural studies of culture employ a semantic model by emphasizing language rather than language *use* or, better, language-mediated *interaction*. Because of the priority given to semantics, social action is at least implicitly conceived to occur in an external relation to semantic structures where people "read" available discourses and then act. Or, initially a more common move in the poststructuralist movement, social action becomes reduced to semantic relations, where people are seen to "manifest" discourses, or discourses are seen to "act through" people. Thus an overemphasis on semantic models undermines studies that want to emphasize human agency and volition in some way, and/or that want to establish a material base to social practice and relations of power (McLaren 1986, Giroux 1988).

The material base of social activity and the volition of the actor can be restored with an approach that takes as primary the pragmatic infrastructures through which all speech acts must take place. All *uses* of discourse take place within localized settings that are negotiated by actors through the employment of distinctive sets of intersubjective rules (Habermas 1981, McCarthy 1978). Such rules are often not themselves directly related to specific discourses—pragmatic rules not are semantic rules. Of course they may be *talked about* by both those who make use of them in interactions and by researchers who study them. And when this happens, particular discourses enter in and actually affect pragmatic rules. But the point is that such rules are distinct from, and are not reducible to, semantic structures, despite the interaction that exists between them.

Pragmatic models locate semantic and narrative analysis within larger cultural contexts implicated by language-mediated interactions. In fact, only pragmatic models are capable of capturing the full meaning of interactions. Austin (1962) presented one of the clearest formulations of this fact by noting that all speech carries meaning at least implicitly through a reference to the activity of the speaker. Locutionary acts implicate the meaning "I am now telling you that. . ." Illocutionary acts implicate the meaning "By speaking thus I . . ." And perlocutionary acts reference an effect created by the speech act that is extrinsic to the act itself (see Austin 1962, 94–107). Hence a reference to the actor, and therefore her social position and the norms and values that cluster about it, is present in all acts. Such references to the actor are pragmatic, rather than semantic, and there may or may not be cultural *names* in existence for the specifics of the actor-reference. References to the actor, moreover, will locate her simultaneously with respect to other possible actor-references carried intersubjectively within the culture under study. These, too, may or may not have specific cultural terms in local discourses. And even when they have been named in the local culture, the full meaning of such pragmatic references consists in *expectations of complex sets of behavior* that are never captured in a purely semantic model. Identity, in other words, is not primarily a function of semantics or discourses, in which people are *named*, but is rather a function of pragmatics, in which people claim their identities through complex displays of behavior.

Searle's work on the conditions necessary for a speech act to take place throws considerable more light on this issue. All speech acts require certain types of conditions. Searle (1969) divides them into three categories (see also Seung 1982, 87). Searle's category of "preparatory" conditions will be the focus of my analysis in this paper. As defined by Searle, these conditions involve cultural (intersubjective) under-standings of authority relationships, norms, and values. By borrowing from the symbolic-interactionist school of sociology, we may add to the picture by noting that Searle's preparatory rules are not simply present in any human interaction but rather must be *claimed* and often *refashioned* on the spot according to cultural conventions or norms. In other words, they are recursive conditions in that a prior intersubjective under-standing of preparatory conditions must exist before they come into play, but bringing them into play is simultaneously to reclaim and (often) to modify them. The way in which a speech act asserts pre-paratory conditions is a fundamental part of the meaning of the act that a semantic model can not capture. And an important feature of preparatory conditions is the identity that the actor claims to occupy.

By employing a pragmatic model to the analysis of culture, we also are in a position to restore a notion of subjectivity with its traditional connotations of agency and volition. Subjectivity, according to my analysis, is not a "positioned" phenomena—not a product of a certain discourse or social location. "Identity," rather, is the positioned phenomena, but it is positioned most fundamentally through pragmatic intersubjective structures rather than through semantic ones. Subjectivity is conceived here to be a form of ontological desire or *telos*—an existential need that motivates actors in their identity claims. Subjectivity is asserted through intersubjective media that makes forms of recognition from others possible. Subjectivity is a category implicit in *all* acts, but it is never exhausted in an act. It always is distinct from any particular identity claimed and usually is engaged in continuously modifying and reclaiming identities as social interaction proceeds.

The question explored in this paper, then, is whether or not preparatory conditions, including identities, display a structure. Is there such a thing as a pragmatic intersubjective structure? I shall argue that there is.

Method

I base my analysis on ethnographic data I collected in Liverpool, England. The ethnography will be described below. My approach is to reconstruct what may first appear to be semantic categories through which the subjects of my study took on various identities. Terms such as "ordinary", "adult," and "teacher," will be discussed semantically and be shown to exist in opposition to other terms ("nonordinary," "youth," "pupil") and to be homologously strung together. As the analysis continues, however, the reader will see that these terms are reconstructed *indicators* of complex pragmatic rule-sets that sometimes were related to the semantics of folk terms used in the discourse of those studied but were not reducible to discourse itself. The terms, rather, refer simultaneously to groups of "setting rules" (a subset I introduce to Searle's "preparatory" conditions) which actors *maintained* through consent to status differentiation. Both types of pragmatic rules are clarified in the discussion.

In addition, I shall argue that each pragmatic identity opposition implicated "third terms" that constitute the basis of the binary distinction. These third terms are something like *implicit thoughts* and in principle can become autonomous in order to support elaborated intersubjective structures of concepts and beliefs. In this study the intersubjective structure of concepts and beliefs drawn upon by the participants was one of logical implication rather than homology and binary opposition. The implicated third terms of pragmatic binary oppositions gave support to a *partially* semantic structure bearing a logical form. It was a partial semantic structure because only some of its key terms were named by the subjects under study. Implicit terms, linked to the pragmatic structures through which interactions took place, often were unformulated and escaped the notice of the actors unless verbal conflicts among them forced their articulation in the rationalization of contested behavior. Thus two types of intersubjective structure are uncovered, one working through homology (where pragmatic analogies across diverse setting categories are at play) and another working through logical implication (where both implicit and explicit semantic categories imply and presuppose each other).

The Ethnography

The ethnographic study upon which the following analysis is carried out was conducted between 1982 and 1984 on participants in an illegal school occupation.[1] The school, Croxteth Comprehensive, served a predominantly white working-class community in Liverpool. It was closed down by the city government in 1982 and was illegally occupied by Croxteth residents in protest. The residents formed a committee called the "Croxteth Community Action Committee" and ran their own educational program for an entire school year with the help of volunteer teachers. At the end of the year, the school was reinstated by a newly elected Labour Party majority in the Liverpool Council. The school continues to operate today.

I was involved personally in the occupation as a volunteer teacher and managed to collect extensive ethnographic material on all aspects of the occupation, the local culture, and the political campaign to win back the school. Because the process of social integration within the school was rife with conflict between local residents, teachers, and students, participants continuously had to articulate and defend many of their assumptions about the nature of schooling, the nature of politics, "proper" social relations, and other matters that came into dispute. My reconstructions are based on both detailed observations of social routines that formed in the school and the discursive accounts that the actors provided each other to defend their various activities and views.

In what follows, I first will describe a series of *pragmatic* binary oppositions used by Croxteth adults to establish settings of interaction. These oppositions revolved around setting-specific identities: identities claimed for particular kinds of interactions. The same people made use of diverse "identity oppositions," as I call them, in diverse settings, but these oppositions were homologously linked. As stated above, it will appear at first that my analysis is of semantic categories, primarily because words are used to describe them. But as the analysis proceeds, it will become clear that the names used for each identity category refer, along with their particular opposition, to interactive *settings* within which identities are claimed through complex behavior.

I then will analyze the third terms implicated in the pragmatic binary oppositions, which I call "axioms." These were unquestioned assumptions that provided the criteria on which the identity oppositions were constructed. Lastly, I will show how some of these axioms were related to "positions": articulated beliefs held by the actors to justify their activities and/or suggest and plan new activities. Positions on the nature of schooling, politics, "proper" authority relations, and so on were intersubjectively linked through rational implication.

The Ordinary-Nonordinary Opposition

When middle-class volunteer teachers arrived at Croxteth to help with the school occupation, they often were surprised and embarrassed by the amount of deference that local Croxteth residents gave them. Although the Croxteth Community Action Committee wished to hold firm control over the political campaign to win back their school, they wished to defer to the teachers when it came to all questions of running its educational programs.

The reason the Croxteth residents deferred to the volunteer teachers ultimately came down to a binary opposition referred to in their setting negotiations with teachers. This was an opposition represented in the discourse of the local residents. As George Knibb, a local resident highly involved in all aspects of the occupation, put it, "I can't say that the kids are doing the right work or the wrong work 'cause I've got no, I don't know, CSEs or O levels[2] meself, I'm just ordinary.... And I don't think there's anyone else in the school that can, on the Action Committee.... I don't think we have the authority to." In this statement George uses a term heard on many occasions in the speech of the local activists: "ordinary." This term was defined in Croxteth in contrast to its opposite, the "nonordinary." Nonordinary people were those who possessed one or more of a number of specific attributes. Particularly important in this set of attributes was educational qualifications, as George notes in his comment, but other attributes counted as well (e.g., a posh accent, a professional job).

The Teacher–Local Adult Opposition

A teacher–local adult distinction was constructed within the occupied school, which was merely a local variation of the ordinary-nonordinary binary opposition. Croxteth residents in the school excluded themselves from decision-making rights over educational matters involving the curriculum and basic academic purposes of education and simultaneously expressed several expectations toward those occupying the status of teacher. These expectations fell within two primary areas: curriculum and discipline. With respect to curriculum, deference was complete, frequently to the amazement of the teachers:

> I mean I can go into a French lesson, uh, something that is supposed to be a French class, and French is one subject I'm not really prepared to teach, . . . and as soon as I go into that lesson I'm announced as "Tony who is going to teach you French"—you know, the assumption is that I can teach French and anything else, that they can't and I can. You know they'd be quite happy, as long as the kids are being taught, they will assume that they're being taught well, to the kids benefit, when in fact it is very much a fill-in. (Tony Gannon, geography teacher)

However, in disciplining students Croxteth residents very soon lost confidence in the ability of the teaches and became critical of their methods. This lack of trust in the teachers' attitudes about discipline became an important feature of the occupation and is discussed below.

Oppositions and "Axioms": Reified Knowledge

Ways of acting out the ordinary person identity in Croxteth culture were simultaneously ways of expecting certain forms of behavior from nonordinary people. The relationship between the two identity complexes determines the behavioral rules associated with each particular identity. However, such a dependency relationship suggests a third term by which actors can determine whether or not a particular interaction is to be structured as an ordinary-nonordinary one. In this case a certain concept of school knowledge was used to fashion the difference between teacher and ordinary adult. I call this perspective of school knowledge "reified knowledge." It is the first example of a type of intersubjective element that I call "axioms."[3]

Croxteth residents constructed their interactions with teachers as interactions with the nonordinary because teachers had qualifications. Qualifications symbolized the possession of school knowledge that in turn was viewed implicitly as a fixed quantity that one either had or did not have.[4] Thus, knowledge (tacitly) was not seen as anything social or fluid, anything fallible toward which pupils or adults could make contributions or offer critiques. It was reified from its origins in social processes (Whitty 1985).

Hence the ordinary-nonordinary opposition, as well as the teacher-local adult opposition, implicated an assumption about knowledge. I call this assumption an "axiom" for two reasons: because of its deeply taken-for-granted nature and its role in supporting less taken-for-granted, more articulated, *beliefs* that I shall call positions. In principle, the reified knowledge axiom was separable from the binary opposition that implicated it and could be articulated and argued for on its own, though this never occurred during my field work in Croxteth.

Class Consciousness and the Social Wage

The ordinary-nonordinary opposition also was related to a form of class consciousness. Claims to being ordinary often were made with a note of pride. Being ordinary was being from the working class, and residents were definitely proud of their class membership. Thus "acting ordinary" was a way of affirming the self, of claiming dignity, and it implicitly affirmed a broader view of class relations.

Moreover, class membership was contrasted discursively with educational achievements. Phil Knibb, the brother of George and the chairman of the Croxteth Community Action Committee, indicated how his determination to remain "ordinary" during his youth ensured his early departure from schooling. Phil had had the opportunity to go to grammar school, but he chose not to go, "because at that time it was a stigma, where we lived in town, to go to college. Because we're from a basically working class area, to go to college, coming home (pause), you had to wear a uniform, to come home like that was bad. So there's no way that anyone wants to go to college." Thus the ordinary-nonordinary opposition linked together a form of class consciousness and pride with an attitude of deference toward teachers. Acting ordinary was accompanied with expectations of positive regard from others, but deference was a part of the style through which such expectations were to be met. The opposition supported contradictory attitudes on the part of the adults who expected their children to work at school and obey their teachers and yet who made claims to dignity by acknowledging their ordinary status and thus their own decisions to leave school early without getting qualifications.

Something of this contradiction was carried over into the perspective the Croxteth activists had of their political campaign to save the school. Though the local activists took over the school and had a group of teachers who had volunteered to serve their campaign as subordinates, they limited their political demands to the return of a school under state control. They had no thought, at the very start of the campaign, of demanding control over the logic of schooling practices—of insisting, for example, on alterations of curricular and/or pedagogic practices to better meet working-class needs.[5] Given their own negative experiences of schooling during their youth, such demands for control or influence over the qualitative features of schooling would appear to be reasonable or even expected by an outsider hearing of such a school takeover. But given the ordinary-nonordinary opposition, such demands did not even appear to be conceivable to the Action Committee during the first months of the occupation.

I call this campaign orientation, or political orientation, "the social wage." It is an example of a "position"—a partially articulated belief consciously held by the activists in full awareness of alternative beliefs. The social wage is a perspective on protest movements in which the purposes and logic of service institutions are assumed to be prerogatives of the superordinates in a hierarchical relationship. Just as trade unions generally organize over the issues of wages and working conditions rather than over having some say in the logic of production, the type of product produced, the most general purposes of the firm, so the social wage orientation in protest movements like the one in Croxteth are geared toward the bare fact of service provision and its quantity, rather than the quality and purposes of services themselves. It is a view of politics homologous to the relationship of trade unions to employers: roughly, workers are to employers as clients are to service administrators and professionals (see Offe 1984, Castells 1978).

Authority Binaries in the Home and Community

Practices constructed through the teacher–local adult distinction put schooling under the teachers' authority. This was especially true with curriculum. However, I already have said that Croxteth adults felt otherwise when it came to questions of disciplining pupils. Most of the volunteer teachers tried to establish order in their classrooms by winning the consent of their pupils to classroom goals. They introduced themselves by their first names to pupils and did not insist on being called "sir" or "miss." They dressed informally and allowed pupils to sit where they liked in the classroom. The style of authority they tried to establish was not a style that Croxteth pupils were used to, and disruptions in the classrooms consequently were frequent.

Croxteth adults correspondingly became very critical of the discipline practices of the volunteer teachers. Their criticisms were focused on the identities claimed by teachers in their interactions with pupils, leading them to state that these volunteers were not really "proper teachers." This conflict revealed a number of additional axioms and related binary oppositions.

"Should" Rules and "How To" Rules in the Community

First of all, adult-youth was another identity opposition in Croxteth, with a hierarchical nature that applied primarily to the domains of the home and community outside the school. This opposition carried rules of authority of a traditional nature, in the Weberian sense of "traditional." That is, one's identity as either adult or youth directly prescribed a normative authority relationship with the adult in the superordinate position. Authority was supposed to be based on status alone; status lines were assumed to be clearly established; and no debates over the grounds of such authority relations were ever conducted. The relationship was homologous to the parent-child relationship in Croxteth. A child should obey a parent because it simply is right to do so.

The identity binaries, adult-youth and parent-child, thus carried "should" rules related to normative axioms. In reconstructed form these axioms could be formulated as the prescription that youth and children should display respect toward (and ultimately obey) adults and parents simply by virtue of the status differences between them. Acceptance of the authority relation by youth was a norm that served as one criteria for judging what *kind* of youth one was (good or bad). "You should obey your (parent, adult, teacher)" was a normative claim rooted in identity oppositions through which pupils were expected to claim dignity.

There were also "how to" rules, or rules of interactive style, that formed a second kind of axiom in the structure. Youth and children were not believed automatically to possess respect for their opposed identities, but rather had to be socialized into displaying such respect. Youth and children were observed many times during my field work to challenge the authority rules, but such challenges worked within the assumptions of the binary oppositions rather than challenged their grounds. It was up to the adult or parent to make sure that youth and children learned and followed the status rules and thus established themselves as worthy of their claims to be an adequate adult or parent. Coercion and bantering were the required style. I often saw adults or parents disciplining their younger counterparts by threatening to "box their ears," "punch their noses," even "knock their heads off." If the threats and bantering were skillfully handled, youth and children gave their consent to the authority, and thus the claimed identity, of the adult.

A third and related axiom can be identified as well. This was the belief that children *need* to be disciplined by adults. Children will not conform automatically to the authority norms pertaining to their status, and it is up to the parent and adult to make sure that they do. If children are not disciplined, they may "turn out bad." This axiom was more complex than the other two in that it was not simply normative, but had an important objective-empirical component to it. Croxteth residents shared a consensus on what it meant for a child to turn out bad: it meant the child would be involved in vandalism, theft, drug usage, and other such behaviors. Thus the axiom made a claim that in principle was *testable*. It was a claim about "the" world rather than about "my" world (an identity claim) or "our" world (a normative claim). It was an implicit theory about the "universal" nature of young people and their maturation.

Homologies between Home and School

In the school, Croxteth residents had expectations of the teacher-pupil relations under formation that were homologous to adult-youth and parent-child relations on the Croxteth estate. In reconstructed form, teachers were to pupils in the school as parents were to children in the home as adults were to youth in the Croxteth community at large. This included the traditional basis of the authority of the teacher, an automatic ascription of authority to status that pupils should accept. Moreover, pupils once again were not expected to consent automatically to this authority relationship—it was up to the teacher to see that they did. Teachers were expected to bring it off through styles of interaction that were similar, though not identical to those used by adults on the estate. The threat of physical sanctions (the cane) and the insistence that the status of teacher be obeyed uncompromisingly were expected of the teaching staff. The "how to" rules were believed to be essentially the same for all three identity pairs.

A Position on the Purpose of Schooling

The homologous relations between the adult-youth and parent-child identities on the Croxteth estate and the teacher-pupil identities in the school supported a position on the nature of schooling. Croxteth residents, unlike the teachers, saw discipline as being more than an instrumental goal necessary only for the primary end of educating youth. They believed instead that discipline was a primary goal of education, an end in its own right. This is a position because it was held within the intersubjective realm of the Croxteth residents *alongside a set of arguments* that they quickly could articulate in its support. The arguments were put in terms of the bad effects that the failure to discipline pupils would have on their character. The full sense of this position was understood only through its connection to the more implicit axioms supporting it (beliefs about the nature and maturation of the child). The connection between a position and other intersubjective elements is one of logical implication rather than homology because the discursive defense of a position will draw up and articulate axioms and other positions that it rationally presupposes. A discursive justification of the belief that schooling exists partly for the discipline and control of youth logically presupposes views about the maturation and nature of the child.

Other Axioms and Positions

So far I have presented a number of binary oppositions, axioms, and two positions (the social wage and schooling for discipline and control) that were features of the intersubjective realm of Croxteth residents who had taken over their school. A few more axioms and positions need to be outlined before the full intersubjective structure may be described.

Schooling for Examinations and Employability

The reified knowledge axiom supported two beliefs, or positions, that had an important bearing on the nature of the school occupation. One was an unquestioning acceptance of the standard British secondary examinations (O levels and CSEs)—the belief that they are a legitimate measurement of successful schooling. The other was the belief that a major reason for going to school is to get jobs rather than to enrich the individual, develop critical awareness, empower students, or other goals commonly endorsed by progressivism or critical pedagogy. The unquestioning attitude held by Croxteth residents toward examinations was not surprising, given their consistent claims to be ordinary and all that implied. Yet it was contradictory, given their own educational histories in which rejection of such formal school goals had played a prominent part. Furthermore, few pupils in Croxteth passed examinations, because of their lack of the appropriate cultural capital. Insisting on examinations[6] during the occupation led to streamed classes with adverse effects for the large numbers of pupils in the nonexamination streams. It fixed the curriculum in a traditional form, and it produced very few passes at the year's end.

The belief that jobs were the primary *academic* purpose of schooling is a position I call "employability." It was implicated by both the reified-knowledge axiom and other features of the ordinary-nonordinary opposition. By first of all viewing school knowledge as something external, objectified, and possessable, local residents managed to distance their identities from educational knowledge—in fact, it kept their identities opposed to it by maintaining their claims to be ordinary people. The view that school knowledge is a sort of possessable object that is useful mainly for making oneself more employable was a way of ensuring that the grounds for one's personal identity and self worth were located outside a cultural sphere that seemed to be under the control of class and territorial others—the nonordinary.

Meanwhile, the belief that a primary goal of schooling is employability was rather ironic in the case of Croxteth, which at the time had one of the highest unemployment rates in Great Britain (roughly 40 percent over all, 90 percent for the sixteen to nineteen-year-old group, Croxteth Area Working Party 1983). It was, moreover, an argument that failed to win the consensus of the pupils to the regime of the school. Most pupils lived in households where long-term unemployment was a well-known phenomenon. One could argue that schooling for empowerment, for greater social awareness, would have been a much more appropriate goal than employability in this context. But it was a goal initially excluded from consideration on the local activists' side because of the cultural factors I have been discussing.

Intersubjective Structure

I have presented a number of intersubjective elements common to the culture of the Croxteth residents who occupied their school and have indicated three categories into which they fall: identity oppositions, axioms, and positions. In this section I will expand the discussion of the structure through which these intersubjective elements implicated each other.

In general terms, we can see that all of the intersubjective elements linked together in supportive or reinforcing ways? Thus the expectations that residents had of proper teacher behavior was homologously supported by their expectations of other superordinate identities routinely claimed in the home and community. Teacher authority was supported furthermore by the axiom of reified knowledge, which served to justify the superordinate position of teacher with respect to both pupil and parent, as well as to differentiate between the two statuses. Reified knowledge, in turn, was an underlying assumption in the belief that examinations are important and valid indicators of schooling success. Examinations played an important role in the ordinary-nonordinary identity opposition that in turn played a part in the social wage definition of the political campaign to save the school. Hence, what I have referred to as identities, axioms, and positions linked together into a supportive, intersubjective structure of reinforcing terms.

All of the intersubjective elements were related to pragmatic rules constituting the negotiated settings within which communicative interactions took place (interactions between local residents and teachers, for example). But some (the identity oppositions and their axioms) were directly implicated features of setting rules, and others (positions) were discursively elaborated "away" from pragmatic structures. With respect to the latter, positions presupposed the third terms in binary identity oppositions, though the connection was usually missed when participants debated points. Yet the vigor with which certain positions were defended in arguments between teachers and local residents is no doubt partially explicable by considering the threat that a challenge to a position posed to the routine structures through which residents maintained their identities and sense of dignity. A challenge to the social wage definition of the campaign, for example, implicitly challenged the ways in which Croxteth residents could be ordinary.

The actual ways in which conflicts between teachers and local residents in the occupied school buildings of Croxteth Comprehensive were resolved are discussed elsewhere (Carspecken 1991). Here I emphasize the formal point: *logical* linkages between intersubjective structures mutually implicated a *prerational* structure of pragmatic identity oppositions. Disputes between abstractly formulated positions on schooling and politics tacitly involved threats to deeper claims to identity that involved existential motivations (first, claims *to exist*, and second, claims to *dignity*).

Conclusions

Changes in Pragmatic Structure

Unfortunately, space constraints prevent me from fully excavating the Croxteth experience for all it can tell about pragmatic structures. The full story of Croxteth Comprehensive has much to contribute in this respect, but the full story cannot be told here. I will, however, mention a few more features of this story in brief to conclude the arguments developed in this paper.

The reader will not be surprised to learn, after reading the above sections, that education in the occupied school of Croxteth Comprehensive initially took on traditional, reproductive forms. This was due largely to the pragmatic infrastructures that ordered social routines in the building. Abstract debates about the way education *should* work were unproductive in Croxteth because of the deep structure of tacit identity oppositions that have been described above.

However, by the end of the school year the unusual experience of working within a school began to bear fruit for Croxteth residents, which should be of interest to professional educators and sociologists of education. Routine social interactions gradually shifted over time, with profound implications for the intersubjective structures I have been discussing. Croxteth activists gradually became aware that their normal ways of claiming the ordinary identity did not fit their new roles within the school, nor their perceptions of classroom practice. The roles were new simply because these activists never before had worked within a school. But the initial way in which the local residents took on new roles was carefully done, in ways that reaffirmed their usual modes of claiming identity—the ordinary identity especially. Yet over time these new roles solidified into altered ways of claiming identities, and the whole pragmatic structure was tacitly shifted. By the end of the year, some of the subtle shifts that had taken place on the pragmatic level came into the activists' discursive awareness and supported a new and growing interest in alternative forms of education. This required the perception and critical articulation of several of the axioms discussed above: reified knowledge, the nature of the child, and others.

Though the nature of these changes and the ways in which they took place are too complex to present here, their implications for the theoretical position developed in this paper can be stated briefly. Changes in *routine interactions* preceded changes in the discourses used to discuss interactions. It was only when certain features of the way of life led by the Croxteth activists altered and solidified into new forms that a critical discourse of schooling could begin. It was change in the possibilities for being a person, in the grounds by which one could claim dignity and existence, that made it possible to examine critically some of the axioms, and the views on politics and schooling they supported. Pragmatics therefore emerges once again as more fundamental than semantics.

Summary

To summarize, structural analyses of culture, and the relation of culture to social practice, can proceed through the consideration of pragmatics as well as semantics. The pragmatic infrastructures through which communicative acts take place display structural properties—in this case a structure of binary oppositions and homologous strings. The structural study of pragmatics perhaps can begin best with a consideration of the identity structures used by actors to define interactive settings and claim public selves. Implicit in pragmatic identity structures are complex rule sets that shape interaction in diverse ways. *Identities are not claimed semantically, by naming the self, but interactively, by displaying intricate patterns of behavior.* Finally, alterations in life routines carry along transformations of the pragmatic infrastructures through which people interact. Such shifts in pragmatic structures may form the basis for articulating new views of life.

Notes

1. I have published a book that provides an historical account and an analysis of this school takeover (Carspecken 1991). The analysis in this paper, however, is new.

2. "O" levels and "CSEs" were British examinations offered to all secondary pupils. Most of the activists from Croxteth has chosen not to attempt these examinations.

3. The presence of the third term in a pragmatic opposition is a link between pragmatics and semantics. It is a prerequisite of the semantic requirements for talking about interactions and giving names to two identities in binary opposition. However, many identity oppositions, constructed in practice, are *not* represented in discourse, and their third terms remain wholly implicit and tacit. Where the respective identities are represented in discourse, the third term itself may or may not be represented discursively, as was the case here.

4. Reified knowledge was an important theme for *both* local activists and teachers; see Carspecken, 1991.

5. A fascinating feature of the campaign, however, was that such attitudes changed by the end of the school year.

6. Teachers also insisted on examinations for their own reasons. A significant minority of them, however, regretted what they considered to be the necessity of offering examinations, and in private interviews these teachers called examinations "instruments of class control." Local residents, by contrast, did not even question examinations during the early period of the occupation. Experiences within the school, however, altered the views of many by the end of the occupation.

7. This was not the case with teachers, however. The intersubjective elements within the teachers' culture clustered into conflicting, nonreinforcing, groups. See Carspecken 1991.

References

Austin, J. L. 1962. *How to Do Things with Words*. Cambridge: Harvard University Press.

Carspecken, P. 1991. *Community Education and the Nature of Power, the Battle for Croxteth Comprehensive*. London: Routledge.

Castells, M. 1978. *City, Class and Power*. London: Macmillan.

Croxteth Area Working Party. 1983. *Croxteth Areas* (Report of the party appointed to consider the needs of the area). Liverpool: City Council.

Giroux, H. 1988. "Postmodernism and the Discourse of Educational Criticism." *Journal of Education* 170, no. 3:5–30.

Habermas, J. 1981. *The Theory of Communicative Action. Vol. 1, Reason and the Rationalization of Society*. Boston: Beacon.

Levi-Strauss, C. 1967. *Structural Anthropology*, trans. C. Jacobson and B. G. Schoef. Garden City, N.Y.: Anchor.

Maybury-Lewis, D. and U. Almagor, eds. 1989. *The Attraction of Opposites, Thought and Society in the Dualistic Mode*. Ann Arbor: University of Michigan Press.

McCarthy, T. 1978. *The Critical Theory of Jürgen Habermas*. Boston: MIT Press.

McLaren, P. 1986. Review of *Postmodernity and the Death of Politics: A Brazilian Reprieve*. *Educational Theory* 36, no. 4:389–401.

Offe, C. 1984. "Legitimacy versus Efficiency." Pp. 130–46 in *Contradictions of the Welfare State*, ed. J. Keane. London: Hutchinson.

Searle, J. 1969. *Speech Acts: An Essay in the Philosophy of Language.* Cambridge: Cambridge University Press.

Seung, T. K. 1982. *Semiotics and Thematics in Hermeneutics.* New York: Columbia University Press.

Whitty, G. 1985. *Sociology and School Knowledge: Curricular Theory, Research, and Politics.* London: Metheun.

11

Constructing the "Other": Discursive Renditions of White Working-Class Males in High School

Lois Weis

A key development in postmodern/poststructuralist and feminist research has been the introduction of issues of silencing and voice into research on schools and schooling (McLaren 1991; Giroux 1991; Lather 1991). We no longer speak of reproduction in terms of relations that sustain and/or challenge the economy, but rather have expanded and challenged these considerations to include issues of voice, power, and privilege, drawing upon the well-known work of Michel Foucault (1990) and others. We speak now of "regimes of truth"—of what is known, not known, practiced and not practiced, because of the very language we employ. Our work has changed greatly since the mid 1970s and is alive with lengthy criticism. For we really do seek to understand both the discourse and practice of those whom we study, as well as our own discourse and practice. The essay by Peter McLaren in this book is a powerful testimony to this. For, I agree, we must keep the focus on ourselves as we ravel and unravel the lives and practices of others.

Excellent work has been done on the dynamics of power and privilege that nurture, sustain and legitimate silencing in schools (Sapon-Shevin 1993; Michelson, Smith, and Oliver 1993). But as we look closely at this work, we cannot help but notice that the move to silence is an ironic and often ineffective move of power. For within the very centers of structured silence can be heard the most critical and powerful, if excluded, voices of teachers and students in public education. Our move to understand both these practices of silence and how such practices and policies are reworked by real people as they move through educational insitutions and our lives must be central to a vital research agenda. All the while, of course, we must continually interrogate ourselves, as authors in this volume and elsewhere do so well (McLaren 1991, Hooks 1990).

Michelle Fine and I (1993) have recently argued that it is important to acknowledge not only policies and practices that silence, but also those that listen closely to the words, dreams, fantasies, and critiques of those who have dwelt historically at the margins. We must listen closely to the "discursive underground"—to the "political critics" who have little access to the centers of power and privilege. These discursive undergrounds flourish at the margins of our schools. We must reach up from the depths of our own academic language and hear their voices, encourage their centering, if we are sincere about our commitment to a democratic public sphere.

When we listen, we learn many things, not all of which we may find appealing. I want, at this point, to invite you into the text that I created from my work in a steel town, a town hard hit by de-industrialization and a restructured U.S. economy. Here I wish to focus on how young white working-class males created "other" at the site of the school. For they did construct the "other" in some very powerful ways, ways that encouraged their own dominance in racial and gendered terms. This setting up as dominant gave most of them per-mission to roam through vast cultural space and essentially "do nothing." For the young white men simply hung out—they, unlike the young women, had few goals, little direction, virtually no sense of possibility.Their energy went largely into construcing the "other"—the black male and female, the white female. In constructing the "other" they were able to distance themselves from this "other," asserting themselves as superior, as fundamentally unlike that which they constructed as abhorrent and/or in need of protection. I do not mean to imply here that these discourses and practices were created without reference to the world outside the peer group. Obviously this is not the case and these young men drew upon historical and current discourses and practices about ethnic minorities and women in general. How these discourses and practices became their own, in a sense, is important, however, and I contend that the process of "othering" is an active one. At this point I invite you into the text.

Freeway

The data presented here were gathered as part of a large ethnographic study of Freeway High School. I spent the academic year 1985–86 in the high school, acing as a participant-observer for three days a week for the entire year. Data were gathered in classrooms, study halls, the cafeteria, extracurricular activities, and through in-depth interviews with over sixty juniors, virtually all teachers of juniors, the vice principals, social workers, guidance counselors, and others. Data collection centered on the junior class since this is a key point of decision when PSATs, SATs, and so forth must be considered.[1] In addition, this is, in the state where Freeway is located, the time when the bulk of a series of state tests must be taken if entrance to a four-year college is being considered.[2]

Freeway embodies trends in the U.S. economy. Occupational data for the Standard Metropolitan Statistical Area for 1960–1980 (the latest year for which data are available) suggest that the most striking decreases in the area are found in the categories of "Precision, Craft, and Repair" and "Operators, Fabricators, and Laborers." These two categories constitute virtually all the so-called blue-collar jobs. When combined, data suggest a relative decline of 22.3 percent in the blue-collar category from 1960 to 1980. A look at some of the more detailed subcategories reveals a more striking decline. Manufacturers, for example, have experienced an overall decline in the area of 35 percent between 1958 and 1982.

Data also suggest an increase in the "Technical, Sales and Administrative Support" category. These occupations constituted 22.8 percent of the total in 1960 as compared with close to 31 percent in 1980, representing an increase of over one-third. Increases in "Service" and "Managerial and Professional Specialty" categories also reflect a shift away from industry and toward the availability of service occupations.

The change in the distribution of occupations by gender needs to be clarified here as well. During this same time period, female employment increased 55 percent, while employment for men decreased 6 percent. For most occupations in the area, a net increase in employment during this period may be attributed mainly to the increase in employed women and a net decrease to a decrease in employed men.

Although the emerging economy has absorbed women at a faster rate than men, the proportion of full-time female workers is still lower than that of full time male workers. Thus, 67 percent of male workers are full time in 1980 as compared with only 43 percent of females. In addition, full-time female workers earned 56 percent of what full-time male workers earned in 1980, and women in sales have average incomes that are only 46 percent of the average income for men. This is particularly important given that a growing number of positions in the Standard Metropolitan Statistical Area are in Sales, and that these are filled disproportionately by women. Such trends are reflective of trends nationwide. A restructured economy has meant that a higher proportion of females is employed in the labor force relative to earlier years, but that females increasingly earn relatively lower wages than males.

In the Freeway area, de-industrialization is exceptionally visible due to the closing of Freeway Steel. The plant payroll in 1960 was at a record high of 168 million, topping 1968 by 14 million. The daily employment was 18,500.

In the first seven months of 1971, layoffs at the plant numbered 4,000, and decline continued into the 1980s. From 18,500 jobs in 1979, there were only 3700 production and 600 supervisory workers left in 1983. At the end of 1983, the plant closed.

The larger ethnography was aimed at unraveling the construction of identities of young white males and females in high school, given the radically restructured economy. What became evident, however, was that these identities, particularly in the case of the young white men, were *absolutely contingent* upon the co-construction of black men and black women, and white women. These co-constructions became a means of asserting themselves—a means of forming their own identities in crucial and concrete ways. Their own heterosexuality, masculinity, and whiteness became their assertions in the face of what they had constructed as "other." These discursive constructions were elaborately braided. What I will present here is the story of that "othering."

Freeway Males

One of the most notable aspects of identity among white working-class males is that of sexism. Paul Willis (1977), for example, argues that male white working-class youth identities are formed at least partially in reaction to that of the ideologically constructed identity of females. Mental labor, for example, is not only less valued than manual labor, but it is less valued because it is seen as feminine. This encourages separate spheres for men and women as well as male dominance. The lads also impose upon girlfriends an ideology of domesticity, "the patterns of homely and subcultural capacity and incapacity," all of which stress the restricted role of women (49).

In terms of the affirmation of male supremacy, Freeway males exhibit the same virulent sexism uncovered in previous studies. This is particularly striking in the Freeway case since young women are weaving an identity which in many ways contradicts that which is woven *for* them by young men (Weis 1990). Although one or two boys seem to exist outside these boundaries, basically white working-class males affirm a rather virulent form of assumed male superiority, which involves the constructed identity of female not only as "other" but also as distinctly "less than" and, therefore, subject to male control. Discussions with males indicate that the vast majority speak of future wives and families in strikingly male-dominant terms. This is in sharp contradiction with the sentiments of young women.

LW: You say you want more kids than your parents have. How many kids do you want?

Bob: Five.

LW: Who's going to take care of these kids?

Bob: My wife, hopefully. Unless she's working too. . . . If she wants to work, we'd figure something out. Day care center, something like that. I'd prefer if she didn't want to. I'd like to have her at home.

LW: Why?

Bob: I think it's up to the mother to do it [raise children; take care of the home]. I wouldn't want to have a baby-sitter raising my kids. Like, I think the principles should be taught by the parent, not by some baby-sitter.

● ● ●

LW: How about your life ten years froirm now; what do you think you'll be doing?

Rob: Probably be married. Couple of kids.

LW: Do you think your wife will work?

Rob: Hopefully she won't have to 'cause I'll make enough money.

LW: Would you rather she didn't work?

Rob: Naw [Yes, I'd rather she didn't work].

LW: Women shouldn't work?

Rob: Housework.

● ● ●

Jim: Yes, I'd like to get married, like to get myself a nice house, with kids.

LW: Who is going to be taking care of those kids?

Jim: Depends how rich I am. If I'm making a good salary I assume that the wife, if she wanted to, would stay home and tend to the kids. If there was ever a chance when she wanted to go someplace, fine, I'd watch the kids. Nothing wrong with that. Equal responsibility because when you were consummating the marriage it was equal responsibility.

LW: So, you're willing to assume it?

Jim: Up to a certain point.... Like if she says I'm going to go out
         and get a job and you take care of the kids, "You draw all
         day" [he wants to be a commercial artist]. "So, I draw; that's
         what's been supporting us for so many years." I mean, if she
         starts dictating to me...there has to a good discussion about
         the responsibilities.

         When both parents work, it's been proven that the
         amount of education they learn, it goes down the tubes, or
         they get involved in drugs. Half the kids who have drug
         problems, both of their parents work. If they are doing terribly
         in school, their parents work.

                              • • •

LW: When you get married, what will your wife be doing?

Lanny: Well, before we had any kids, she'd be working, but if we had
         kids, she wouldn't work, she'd be staying home, taking care
         of the kids.

                              • • •

Seth: I wouldn't mind my wife working as far as secretarial work
         or something like that. Whatever she wanted to do and she
         pursued as a career. If there was children around, I'd like her
         to be at home, so I'd like my job to compensate for just me
         working and my wife being at home.

                              • • •

LW: Do you think your wife would want to work?

Sam: I wouldn't want her to work.

                              • • •

LW: Let's say you did get married and have children, and your
         wife wanted to work.

Bill: It all depends on if I had a good job. If the financial situation
         is bad and she had to go to work, she had to go to work.

LW: And if you got a good job?

Bill: She'd probably be a regular woman.

LW: Staying at home? Why is that a good thing?

Bill: I don't know if it's a good thing, but it'd probably be the
         normal thing.

It is striking in the above that these young men have constructed women as caretakers and themselves as the sole providers. It is particularly key that these young men expect their wives to be home taking care of the children once children are born. In fact, one of the boys brings to bear what he sees as scientific evidence to argue that "It's been proven. . . half the kids who have drug problems, both of their parents work; if they are doing terribly in school, their parents work." They wish to see their own income sufficient to assume sole support of the family. This dominance in the work place and in the family is set up in relation to women. They have constructed women in a panicular light, despite home lives which contradict this and, to some extent at least, competing discursive messages in the wider society about women in the work force.

Only a handful of boys constructed a future other than that above. Significantly, only one boy constructed a future in which his wife *should* work, although he does not talk about children. A few boys reflect the sentiment that marriage is a "ball and chain," and one boy said the high divorce rate makes marriage less than attractive.

LW: What kind of person do you want to marry?
Vern: Someone who is fairly good-looking, but not too good-looking so she'd be out, with other people screwing her up. Someone who don't mind what I'm doing, let me go out with the guys. I won't mind if she goes out with the girls either. I want her to have a job so she ain't home all the time. 'Cause a woman goes bonkers if she's at home all day. Give her a job and let her get our of the house.
          . . . People tended to get married as soon as they got out of school, not as soon as, but a couple of years after. I think people nowadays don't want to get married until twenty, thirty.
LW: And that's because of what?
Vern: They've seen too many divorces.

It is noteworthy that Vern is the only boy to discuss divorce as an impediment to marriage. Almost every girl interviewed discusses divorce, and it is a topic of conversation among young women. Despite Vern's relatively more open-minded attitude toward females, it is significant that he still envisions himself "allowing" his wife to work, and sees his role as one of controlling her time and space. He does not, for example, want her to be "too good-looking" because then she would be out, with "other people screwing her up." He also notes that he "does not mind" her going "out with the girls," and that he wants "her to have a job so she ain't home all the time."

The boy below expresses the sentiment that marriage is "ball and chain", and that he, therefore, wants no part of it. Only a couple of the boys expressed a similar sentiment or elaborated the theme of "freedom" associated with being single. Again, this is unlike the girls.

Tom:	I don't want to get married; I don't want to have children. I want to be pretty much free. If I settle down with someone, it won't be through marriage.
LW:	Why not?
Tom:	Marriage is a ball and chain. Then marital problems come up, financial problems, whatever. I don't really want to get involved in them intense kind of problems between you and a spouse. . . .To me it's a joke.
LW:	Tell me why you think that.
Tom:	Well, I see a lot of people. I look at my father and mother. They don't get along, really.

The vast majority of boys at Freeway High intend to set up homes in which they exert control over their wives—in which they go out to labor in the public sphere and their wives stay at home. Only a few question the institution of marriage, and only one begins to question a fundamental premise of patriarchy—that women's place is in the home and men's place is in the public sphere. As noted above, however, even this one boy sees himself largely controlling the actions of his wife. Central to the boys' identity, then, is the establishment of male dominance in the home/family sphere as well as in the paid labor force. It must be understood that the construction of a male dominant identity is absolutely dependent upon the construction of women as unable to take care of themselves monetarily and as having full responsibility for the day-to-day activities of children. Young white men strip, in a sense, the female subject. As Vern notes, he wishes to marry someone "who is fairly good looking, but not too good looking so she'd be out *with other people screwing her up*" (my emphasis).

As young men weave their own form of material cultural superiority vis-i-vis women, they are encouraged by a larger society and societal institutions, such as schools, which concur. In this working-class school, there is simply no sustained challenge to the vision of male dominance woven by male youth. Although young white working-class women challenge this vision in their own privatized fantasies about their future lives, they neither challenge the men publicly nor under-stand that they will have to focus their energies collectively if their private challenges to the social order have any chance of succeeding. In many cases the school actively aides in the construction of male dominance (Weis 1990).

Racism and the Construction of the "Other"

Freeway is a divided town, and a small number of Arabs and Hispanics live among blacks largely on one side of the "tracks," and whites on the other, although there are whites living in one section of Freeway just adjacent to the steel mill, which is in the area populated by people of color. Virtually no people of color live in the white area, unlike large American cities where there are pockets of considerable mix. Most African-Americans came from the south during and after World War II, drawn by the lure of jobs in the steel plant. Having been relegated to the dirtiest and lowest-paid jobs, most are now living in large public housing projects, never having been able to amass the necessary capital to live elsewhere. Although I have no evidence of this, I also assume that even had they been able to amass capital, mortgages would have been turned down if blacks had wished to move into the white area. Also, there is no doubt informal agreements among those who rent not to rent to blacks in the white areas. Today most project residents receive welfare and have done so for a number of years.

It is most striking that people of color are used as a foil against which acceptable moral, and particularly sexual, standards are woven among young white men. This weaves in and out of a protectionist stance taken vis-à-vis white women. The goodness of white is always contrasted with the badness of black—blacks are involved with drugs; blacks are unacceptable sexually; black men attempt to "invade" white sexual space by talking with white women; black women are simply filthy. The boundaries of acceptable behavior are drawn, for white men, at what becomes defined as black. Although there are numerous black athletes at Freeway High, I never heard discussion of this among young white men. Academics is not highly valued at this school, so good black students would not be noted either. There is a virtual denial of anything at all good being identified with blackness. While masculinity, then, is constructed *by* white men, both in relation to black men and black women, and white women. How these groups intersect in this con-struction will be explored below. Once again, as with white women, discursive messages in the larger society as well as those filtered through the insitution itself have a hand in shaping these constructions. They are not woven solely through the thinness of peer interactions, disconnected from historically rooted societal constructions. On the contrary, although it is not my intention to explore this issue here. Much of the expressed racism in this class fraction centers around "access" to women, thus serving the dual purpose of constructing blacks *and* white women:

Jim: The minorities are really bad into drugs. You're talking everything. Anything you want, you get from them. A prime example, the _____ ward of Freeway; about twenty years ago the _____ ward was predominanly white, my grandfather used to live there. Then Italians, Polish, the Irish people, everything was fine. The houses were maintained; there was a good standard of living....

  ...The blacks brought drugs. I'm not saying white people didn't have drugs; they had drugs, but to a certain extent. But drugs were like a social thing. But now you go down to the ward; it's amazing, it's a ghetto. Some of the houses are okay. They try to keep them up. Most of the homes are really, really terrible. They throw garbage on the front lawn; it's sickening. You talk to people from [surrounding suburbs]. Anywhere you talk to people, they tend to think the majority of our school is black. They think you hang with black people, listen to black music.

  ...A few of them [blacks] are starting to go into the _____ ward now [the white side], so they're moving around. My parents will be around there when that happens, but I'd like to be out of there.

                                   • • •

LW: There's no fighting and stuff here [school], is there?
Clint: Yeah, a lot between blacks and whites.
LW: Who starts them?
Clint: Blacks.
LW: Do blacks and whites hang out in the same place?
Clint: Some do; [the blacks] live on the other side of town.

  ...A lot of it [fights] starts with blacks messing with white girls. That's how a lot of them start. Even if they [white guys] don't the white girl, they don't like to see...
LW: How do you feel about that yourself?
Clint: I don't like it. If I catch them [blacks] near my sister, they'll get it. I don't like to see it like that. Most of them [my friends] see it that way [the same way he does].

LW: Do you think the girls encourage the attentions of these black guys?

Clint: Naw. I think the blacks just make themselves at home. They welcome themselves in.

LW: How about the other way around? White guys and black girls?

Clint: There's a few that do. There's people that I know of, but no one I hang around with. I don't know many white kids that date black girls.

• • •

Bill: Like my brother, he's in ninth grade. He's in trouble all the time. Last year he got jumped in school....About his girlfriend. He don't like blacks. They come up to her and go, "Nice ass," and all that shit. My brother don't like that when they call her "nice ass" and stuff like that. He got suspended for saying "fucking nigger"; but it's all right for a black guy to go up to whites and say stuff like that ["nice ass"].

          ...Sometime the principals aren't doing their job. Like when my brother told [the assistant principal] that something is going to happen, Mr. _____ just said, "Leave it alone, just turn your head."

          ...Like they [administrators] don't know when fights start in this school. Like there's this one guy's little sister, a nigger [correction]—a black guy grabbed her ass. He hit him a couple of times. Did the principal know about it? No!

LW: What if a white guy did that [grabbed the girl's ass]?

Bill: He'd probably have punched him. But a lot of it's 'cause they're black.

It is important to note in the above the ways in which several discursive separations are occurring. To begin with, once again, white men are construcing women as people who need the protection of men. The young men are willing to fight for their young wormen so that if anyone says "nice ass," it is legitimate to start a fight. Black men, in turn, are being constructed as overly sexualized. They "welcome themselves in"; they behave in ways that are inappropriate vis-à-vis white women. It is very important here that the complaint is about intruding onto white property. It is not only that women are being defended from the inappropriate advances of oversexualized blacks. Rather it is the fact that *black men are invading the property of white men that is at issue here.* Furthermore, the discursive construction of black men as oversexualized enables white men to elaborate their own appropriate heterosexuality. By engaging in this discursive construction of black men, they are asserting their *own* heterosexism and what they see as appropriate homophobia, since only heterosexual men presumably would be threatened by this form of intrusion. Thus at a time of heightened concern with homosexuality (by virtue of their age and the collective nature of their lives), these boys can assert virulently and publicly their concern with black men, thus expressing their own appropriate sexuality as well as their ability to "take care of their women." There is a grotesqueness about this particular set of interactions, a grotesqueness that enables white men to continue to define themselves as pure and straight, while defining black men as dirty and oversexualized, almost animal-like. The white female can then be, once again, put on a pedestal (read, stripped of her subject), although their own behavior certainly contradicts this place for white women. It is most interesting that not one white female ever constructed young black men as a "problem" in this regard. This is not to say that white females are not racist, but this discursive rendering of blacks is quite noticeably under the cultural terrain of white men, at least at this age. If one accepts that these men are constructing themselves as providers and protectors of white women, then it is arguably the case that they are also constructing for women the discursive rendering of blacks described here. The young women, in turn, have no particular discursive rendering of blacks at all.

Observational data support the notion of racism among white youth. This is mainly directed toward blacks, although, as the excerpts below indicate, racism surfaces with respect to Arabs as well. There is a small population of Yemenites who emigrated to Freeway to work in the steel mills, and this group is targeted to some extent also.

Social Studies, Social Studies, 26, November 1986*

Sam:	Hey, Abdul, did you come from Arabia?
Abdul:	Yeah.
Sam:	How did you get here?
Abdul:	I walked.
Sam:	No, seriously, how'd you get here?
Abdul:	Boat.
Sam:	Where'd you come from?
Abdul:	Saudi Arabia.

Sam: We don't want you. Why don't you go back.
[no comment]

• • •

Social Studies, 11, December 1986*

Ed: Do you party, Nabil?
Nabil: Yeah.
Paul: Nabil, the only thing you know how to play is polo on camels.
[Nabil ignores]

• • •

English, 2, October*

LW: [To Terry, who was hit by a car two days ago]. How are you?
Terry: Look at me [*sic*] face. Ain't it cool? [He was all scraped up.]
LW: What happened?
Terry: Some stupid camel jockey ran me over in a big white car. Arabian dude.

Most of the virulent racism is directed toward blacks, however. The word "nigger" flows freely from the lips of white males, and they treat black females far worse than they say black males treat white females.

At the lunch table, 21, February 1986*

[discussion with Craig Centrie, research assistant]

Pete: Why is it [your leather bag] so big?
Mike: So he can carry lots of stuff.
CC: Yes, I bought it because my passport would fit in it.
Pete: Passport! Wow—where are you from?
CC: Well, I'm American now, but you need one to travel.
Pete: Can I see? [He pulls out his passport. everyone looks].
Mike: This is my first time to ever see one. What are all these stamps?
CC: Those are admissions stamps so [you] can get in and out of countries.
Mike: Look, Pete, N-I-G-E-R-I-A. [pronounced Niggeria]. Yolanda [a black female] should go there. [everyone laughs]
Pete: [Did you see any] crocodile-eating niggers? [laughter]

• • •

In the Lunchroom, 21, January 1986*

Students [all white males at the table] joke about cafeteria food. They
then begin to talk about Martin Luther King Day.

Dave: "I have a wet dream—about little white boys and little black
          girls." [laughter]

• • •

In the lunchroom, 7, March 1986*

Once again, in lunch, everyone complains about the food. Vern asked
about a party he heard about. Everyone knew about it, but it wasn't
clear where it would be. A kid walked past the table [of white boys].

Clint: "That's the motherfucker. I'll whoop his ass." The entire table
          goes "ou' ou' ou'."

CC: "What happened with those tickets, Pete?" [Some dance
          tickets had been stolen.]

Pete: "Nothing, but I'm pissed off at that nigger that blamed me."

Pete forgot how loud he was speaking and looked toward Yolanda [a
black female] to see if she reacted. But she hadn't heard the remark.

• • •

At the lunch table, 12, February 1986*

Mike: That nigger makes me sick.
Pete: Who?
Mike: You know, Yolanda.
Pete: She's just right for you, man.
Mike: Not me, maybe Clint.

• • •

At the lunch table, 12, February 1986*

About two minutes later, Darcy [a black female] calls me [CC] over.
"What's your name?"

CC: Craig, what's yours?
Darcy: It's Darcy. Clint told me a lie. He said your name was Joe.
          Why don't you come to a party at Yolanda's house tonight?"
Yolanda: "Why don't you just tell him you want him to come."
          [everyone laughs].

Clint: Well, *all right*, they want you!
Pete: What do you think of Yolanda?
CC: She's a nice girl. What do you think?
Pete: She's a stuck up nigger. Be sure to write that down.

• • •

[A group of males talk about themselves.] "We like to party all the time
and get high!" [They call themselves "freaks" and "heads."] [about
blacks] "They are a group unto themselves. They are all bullshitters."

• • •

At the lunch table, 12, February 1986*

Much of the time, students discussed the food. Vern talked about the
Valentine's Day dance and began discussing getting stoned before the
dance.

CC: "Do you guys drink at the dance, too?"
Pete: "No, I don't know what they would do to us [everyone
            laughs]. There probably wouldn't be any more dances."
Yolanda and friends walk in. Yolanda and a friend were wearing exactly
the same outfit.
Clint: "What are you two—the fucking Gold Dust Twins?"
Yolanda: "Shut the fuck up, 'boy' " [everyone laughs]."
            Quietly, Pete says, "Craig, they are nasty."
CC: "What do you mean?"
Pete: "You don't understand black people. They're yeach. They
            smell funny and they [got] hair under their arms."
Clint, Pete, Mike and Jack all make noises to denote disgust.

The males spend a great deal of time exhibiting disgust for racial
minorities, and at the same time, asserting a protective stance over white
females vis-à-vis black males. They differentiate themselves from black
males and females in different ways, however. Black males are treated
with anger for invading *their* property (white girls). Black females, on
the other hand, are treated with simple disgust. Both are seen and
interacted with largely in the sexual realm, however, albeit for different
reasons and in different ways.

It is also significant that white males elaborated upon sex largely
in relation to blacks. Certainly their own identity is bound up with
sexuality but this sexuality comes through most vehemently and con-

sistently in relation to black males and females. They use sexuality as a means of "trashing" black males and females, and setting themselves up as "different from" them in the sexual realm. Thus black sexual behavior, both male and female, is seen as being inappropriate—unlike their own. While sexuality is certainly elaborated upon in relation to white girls (and obviously encoded in discussions about children), such discussions do not exhibit the same ugliness as those involving blacks and the constructed sexuality of blacks. It is significant, for example, that when a group of white males was discussing Martin Luther King Day they said, "I have a wet dream—'bout little white boys and little black girls." It is even more significant that Pete said, "You don't understand black people. They're yeach. They smell funny and they [got] hair under their arms". Blacks are talked about largely in terms of sexuality, and sexuality is talked about to a great extent in terms of blacks. Blacks are used to demonstrate the boundaries of acceptable sexual behavior (in that black behavior is unacceptable) and provide a means of enabling whites to set themselves up as "better than" (more responsible, less dirty and so forth) in this area. Although white boys do say, as I noted above, "nice ass" to white girls, they do not see this as contradictory to their embedded attitudes toward black sexuality, given that they feel that white girls are their property to begin with. Black sexuality is simply negative; their own sexuality is, in turn, seen as positive. *In the final analysis, white males elaborate an identity in relation to the ideologically constructed identity of both black male and black female.* In other words, white males elaborate their own identity in relation to the identity that they construct for others, in this case, black male and black female. In so doing, they set themselves up as "other than" and "better than" each group.

Young white men spend a great deal of time expressing and exhibiting disgust for people of color. This is done at the same time as they elaborate an uninvited protective stance toward white women. In a sense, these young men "are inviting themselves in" to white women's lives in the way that they accuse black men of "inviting themselves in" to these same young women's lives. Of course, for the white men they draw the bounds of acceptability at their *own* actions, denoting as unacceptable the ways in which they envision black men "inviting themselves in." Their discursive rendering of blacks takes a distinctly genderized form. Black males are treated with contempt for invading their property (white girls), thus enabling these men to draw distinctions between their own sexual behavior and that of blacks, as well as drawing themselves out as coming to the aid of the "damsel in distress." In addition, these episodes enable a discursive rendering of themselves as *definitely* heterosexual. Black females are treated with simple disgust; seen as beyond the boundaries of what is an acceptable heterosexual object. Thus, Pete states that "they smell funny and they (got) hair under their arms." The disgust is evident, as these young men discursively elaborate the African-American as highly sexualized and physically gross. It also sets black women up as "something" that anyone can do anything with sexually because they are beyond the limits of acceptable heterosexual practice (witness the Martin Luther King "chant").

It is significant that young white men elaborate their own sexuality largely in relation to blacks. Black men and women are the foil against which they set up their own heterosexuality as well as their own ultimate desire for stable two parent families. White women are, on the other hand, largely talked about in terms of family and children. While there are certainly gross discussions about young white women as well, these pale in contrast to the discussions about black women. Blacks are used largely to express contempt and, at the same time, encourage young white men to set themselves up as "pure" in relation to people of color. "I have a wet dream- -about little white boys and little black girls" undermines the seriousness of the black struggle, turning it filthy. Thus, when young white working-class men say 'nice ass" to white girls, it is okay, because it is somehow different than when blacks do it. Also, of course, white women are seen as the property of white men, therefore making it all the more acceptable for them to say and do anything they like.

Conclusion

In this essay I have traced the drawing of "other" as young white working-class men form their own racial, class, and gendered identity. In order to form themselves as white and male, they simultaneously construct the white female "other" as well as the black male and female "other." Their own construction of self is intimately bound up with the discursive construction of "other." The ways in which these types of constructions take place are critically important. For the white working-class male, at least in this particular sector of the country, the construction of blacks takes on central importance. Ultimately, these young white men will enter aduldood with very racist constructions of people of color which they created (in relation, of course, to the material and discursive constructions of people of color in the society at large). Such constructions will be difficult to dislodge, particularly since they are so intimately braided with their own sexuality. Whiteness, then, is constructed in relation to constructed black sexual filthiness, at least in this class fraction. While certainly later experiences in the work force and so forth, will layer on top of this, perhaps altering it a bit (or reinforcing it through similar constructions in adult life), we must take pause at the real meaning of sexism and racism and their depth when this occurs. This is not, of course, to deny the very real material issues surrounding racism and sexism in this country. However, discursive constructions are key, as Michel Foucault argues. They set limits on what is imagined as possible. Listening to the voices of young white working-class men pries open a reality of racism, in particular, and the ways in which racism is linked to expressed heterosexuality and male dominance for whites that may be far deeper than we imagined. As scholars dedicated to the opening up of democraic public space, we certainly have our work cut out for us.

Notes

1. The Preliminary Scholasic Aptitude Test (PSAT) and Scholasic Aptitude Test (SAT) are administered by the Educational Testing Service in Princeton. Most four-year colleges require the SAT for entrance.

2. The governing body of the state educational system administers a series of tests that must be taken in high school if entrance to a four-year college is desired. Not all students take these tests, of course, the track placement often determines whether the tests are taken.

References

Foucault, Michel. 1990. *The History of Sexuality: An Introduction*. New York: Vintage Books.

Giroux, Henry. 1991. *Postmodernism, Feminism and Cultural Politics*. Albany: State University of New York Press.

hooks, bell. 1990. *Yearning*. Boston: South End Press.

Lather, Patti. 1991. *Getting Smart*. New York: Routledge.

McLaren, Peter. 1991. "Schooling the Postmodern Body," Henry Giroux, ed. *Postmodernism, Feminism and Cultural Politics*. Albany: State University of New York Press, pp. 144–47.

Michelson, Roslyn Arlin, Stephen Smith, and Melvin Oliver. 1993. "Breaking Through the Barriers: African-American Job Candidates and Academic

Hiring Process," eds. Lois Weis and Michelle Fine. *Beyond Silenced Voices*. Albany: State University of New York Press, pp. 9–24.

Sapon-Shevin, Mara. 1993. "Gifted Education and the protection of Privilege: Breaking the Silence, Opening the Discourse," eds. Lois Weis and Michelle Fine. *Beyond Silenced Voices*. Albany: State University of New York Press, pp. 25–44.

Weis, Lois. 1990. *Working Class Without Work: High School Students in a De-Industrializing Economy*. New York: Routledge, Chapman and Hall.

Weis, Lois and Michelle Fine. 1993. *Beyond Silenced Voices*. Albany: State University of New York Press.

Willis, Paul. 1977. *Learning to Labour*. Westmead: Saxon House Press.

12

*Reflections of a Critical Theorist in the Soviet Union:
Paradoxes and Possibilities in Uncertain Times*

Wendy Kohli

Contradictions in Context

The Soviet Union in 1991 is not the hopeful place it was when
I first visited there in 1987.[1] As I write this essay, the economy lurches
problematically, even dangerously, toward the welcoming arms of the
"free market." Diverse sectors of the population grow increasingly
uneasy about the apparent reassertion of power and influence of the
KGB and the military. There is evidence of government media
censorship again, although not to the extent of pre-Gorbachev days.
Civil war is on the lips of many, especially in republics far from the
center, Moscow. And intellectuals once again ponder their uncertain
futures.[2] The hopes and dreams of the early days of *perestroika* and
glasnost have turned to bitter recriminations against the man who set
the processes of democratization in place. Things change. Things stay
the same.

I think of my first trip to Red Square. As a student of the Russian
Revolution and a "believer" in the emancipatory possibilities of those
young radicals, I was moved to tears at the sight of such power, hope,
possibility, and tragedy. What happened to *that* dream? Could the years
of Stalin terror or Brezhnev stagnation have been foretold? Were the
seeds of the Soviet socialist failure planted in those early expulsions
of anarchists and democrats? What kind of socialist fixture is possible
now? Is (was?)[3] *perestroika* no more than another cruel tease similar to
the Khrushchev "thaw" two decades ago? *Is* there a future for democratic socialism in the Soviet Union?

Before 1987 I did not much care about the future of the Soviet
Union. I long ago had excluded that country from my intellectual or

political interests. For me, it had became the tragic symbol of everything
that should be avoided in the world-historical struggle for freedom and
social justice. My formative political education drawing primarily on
anarchism and Critical Theory, especially the work of Murray Bookchin,
Theodor Adomo, Max Horkheimer, and Jürgen Habermas, provided
strong criticism of most of what the Soviet Union had become. And
my feminist commitments substantially enlarged that critique as I saw
the massive bureaucratic State and Communist Party system in the light
of patriarchal domination and masculinist militarism.

Then with my first trip to Moscow, Leningrad, and Tblisi, Georgia,
something changed. Coming face-to-face with people who had been
only cold, gray, ideological abstractions for me up until then forced a
shift in my stance. The Soviet Union was at once much more and much
less than I had been led to believe—by the propaganda of the U.S. media
and educational system, as well as by my colleagues on the left. I began
to glimpse the multiple realities of the situation there, to pierce the thick
veils of fear and formalism that disguised the authentic beliefs and
feelings of individuals and to grasp the power of "official" discourse
and its counterforce, the "unofficial." I also apprehended, with deepening anger, the degree to which the U.S. government systematically
had distorted most communication about that country in order to serve
the interests of our "military-industrial complex."

These realizations did not erase the evidence of a repressive
system, nor cause me to reformulate dramatically my analysis of Soviet
socialism. In many instances they actually reinforced the evidence. But
at the same time they did remind me of the complexities of lived situations, especially in a society as expansive and diverse as the USSR. And
they did reveal some interesting contradictions. With many of my new
Soviet friends and colleagues, I often was the only person who could
see *any* positive qualities in socialism. The word and its associated
practices had become so tarnished that most intellectuals I met felt only
bitter cynicism about a system that once held so much promise. I also
was one of the few people in the circles in which I moved who could see
clearly the underside of capitalism, including its tragic historical effect
on Soviet life resulting from the dangerous and debilitating arms race.

At the same time, the more I experienced, albeit in my privileged
way, the daily grind of life in the USSR, the more I understood the
frustration and feelings of betrayal that my friends felt toward a system
ruled by a corrupt party elite and cheapened by its hollow slogans. In
that context, the "West" looked better and better to me as well; however,
niether was good enough to fundamentally alter my critique of
capitalism nor to stop my visits to the Soviet Union. There was still

too much to learn and to share. I was eager to find out more about the society in general, the educational system in particular, and the hegemonic influence of Marxism-Leninism on both. What and where were the "critical openings" in that discourse? How was opposition expressed? What did it mean to be a "critical" educator or to do critical research in the paradox-filled country known as the contemporary USSR?[4]

Critical Theory/"Critical" Moments

I found myself looking for "comrades"—those intellectuals who were critical of Stalinism *and* monopoly capitalism—and of all the cultural baggage each of those systems brings.[5] Where was critical pedagogy, cultural studies, or feminist materialism? Certainly, I queried, there must be a tradition in the Soviet Union that paralleled the "progressive left" movements of Eastern Europe? Certainly there must be scholars, poets, writers, and activists who remained committed to the revolutionary ideals of 1917 and who saw the possibility of resurrecting those ideals at this historic moment; those not seduced by the fetishism of the market or the "cult of individualism" necessary for those market forces to go unchecked; those who did not hold to a technocratic, positivistic understanding of science; those who were not on a retrograde to the Orthodox Church or the monarchy? Yes, there are such people alive and well in Moscow, Leningrad, and some of the other cosmopolitan centers. As one contemporary "critical Marxist" reminds us, "Soviet society has never been as monolithic as it was presented by Stalinist ideology or the oversimplified Western conceptions of totalitarianism. Numerous interest groups, forming within and outside the apparatus of power, have always exerted influence on decision-making and engendered a variety of conflicts" (Kagarlitsky 1990, 337).

One segment of opposition is the intellectuals who came of age during the Khrushchev "thaw" and had access to some of the work of the Frankfurt School, including that of Adorno and Marcuse. The influence of these theorists as well as the "critical" Marxism of George Lukács and Karl Korsch can be felt in the era of *perestroika*. This generation of "Khrushchev critics" carries on a strong tradition in the history of the postrevolutionary society. To understand the importance of these critics in the Soviet, or, more accurately, the Russian context, it is important to distinguish the term *intelligentsia* from Western notions of *intellectual* or *academic*, for they are not synonymous. As Kagarlitsky (1988) indicates, the intelligentsia "formed out of various social classes and [was] held together by *ideas*, not by sharing a common profession or economic status" (14–15). They were moved to act by *moral and social ideals*. Kagarlitsky, himself a young member of the Moscow intelligentsia and one of the few "neo-Marxists" writing in the Soviet Union today, was imprisoned under Brezhnev in 1982 for acting on his moral and social commitments. He finished *The Thinking Reed*, an impressive history of intellectuals in the Soviet Union just as he was arrested along with many other activists who had founded "new left" groups and *samizdat* journals (Kagarlitsky 1990, 344). Because of his uncommon status, those working with the *New Left Review* in England "courted" him and subsequently published two of his texts.

In his first book, Kagarlitsky (1988) provides a substantial narrative of the rich "living traditions of social criticism" rooted in the nineteenth century and revived, to greater or lesser degrees, in the decades of the twentieth century. Contrary to Lenin's dictum, he argues that "there can be no doubt that the bearer of the revolutionary principle in Russia, right to the end of the nineteenth century, was *not any definite class, . . . but the intelligentsia*" (21, emphasis added). And, he asserts, it was from the time of the Decembrists Movement in 1825 that this "intelligentsia crystallized" and became a permanent part of Russian political life (14).

The changes initiated by Gorbachev are best understood in the context of the historical development and activity of the intelligentsia. From its roots in December 1825, through its role in early twentieth century revolutions, and its renaissance under Khrushchev, 1990, the Soviet intelligentsia "has prepared the ground for restructuring" (Zaslavskaya 1990, 174). This is not, however, an argument for an intellectual elite to govern the country. Quite the contrary. For both Kagarlitsky and Zaslavskaya, any reformist agenda must find "a mass base for the transformations. . . .What is needed is not a boost to the social egoism of "advanced" (and essentially the most prosperous) social groups but, on the contrary, a struggle to gain their utmost solidarity with the wider masses" (Kagarlitsky 1990, 359).

At the same time, however, it is important to recognize the significance of an entire generation of thinkers who were nourished on and who refined multiple forms of criticism of communist orthodoxy (Zaslavskaya 1990, viii). It was they who "held on to their socialist values" through the repressive years of Stalin and who preserved their "moral nucleus" in the face of Stalinist terror. Although there have been "decades of bureaucratic control of academic institutions, . . . no bureaucracy could *completely* prevent intellectuals from thinking creatively"(3). It was such committed socialist democrats who I wanted to find in the field of educational theory and practice.

"Doing" Critical Educational Theory at Moscow State University

After two nonprofessional visits to the Soviet Union, I decided to spend more time there working in areas related to my own scholarly interests in critical educational theory. I did not intend to become a specialist in Soviet education, to switch to comparative education, or to become a sovietologist. Mine was a modest goal of finding a hospitable place in an academic setting that would provide me with a more in-depth grasp of the educational system and the world of Soviet educational scholarship. Also, I wanted the opportunity to lecture on the U.S. educational system, critical pedagogy, and teacher empowerment.

By the summer of 1989, I was fortunate to qualify for a faculty exchange between te SUNY university system and Moscow State University (MGU). MGU is the largest and most prestigious university in the Soviet Union, located in the Lenin Hills overlooking the center of Moscow, and housed in a powerfully massive architectural tribute to Stalin that is vaguely reminiscent of the Empire State Building. MGU is similar to most U.S. research universities in that faculty members are expected to do research, work with doctoral students, and teach. I requested a placement with the department (*kafedra*) of Theory and Practice of Communist Education (or Upbringing) within the faculty of the School of Philosophy (*Filosofsku fakul'tet*) having been told it was the closest thing to a department of philosophy they had at that time.

Communist "Upbringing"

The Russian Revolution brought a new vision of society and with it a new conception of "man" [*sic*]. It was the task of the revolutionaries to create institutions and social practices that produced this "new Socialist man" with a socialist consciousness. This required "sciences, social services and education that conveyed the worldview underlying a socialist commitment" (Popkewitz 1984, 61). Marxist-Leninism was the world view on which young people were to be "brought up." My host department at MGU had a historical role in reproducing this worldview: the onerous (and once very prestigious) task of educating researchers and college teachers whose specific academic work was to create the ideological apparatus of Marxism-Leninism at all levels of the educational system through such required courses as "Scientific Communism" and "The History of the Communist Party." All of the faculty in this *kafedra* were Communist Party members, and many of the graduate students aspired to that as well. My host professor was a former general in the KGB and now an educational theoretician in semiretirement. Needless to say, for a person who until 1987 had virtually no interest in or sympathy for the Soviet Union, its bureaucratic form of socialism, or its official rendering of Marxism-Leninism, I found this placement a challenge indeed. I was "in the belly of the beast."

It became clear to me that this *kafedra* represented one of the more "conservative"[6] positions in the shifting political sands of Soviet life. I also came to learn from colleagues in other institutes and departments of the university that my host department was a laughingstock for most "liberal" or "progressive" thinkers. The "Scientific Communism" courses that everyone in secondary and postsecondary education is required to take long ago had lost their credibility with much of the intelligentsia. The department, aware of its loss of standing in certain circles, and prodded by the dean, made an effort to gain back some legitimacy in the Gorbachev era by changing its name to "Problems in Education and Culture." Unfortunately, everything else remained the same. For many outside the department, this renaming was just another example of the entrenched "apparatchiks" putting old wine in new bottles.

I felt I was in a time warp when talking with these faculty committed to the orthodoxy of "communist upbringing"; it was like being in a Leninist version of *Back to the Future*. The attitudes and general demeanor of most of the faculty smacked of another time, a static and smug era with only a hint of self-doubt, reflection, or criticism. Their views on Gorbachev, though polite for their visiting American, were laced with cynicism and sarcasm. Even though I had a long-standing allegiance to the revolutionary ideals of 1917 and *not* to "bourgeois imperialist" capitalism,[7] the gap between what I took to be their rigid, reified, nondialectical instantiation of those ideals and my critical understanding of Marxism and Leninism proved unbridgeable. I wondered if, when, or where I would find anyone with a "critical" perspective.

Marxism-Leninism, Philosophy and Science: Where is the Critique?

Up until very recently in the USSR, philosophy was synonymous with Marxism-Leninism, and the principles of Marxism-Leninism served as the foundation for the entire Soviet educational system. The teaching of this "orthodox" philosophy was supported officially at all levels and was the ideological framework that defined scientific research. It is impossible to understand the scope, purpose, and limitations of educational research in the Soviet Union without addressing the influence of this Marxist-Leninist worldview.

Marxism-Leninism generally is divided into three parts: dialectical and historical-materialist philosophy, political economy (Marxian economic theory), and "Scientific" Communism (social and political theory of Marxism-Leninism) (Scanlon 1985, 22). Much of the established party elite, including a large segment of the academic community, believed or professed to believe until very recently that this Marxist worldview "is the only adequate intellectual orientation for modern man" (22). This is not to say that, as already noted, there were no theoretical or practical disagreements. But now in the era of *glasnost*, the official consensus finally is breaking down as more conceptual problem areas are being discussed openly, including the "identity of philosophy itself" (21). Scanlon describes the identity problem as such: "The central issue concerning the nature of philosophy in the post-Stalin period has been the question of the relationship between philosophy and science. If...a philosophical system is expected to provide an objectively true description of reality, how is philosophy to be distinguished from the sciences? Or is it itself a science? If philosophy is a science, how is it related to and distinguished from other sciences? And what is it if *not* a science?" (26).

The implications of these contested themes for research and educational practice are profound if, as Popkewitz (1984) argues, "Marxist-Leninist thought provides the framework for the formation of science...[and that] science is to serve directly the policy goals of the state" (59). Through examining what counts as "science," educational researchers would be forced to examine, more explicitly, the methods and purposes of their work, their epistemological assumptions and the relationship between knowledge and interests—especially the interests of the State apparatus. This would require a reflective critique of their work and of the ideological framework defining it. It could require critical theory, the work of the Frankfurt school.

"The Latent Positivism of Marx"

To speak of critical theory in any meaningful way with regard to educational research in the Soviet Union, we must come to terms with the scientistic, technocratic, and authoritarian tendencies of the dominant ideology and of the political and research practices derived from it. It must be acknowledged that Marxism, very soon after the revolution, was transformed from an analysis of critique and opposition to an ideology of power, prediction, and control (Popkewitz 1984, 60). The work of Jürgen Habermas and Albrecht Wellmer provide a powerful framework through which to understand this transformation.

Drawing on Habermas's analysis of knowledge and interests,[8] Wellmer (1974) developed a critical view of Marx's philosophy of history and demonstrated how it led to the "misconception of ideology-critical social theory as a 'science' in the same sense as the natural sciences"(68). What followed from this misconception was "an erroneously techno-cratic interpretation of his [Marx's] theory" that served well the adminis-trative and technical interests of the State in the controlling hands of the Communist Party (69). Wellmer's analysis follows in the tradition of his teachers, Horkheimer and Adorno, in criticizing the "objectivistic tendencies of Marx's conception of revolution" (129). In *Dialectic of Enlightenment*, Horkheimer and Adorno (1972) not only "produce a profound historico-philosophical critique of capitalist society. . .and the liberal capitalism criticized by Marx [but also] *its state-capitalist and state-interventionist heirs*" (Wellmer 1974, 129–130). The Soviet Union is the principal "heir" to this administrative throne of technical rationality and state power. One of the primary (and most resistant) targets of *perestroika* is the party apparatus with its accompanying technical-instrumental interests. Party bureaucrats, especially those in leadership positions within state agencies, have the most to lose from a democratization process, from *perestroika*. One such mammoth bureaucracy is the Academy of Pedagogical Sciences (APS), the all-union organization that sanctions much of the educational research done in the Soviet Union.

Critical Openings in the Academy of Pedagogical Sciences

There is no agency or institution in the United States that is directly analogous to the APS. As the "central body for research and developments (Tabachnick, Popkewitz, and Szekely 1981, 7), it resem-bles in part the former National Institute of Education (NIE) and current Office of Educational Research and Improvement (OERI) division of the U.S. Department of Education. And with an elected membership of prestigious "academicians," it also has some similarity to the National Academy of Education. The Presidium of the Academy, as the primary policy and governance unit, oversees the work of at least fifteen research institutes, each with the responsibility for planning and implementing distinct lines of research such as special education, educational psychology and general pedagogy, and curriculum.[9] Each institute has a director and several sector heads. Similar to our government-funded research and development centers, these institutes employ dozens of trained scholars whose primary function is to do educational research that conforms to the current policies of the Soviet government and promotes the development of socialist society. It also must conform to the internal politics of the institute and the APS bureaucracy.

Research institutes vary in academic respectability and prestige, depending, to a large extent, on the status of the director. Similar to many division heads in the U.S. Department of Education, institute directors in effect are "political appointments" serving at the pleasure of the presidium of the Academy. To land what is considered a plum position at one of these research institutes, one must be exceptionally good at his/her work, and/or well-connected to one of the elected academicians and/or party member. "Scientific workers," as most researchers are called, have relatively high occupational status in the society and the scientific work they do is considered important by other professionals. As an outsider, however, it often was difficult for me to ascertain what was fact and what was fiction about the reputation of the research being conducted. Quality varies from "sector" to "sector" and institute to institute. Prior to *glasnost*, the research had to conform to the dominant party line. A researcher in Comparative Education at the Institute for General Pedagogics, for example, indicated that in her first sixteen years working there, not one of her articles would have been published if it conveyed positive renderings of educational systems in England or the United States, the countries she studied. It has been only within the past four years that a more "pluralist" policy has been in effect. Similarly, all research articles had to begin with a gratuitous, if not genuinely heart-felt, nod to recent official proclamations or party policy statements.[10] And discrimination based on nationality and ethnicity is still a factor in institute politics. For example, in many places it is well known that if you are Jewish, there is no chance for you to ever gain a leadership position in your institute, regardless of your academic record.

Since the onset of *perestroika* the Academy of Pedagogical Sciences has come under considerable attack from outside the educational establishment as well as from within its own constituency. In 1988 the internal criticism led to the formation of a "temporary research collective," Vremennyi Nauchno-Issledovatel'skii Kollektiv (VNIK) that was charged with developing a new philosophy of education for the USSR and for proposing alternatives to the centrally-driven practices and policies of the entrenched, party-controlled bureaucracy. VNIK, led by Eduard Dneprov, who now serves as the minister of education for the Russian Federation, represented an "opening" for oppositional discourse. In 1990, many researchers from this collective under the leadership of Dneprov formed a new institute, the Center for Pedagogical Innovations. Just in its first year, it remains to be seen if the experimentation done through this center or the conceptual papers produced by this collective of critics will have much effect on Soviet educational research and practice or on the organizational practices of the Academy of Pedagogical Sciences (Kerr 1990, 27).

Resistance to change remains a powerful obstacle. From my interviews with members of VNIK, as well as those who were skeptical or critical of its purposes, I was struck with the depth of despair and cynicism that permeates the educational academic community. Reform is slow, the problems overwhelming. And the administrative control by the party apparatus still is powerful, even with some "liberal" appointments.[11] The APS, particularly its International Department, still has considerable power to decide which researchers will be supported for travel abroad, a coveted opportunity for everyone in a society that has had such severe restrictions on travel.[12]

The APS leadership also has substantial control over which research themes and researchers receive official legitimation and support.[13] For example, at a recent APS-sponsored conference, "Humanizing Education in the Soviet Union," which I attended with fifteen other U.S. philosophers of education, not one of the prominent Soviet educational reformers from VNIK was invited to attend, even though much of their work is focused just on that theme. Those in attendance were the friends and generational-colleagues of the conference organizers, all with similar ideological commitments and institutional status.

Educational and social science research has suffered greatly from this kind of ideological rigidity within the academic establishment. For decades, any lines of research that were perceived by officials to "go against the grain" of the orthodoxy were disallowed. For example, the discipline of sociology was outlawed because it had the potential to undermine Marxism-Leninism. Only in the past four years has there been approval for the reestablishment of sociology departments and institutes, along with such previously banned research methodologies as opinion polls. Through observations and interviews with various researchers, I was struck with their strong reliance on and belief in "scientific" methods, that is, quantitative research methods. Qualitative and ethnographic approaches are used rarely, if at all.[14] They have been considered too subversive by officials, too "interpretative."

The Contradictory Nature of "Apolitical" Critique

Many intellectuals I met took an "apolitical" identity/stance. Most of these colleagues, coincidentally, were attached to one or another of the psychological institutes affiliated with the Academy of Pedagogical Sciences. Virtually every scholar who identified as a psychologist—whether social, educational, or clinical—eschewed politics, particularly socialist or Marxist politics of any kind. As much as I resisted the "hard-line" ideologues in the Department of Upbringing, I could not fully embrace the political commitments (or lack thereof) of the psychologists. Although I understood their virtual wholesale reaction against the reified socialism, bureaucratic controls, and state repression that had shaped Soviet life to a greater or lesser degree since the 1930s, I am too steeped in critical theory to accept their stance unchallenged. The focus of most of their work was on "individualism," "the creative personality," or some equivalent focus on the person as a "unique soul." Of course there were multiple interpretations of these themes, particularly among the psychologists who were informed by the work of Lev Vygotsky and who understood the dialectical development of the individual in a social context. Nevertheless, among many of the younger academics, there was a distinct retreat from "ideology" and most certainly from Marxism. They had no interest in "saving the baby" while disposing of the "bath water." Yet, at the same time that they rejected the political ideology of Marxism-Leninism, they held on to its technocratic scientism. Like their colleagues doing educational research, their work followed a most positivist conception of "scientific rigor."

Is the Future Postmodern?

This "apolitical" voice was echoed at the Institute of Philosophy in Moscow, one of the most prestigious institutes affiliated with the Academy of Sciences, and in the Department of Religion and Philosophy at Leningrad University. Instead of focusing on the psychological development of the "individual," however, many of the current generation of sophisticated young philosophers are drawn instead to the religious and spiritual development of the person or to postmodern discourse and its "politics of subjectivity." For the past three years there has been an impressive parade of contemporary critical and postmodern scholars coming to Moscow; they include Frederic Jameson, Jürgen Habermas, Susan Buck-Morss, and Jacques Derrida. The Moscow institute also sponsored an international conference on Heidegger in the fall of 1989, and a conference on "Language and Text: Ontology and Reflection" is being planned in Leningrad for 1992. Critical theory, especially the work of Jürgen Habermas, received a respectful hearing by these scholars, but they resonated emotionally and intellectually to the work of Deleuze, Foucault, and Derrida. For them, Habermas was too "systematic" and still "too connected to the Marxist project."

At each institution where I held seminars on Critical Hermeneutics and Critical Pedagogy, I was confronted with audiences searching for new schemas for understanding their world. Some embraced the nihilism of Nietzsche,[15] others the religious foundationalism of the Russian Orthodox Church. It was inconceivable to them that socialism and any theory informing it could have a "critical moment." For them it was pure ideology, dogmatism. Given the reification of Marxist theory in the Soviet system, the poor and limited translations of the writings of Marx, and the brutal regimes that acted in his name, their sentiments were not surprising. Many of these young scholars are the sons and daughter of the "Khrushchev era" intelligentsia who now challenge the neo-Marxist commitments of their parents and remind them of the persistence of the corrupt "circulation of power" in the Soviet bureaucracy. Marxist theory in any form is "dirty" to them and "dangerous." But their position causes me no small amount of concern. I wonder, really, if it is any more dangerous than having an entire generation of talented scholars disengage from the political arena and adopt a "pure" stance in the name of individual freedom, *glasnot*, and spiritual development, while the technocrats and bureaucrats consolidate their power? At this time of cultural, political, economic, and social crisis in the Soviet Union, can this privileged stance be afforded? Once again we confront that revolutionary question of praxis: What is to be done? Things change. Things stay the same.

Notes

1. I make no claim to be a "specialist" on the Soviet Union. In fact, the more I know about that vast and contradictory place, the more impenetrable it seems. I also want to avoid the pretense of speaking for the whole of the "Soviet people." My primary social and research context was a small segment of the educated elite who brought their own limitations to any dialogue or experience. Finally, although not explicitly making parallel criticisms of the United States in this essay, I have learned that there are many problematic tendencies in common between the two super powers.

2. A reflection of this uneasiness is a braindrain to the West. In just the past few weeks, as only one example among many, I have been asked by several established academics to secure "some kind, *any* kind of visiting professorship" for them. They seem tired of waiting for the long-promised economic recovery or democratic reforms and want a respite from the stress.

3. Some colleagues in Moscow are already describing the time in which they now live as "Post-*perestroika*."

4. When I use the term *critical*, I am heavily influenced by the Critical Theory of the Frankfurt School. Nevertheless, in the context of the Soviet Union where the influence of the Frankfurt School has been limited, I am extending and broadening my use of critical to include multiple and even contradictory oppositional moments and voices.

5. I want to thank my colleagues in the United States who have shared with me their insights and research experience in the Soviet Union. They include Susan Buck-Morss, Julie DeSherbinin, Dmitrii Khanin, Thomas Popkewitz, Nancy Ries, and John Ryder.

6. Conventional political labels and categories have been turned on their heads in the current Soviet context. Those who we in the West might call the "far left," those committed to orthodox communism or socialism, are perceived to be on the "far right" now in the Soviet Union because of their "conservative" tendencies.

7. While I was at MGU I was told that the derogatory terms *bourgeois* and *imperialist*, often used toward the United States, "were no longer used." This was corroborated in other contexts as well.

8. See, for example, Habermas's *Knowledge and Human Interests* (Boston: Beacon Press, 1971).

9. As of this writing, the APS has undergone several recent reorganizations. New institutes are forming and old ones are being transformed or phased out.

10. It is important to note that those who "went along" with official discourse often did so out of fear for their lives and the lives of their families. This is a degree of systematic intellectual policing that, I think it is safe to say, we in the United States have not experienced. Here we are simply ignored.

11. For example, Vasily Davydov was appointed the vice-president of the Academy. Davydov, a Vygotskian psychologist, was out of favor in the Brezhnev era but has assumed considerable influence in the Gorbachev regime.

12. It is commonly assumed that the administrators in the International Department are either actual members of the KGB or are expected to make reports to the KGB.

13. This is similar to much of the grant-making that goes on through the U.S. Department of Education. Officials of the Reagan administration, for example, created an "acceptable researcher" list from which to select grant winners.

14. A colleague of mine, Nancy Ries, finishing her dissertation in anthropology at Cornell University, may be the first foreign academic allowed

to do ethnographic research in the Soviet Union on Soviet culture, values, and beliefs.

15. As Susan Buck-Morss recounted, with no small amount of irony, "Nietsche and Foucault would travel well there."

References

Horkheimer. M., and T. Adorno. 1972. *Dialectic of Enlightenment*. New York: Herder & Herder.

Kagarlitsky, B. 1988. *The Thinking Reed: Intellectuals and the Soviet state from 1917 to the Present*. London: Verso.

————. 1990. *The Dialectic of Change*. London: Verso.

Kerr, S. 1990. "Will Glasnost lead to Perestroika? Directions of Educational Reform in the USSR". *Educational Researcher* 19, no. 7:26–31.

Popkewitz, T. 1984. *Paradigm and Ideology in Educational Research: The Social Functions of the Intellectual*. London: Falmer.

Scanlon, J. P. 1985. *Marxism in the USSR: A Critical Survey of Current Soviet Thought*. Ithaca: Cornell University Press.

Tabachnick, B. R., T. Popkewitz, and B. Szekely. 1981. *Studying Teaching and Learning: Trends in Soviet and American Research*. New York: Praeger.

Wellmer, A. 1974. *Critical Theory of Society*. New York: Seabury.

Zaslavskaya, T. 1990. *The Second Socialist Revolution*. Bloomington: Indiana University Press.

13

Participatory Action Research and Popular Education in Latin America

Carlos Alberto Torres

One of the signal developments in educational reform over the past two decades in Latin America has been the ascendancy of popular educational participatory action research. Popular education and participatory action research are two central traditions of nonformal education in Latin America. Popular education is highly critical of mainstream education, seeking to empower the marginalized, the disenfranchised, and the poor. Participatory action research combines research, educational work, and social action. These paradigms share a number of epistemological, theoretical, methodological, and political elements, and both paradigms have been influenced by the works of the Brazilian educator, Paulo Freire. This article discusses the origins of participatory action research, its basic premises, its main differences compared with non-participatory research, and some practical and critical conclusions that can be derived from these origins, theoretical-political premises, and epistemological foundations.[1]

Foundations: Paulo Freire, the Critique of Pedagogical Positivism, and Social Transformation

For Freire, the principal concerns of adult education are not pedagogical or methodological in the strictest sense, but are related to its political application as a form of advocacy for oppressed social groups. Adult education programs in Latin America are designed explicitly as mechanisms or instruments for pedagogical and political involvement with the socially subordinated sectors of the population. Following Freire, adult education constitutes a pedagogy for social transformation; in this sense it describes its educational project as a form of "cultural action." The central objective of cultural action can be described by the term *conscientization*.

The specificity of conscientization in the original Freirean proposal rests on the development among students and teachers of critical consciousness as forms of class knowledge and class practice: that is, educational and research processes that constitute part of the "subjective conditions" for the project of social transformation (Brandão 1982, 93–104; C. Torres 1980a, 1980b). Freire describes critical consciousness:

> The first level of apprehension of reality is the "prise de cons-
> cience." This awareness exists because as human beings we are
> "placed" and "dated." As Gabriel Marcel used to say, men are with
> and in the world, looking on. This "prise de conscience," however,
> is not yet critical consciousness. There is the deepening of the
> "prise de conscience." This is the critical development of the "prise
> de conscience." For this reason, critical consciousness implies the
> surpassing of the spontaneous sphere of apprehension of reality
> by a critical position. Through this criticism, reality appears to be
> a "cognoscente objectum" within which man assumes an episte-
> mological position: man looking for knowing. Thus, critical
> consciousness is a test of environment, a test of reality. To the
> extent that as we are conscientizing, we are unveiling reality we
> are penetrating the phenomenological essence of the object that
> we are trying to analyze. Thus, critical consciousness means
> historical consciousness. In the last analysis, class consciousness
> is not psychological consciousness. Nor does it mean class
> sensitiveness. Class consciousness has a strong identity with class
> knowledge. But as it happens, knowledge does not naturally exist
> as such. (Freire 1980, 74; my translation)

Knowledge, for Freire, is a social construction; it constitutes a process of discursive production and not merely an end product consisting of an accumulated cluster of information or facts. Freire's understanding of knowledge as a dialectics of oppositions is fundamentally at odds with traditional-idealist and positivist epistemology.[2] Freire's pedagogy emerged as a critique of the traditional (authoritarian) educational para-digm, but also of its competitor in the region, positivism,[3] which was gaining ground in Latin America during the 1950s and 1960s. He proposed a nonauthoritarian and directivist pedagogy of liberation as an overt challenge to existing pedagogical models that he regarded as forms of "banking education" that treated knowledge as isolated, ahistorical facts simply to be "deposited" into the minds of the students as a banker might deposit funds into an account. Freire's conception of pedagogy held that the teacher is at same time a student, and the student is a teacher. While the nature of their knowledge may differ, as long as education involves the dialectical and reciprocal production of knowledge, and not merely the transmission of facts, students and teachers will share a similar status and will be linked through a pedagogical dialogue characterized by horizontal relationships. Freire's educational agenda is not necessarily carried out in a classroom but functions in a "culture circle," where emphasis is placed on *sharing* and *reflecting* critically upon the learner's experience and knowledge, both as a source of rough material for analyzing the "existential themes" introduced by critical pedagogy, and as an attempt to demystify existing forms of false consciousness.

The main characteristic of liberation pedagogies in Latin America has been their resistance to be incorporated into the formal apparatuses of the capitalist state. Ideally this resistance is designed to bring a political regime to power that is sympathetic to the interests and demands of the popular sectors. Important differences exist between Freirean educators and the bureaucrats, decision makers, and teachers who are responsible for reproducing the structures of the larger educational system. The knowledge-guiding interests of most traditional educational approaches in Latin America continue to be circumscribed by an overemphasis on the methodological procedures of classroom instruction that are informed largely by an instrumental procedures of classroom rationality (Mezirow, 1977, 1981, 1990; C. Torres 1991a).

Insofar as the state and the school system in Latin America represent instruments of ideological mediation and control, pedagogies of liberation have developed a "hermeneutics of suspicion" with respect to state institutions. Implementation of Freirean-like approaches have occurred throughout Latin America for more than 20 years and recent studies reveal that most radical educators prefer to design nonformal and nongovernment organization-sponsored educational ventures rather than working within state-sponsored educational institutions. It is only recently that interventions in school settings known as *public popular schooling* have been advanced by Freirean educators (Gadotti, 1990); and most of these have taken place in the context of Brazilian debates on school autonomy.[4] Not surprisingly, many of the representatives of this pedagogy have worked, politically and professionally, within political parties, universities, and research centers, as well as with organizations that have originated in or are linked to churches.

A natural compatibility exists between pedagogies of liberation and the field of nonformal education in Latin America (La Belle 1986).

Even the so-called psychosocial method For adult literacy training[5] has a clear place for practice and experimentation within nonformal education, while its applicability in elementary or secondary education, for example, still is controversial. The reasons for the controversy surrounding nonformal education are many. For instance, in formal educational settings in Latin America, the power of a teacher who is responsible for evaluating students' progress, such as grading school work or attaining class discipline in school settings, differs sharply from the classical Freirean facilitator in a cultural circle working with consenting and self-motivating adults. While the members of a thematic research team (such as the one coordinated by Paulo Freire in El Recurso, in Santiago de Chile) work in the context of a poor (peasant, workers, marginal) community where a consensus already exists on educational practices (or cultural action) that may lead to conscientization, it is too optimistic to assume that a similar consensus may exist in an inner-city urban classroom, or that every classroom is linked organically to a community experiencing the same generative themes.[6]

In spite of these, and perhaps other differences, the implications of Freire's proposal for schooling are vast. Consider, for example, the idea of utilizing the needs of the communities as prime material for the design of vocabulary for literacy programs or the teachiug of sciences, social studies, or mathematics (Shor 1987). To implement this community-based curriculum in the classroom, or to practice pedagogy as a form of cultural politics (Giroux and Simon 1988; McLaren and Leonard 1993), will undermine simultaneously the power of "curriculum experts," school administrators, and state bureaucracies, while eventually giving back to the individual teacher the control over what goes on in the classroom (Bates 1986). Understandably teachers' control in the Freirean-based classroom or cultural circle often will be in contradiction with attempts to control curriculum and school practices by other segments of civil society (special interest groups, business groups, social movements) or by bureaucratic regimes of the state.

From the perspective of cultural politics, curriculum control and teacher autonomy are related issues that eventually could spark a wholesale change within school organizations and administrations. Obviously, in the context of debates over school excellence that focus on international competition within the corporate marketplace, the research projects and policy initiatives generated by a liberating pedagogy will be disruptive of any school "ethos" based on the premises of creating a corporate culture and the technical discourse of mana-gerialism (Bates 1986). In the context of adult education, a pedagogy of liberation is not only more closely linked to the needs of communities and possesses the curricular and organizational flexibility that the rigid school system may lack, but it "has proved to be of great importance as an instrument of mobilization and the development of political consciousness in diverse experiments in the transition to socialism, as was the case in Cuba and Nicaragua" (C. Torres 1990, 9).

In fact, the development of approaches to liberation pedagogy within the area of adult education largely was responsible for the origins of participatory action research in Latin America. Pablo Latapí (1988) argues that participatory methodologies have been developed not in a linear fashion but through competing claims for alternative methodologies, including *thematic research* (Freire's original approach); *action research* (proposed by the respected Colombian sociologist Orlando Fals Borda, who bases his claim on the notion of popular science); *militant research*, which emphasizes the political component of action-research methodologies (well represented in the work of Miguel and Rosiska Darcy de Oliveira, members of the IDAC, an institute founded by Freire and a group of Brazilian exiles in Geneva); and, finally, *participatory research* also known as *participatory action research* (Carr and Kemmis 1986; Duke 1985; Hall and Kassam 1985).

Participatory action research in Latin America has received important support from a growing number of scholars who are becoming influenced by work being done in continental social theory. For instance, representatives of the Frankfurt School (Habermas, Adorno) have questioned conventional social research approaches based on positivist and empiricist assumptions. Dialectical, phenomenological, and hermeneutical views have suggested different epistemological foundations for research and practices in education. New qualitative evaluation methods slowly but steadily have advanced in Latin America, challenging falsifiability or hypothesis-testing approaches (Esmanhoto, Klees, and Werthein 1986).

Participatory action research in Latin America has been inspired deeply by Freire's thematic investigation and generative word methodologies. The object of thematic investigation is to construct generative themes or expressions that result from disadvantaged groups reflecting on their needs and concerns. The purpose is both to facilitate educational programming and to develop a conscientizing cultural action. Thematic investigation (investigation-education) occurs in three stages: *an eminently investigative phase, an eminently pragmatic phase,* and *an eminently pedagogic phase.* Techniques of thematic investigation include *reduction, codification,* and *decodification* (C. Torres 1980b).

Thematic investigation and participatory action research were connected especially to the agrarian reform projects developed at the beginning of the 1960s in Latin America. The beneficiaries of this research strategy included workers, peasants, and indigenous peoples, as well as community and spontaneous settlements in fiscal lands (particularly in the 1960s and 1970s). Freire's work for the Instituto of Training and Research in Agrarian Reform (ICIRA) in Santiago de Chile, supported by the Food and Agriculture Organization (FAO), the United Nations Development Program (UNDP), and the Chilean government was involved with campesinos in El Recurso, groups in rural communities undergoing accelerated agrarian reform. By the late 1970s, a shift in the orientation and clientele of participatory action research occurred, and a focus was placed on the organization of the urban-marginal sector, instead of the peasantry, as well as on heterogeneous urban and rural groups with organizational potential. Marcela Gajardo (1985) has revealed a gradual movement from projects in the rural sector to urban projects. This shift accompanied the process of political and social democratization in Latin America, which brought about a redefinition in the focus of research strategies. During this time, researchers began to examine problems such as critical levels of poverty that were growing in the urban areas at a faster pace than in the rural areas, hence producing serious unrest among large segments of the urban populations (Gajardo 1985, Latapí 1987).

During the last few years, Latin Americans in numerous countries have witnessed growing poverty, marginality, and unemployment in the formal economy, exacerbated by the combined strains of the external debt and fiscal crisis of the state. In the public sector there exists a growing process of marginalization, and popular education projects are taking additional steps to promote both conscientization and the political organization and mobilization of the poor, and to contribute to local economic reforms (Razeto 1990).[7] The demands and challenges for participatory action research and popular education projects related to this new, emerging popular economy and its so-called *factor C*,[8] are formidable (Goldenberg 1990, Razeto 1990).

In summary, the origins of participatory action research in Latin America are related to the contribution of Paulo Freire, his critique of positivist and scientific pedagogy, and his method of thematic research. In addition, participatory action research emerged out of the dynamism and socio-political conditions of the 1960s, with the dynamics of social transformation unleashed by the Cuban Revolution, and the process of reformist change sponsored by the Alliance for Progress (C. Torres 1990). In education, new approaches were developed, including the paradigm of popular education. Participatory action research projects now often are developed in the context of popular education, defined by Freire in the following terms: "Popular education postulates, then, the effort of mobilizing and organizing the popular classes with the goal of creating a popular power" (in R. Torres 1986, 59).[9] Had Freire anticipated the changing economic conditions in Latin America that have occurred in less than a decade after this dialogue with Rosa Maria Torres, it might have provoked him to reconsider his definition of popular education to include the notion of a new popular economy.

Participatory Action Research and Popular Education

I have argued elsewhere that popular education projects

arise from a political and social analysis of the living conditions of the poor and their outstanding problems (such as unemployment, malnourishment, poor health) and attempt to engage the poor in individual and collective awareness of those conditions. Second, they base their educational practice on collective and individual previous experiences (as previous knowledge), and they work in groups rather than on an individual basis. Third, the notion of education provided by these projects is related to the concrete skills or abilities that they try to instill in the poor...and these projects strive to arouse self-reliance among the participants. Finally, these projects can be originated by governments, as in Colombia and Dominican Republic or, as in Nicaragua, with the collectives of popular education, and they may be directed toward adults as well as children. (Torres 1990, 9–10)

There is ample evidence that many of the projects of participatory action research have been developed within the popular education movement in Latin America, and both have been influenced by Paulo Freire's political philosophy of education and theory of knowledge. Members of the Institute for Cultural Action (IDAC) have posed what I consider to be the generic framework of participatory action research:

The frame of reference of our political-pedagogical action is the desire of living and constructing, in each concrete situation, a pedagogy of the oppressed. That is, to experience an educational practice in which, always starting from the realities and interests of those with whom we work, we seek a process of acquiring knowledge and means (instruments) that will increase their power of intervention over reality. This option of the base of education as conscientization explains the diversity of the concrete involvements and commitments of IDAC and, at the same time, the coherence of our methodologies for working in the most diverse contexts. (Freire et al. 1980, 9–10; my translation)

The IDAC carried out a number of international projects, different in terms of the historical and geographical contexts involved and the level of precise educational demands. Thus we find projects such as the 150 hours of paid educational leave designed by the Italian workers from 1971 ot 1973. These workers struggled to implement an education program that could be dedicated to specific learning activities, spread out over three years, and with paid leave; they achieved their objectives in the collective national work contract for the Italian metal workers in April 1973. Another project of the IDAC included the struggle of the feminist movement in Geneva (Switzerland) in the early 1970s; still another involved the PAIGC (African Party for the Independence of Guinea and Cap Verde) liberation movement in Guinea-Bissau between 1973 and 1976. How can a methodology emphasizing social action be so coherent in such diverse contexts? What are the theoretical, methodological, and technical elements that can account for this coherence? Perhaps the answer lies in the basic premises of participatory action research. Gajardo (1982) has suggested the following elements as central axes of participatory action research:

1. Participatory Action Research (PAR) starts from social and political intentionality which is explicit and articulated in solidarity with the dominated and pour classes and groups of the society;
2. PAR assumes a combination of research processes that include popular participation;
3. The incorporation of researchers and the population being studied into the same research process is an important premise of PAR;
4. The constitution of education and research activities in a socially organized base or group constitute a *sine qua non* condition of PAR;
5. At an epistemological level, PAR assumes an understanding of knowledge as an instrument of social transformation, postulating a strong critique of the separation of theory and practice;
6. A further epistemological premise of a PAR project is the incorporation of critical theory in order to establish a critique of methods and techniques that prevent a dialectical understanding of the object/subject relation in the educational/research process;
7. The endorsement of action research projects that exhibit an holistic vision—a vision of the concrete totality—that critically challenges

the partial, parceling, or unidimensional visions of social reality is a fundamental tenent of PAR;

8. A natural result of PAR projects will be the sponsoring of a systematic movement of consciousness-raising in the population studied;

9. And above all, the distinctive trait of a PAR project is the encouragement of the *participation* of the members of the popular sectors. In this regard, the following would be the most important criteria for sponsoring participation:

> 9.1 participation beginning with an initial feedback of information;
>
> 9.2 participation beginning with data gathering;
>
> 9.3 participation throughout the project on a theme proposed by the researcher,
>
> 9.4 participation throughout the project on a theme proposed by the group itself;
>
> 9.5 participation in the research stemming from the educational action;
>
> 9.6 participation in understanding of the milieu of the political community and in the exercise of revindicative actions;
>
> 9.7 participation in the design of self-management mechanisms of political organization, including economic organization (Barquera 1986, Gajardo 1982, Werthein and Argumedo 1986).

When we speak about strategies for emancipatory education and participatory action research, we are speaking of a succession of small experiments that generally take place in an unplanned or unorganized manner, in diferent regions of a country or in different communities within a region; through different channels of communication and across varying institutions; respondong to different pedagogical criteria, to different political-cultural visions, to different political practices, to different "generative themes" of political conflict, and to different experiences of social struggle among both beneficiaries and promoters.

Let us refer again to the examples provided by the experiences of IDAC. In general terms, despite the heterogeneity (geographic as well as historical) of the experiences, several common denominators exist.

1. Participatory action research (PAR) deals with political-pedagogical proposals that are born out of social struggles; that is, it deals with

pedagogical actions that are inscribed in the process of social, political, and economic defense of the rights of the poor.

2. PAR results from an *inductive* process arising from the description and analysis of real and lived situations emerging from the concrete everyday life and work experiences of the participants. The participants will try to explicate these experiences and critically reflect upon them within a more complex frame of reference.[10] Here the researchers often draw upon existential and phenomenological research initiatives.

3. The fundamental objectives of PAR are: (a) to achieve an understanding of the mechanisms and regularities which explain the functioning of social reality; that is, to provide a historical-structural focus; (b) to support the acquisition of knowledge, abilities, and skills that are helpful in the interpretation and transformation of that social reality; (c) to support a methodological work that takes into consideration the thought and language structures of the participants, with a particular emphasis on improving their verbal and language skills.

4. The fundamental moments in PAR include:

   (i) Collective classification of the objectives of the research (process analysis, demands, and claims that motivated the starting of this pedagogical phase). I wish to stress that this is a collective task rather than the task of individual researchers:

   (ii) A review of the personal history of each participant, placing these within a global framework (regional, national, corporative); listing all the problems that affect the members of the group and discussing them. Here the interdisciplinary perspective of the research team is essential. Similarly, the use of concepts, techniques, and theories from the social sciences, as well as nontraditional didactic materials, is extremely important;

   (iii) Specification of the generative theme. Here the range of options is as broad as the range of mechanisms of social exploitation and domination that exist in the diverse historical-political contexts under investigation. In describing IDAC's experience, Freire and coauthors mention the following among other broad generative themes: (a) the factory and the worker; (b) the health of the worker; (c) the city-countryside contradictions; (d) the relations between workers and the state, (e) the methods of communicating information and the worker's culture (Freire et al. 1980);

(iv) The last stage consists of a final synthesis and inventory of the experience, which is not necessarily going to be evaluated (i.e., by means of examinations and/or marks) and/or certified. The aim is to establish in a systematic manner answers to questions such as: What action should be taken as a response to the generative theme? In what direction should the research proceed, and how can this be accomplished?

There are epistemological, philosophical, and methodological problems associated with participatory action research (Latapí 1986, 128) and popular education (La Belle 1986, C. Torres 1990). Eventually, some questions can be traced to the Freirean origins of these paradigms. In the following sections I will discuss the relationships between participatory action research and the state and the challenge of participatory action research for traditional educational researchers in Latin America.

Participatory Action Research and the State: Questions and Queries

Is it possible to launch a participatory action research process *from* and *within* the educational agencies of the capitalist state? All complex and large organizations such as the state apparatus work through a series of legal norms, institutional routines, control levels (hierarchical, budgetary, and so on), hierarchical communication networks, and so forth, that reflect the bureaucratic practices of formal organizations. Thus, given the increasing bureaucratization of the state agencies, under what conditions is it possible to carry out participatory action research—which is eminently impressionist, spontaneous, micro-oriented, naturalistic, and decentralized by nature—in the context of normative environments that are centrally planned and controlled by a corporative managerial culture?

A second theme is equally important. From a Gramscian perspective, every State assumes the role of synthesizer of the basic ideological principles that form a nation, the integration of the social groups, and the formation (civic, political, and educational) of its citizens. Historically, this has implied activities ranging from propaganda to social control, from controlled mobiiization to repression, from assuming initiatives !or claims) based or anchored in the civil society to proposals attempting to modify the very foundations of such societies.

Are these political, symbolic, and material state-induced processes compatible with the preconditions, assumptions, objectives, and strategies of participatory action research based on emancipatory interests? In other words, can participatory action research be implemented within state institutions without contradicting its liberal-capitalist foundations or the prevailing technical interests that guide policy planning that are grounded in a technocratic rationality? Under what conditions is there room within the capitalist state for allowing or legitimating research and educational practices that potentially or directly challenge its organization of power and its social relations of production?

These queries address substantive problems concerning the actual link between political power and participatory action research. Without a doubt, one of the most important contradictory relations results from the interaction between planning (educational, social) and mobilization and the political participation of the individual as a citizen. Are there acceptable degrees of freedom within the democratic state to implement participatory action research that may lead, in turn, to alternative forms of citizenship education? If that is the case, what are the political conditions for its reconstruction and production?

There are not clear-cut answers to these questions. However, any discussion of the relationships between participatory action research and the state implies a discussion of the role of qualitative researchers and intellectuals in the production of knowledge and power.

Participatory Action Research and Traditional Intellectuals

How can it be possible to carry out participatory action research in Latin America if researchers (teachers, professors, students) have been trained (professionally and ideologically) to perform traditional, nonparticipatory research roles? Participatory research, to be successful, may need new epistemological approaches.

Let us take as a premise the idea that theories, methods, and research techniques, related to academic research in the social sciences, have been and continue to be in Latin America (and perhaps elsewhere) dominated by positivist or even vulgar empiricist paradigms. Positivist methodologies assume: a predetermined set of methodological sequences in the research process (i.e., delimitation of a general theoretical framework, selection of specific hypothesis, testing or experimentation, and so on); prespecified ways of linking theory, data, and interpretation;

a dominant testing logic and standardized research techniques (i.e., deductive or probabilistic models of explanation); and a common means of presentation and dissemination of research products (research papers, articles, books, workshops, and other forms).

Participatory action research involves an "epistemological rupture" that signals a move away from the limitations of positivistic and vulgar empirical models and the beginning of a new type of practice which, provisionally, I will refer to as historical-structural. Historical-structural research differs from positivistic research in the following ways:

1. It is guided by a notion of a concrete totality (Kosik 1976).
2. It is assumed to be virtually impossible to separate in a clear-cut fashion politics from research, thus challenging the sharp distinction found in mainstream research between empirical facts and values. Facts are viewed as socially constructed, while values are considered socially introjected (thus depending on cultural capital or habitat/habitus, or intellectual, institutional and organizational milieu, political socialization experiences, and so on). The researcher's values always are self-reflexively present in the process of research and policy making.
3. The issues of class, gender, and race differentiation are taken very seriously, not only in terms of the analytical strategy, but also in terms of the axiological principles that originate and orient the research endeavor.
4. The notion of scientific objectivity is considered problematic.
5. A number of ethical and moral considerations exist about how the research (and by implication research findings) is employed in the process of restructuring new forms of social organization and knowledge production.
6. A theory is considered "dialectical" and is never subordinated to the positivistic logic of mainstream research and research techniques.

I believe that there exists increasing evidence for this "epistemological rupture" in research environments dealing with schooling issues (as well as other academic environments) throughout Latin America over the past twenty years. A concrete example in the field of education is the burgeoning growth of qualitative and naturalistic research among Latin American education researchers.

Even from an historical-structural perspective, epistemological challenges persist. For instance, how is it possible for the researcher to break the dichotomy between the subjectivity of the researcher and the subject (and object) that is researched, or between theory and practice? Furthermore, what possibility exists for successfully combining participatory action research methodologies with a historical-structural paradigm in challenging the established positivist paradigm in Latin American social science? Are there any epistemological rules that permit the researcher to combine (without authoritarianism, manipulation, or proselytism) research based on historical-structural analysis with participatory action research, using the criteria for promoting participation mentioned earlier? What conditions need to exist for this to happen? Is it possible to gain legitimacy for this new epistemology within the democratic state and communities of established scholars within Latin America? Do we need a new methodological *metanoesis* (a total change of mental action) for all those involved in scientific research, capable of addressing this contradictory transformation of the research process?

The dialogue over these questions remains open. Participatory action research in Latin America is becoming a major contributor to emancipatory education movements that take place in nonformal educational settings. At the same time, and in spite of its limitations and myths (Latapí 1988), it will call into question not only the present organization of social science in undergraduate as well as graduate training in education but also the basic epistemological assumptions of established educational research—and even the main aims of emancipatory education itself.

Not by chance, participatory action research methodologies have failed to assume a central place in teaching and research in schools of education in Latin America. They are considered by many mainstream educational researchers, to paraphrase Kant, as deviations from practical reason. Freire (1975) is very clear, however in linking practical reasoning with the project of conscientization:

> If conscientization cannot be produced without the revelation of objective reality, as an object of knowledge for those subjects involved in the process, then this revelation—even when it is a clear perception of reality—is still insufficient for an authentic conscientization. In the same way that the epistemological cycle does not end in the degree of acquisition of already existent knowledge, but rather continues through the stage of creation of new knowledge, neither can conscientization be stalled in the mode of revelation of reality. It is authentic when the practice of revealing reality constitutes a dynamic and dialectic unity with the practice of transforming reality. (28; my translation)

Considering its origins, premises, and intentionality, participatory action research can make an important contribution to problem-posing education and conscientization projects throughout Latin America. While both approaches represent political agendas that have yet to receive the necessary scientific legitimation for adoption by mainstream educational researchers, the growing fiscal and environmental crisis in Latin America soon may generate a more urgent interest in forms of research designed to promote social change. There are few other options left.

Notes

1. In describing participatory research I will use extensively the work of Chilean sociologist, Marcela Gajardo (1982), one of Freire's earlier collaborators.

2. I use *epistemology* for its convenience. However, Freire's approach is more a theory of knowledge in general than it is a theory of scientific knowledge (thus *epistemology*).

3. The positivist or logical-empiricist approach to the human sciences is based on several premises: (a) that theory and science can be defined in a unitary manner; (b) that it follows for the most part a model of natural science; (c) hence it is base mostly on experimentation (or quasi-experimentation) and measurement; and (d) it employs causal explanations, often connected to mathematical models or manipulation of statistical analyses.

4. A discussion of *escola pública popular* (public popular schooling) can be found in C. Torres 1991b; Gadotti 1990.

5. Freire always has rejected the notion of a psychosocial method, arguing instead that he proposed technical and methodological suggestions for literacy training, rather than a formalized method.

6. A generative theme is an existential and crucial daily life situation for members of a given "oppressed" community. When a generative theme is discovered through thematic investigation and is codified, it becomes a knowledgeable object mediating between knowing subjects, and it then leads to discovering "generative words" (selected based on their syllabic complexity and richness), the basis for the Freirean literacy training process.

7. The term *popular economy* refers to the production, distribution, exchange, and consumption of goods by the popular social sectors (e.g., the poor, marginalized, disenfranchised groups) in Latin America societies. Different in nature (and perhaps in behavior) from the formal labour markets and the formal economy at large, popular economy usually has been characterized as

informal or nonformal economic sectors, or as part of the subsistence strategies of the poor. However, there are a number of reasons why these characterizations based on informality or subsistence factors may be misleading (Razeto 1990, Sáenz 1989).

8. The new economic rationality of popular economy includes what is called *factor C*. Following the traditional distinction of economic factors (i.e., K for capital, L for labor), Razeto argues that the peculiarity of popular economy is the presence of *factor C*, that is, the economic units have an element of *community, cooperation, collaboration,* and *collectivity* that build a sense of solidarity. Razeto terms this axiological and psychological factor as *factor C* of the popular economy because most of the words, in Spanish or English, begin with the letter *C* (Razeto 1990, 83).

9. For more discussion see C. Torres 1990, 110–11.

10. See Miguel Darcy de Oliveira in Freire et al. 1980, 15–37.

References

Barquera, H. 1986. "Una revisión sintética de la investigación participativa" [A synthetic review of participatory research]. Pp. 33–72 in *Investigación participativa: algunos aspectos críticos y problemáticos*, coord. C. Picón. Patzcuaro, Mexico: CREFAL.

Bates, R. 1986, April. "Instructional Leadership and Educational Control: A Cultural Perspective." Paper presented at the 67th annual meeting of the American Educational Research Association, San Francisco.

Brandão, C. R. 1982. "Lutar com a palavra" [The word as weapon]. Rio de Janeiro: Graal.

Carr, W., and S. Kemmis. 1986. *Becoming Critical. Education, Knowledge and Action Research* London: Falmer Press.

Duke, C., ed. 1985. *Participation Research* (Canberra Papers in Continuing Education). Canberra: Australia University Centre for Continuing Education.

Esmanhoto, P., S. Klees, and J. Werthein. 1986. "Evaluación educacional: tendencias hacia el desarrollo de enfoques participativos" [Educational evaluation: Trends toward development of participatory approaches]. Pp. 73–98 in *Educacion y participación*, ed. J. Werhein and M. Argumedo. Brasilia: Instituto Interamericano de Cooperación para la Agricultura, Ministério da Educação. Secretaria de Ensino de Primeiro e Segundo Graus.

Freire, P. 1975. "La concientización desmitificada por Freire" [concientización demystified by Freire]. *Revista Sic* 38:164–66.

———. 1980. "Conscientizar para liberar" [Conscientization for liberation]. Pp. 73–84 in *Educación y concientización*, ed. C. A. Torres. Salamanca: Sígüeme.

Freire, P., et al. 1980. *Vivendo e aprendendo. Experiencias do IDAC en educação popular* [Living and learning: IDAC's experiences in popular education]. 5th ed. São Paulo: Brasilense Editora.

Gadotti, M. 1989. *Convite a leitura de Paulo Freire* [Invitation to read Paulo Freire]. São Paulo: Editora Scipione.

———. 1990. *Uma só escola para todos. Caminhos da autonomia escolar* [One school for everyone: Paths of school autonomy]. Petropolis: Editora Vozes.

Gajardo, M. 1982, March–April. "Evolución, situación actual y perspectiva de las estrategias de investigación participativa en América Latina" [Evolution, current situation and perspectives of participatory research in Latin America]. Punta de Tlalca, Chile: Facultad Latinoamericana de Cieucias Spciales (FLASCO)—Programa de Interdisciplinario de Educacion.

———. 1985. *Teoría y práctica de la educación popular* [Theory and practice of popular education]. Michoacán, Mexico: Programa Regional de Desarrollo de la Educacion (PREDE)—Organization of the American States (OAS)—Centro Regional para la Alfabetización Funcional de America Latina (CREFAL)—International Development Research Centre (IDRC).

Giroux, H., and R. I. Simon. 1988. "Schooling, Popular Culture, and a Pedagogy of Possibility." *Journal of Education* 170, no. 1:9–26.

Goldenberg, O., comp. 1990. *Economía popular: de la protesta a la propuesta* [Popular economy: From protest to proposal]. Heredia, Costa Rica: Editorialpec.

Hall, B., and Y. Kassam. 1985. "Participatory Research." Vol. 7, pp. 3795–3800, in *International Encyclopedia of Education: Research and Pactice*, ed. T. Husen and T. M. Postlewaite. London: Pergamon.

Kosik, K. 1976. *Dialéctica de lo concreto* [Dialectics of the concrete]. Mexico: Grijalbo.

La Belle, T. J. 1986. *Nonformal Education in Latin America and the Caribbean. Stability, Reform, or Revolution?* New York: Praeger.

Latapí, P. 1986. "Algunas observaciones sobre la investigación participativa" [Some observations about participatory research]. Pp. 125–31 in *Investigación participativa: algunos aspectos críticos y problemáticos*, coord. C. Picon. Pátzcuaro, Mexico: Cuadernos de CREFAL 18, Centro Regional para la alfabetización funcional de América Latina.

————. 1987. "Poverty and Adult Education in latin America. Prospects for Year 2000." University of Alberta, Edmonton.

————. 1988. "Participatopy Research: A New Paradigm?" *Alberta Journal of Educational Research* 34, no. 1:310–19.

McLaren, P., and P. Leonard, eds. 1993. *Paulo Freire: A Critical Encounter.* London: Routledge.

Mezirow, J. 1977. "Perspective Transformation." *Studies in Adult Education* 9, no. 2:153–64.

————. 1981. "A Critical Theory of Adult Learning and Education." *Adult Education* 32, no. 1:3–24.

————. ed. 1990. *Fostering Critical Reflection in Adulthood: A Guide to Transformative and Emancipatory Learning.* San Francisco: Jossey-Bass.

Razeto, L. 1990. "Economía de solidaridad y organización popular." Pp. 70–96 in *Educación comunitaria y economía popular*, comp. F. Gutierrez. Heredia, Costa Rica: Editorialpec, Friedrich Ebert Stiftung, International Community Education Association.

Sáenz, A. 1989. "Informal Labor Markets and Education." University of Alberta, Edmonton.

Shor, I. ed. 1987. *Freire for the Classroom. A Sourcebook for Liberatory Teaching.* Portsmouth, N.H.: Boynton/Cook.

Shor, I., and P. Freire. 1987. *A Pedagogy for Liberation. Dialogues on Transforming Education.* Amherst, Mass.: Bergin & Garvey.

Torres, C. A. 1980a. "La sociología de la cultura y la crítica pedagógica de Paulo Freire" [Sociology of culture and the pedagogical criticism of Paulo Freire]. Pp. 315–49 in *Sociología de la educación: tendencias contemporáneas*, ed. G. Rivera and C. A. Torres. Mexico: Centro de Estudios Educativos.

————. 1980b. *Educación y concientización* [Education and conscientization]. Salamanca, Spain: Ediciones Sígueme.

————. 1990. *The Politics of Nonformal Education in Latin America.* New York: Praeger.

————. 1991a. "Instrumental Rationality and Adult Education Policy in Canada: Policy-makers' Views and Policy Rationales in the Province of Alberta." University of California, Los Angeles.

————. 1991b, April. "Educational Policy and Social Change in Brazil. The Work of Paulo Freire as Secretary of Education in the Municipality of São Paulo." Paper presented at the American Educational Research Association,

Chicago. [*Comparative Education Review,* 1994, 38, 2, pp. 181–214 as "Paulo Freire as secretary of education in Sáo Paulo, Brazil"]

Torres, R. M. 1986. *Educación popular: Un encuentro con Paulo Freire* [Popular education: An encounter with Paulo Freire]. Quito: Centro de Educación y capacitación del campesinado del Azuay (CECCA), Corporación Ecuatoriana para el Desarrollo de la comunicación [CEDECO].

Werhein, J., and M. Argumedo, eds. 1986. *Educación y participación* [Education and participation]. Brasilia: Instituto Interamericano de Cooperación para la Agricultura, Ministério de Educação. Secretaria de Ensino de Primeiro e Segundo Graus.

14

We Can Reinvent the World[1]

Paulo Freire and Moacir Gadotti
Translated by Rudolf Wiedemann

The educator Paulo Freire does not like being interviewed. He complains about the journalists distorting his declarations. Announcing the pedagogic project he intended to introduce when he assumed the Municipal Secretariat of Education in the City of São Paulo in 1989, a headline in a big São Paulo newspaper declared the following day: "From now on writing wrong will be correct."

To overcome that resistance *Nova Escola* magazine had an idea: what about inviting Moacir Gadotti, also an educator, personal friend and chief-of-cabinet in Paulo Freire's secretariat, to talk to him? That would have the additional advantage of providing a more open and richer conversation, a dialogue between two educators deeply committed to transforming Brazilian schools.

It worked. The outcome was a lesson of life, with Paulo Freire using his sharp intelligence to reflect upon his experience as secretary of education, upon the course of public schooling, upon freedom and democracy, and to speak about his hope which he portraits in the book *Pedagogy of Hope—A Re-encounter with Pedagogy of the Oppressed* (Paz e Terra). The hope that it is possible to put an end to oppression, miscry, and intolerance and to transform the world into a place that is more agreeable and more just to live in. "Hope makes part of me just like the air that I breathe," he declares.

Being the most important Brazilian educator, known and appreciated all over the world, Paulo Freire has already written more than thirty books, among them *Pedagogy of the Oppressed* in 1968, a milestone in Brazilian pedagogy and which has influenced educators in all parts of the world. At the age of seventy-two, Freire continues producing at an impressive rate. Since he left the secretariat in 1991 he has already written four books—*Education in the City* (Cortez); *Teacher Yes, Auntie No—Letters to Those Who Dare to Teach* (Olho D'Agua) and *Politics and Education* (Cortez), besides *Pedagogy of Hope*. He is finishing the fifth book, which will be called *Letters to Cristina*. Cristina is a niece of his, also a teacher, to whom he used to write during his exile.

Due to his liberating pedagogy and his political militance, Paulo Freire was exiled after the military coup of 1964. He returned to Brazil in 1980, after an amnesty. Being in exile he developed projects in several countries in Latin America, Europe, Africa and lectured at Harvard University in the United States. Most of the time he worked for the World Church Council with headquarters in Geneva.

Nine years after his return he assumed the Municipal Secretariat of Education of the City of São Paulo during the government of Luiza Erundina from the Workers' Party. He occupied the job for two-and-a-half years. He has been the target of accusations from the current São Paulo municipal administration, headed by Paulo Maluf, which are similar to the ones which were made against him during the military regime: accusations of developing a pedagogic proposal that is politicized and ideological. Paulo Freire defends himself against these accusations in his discussion with Moacir Gadotti, another important Brazilian educator and author of fifteen books. His latest two books— *History of Pedagogic Ideas* (Atica) and *Pedagogy of Praxis* (Paulo Freire Institute)—have come out recently.

Moacir Gadotti: Brazilian people are living from their hopes. However, one after the other have been lost and there has always been frustration afterwards. That happened with the direct-elections-now movement, with the Constitutional Assembly, with Collor....Today we are living a moment of uncertainty, it seems that the ground we step on is moving and that we, in Brazil, cannot see tomorrow. Where does the hope that it is possible to transform the world that you refer to in your book *Pedagogy of Hope*, come from?

Paulo Freire: Although succinct, it is a question that requires reflection upon ourselves. What are we in the world? John, Mary, Charles? It does not matter the social class, although it has a considerable influence upon the way we are. But what are we, why are we, how are we, who are we? This gives me the chance to make comparisons. For example: I am looking at my small backyard now and I see other living beings there, but of natural order—a jaboticaba and the kennel where Jim is, a German shepherd dog—and I can already establish comparisons among how I am, how the jaboticaba is and how Jim is. Without going too far, I come to a first conclusion that the relationship existing between me and my jaboticabas and between me and Jim is not the same as the one between me and you. There is a different quality in these relationships. A second conclusion is that I can take as a reference, to distinguish myself from the other two beings (Jim and the jaboticabas), that—although all three of us are finite, unfinished, uncompleted, imperfect—only I know that we are finite, unfinished and uncompleted. The jaboticaba does not know. It has another kind of knowledge.

Gadotti: That is what you want to say when you write in your book "I am hopeful by existential imperative" ?

Freire: That's it, too. I am hopeful because I cannot give up being hopeful as a human being, This being that is finite and that knows that it is finite is—due to the fact that it is unfinished knowing that it is so— necessarily a being that is in search. It does not matter that the majority is not seeking. Not seeking is the result, the immobilism imposed by the circumstances in which we could not seek. However, it is not the being's nature. Therefore, the large suffering masses, more immersed than emersed in the social, political, and economic reality, as I call it in *Pedagogy of the Oppressed*, are prevented from being. Therefore, they become apathetic. Hope does not flourish in apathy. Struggling for hope is up to the pedagogue, the philosopher, the politician, to those who understand the reason of the masses' apathy—and sometimes the reason for their own apathy. I cannot give up hope because I know, first of all, that it is ontologic. I know that I cannot continue being human if I make hope disappear and the struggle for it. Hope is not a donation. It is part of me just as the air that I breathe. Unless there is air, I will die. Unless there is hope, there is no reason for history to continue. Hope is history, do you understand? At the moment you definitely lose hope you fall into immobilism. Then you are as much a jaboticaba as the jaboticaba itself.

Gadotti: Is hope a mark, is it the ontological expression of the human being?

Freire: Hope is an invention of the human being that is part of our nature today, that has been constituted historically and socially. That means, hope is a project of the human being and is also the viabilization of the project. Therefore, dictators annihilate—as much as they can—the masses' hope. Sometimes under fright, fear, terror. Sometimes under assistentialism [state charity]. I am not against assistance because it is not possible that you can see a person dying and not give him bread because it would be assistential. This is wrong, it is a crime. What we cannot be is assistentialists, which means transforming assistance into a strategy. As a tactic, however, it is absolutely valid.

Gadotti: What is new about your new book and what remains from *Pedagogy of the Oppressed*?

Freire: Many things have remained. Besides belief and hope, a respect for a conviction of the importance of the role of subjectivity has remained. When the Marxists— and also the non-Marxists—of a purely mechanistic nature of thinking used to criticize me in the 1970s, they accused me of being, idealistic, Kantian, in the best of the hypothesis of being neo-Hegelian, due to my proposals of conscientization, which came into conflict with the idea that the superstructure conditions consciousness. Today we see emerge secure and serious criticism of that mechanistic explanation of Marxist origin, which had not been competent to explain the proper role of its struggle against the capitalist project—a struggle in which it annulled the individual's liking, the individual's fear, the individual's pleasure, the individual's presence.

Gadotti: So you continue criticizing this mechanistic explanation which sustains the thesis of the human being's inexorability and the idea that there is a succession in history that will inevitably lead to socialism?

Freire: Of course. Just look at the enormous contradiction in this inexorability: people used to quarrel about inexorability. If the event will come tomorrow anyway, why should I die today struggling for it? I will wait. This mechanistic hypothesis should even lead to apathy. And it has been proved that it is not like that.

Gadotti: Look what a strange thing: in *Pedagogy of Hope* you say that "class-struggle is not the motor of history, but certainly is one of them." You—who was criticized in *Pedagogy of the Oppressed* for not using the term class-struggle—know that now you will be criticized for using it.

Freire: That is interesting. Do you know one of the risks we will encounter at the beginning of the millenium—and which we already encounter today? It is that many people from the left were so impacted by the fall of the Berlin Wall that they lost their parameters and feel themselves immobilized. These people are perplexed about history, precisely because they thought that tomorrow was inexorable. They did not have time to reconstruct and rethink themselves.

Gadotti: But what are these risks?

Freire: First of all, the risk that a minority of these people manage to get into power and reactivate, odiously, Stalinist manners. The second risk is that some of those who have been impacted fall into such immobilism that they begin to believe in the neo-liberal discourse: that the struggle between the social classes has come to an end, that ideology has come to an end, that history has come to an end. This second group constitutes an enormous danger to progressivity itself, and strengthens the majority of the right and the minority of the left that intends to reactivate Stalinism. A third risk we will have to encounter at the beginning of the millenium due to this historic disorder is exactly the power of neofascism, which has been growing especially in Europe but also in the Third World (see the outbreak of neo-Nazism in São Paulo, the threats of killing people from the northeast of Brazil, the racism from the right). It is a frightening threat that is of a material nature but above all distant from that preoccupation. It has to be discussed at primary school, in the children's own language.

Gadotti:	You have also been worried about about sectarianism, haven't you?
Freire:	In *Pedagogy of Hope* I advance a little in relation to *Pedagogy of the Oppressed*, where I had already criticized sectarianism. There I had been radical and not sectarian. Today I consider myself more radical—and even more distant from sectarianization. It has been historical experience and, therefore, political and social experience that has taught me that I have to convince myself of not being so sure about my convictions. Instead of killing the adventure of hope within me, this certainty about uncertainty, about uncertainty's search, has lead me further on toward the adventure of hope. That means, at the moment I discover that I cannot be any longer so sure about my convictions, I hope that I will discover a bit of light in the uncertainness. So I will be more curious, more inquiring, more competent. And this will necessarily cause me to be more nonconciliatory; to understand the difference and not to deny it.
Gadotti:	What is the meaning of respecting the difference? Is it just as the bourgeois ideology says, respecting the poor, respecting the blacks....?
Freire	It is about getting into his or her skin and learning too.
Gadotti:	In the book *The Mestizo Philosophy* (Nova Fronteira), that is fantastic, the French educator Michel Serres affirms that all of us are mestizos and that there is no education unless one can understand—more than understand, assimilate—another culture that is not one's own. Do you agree?
Freire:	The position I call substantively democratic sets out to understand a need. It is not like a favor. It is necessary to understand someone different from me if I want to grow. Therefore, my radicality ends in the the present moment, Gadotti, the moment when I refuse to understand that which is different from me. When I understand that which is different, I discover that there is antagonism, which is the more radically different, I also discover that even with the antagonism I learn. Therefore, I cannot close myself sectarianly. Intrinsically, my quarrel is not against the others; it is against myself, in the sense of not allowing myself

to fall into sectarianization. And sectarianization is the negation of the other, the negation of the contrary, the negation of the different, the negation of the world, the negation of life. That means, nobody can stay alive if he or she sectarianizes him or herself. Note how Stalinism was antilife, how Nazism was antilife. And democracy is only authentic when it is life. And the latter is only life when it is mobile, when it is afraid. It is necessary to open oneself as much as possible to emotions, joy, desires, even to the antilife of scientificism. Scientificism is antilife because this dream of an absolute rigorousness of knowledge against the non-rigorousness of knowledge is the negation of life too.

Gadotti: In *Pedagogy of Hope* you approach the question of women, of the pitfall that language represents, for example, when we affirm that men make history or when we say—to defend ourselves against certain questions which women ask about the use of language—that the woman is necessarily included when I speak of man. How can we escape from this pitfall?

Freire: First of all, we have to acknowledge that language is a social production, with an individual presence in that social production. In the second place, language is an ideologic body: It is not possible to think of language without ideology and without power. In the third place, grammar itself is born historically as a regulation of the powerful, of the one who has got power. It is obvious that in machist cultures language is molded according to that machism. In a progressive perspective it is absolutely fundamental that language is also reinvented, because it is not possible to democratize a society, leaving away one of the fundamental aspects of society's tasks, the one of human language. At a time of searching for equality, of overcoming restrictive ideologies, it is not possible that there remain syntaxes prohibitive to women. Some time ago, talking to an audience of fifteen hundred women, I suddenly saw the face of a man and said: "Todos vocês" [masculine plural for "all of you"]. This is not grammar. This is ideology. I really have to say "todas vocês" [feminine plural]. I write in that book that it is possible that someone could say that the invention of language, before the invention of social structures, was pure idealism. It is not. At the moment you do not consider history as determinism but as possibility, reinventing language becomes part of reinventing the world. So you can even begin with the struggle of reinventing language.

Gadotti: This question is linked to another pitfall of language which you explain in your book *Teacher Yes, Auntie No.* On page 25 you say: "The attempt of reducing the woman teacher to the condition of auntie is an innocent ideological pitfall through which—trying to give the illusion of sweetening the teacher's life—one tries to smooth her capacity of struggling to divert her in her fundamental tasks." What do you want to say to that?

Freire: That one mustn't take away from the female teacher the duty of being a teacher, the duty of loving not only the child but the process itself, of which she forms a part as one of the subjects, that is teaching, that is formation. What she must know is that when she is called auntie, in the kernel of this auntie there is—not always lucidly to the headmistress—the following: auntie cannot go on strike. The more you reduce professionalization to parental affection the less the teacher will be able to struggle. At least that is what ideology is expecting. I also say that she may like being an auntie and may prefer being called auntie. Nothing against that. However, she must know about the ideological artifice when she is called auntie.

Gadotti: Another preoccupation expressed in the book concerns the children's cultural identity, which school ignores. Given this system of just one idea of culture, a monocultural curriculum, what can a teacher do in the classroom in order to transform this school and this curriculum?

Freire: A large number of male and female teachers feel absolutely handcuffed by an authoritarian administration. This form of administration encourages the female teachers to become aunties, the concept by which they explain or accommodate themselves to the immobilism that authoritarianism expects from them. However, I believe that it is possible to practice popular education at school. Of course, swimming with the stream is one thing and swimming against it is another thing. If one has an open-minded, democratic administration, one will be swimming with the stream if one defends a number of open political-pedagogical positions. And one will be swimming against the stream if the concept of participation is forbidden, is a sin. It is difficult then to defend participation and, above all, to live participation. However, it is possible.

Gadotti: As a teacher, what would you do in the classroom?

Freire: One of the things the teacher should do is, for example, understanding culture in a multicultural way, commenting with the students on the differences and pointing out that this part of the curriculum is not universal, it has its regional dimensions, even of the family, and there also enters the class problem. It is also necessary to know how to reinvent language, to understand the diversity of its syntaxes, to recreate language in a correct form. As a teacher one witnesses its shape every day and understands very well the dialectical relation between tactics and strategies. That means, one has the strategic dream that is multiculturality, but one must have tactics to talk about it, because one may fall into exaggerations in one's discourse—which are idealistic, voluntaristic—and one might lose one's job. And it is not the question of losing one's job; you have to maintain your job and help your dream come true. I think there aren't any formulae for that. Every day one has to recreate one's tactics to overcome the exclusivism of a narrow cultural comprehension.

Gadotti: Your experience at the Secretariat of Education has given you a strong impulse to write. What are your plans for the next fifty years?

Freire: I wish I had these fifty years. . . . At the moment I am writing a book I like very much, which is full of affection, which will be called *Letters to Cristina*. Cristina is a niece of mine who has been in correspondence with me since her childhood, when I was in exile. One day I got a letter in which she wrote: "Until today I have heard about uncle Paulo from my mother, my father, and my grandmother. And now at university I start to get to know another Paulo, through somewhat frightening references (we were still under military dictatorship); not any longer of uncle Paulo but of the educator Paulo Freire. And I am so interested in learning about Paulo Freire, uncle of all the others not only mine, that I'd like to ask a favor: send me letters about your life, about your childhood." I thought it was great and I answered her that I would do that.

Gadotti: And after that book?

Freire: I dream of writing an essay about Amilcar Cabral [revolutionary leader who founded the liberation movement of Guiné-Bissau and Cabo Verde in Africa]. I think it is very opportune working a bit on that. At a moment when people think that there will never again be a revolution, I, on the contrary, do believe that there will be one. Not the day after tomorrow and not like those we have already had. We must understand that history has not come to an end. What has come to an end is the way of making history. Today we have begun living a new way of being historical and we must notice that. We must do everything we can to make that clear.

Gadotti: Talking about making things clear, what do you say about the criticism that the current municipal secretary of education, Solon Borges dos Reis, has made of the previous administration, of which we formed a part? He announced the deactivation of MOVA [Adult Literacy Movement] because it had political-ideological objectives. He also intends to work more with professionalization, in contrast to those of us who worked more with school autonomy and participation—words which, according to professor Solon, are associated to the liberating pedagogy of Paulo Freire. He says that he will give emphasis to pedagogy for responsibility. First of all, I have to point out that Professor Solon has the obligation of trying to affirm his administration as secretary in the

position and political-pedagogical option he has,
which the government he belongs to has. In this sense
he is as political as we are. The neutrality he refers
to does not exist. He is not neutral. He is trying to
canalize his administration not only into a pedagogic
perspective but into a political-ideological option that
diverges from ours, that is opposed to ours. It is his
right. By the way, he confesses that when he says that
"the values of the Workers' Party administration are
not the values we want for education."

Freire: Exactly. In the book *Politics and Education*, there is an
article on education and responsibility in which I
discuss the comprehension of reponsibility associated
with education and emphasize the question of the
political option, of the need for pedagogical
responsibility. I defend Professor Solon's right to
defend his option. Therefore, I also say in that article
that it is not possible to have rigorous administrative
continuity when a conservative administration
succeeds a progressive administration. How can I, an
educator who considers himself as progressive,
continue a reactionary work? And how can a
reactionary, a conservative person, continue a
progressive work? There are very few purely administrative aspects. Any administrative problem is
illuminating and founds a political question. For
example, the priorities are political, ideological.

Gadotti: This fact does not strengthen the idea that is
important, indeed, to strengthen the political-
pedagogical proposals of the schools themselves, so
that they can further administrative discontinuity.

Freire: I think so, but that also concerns the political power
of those who are in the central administration. For
example, how can a conservative administration, first
of all, accept the proper idea of school autonomy? It
cannot, for one of the characteristics of conservativism
is exactly a centralization of power. When you ask
what the meaning of school autonomy itself is, the
answer has a political and ideological starting point.
It is not a question only concerning administration
sciences, it is not a question the answer of which
depends on pedagogy. The education practice will

reflect the political-ideological dream of whoever defines autonomy. Something else: it is absolutely wrong to say that we did not make an education for responsibility or responsible education. However, our responsibility was based on other values. Our responsibility had to do, above all, with ontology, with the human being's quality of being. My responsibility concerns that. Therefore, I speak of ontology. I am responsible in my educational practice in the sense of helping myself and helping others become more. And it is not possible to become more without liberation. Thus, a pedagogy of liberation is profoundly responsible.

Gadotti: What is the difference between pedagogy of liberation and the one that is being put into practice?

Freire: The difference between the first one and the latter, which is said to be responsible—and which is as responsible as we are—is that the conservative one is responsible in relation to the interests of the dominant group. To argue, however, that to be responsible in relation to the interests of the dominant group is the only measure of responsibility is absurd. I can't say either that we are the only responsible ones. However, I have to distinguish at which point I am responsible. My utopia is not the conservatives' utopia. The conservative wants to preserve, therefore, he is reactionary—for it isn't necessary to preserve what is legitimate; one struggles for preserving what is illegitimate.

Gadotti: What balance would you make today of what was done during your administration?

Freire: I don't have any balance, but if you ask me if I regretted something, I would tell you that—despite the legitimacy of regret—I don't regret anything. I would do the same thing again. When we came together to administer the Secretariat, we didn't think that we were the greatest educators in the State. None of us thought that for that reason only we would be able to do something positive. None of us thought that we had been chosen by God to save education in São Paulo and in Brazil later on. What we knew was that we were doing the job seriously and we would bet, without any false modesty, that we were able. And we had political options. We knew, for example, that we defended the idea that a school, being public, should become a popular school. And you, Gadotti, added that it was necessary to make clear what the popular was: when we want public school to become popular, efficient, democratic, we don't think of making a bad school for the children who were born rich. We were convinced that we should make a school that, having the taste, the smell of the popular, wouldn't have disgust for the bourgeoisie. We wanted that school to have a Brazilian face, therefore, an open school, happy, critical, one that would encourage the children's creativity and not their fear. Therefore, we needed an administration which would also be like that. It is not possible to think of the democratic dream of school having an authoritarian administration.

Gadotti: Therefore, you encouraged changes in the structures of power at the Secretariat?

Freire: We made a structural change through which the secretary possibly lost 60 percent of the arbitrary power it had. I couldn't even appoint a school secretary. There were indications from the base. Unless we break with the colonial character of the administration—in which it was even up to the secretary to deal with the teacher who had missed lessons in the month of September the year before— one cannot speak of school autonomy. We searched for the School Councils, created by Márion Covas in 1985 and archivated by Jñio Quadros. The School Councils were an extraordinary step towards the parents, the pupils, and the teachers achieving a place that exceeded the headmaster's power.

Gadotti: Do you think that this desire for freedom, autonomy, and participation is a mark left by your administration that will persist?

Freire: I believe in that. Even if this desire will suffer moments of suffocation, where it will feel that it cannot express itself. For in the end, the desire of being forms part of the ontology of being. Nobody can decree that men and women stop dreaming. That is a dictator's business.

Notes

1. Reprinted from *Nova Escola*, ANO VIII, No. 71, Novembro, 1993, pp. 8–13.

15

Collisions with Otherness:
"Traveling" Theory, Postcolonial Criticism, and the Politics of Ethnographic Practice—The Mission of the Wounded Ethnographer

Peter L. McLaren

Qualitative Research as a Discourse of Power[1]

...the most eloquent parts of the work [traditional philosophical works] are the wounds which the conflict in the theory leave behind.

—T. W. Adorno, "Der Wunderliche Realist: Uber Siegfried Kracauer"

This essay will discuss qualitative research in general and critical ethnography in particular from the perspective of new developments within critical social theory over the last several decades, particularly neo-Marxist and poststructuralist variants of critical postmodernist discourse.[2] Those strands of more orthodox anthropological fieldwork, including both liberal and conservative accents, that continue to enjoy uncontested power in contemporary educational research situate the challenge of field analysis in largely instrumental terms, or in what the Frankfurt School theorists refer to as "instrumental rationality." From the perspective of a defanged and defamed modernism, ethnographic research generally has been normalized to mean those practices in which researchers engage in order to gain entry into the field site, establish an ongoing rapport with subjects through the generation of a reciprocal trust, maintain the confidence of the subjects, and achieve a longevity in the field by remaining as unobtrusive as possible, sometimes affecting an almost bold detachment to the point of self-effacement. In so doing, they attempt to construct representations of social life that both mirror and explain the events that transpired throughout their fieldwork practices.

The general assumption upon which this essay is founded cuts against the grain of this traditional approach to ethnographic research and attempts to stand outside of the policing structure of its sovereign discourses. Operating within an anthropological subterrain where subjects of the anthropologist's gaze rarely assume their appointed roles and places, and where unconventional alliances can be made between descriptions and meanings, this essay takes the position that ethnographic research and the production of knowledge is never self-authenticating or self-legitimating. Debate over issues of meaning construction becomes inexorably bound up with questions of language and interpretation, the knowledge/power nexus, and the sovereign "logocentric" discourses of modern scientific rationality. As a form of praxis, ethnographic research neither determines its own effects nor speaks its own truth in a manner that transcends its relation to the metaphors that constitute its meanings. For example, normative definitions of woman, man, colonizer, colonized, researcher, informant, and so on enforce particular ideological exclusions and promote an insider politics that often freezes and ossifies difference. This is so because within modernist theoretical discourse, binary oppositions enforce a dependent hierarchy where one of the two terms forcefully restricts, undermines, and usurps the meaning of the other and produces ideologically disfiguring effects (Hammer and McLaren 1991).

In a recent essay in *Out There: Marginalization and Contemporary Cultures*, Cornel West (1990) asserts that "one cannot deconstruct the binary oppositional logic of images of Blackness without extending it to the contrary condition of Blackness/Whiteness itself" (29). He notes further that "social theory is what is needed to examine and *explain* the historically specific ways in which 'Whiteness' is a politically constructed category parasitic on 'Blackness' " (29). Consequently, it is the historical meanings linked to these terms that need to be placed under theoretical stress such that the terms may not simply be reversed but rather subverted (Hammer and McLaren 1991).

It is the transparency of whiteness and maleness that makes it possible for white male researchers to arrogate to themselves the exclusive right to "nominate" all other groups while monumentalizing their own. Those groups that do not fall into the category of white or male are positioned irrevocably as *Other*; and this category of *Other* must be assumed or internalized in order for peripheralized groups to become part of the totality.

Viewed from both a poststructuralist and ethnosemiotic vantage point, ethnographic research and the production of qualitative meaning needs to be extended beyond the prevailing logocentric and humanistic *anthropologos* that informs its central axioms and to be taken seriously within the context of the following question: Under what conditions and to what ends do we, as educational researchers, enter into relations of cooperation, mutuality, and reciprocity with those whom we research?

Most of the discussion in the remainder of this essay follows an assertion frequently associated with the disciplinary trajectory known as *critical ethnography*: that field research is the creature of cultural limits and theoretical borders and as such is implicated necessarily in particular economies of truth, value, and power (see Kincheloe 1991, McLaren 1986, and Simon and Dippo 1988). Correlatively, I want to address the antecedents and implications of recent perspectives in critical social theory in connection with formulating a new conception of ethnographic work.

We are conducting research at a time of moment-to-moment apocalypse; in the future anterior where we feel nostalgia for a time that has not yet arrived and whose realization is structurally impossible. It is a time of cultural implosion that not only affects the subjectivity of the researcher but also the placeless terrain of theory itself. Specifically in this postmodern era of blurred genres, we are witnessing the " 'literaturization' of the social sciences" (Loriggio 1990, 235) and a "welding of the literary and the sociopolitical" (Manganaro 1990, 35). Intersections between the Anglo-American philosophical tradition and European social theory have yielded creative implications for our understanding of social life. For instance, Manganaro's book, *Modernist Anthropology: From Fieldwork to Text*, cogently illustrates intellectual affinities and a continuity of ideas among work carried out by surrealist sociologists, poststructuralist semiologists, deconstructionist theorists, and continental ethnologists. Similarly, it is not difficult to tease out among these various strands of contemporary theory what Manganaro (1990) calls "new hybridic possibilities for cultural critique" (45).

Examining ethnography in light of this new mapping of anthropological research, I suggest that new understandings that have implications for an emancipatory social practice can develop if researchers are able to situate and analyze field research as textual strategies and discursive practices that ineluctably are entangled within larger structures of power and privilege. In this view, knowledge is understood as a social text made up of competing rhetorical strategies. The current postmodern perspective of knowledge production that

emphasizes experience, subjectivity, reflexivity, and holistic understanding can, of course, be situated in German romanticism—a movement that grew out of a dissatisfaction with and criticism of the
Enlightenment search for general laws and scientific rationality. The
crisis of representation in current anthropological discourse can be
linked to both strengths and limitations within the romantic tradition
in anthropology (a tradition that has been chronicled in recent books
such as Michael Jackson's *Path toward a Clearing: Radical Empiricism and
Ethnographic Inquiry*, Renato Rosaldo's *Culture and Truth: The Remaking
of Social Analysis*, and George W. Stocking's *Romantic Motives: Essays on
Anthropological Sensibility*).[3] My emphasis in this essay is on how the
postmodern turn in anthropological theory has effected this crisis of
representation and on the implications the crisis holds for the practice
of critical ethnography.

A way of pitching the perspective that has resulted from the
revolution in critical social theory over the last several decades is to make
the claim that field researchers undertake their projects not just *in* a
field site, but *within a field of competing discourses that help structure a
variegated system of socially constituted human relationships*. The field site
no longer can be considered simply the geographical location of the
study; it also is the location where geopolitical vectors of power crosscut
the cultural terrain under investigation. The field site additionally maybe
considered *the site of the researcher's own embodiment in theory/discourse
and his or her own disposition as a theorist, within a specific politics of location*.
Here it should be recognized that discourses do not simply reflect the
field site as a seamless repository for transcriptions of a pristine "source"
of cultural authenticity, but *are constitutive of such a site*. In other words,
fieldworkers always are cultural workers who engage not just in the
analysis of field sites but *in their active production* through the discourses
used to analyze field relations. The cultural terrain of the field site is
never a monadic site of harmony and control, but is a disjuncture,
rupture, and contradiction that is better understood from a research
perspective as a contested terrain that serves as the loci of multivalent
powers (McLaren 1994). It is within this context of framing our concept
of field relations and research that we can situate more critically our
role as field researchers.

This perspective shares some of the insights of recent feminist and
critical approaches to anthropological research that probe the nature
of representation and power relations themselves, a perspective that
shifts the emphasis of anthropology from a fieldwork-based "science"
of culture to a form of textual analysis in which knowledge is viewed
as an interlaced network of conflictual and arborescent discursive

practices, forms of ideological production, and what Giroux (1990) has termed modalities of ethical address (see also Britzman 1991; Clifford 1987; Clifford and Marcus 1986; Mascia-Lees, Sharpe and Cohen 1989; McLaren 1994; and Van Mannen 1990).

Discourses, as I am referring to them here, are modalities that to a significant extent, govern what can be said, by what kinds of speakers, and for what types of imagined audiences (Weedon 1987). They are social practices that constitute both social subjects and the objects of their investigation. The rules of discourse are normative and derive their meaning from the power relations of which they are a part. That is, discourses *organize a way of thinking into a way of doing*. They actively shape the practices that the discourses serve. But they always are indexical to the theoretical perspectives of the researchers and their intepretations. In other words, there exists no single privileged and perdurable set of research practices whose name is "field relations."

Modernist ethnography is preoccupied with locating through description and analysis the identity of research subjects from a position of intelligibility that either refuses to locate the agency of the researcher or falsely assumes that the researcher speaks from a unsullied, prediscursive and stable site untouched by the very discourses used in the research process. That is, the "onto-epistemological" tradition within ethnography fails to recognize that the identity of the researcher *qua* researcher is both a discursive fiction and a social practice. The discursive tools of analysis used to uncover the authenticity of the studied "other" become the unconscious predicates of the researcher's own identity and subjective disposition (politics of location) in the field. A poststructuralist approach to critical ethnography, on the other hand, refuses the imposition of an epistemological construction of the identity of both the researcher and the researched that the tradition of Western epistemology has produced as a series of established, hierarchical binarisms: the knower and the known, the subject who inquires and the object of inquiry, the researcher and the researched (Butler 1990, 144). The critical poststructuralist ethnographic practice I am both summarizing and advocating calls for a radical reconceptualization of culture as a field of discourse (see Clifford and Marcus 1986) that is implicated in relations of power and is constituted by normative understandings; such a perspective can enable researchers to understand field relations better as social practices that are not immediately present to themselves. As ethnographic researchers, we actively construct and are constructed by the discourses we embody and the metaphors we enact (McLaren 1994, 1989). We are, in effect, both the subject and the object of our research. It is within this context that we

unconsciously strive as field researchers to create an atmosphere of place
and tradition that will act as a lure to the "right" kind of informants—
those who will be compliant with our research agenda by conforming
to our normative understanding of them.

I am suggesting that it is extremely tempting to absolutize or
totalize the groups we study, to see them as existing homogeneously,
rooted in particular world views, and to ignore the way in which power
operates as a regulating force that centralizes and unifies often
conflicting and competing discourses and subjectivities (cf. Giroux 1988,
McLaren 1989). There is, of course, something rather estranging in all
of this, something perhaps duplicitous. This is why it is vitally important
that we connect empirical data to the discourses that produce them and
that, at the same time, produce our subjects under study. In so doing,
we can attempt to engage in a form of theoretical decolonization; that
is, in a critical way of unlearning accepted ways of thinking, of refusing
to analyze in the mode of the dominator while at the same time paying
attention to the dangers of assuming the sponsorship of a postcolonial
elite. Such a task is but a first step to the larger goal of transforming
our field relations and research efforts within the context of a politics
of difference and vision of social justice (McLaren, in press).

Shipwrecked against Infinity: Field Relations as Competing Discourses

The discourses of ethnographic research consist of rhetorical tropes
that both reflect and shape the way in which we consciously and
unconsciously identify ourselves with our role in the field and with
the subjects of our study. Mainstream research and field relations
become, in the context I have set forth, an appeal to a *particular
understanding* of reality that is deeply rooted in what moves us to take
for "human" what is merely the discursive form of humanity in our
society. We often situate ourselves as field researchers by viewing
ourselves as a paradigm of humanity and then construct the origins
of this universal presence in our selected ethnographic methodologies
(cf. Litchman 1982). The discourses of ethnographic research may, in
fact, possess the power of truth, but in reality they are historically
contingent rather than inscribed by natural law; they emerge, in other
words, out of social conventions, but they always are profoundly
implicated in the question of the ethical formation of the self and other.

Postmodern criticism has certainly posed a challenge to critical
ethnography. Aspects of Western culture epistemologically codified in
ethnographic breviaries of the past and valorized by the authorial
signatures of, for example, Weber, Durkheim, and Parsons, are now

being refigured and recodified by a postmodern epistemic skepticism of dissolving certainties, splintering subjectivities, multiple voices, and the molecularization and disaggregation of the self (the politics of one's "addressivity"). The role of critical ethnography within the context of postmodern thought is to redefine agency and political activism outside of the notion of the unitary, monolithic (and often incorrigible) subject of history. As Rosi Braidotti has recently remarked in the context of feminism: "the conceptual challenge [of postmodern theory] consists in upholding the idea of the subject as a dazzling collection of integrated fragments, while also defending the specificity of the female subject as a theoretical, libidinal, ethical and political agent." (1991, pp. 281–282). Conquergood adds that "The presuppositions of pattern, continuity, coherence, and unity characteristic of classic ethnography may have had more to do with the West's ideological commitment to individualism than with on-the-ground cultural practices" (1991, p. 184). Fieldsites, like subjects, are not unified wholes but borderlands and zones of contest that can best be understood through forms of meta-rhetorical criticism.

Postmodernism's shattering of the monumental criteriologies and classificatory schemes associated with ethnographies grounded in a modernist Romantic idealism has created a self-referential world of theoretical abstraction—of signs and simulations—that retrospectively confers the sanctity of its own criticism. One way of negotiating through the labyrinthine trajectories of postmodern criticism has been undertaken by John and Jean Comaroff whose endorsement and development of a neomodern historical anthropology has attempted to rethink the modernist ethnographic project in light of postmodern assaults on logocentric research.

Describing anthropology in general as "a historically situated mode of understanding historically situated contexts, each with its own, perhaps radically different, kinds of subjects and subjectivities, objects and objectives" (1992, pp. 9–10), the Comaroffs assert that it is "impossible ever to rid ourselves entirely of the ethnocentrism that dogs our desire to know others, even though we vex ourselves with the problem in ever more refined ways" (p. 10). Their neo-modern approach to "doing ethnography" criticizes the "decontextualized exchange between anthropologist and informant" and the woeful reduction of ethnography to the experiencing subject of modern, western humanism as well as the reduction of the anthropological enterprise to an "ethnocentric interview" (p. 10).

The work developed by the Comaroffs is politically and conceptually anchored in the task of operationalizing the concepts of

ideology, hegemony, and power (in both the latter term's agentive and
nonagentive modes) as a "cogent way of speaking about the force of
meaning and the meaning of force—the inseparability, that is, of power
and culture" (p. 28). They attempt to "disinter the processes by which
disparate, even divisive, discourses [are] fused into a consistent
ideology" (p. 35), by means of a "neomodernist method that takes
seriously the message of critical postmodernism yet does not lose the
possibility of social science; that takes to heart the lessons of cultural
Marxism, seeking a conception of culture that recognizes the reality
of power, yet does not reduce meaning to either utility or domination;
that builds on the techniques of cultural history, pursuing the dialectic
of fragment and totality without succumbing to brute empiricism; that,
above all, proceeds, as it must, by grappling with the contradictions
of its own legacy, seeking to transcend them—if only provisionally and
for the moment" (p.45)

The Comaroffs contend that ethnography is concerned with
situating the gestures of others within the often seemingly arbitrary
systems of signs and relations of power and meaning that animate them.
Of importance therefore is the dialectical interplay of these systems
(dialogics is subsumed here within dialectics). Texts must be understood
within contexts and equations of power and meaning must be assigned
value. Finally, what must be comprehended is that contexts and values
are also analytical constructions that reflect the anthropologist's own
assumptions about the social world (pp. 10–11). We must not abandon
analytical constructions simply because they can never serve as realist
transparencies. Rather, we must seek to understand how collective
worlds are made and fashioned dialectically. Culture, in this view, is
defined as "a field of contest" one that is "often a matter of argument,
a confrontation of signs and practices along the fault lines of power"
(p. 18). We must recognize that modern ethnography has inherited the
discourse of the colonizer through a dialectic of domesticity which treats,
for instance, inner-city 'others' as "undomesticated primitive lands", as
the bestial African bush, as objects of a "civilizing mission" that attempts
to domesticate "that part of the metropole that had previously eluded
bourgeois control" (p. 293). We need to always be conscious of the
political and ethical consequences of our own unstated assumptions
as researchers and those assumptions which have unconsciously
shaped the language of analysis which we have inherited.

Knowledge and the Body

Consequently, it is important to pursue this question: If discourses
are not grounded transcendentally, and if they are not mappable by

intellection, how, in fact, are they grounded? Recent research on the body suggests that knowledge is grounded through forms of embodiment. The concept of the body as a site of cultural inscription is growing in prominence as a topic of investigation among contemporary social theorists. Efforts are being made to uncouple the idea of the feminine body/subject and the Black and Latino body/subject from the negative and unspoken Other and to recognize the body as a site of *enfleshment*—that is, as a site where epistemic codes freeze desire into social norms. In other words, bodies are becoming recognized and explored as socially situated and incarnated social practices that are semiotically alive. However, I should add that the importance of understanding the body is not for researchers to turn it into a textualized semiotic laboratory, but rather to recognize knowledge as a typography of embodiment; that is, to recognize the body as the grounds for all our intersubjective relationships with the subjects of our investigations and for our affective investment in our own research projects. We cannot separate the body from the social formation, since the material density of all forms of subjectivity is achieved through the "micropractices" of power that are socially inscribed into our flesh (McLaren 1994, 1995).

As Allen Feldman reports in his brilliant ethnography of political terror in Northern Ireland, *Formations of Violence* (1991), the body is "the factored product of the unequal and differential effects of intersecting antagonistic forces" (176) that "coheres into an economy of the body" (177). Although the body is the product of history, it is, through the workings of the subject, also the shaper of history. Ethnography in my estimation should help produce those forms of agency necessary for the transformation of forces and structures of oppression. Feldman's formulation of agency is important: "Exteriority folds the body, but agency, as a self-reflexive framing of force, subjectivates exteriority and refolds the body. It is not only a matter of what history does to the body but what subjects do with what history has done to the body" (177).

It is important that ethnographers engage the means by which discourses "live" inside of both "us and them" as linguistic and extra-linguistic mediations. Our capacity as researchers to understand the body as an effect of power/knowledge relations and also as a site of their articulation can help us to escape the political paralysis that often accompanies the poststructuralist recognition that values, desires, and practices always originate elsewhere in predisclosed structures and in conditions not of our own making. In other words, while it is true that our desires and intentions and those of our subjects never can be completely mapped or made conscious, and while they are certainly mediated by competing sets of discursive practices and relations, this should not compel us as researchers to assume a passive, passionless, and politically inert role. Nor should it be an occasion for a voluntaristic denial or abandonment of hope—a sanctioned refusal to upstage despair in the face of the dominant culture's persistent demonization and naturalization of the Other.

If the objectivist program in the social sciences was grounded in empirical studies, the postmodernist approach to research is grounded in the metaphoricity and tropicity of all discourse. Metaphor and polyseme form the cornerstones of what George Lakoff calls "experiential realism" and what Mark Johnson calls "embodied, nonpropositional, and imaginative meaning" (cited in Frank 1990). Metaphor and polyseme are constituent not only of speech but also of thought, and we can trace our embodiment in knowledge preverbally to our early experiences of balance, containment, forces, cycles, and so forth that become our image schemata and which in turn inform our propositional logic (Frank 1990, 158). As Arthur Frank (1990) notes, understanding and knowledge are projections of embodied image schemata that are multivocal, yet can form the basis of mutual understanding, since bodily experience is shared. Cartesian philosophy managed to overlook the fact that validity claims can no longer afford to exclude the body. In fact, I would go so far as to say that theoretical knowledges constitute externalized metaphors of the body; they form the prostheses of the body, artifacts that offer strategies of desire; they advocate; as embodied metaphors, metonymies, and images based on experience, they solicit; they seduce; they hypnotize; they cannot be considered lifeless nor can they be considered objective.

This is why our research agendas with their accompanying theoretical formulations must be situated within the ideological boundaries and discursive borders that constitute their respective projects. A project is more than a subjective disposition, rather it constitutes a political imperative grounded in an ethical discourse (McLaren, 1994). The ethical project known as critical ethnography is one that does not emerge transcendentally in textual forms detached from perception, bodily experience, and the friction of social reality. It is an ethics that emerges concretely *from the body, is situated in the materiality and historicity of discourse, in the call of the flesh, in the folds of desire*. It is an imperative that presupposes an answer, in a response *from the other*. If the way in which metaphors are grounded in bodily experience becomes part of the theoretical structures through which we perceive the world, and if such structures bring about changes in the way we act in the world, then it is important for critical ethnographers to utilize an ethics fully grounded in the body (see Chambers 1990, McLaren 1995). Such an ethics must be understood as the product of competing discourses and must refuse either to abandon or fetishize the voice of the marginalized.

Knowledge and Truth

There is another perspective from which knowledge must be analyzed and understood, and that is in the lived relation of knowledge to truth. I am suggesting here, along with Foucault and others, that the constraints of discourse, that the very act of signification, constructs an impassable and implacable division posed by alterity; discourse itself creates barriers or constraints at the point at which its own situatedness in social relations becomes apparent. This suggests that Truth cannot be spoken of in the absence of power relations, and each relation necessarily speaks its own truth (Foucault 1980). Another way that ethnographers and field researchers can begin to think of the "truth" of their work is not to render knowledge as something ultimately to be discovered, but rather as social texts that are relationally produced in a multiplicity of mutually informing contexts. When such truths become official, when they are presented as discourses of sanctioned legitimacy, then they often serve as an impediment to further truth and must therefore be deformed—even perverted—by rhetorizing moves on the part of the researcher that deconstruct their metaphysical bearings. Representation is always re-presentation within particular ideological configurations.

If every signification constitutes a mask (Levinas 1981, Patterson 1990), then the way to truth becomes the absolute pursuit of alterity— to probe the totality of otherness. Patterson (1990) writes that "in its alterity, truth belongs to what we shall have been, in the light of what we are in the process of becoming." Truth is "that juncture where the *not yet* of alterity proclaims itself" (302). Further, truth "is not what we try to find out but what we endeavour to become." That is, "truth is not what we know but what we are not yet" (303). It is the process of becoming "other" to one's "I."

Of course, the pursuit of alterity is fraught with danger. As Gayatri Spivak (1990) argues, the postcolonial elite consisting mainly of metropolitan intellectuals must persistently unlearn their privilege in the context of a neocolonial world in order to engage the truth of otherness.

Research as Advocacy

Critical ethnography contests the epistemological closure of the so-called objectivity and scientificity of mainstream ethnographic research (Lather 1986, McLaren 1986). Typically, critical ethnographers do not shrink from the charge of perspectivism; rather, they openly contest those discourses which attempt to occlude the historicity and partisanship characteristic of the analysis of social life (Kincheloe 1991, McLaren 1986, Simon and Dippo 1988). Critical social inquiry situates its project in a nonobjectivist view of knowledge that challenges certain ethical standards and imperatives of the dominant culture (Bennett and LeCompte 1990).

Within the discourse of science, explanation surpasses understanding and empathy (Agger 1989). Read from the perspective of critical ethnography, such an emphasis is highly problematic which is not to suggest that questions of validity, verifiability, and explanation are not important (Lather 1986, Simon and Dippo 1988). However, critical ethnographers have made their position on knowledge quite clear: They cannot hide the word's inherence in the constitutiveness of an ingress to the world—a position which, rather than vitiating the objectivity of knowledge, underscores its insinuation in human interest and social power (Kincheloe 1991; McLaren, 1995). Consequently, they raise a fundamental question: What social effects do you want your evaluations and understanding to have?

Mainstream social science forswears its own ideological constitutivity, but its discursive underpinnings are clear; the problem is that researchers who work within its limits refuse to acknowledge the interests that such research serves. As Ben Agger (1989) notes, research is never disinterested, but rather must always narrate its own ideological contingency within networks of power relations. Agger rightly objects to the analytic cleavage of description and exhortation, the temporal separation of knowledge and desire, the sundering of analysis and social criticism, and the refusal of researchers to examine their textual practices as imaginative fictions.

It is necessary here to assert that all research—qualitative or quantitative—exists as a form of rhetoric, but not as "mere" rhetoric. As Bruce Robbins (1990) maintains, rhetoric involves much more than merely technical or pure instrumentality prostituting itself in the service of any user without a sense of critical oppositionality or narrative anchoring in the common good. Rather, rhetoric's limits belong to the domain of social theory, and its perpetually destabilizing function and indeterminacy should not be linked solely to language and tropes but to "the contingencies of action, of historical audience, and of politics" (10). That is, rhetoric necessarily foregrounds the public issue of value and accountability.

As a defense of the rhetoricity of research, Agger (1989) argues against what he terms "methodological pluralism." According to Agger, methodological pluralism assumes that the world is really all one piece but can be read differently through different sociological approaches. In other words, the same world can be explained differently; it is all simply a question of the researcher's ontological coordinates. This view prevails in so many courses in educational research, especially during instances in which prospective researchers are invited to conceptualize the educational and social milieu according to functionalist, interpretivist, and conflict theories. The problem with explaining the social world through these three somewhat overlapping conceptual lenses is that it "assumes a single, simple world named differently" and therefore "misses the constitutiveness of writing entwining a theory of being and explanation" (315).

What Agger underscores with such sharpened insight is that when the researcher neglects how the relationship between subject and object has been historically produced within a nexus of power relations, the world's own self-understanding then becomes the basis of the researcher's criticism of the social world, and thus critical writings can become dismissed and domesticated and ultimately discarded as weakened versions of other forms of analysis. Critical ethnographic knowledge becomes, in this view, just another "gloss" on reality. And presumably the classroom instructor, who is standing in a site unspoiled by ideology, can invoke "conflict theory" as one item in an entire menu of theoretical perspectives on the world. Structural functionalism, phenomenology, or conflict theory become one of the many "lenses" through which to look at the world, or one of the many "hats" the liberal researcher wears to show that he or she is willing to see the world from all sorts of research perspectives—even radical ones. Epistemological pluralism is really a form of neopositivism—a perspective that always is "preontologically available" for the researcher to read the world. Yet the centrist position of slicing up the world into its functionalist, interpretivist, and critical pieces really works to usurp critical research under a liberalism that locates it as an example of the "openness" of the social system. Critical research thus becomes "ironically a genuflection to an *uncritical* discipline" (Agger 1989, 316).

Research practices undertaken in a critical mode necessitate recognizing the complexity of social relations and the researcher's own socially determined position within the reality that one is attempting to describe. A failure of such a recognition can conjure into being the concretely elaborated idea of the researcher/outsider as master of the discourse *on* schooling, on the one hand, and on the other hand, the figure of the hapless teachers and their students who not only are prevented from becoming authorities on the discourse *of* schooling but also are left as vulnerable, unwitting victims of the outsider/researcher's study.

The status of field researchers as truth-bearers from the culture of maleness and whiteness putatively embues them with an impartial and rational intelligence, reinforces the idea that the teacher's anecdotal logics and local knowledge are of lesser status, and binds power and truth together in such a way as both to privilege and normalize existing relations of power. This only habituates teachers to the established direction of educational research and the cultural-political regime of truth ascribed to by the dominant culture. This is precisely why it is important to enter field relations collaboratively rather than purge difference through the universal calculus of putatively disinterested objective analysis. The field researcher needs to share with his or her subjects the discourses at work that are shaping the fieldsite analysis and how the researcher's own personal and intellectual biography is contributing to the process of analysis.

Mainstream ethnography is based on the concept of the authorial masculine subject and is structured in unconscious desire as forms of realist narrativity. Patricia Ticineto Clough has convincingly argued that the narrativity undergirding mainstream ethnographic research—i.e., the researcher's unconscious complicity in the process of reading and writing and in the formation of institutional forms of discursive authority—subjugates the researcher to an oedipal logic that nurtures a unified, masculinist, and 'heroic' identity. Discursive authority is narratively constructed in the masculine figure through forms of sexual politics and practices of disavowal and displacement. In other words, ethnography has been one of the conceptual weapons used against women through the construction of phallologocentric thought and the reproduction of the male/famale dichotomy (Clough, 1992).

While the subjectivities of ethnographers may be thought of as fluid, molar, desiring machines (after the post-structuralist conceptualizations of Deleuze and others) it is important to remember that capitalism has a profound capacity to historically organize desire in specific phallologocentric modes of subjectivity and zones of sociality. That is, the unconscious structures of subjectivity are organized and symbolically ordered so as to secure among subjects particular forms of ideological complicity. When I talk about constituting the ethnographic subject and the subject of ethnography within new spaces of possibility and modes of subjectivity, I refer to the necessary abolition of present exploitative capitalist social relations of production and the struggle for democratic social relations on a socialist model. I also refer to the importance of a non-phallocratic sexuality. In saying this, however, I want to reiterate Rosi Braidotti's warning that "the proper task of men who intend to deconstruct phallic premises should be to speak as singular men, not as representatives of Mankind, and develop a new way of thinking masculinity" (1991, p. 123).

Conversations with Silence: The Discourse of the Other

Poststructuralists acknowledge explicitly that meaning consists of more than signs operating or being operated in a context. Rather, there is a struggle over signifying practices. This struggle is eminently *political* and must include the relationship between discourse and the contradictions involved in subjective formation/the formation of subjects (Butler 1990, 145). According to poststructuralism, we construct our selves, our identities, through the availability and character of signs of past and present events as well as possible futures. That is, the parameters of the human subject vary according to the discursive practices, economies of signs, and subjectivities (experiences) engaged by individuals and groups at any historical moment. We need to jettison the outmoded and eminently dangerous idea that we possess as researchers a timeless essence or a consciousness that places us beyond historical and political practices. Rather, we need to understand our "working identities" as an effect of such practices. Our identities as researchers are not fettered to or dependent upon some transcendental regime of truth beyond the territory of the profane and the mundane. In other words, our identities are constitutive of the literacies we have at our disposal through which we make sense of our day-to-day politics of living.

Consequently, when considering the characteristics that are constitutive of the researcher or those being researched—the "insiders" and "outsiders" of the research process—it is important not to fall into the trap of essentializing either one. This position emphasizes that those with whom the researcher works are always necessarily partners in the research and are not inert referents abstracted from social history and practice; that is, referents isolated by the research process and separated from the concreteness of heteroglossia, the socioeconomic and the historical. Trinh Minh-ha (1988) articulates a view of the subject (as researcher, as researched) that speaks to a refusal to naturalize the *I*:

The moment the insider steps out from the inside she's no longer a mere insider. She necessarily looks in from the outside while also looking out from the inside. Not quite the same, not quite the other, she stands in that undetermined threshold place where she constantly drifts in and out. Undercutting the inside/outside opposition, her intervention is necessarily that of both not-quite an insider and not-quite an outsider. She is, in other words, this inappropriate other or same who moves about with always at least two gestures: that of affirming "I am like you" while persisting in her difference and that of reminding "I am different" while unsettling every definition of otherness arrived at. (76)

One of the most important tasks in which a field researcher can engage is understanding and transforming the various ways in which his or her own subjective formation privileges certain discourses that unwittingly construct subjects as the Other. Iris Young (1990) argues that the cultural imperialism of the researcher not only provides and insists on only one subject position, that of unified, disembodied reason identified with white bourgeois men, but it promotes members of culturally imperialized groups to devalue themselves and other oppressed groups. Groups who are researched by metropolitan ethnographers often learn to devalue members of their own groups and other oppressed groups by internalizing the cultural knowledge that dominant groups "fear and loathe them." However, oppressed and marginalized groups do not simply assume the dominant subjectivity toward themselves and other members of the groups with which they identify; they also live a subjectivity different from the dominant subject position that they have derived from their positive identification and social networks with others in their group. The dialectical relationship between these two subjectivities—"the point of view of the dominant culture which defines them as ugly and fearsome, and the point of view of the oppressed who experience themselves as ordinary, companionate, and humorous"(148)—represents what Young calls "double consciousness."

Before engaging in fieldwork relations and analysis, researchers need to become aware of how they unwittingly can become complicitous in the hostile displacement of minorities as those who possess a prehistorical surplus of culture that celebrates the distance that middle-class whites have evolved (e.g., have become rational). Educators, like ethnographers, often fall into the mistake of regarding "authentic" culture as something that distinguishes them from those they are studying. The Other therefore becomes a cultural generality that accounts for the ethnographer's "difference." That is, the Other becomes invasive and corrosive of the researcher's self-contained subjectivity. Put another way, the proliferative and meretricious figure of the Other becomes in this case a cultural fiction that allows educators and researchers to ignore the partiality of their own perspectives that assign cultural "otherness" to certain groups in order to render invisible how such a practice often is a form of ideological violence and an exercise of the power to dominate. A miasma of smoke often is exhaled by our field research, obscuring the political and ethical ramifications entailed by our analyses, but easily overlooked, absorbed, and displaced by the Eurocentrism and androcentrism found in our research traditions.

Ethnographic research needs to be so checked in order that it not fall prey to the privatization of self-absorption due to the narcissism of the researcher, a narcissism which, as a form of regenerative barbarism, assumes the researcher's own subjectivity and human agency to be the privileged reference point for judging not only the cultural and social practices under his or her gaze but those who engage in them. Such a form of engagement amounts to little more than a form of ethnographic vampirism, an imperialist and imperious act of ethnographic voyeurism and cultural appropriation. This process is spelled out by Marianna Torgovnick (1990) in *Gone Primitive: Savage Intellects, Modern Lives*. Torgovnick makes a compelling case against the damaging effects of the colonial imagination formed out of the sovereign Eurocentric archives of the imperialist West, an imagination that has profound implications for the practice of ethnography undertaken in the spirit of modernism, where certain groups become othered and devoiced through the "male-centered, canonical line of Western primitivism" (248).

We need to move beyond the perspective that James Clifford (1987, 122) has identified as "salvage ethnography" (recording the languages and lore of disappearing peoples) and represented by the works of Boas, Kroeber, and others, studies that attempt to "rescue authenticity out of destructive historical change." Such a perspective argues Clifford, allows human differences to be "redistributed as separate, functioning cultures." The "ethnographic present" that is constructed by Western researchers, largely white males, as a point of reference for judging the worth of varying degrees of "primitiveness" is what keeps ethnic groups buried in the past and "marginal to the advancing world system." The "lowly" knowledge of the ethnic minority becomes, in this view, helpful to us only in terms of "aesthetic appreciation." As educational researchers, we must cease to attribute to certain groups "mythical consciousness" while we reserve "historical consciousness" for ourselves; in addition, we should welcome the day when the dominance of modernist dichotomies of literate/nonliterate, developed/underdeveloped, and so forth, have substantially ebbed. Similarly, it is necessary that we cease to characterize ourselves as "dynamic and oriented towards change," while those from nonwestern societies constantly "seek equilibrium and the reproduction of inherited forms" (Clifford 1987, 125).

One way out of this dilemma is suggested by Iris Young (1990), who argues against constructing totalizing and monolithic representations of difference by encouraging representations of subjects as plural, shifting, and heterogeneous and helping to confront "the very desire to have a unified, orderly identity, and the dependence of such a unified identity on the construction of a border that excludes aspects of subjectivity one refuses to face" (155). This perspective on cultural identity and difference is implicit in the pointed reminder by Trinh (1988) that "what is at stake is a practice of subjectivity that is still unaware of its own constituted nature, hence, the difficulty to exceed the simplistic pair of subjectivity and objectivity; a practice of subjectivity that is unaware of its continuous role in the production of meaning, as if things can make sense by themselves, so that the interpreter's function consists of only choosing among the many existing readings. . ." (77).

We have seen among ethnographers an inordinate emphasis placed on rationality and intellectualization that has provoked them to overlook the specificity of the investments that the so-called masses or primitives make in everyday social life, not to mention the ideological investments of the ethnographers themselves. Valerie Walkerdine (1986) considers this emphasis on the part of qualitative researchers to be the result of the Cogito "which culminates in the scientific management of populations, the power/knowledge of the modern social world" (196). She writes that, "Rather than seeing the pleasures of 'the masses' as perverse, perhaps we should acknowledge that it is the bourgeois 'will to truth' that is perverse in its desire for knowledge, certainty and mastery. This is the proper context in which to understand the *desire* to know the masses, the voyeurism of the (social) scientist" (196).

As researchers we must avoid what Renato Rosaldo (1989) calls "imperialist nostalgia," which is a nostalgia for the traditional colonized culture before it was destroyed by agents of colonialism, "where people mourn the passing of what they themselves have transformed" (69). We must not become elegists lamenting the disappearance of our imperial inheritance, which saw pastoral primitives as objects of bourgeois curiosity and pathos. Consequently, when field relations are undertaken, they must be undertaken in such a way *as to narrate their own contingency, their own situatedness in power/knowledge relations*. But I would caution against often fashionable calls for autocritique through more autobiographical and dialogical forms of writing that demand writers acknowledge the biographical and sociological contexts surrounding their modes of analysis. Epistemologically, reflexive forms of writing fall into the trap of assuming that any text is really a description of the author's subjective experience of whatever he or she is writing about. As Larry Grossberg (1988, 66–67) points out, many of the calls for autocritique make the mistake of assuming that the interpretation of the text must be measured by how "accurately" it represents reality. This assumption too often leads to damaging consequences for ethnographers and their readers. These include the reinscription of the privileged place of the author's experience, the undermining of critical authority and the potential for texts to become forms of strategic intervention and social transformation, and the forcing of authors into an endless production of self-determined interpretations.

The primary referent for the empowerment of those who have been deemed lesser or unredeemed should not be their moral strangeness or displacement outside the boundaries of the familiar, but rather *the establishment of criteria that can distinguish claims of moral superiority which we exercise as outsiders*. That is, the Others have a hermeneutical privilege in naming the issues before them and in developing an analysis of their situation appropriate to their context (cf. Mihevc 1989). The marginalized have the first right to name reality, to articulate how social reality functions, and to decide how the issues are to be organized and defined (Mihevc 1989). Critical ethnography has a tendency to become evangelizing, and to enunciate its call for liberation as if it were the sole theoretical representative of the oppressed. But this warning against metaphysical seduction should not prevent the researcher from giving up all critical authority in interpreting how the reality of the marginalized has been named and voiced and in analyzing the social consequences that follow.

Ethnographers must accept the responsibility that comes with giving the world meaning and for providing critical spaces for subjects to understand the literalness of the reality in which their subjectivities are inscribed, the contexts through which such a reality is articulated, and how their experiences and those of the researcher are imbricated in contradictory, complex, and changing vectors of power. Of course, as ethnographic researchers it is important to be aware of the controlling cultural mode of our own research and the ways, often multifarious and unwitting, in which our subjects and our relationship to them become artifacts of the epistemes that shape the direction of our theorizing. These debilitating forms of ethnographic capture occur by fixing the conceptual world in a particular way through selecting *particular* discourses from a cultural range of possibilities. The invisibility of the dominant ideology in its own privileging norms (made possible by a generally accepted mimetic theory of representation) enables the dominant group to reinvent the group it is studying for its own purposes. The cloaking device is not "merely" rhetoric, but is the way in which language is embedded in social practices and relations of power.

Judith Stacey (1988) warns of the potential for the ethnographer to manipulate and betray the subject. At least some of the manipulation and betrayal of the subject can be avoided by avoiding the romanticism of "yearning to know the 'Other' " (Mascia-Lees, and Sharpe, and Cohen 1989) and locating the "other" in oneself through self-reflection (Stacey 1988, 26). These temptations of the field researcher can be potentially subversive of critical anthropology's own political agenda by "turn[ing] ethnographers into the natives to be understood and ethnography into virgin territory to be explored" (Stacey 1988, 26). The ethnographic project needs a "politicaily reflexive grounding" without which "the 'Other' can too easily. . .reconstituted as an exotic in danger of being disempowered by that exoticism" (30).

In Benita Parry's (1987) terms, a critical research practice must do more than simply repossess "the signifying function appropriated by colonialist representation" or demystify or deform the rhetorical devices that "organize capitalism's discursive field" (28). Rather, the founding concepts of colonialism's "received narratives" and "monolithic figures and representations" must be refused rather than recoded in another tale of neocolonialism.

Of course, in attempting to dislocate the fixity of Eurocentric, sovereign narratives that structure our practice as theorists, it is impossible to remain totally outside the Western frame of reference, and this is certainly not what I am suggesting. As Spivak (1989, 1990) notes, it is important to speak "from within" emancipatory master narratives while simultaneously taking a distance from them. At the same time, it is important not to fall prey to hegemonic nativist counternarratives that make one complicitous with the forms of oppression one is struggling against. Gloria Anzaldúa (1990) refers to the task ahead as one of trying to formulate marginal theories

> that are partially outside and partially inside the Western frame
> of reference (if that is possible), theories that overlap many

"worlds." We are articulating new positions in these "in-between," Borderland worlds of ethnic communities and academies, feminist and job worlds. In our literature, social issues such as race, class and sexual difference are intertwined with the narrative and poetic elements of a text, elements in which theory is embedded. In our *mestizaje* theories we create new categories for those of us left out or pushed out of the existing ones. We recover and examine non-Western aesthetics while critiquing Western aesthetics; recover and examine non-rational modes and "blanked-out" realities while critiquing rational, consensual reality; recover and examine indigenous languages while critiquing the "languages" of the dominant culture.... If we have been gagged and disempowered by theories, we can also be loosened and empowered by theories. (xxvi)

Critical ethnographers need to develop the will and the competence to reposition their sites of enunciation and narrative authority and to make choices outside the comfort and danger of an *a priori* standard based on Western, monocultural and universal constructions of identity and difference. It also is essential that ethnographic researchers act *with* the oppressed, not *over them* or *on behalf of* them. Critical ethnography must be *organic to* and not *administered upon* the plight of struggling peoples. Field researchers constantly should place themselves in relations of "risk for knowledge," which means assuming a stance toward field research that is not founded on political deceit or moral absolutism.

We are all on this sad journey together. We glance around at each other and exchange smiles that are most often quite sad and sometimes desparately sweet but, for the most part, our longings for contact and our yearning for comprehension go unfulfilled. There is a strange tragedy associated with doing ethnographic research because as we try desperately to explain the mystery and the pain of our displacement from each other, we are always reminded that any explanation of the 'other' makes impossible but necessary demands on us to gain a deeper understanding of what's motivated us to become researchers in the first place. And for this we need to see our hearts in the dusky light of that which can't be explained through *écriture* or *critique engagée*.

It is important in this context that the field researcher not use the field as a site for his or her psychotherapy or a *mise-en-scène* where his or her own politics of difference is reduced to an essentializing confrontation with otherness such that difference remains fetishized and pleasurably infantilized and eroticized for Western consumption around the nodal points of a McWorld of cultural homogenizations. Yet at the same time, the ethnographer needs to recognize that the techniques of gaining objectivity in the field often serve as rituals to protect researchers from the necessary *wounding* needed to acknowledge and promote interconnections between their lives and the lives of those whom they study.

In 1916, Ford Motor Company's English School Melting-pot ceremony saw foreign-born Ford employees directed into a symbolic 'melting-pot' dressed in American clothes and proudly carrying the American Flag (Sollors, 1986). Ethnographers may laugh at the crude obviousness of this ritual drama of redemption and rebirth, this slaying of the foreign self so that it can emerge in its hallowed and pristine American incarnation. They are, however, recuperating this ritual when they fail to interrogate the governing ideological frames that shape their research and the interests they serve. Interrogation leads to discomfort as one identifies the ways in which the "other" has been constructed out of the fear and hatred of the self within a Manichaean universe of binary oppositions wherein "otherness" is expelled as repugnant and savage. A wounded ethnographer is one who feels the pain and appreciates the joy of the "other" while refusing to disown culpability for the production of the colonizing subject and the mythopoetics of imperialism that marks its discursive inscription. Such disowning leads to a desire for transforming the discursive and material conditions that mark relations of exploitation and oppression. Self-inflicted wounding, however, is the fashionable bourgeois stigmata worn by the guilt-ridden liberal ethnographer who seeks redemption but is unwilling to work for it and has no place in a postcolonial ethnography of resistance.

One of the most significant challenges for critical ethnographic work, and qualitative studies in general, is to begin to rethink the categories we use to shape the problematics of our research. What is especially problematic in Western, ethnographic practice is its *ocular centrism* (Clough, 1992) its emphasis on looking, on its masculinist, colonial gaze that presumes a stable, external world to be explained, that transforms dark-skinned informants into scopic sites of sexualized, racist mythology—a white mythology grounded in an imperial specular epistemology and perspectivalism. We need to move beyond a dialectics of the white visual witness and construct a anti-colonial, anti-racist and liberatory dialectics of hearing, touching and tasting the other beyond their inscription in colonial texts.

Critical ethnographers need to recognize that too often the notion of "otherness" is a means of marketing "savagery" in the name of research, an attempt to render "otherness" as the recrudescence of archaic barbarism, to culturally annex "them" for the benefit of "us."

Why do white, male researchers think that they are less "ethnic" than the darker-skinned populations who are the objects of their research? While it is true that Eurocentric culture is based on a denial of its own violent, racist formation, we cannot really frame "researcher/other" as a binary opposition, since what we are witnessing in the exchange between the researcher and the research subject is a collaborative construction, not absolute differences (MacCannell, 1994). Within this construction, however, ethnographic researchers need to interrogate the repressed "Otherness" contained in their own presuppositions of identity as researchers so that such a collaboration does not work to undermine their emancipatory intentions and practices (cf., hooks, 1993).

In conclusion, I am arguing that ethnographic research must take into consideration its form of analysis as a narrative practice that is institutionally bound, discursively situated, and geopolitically located. What critical postcolonial ethnography needs at the present historical moment is not simply another means of constructing a knowledge of the partial, the particular, and the contingent, but new forms of theoretical practice that can engage difference without absorbing, accommodating, homogenizing, or integrating it into the totalizing schemes of Western essentialist ethnographic practices. We need to resist facile forms of postmodern detailism and anecdotalism and refuse the appropriation of difference into totalizing identities by ontologizing Otherness and thereby sublating the Other within itself through a violent act of self-possession (R. Young, 1990). One way that ethnographers can avoid the tyranny of cultural imperialism is by fashioning themselves as ethical subjects who both acknowledge and respect the heterogeneity of the Other not by stepping outside of Western culture but rather, as Robert Young (1990) suggests, "by using its own alterity and duplicity to effect its deconstruction" (119).

Is the ethnographer as a postcolonial 'radical critic' simply someone who willfully opposes the hegemony of the dominant culture from the 'inside'? or are ethnographers in a very fundamental way complicitous in repeating the very structures of domination that they oppose? Is the answer to create a new language of analysis or simply destroy the established linkages between power and knowledge that have been secured through current relations of privilege and exploitation? Is it a choice between poiesis and praxis or their combination?

Stephen Yarbrough (1992) suggests that critical consciousness must necessarily engage in self-negation. He remarks: "Reflecting on itself, critical consciousness gradually sees itself for what it is: an originating, oppositional, agonistic, destructive, self-seeking, self-perpetuating, even traitorous longing for power and place. Thus critical consciousness 'wanders' according to a kind of logic" (p. 165). This logic, writes Yarbrough, continually displaces itself as consciousness approaches the act of criticism. When it recognizes that what it opposes are really forms of itself, it must negate itself. This is the point at which critical consciousness truly becomes criticism. Yarbrough adds that "When critical consciousness realizes that *it* is the cause of disharmony, that it alone produces the very conditions it opposes, and that it alone can contain its destructiveness, then it can truly become critical" (p. 165). The values that the ethnographer-as-critic seeks to displace are always her own, and when this is realized, criticism has the choice of negating itself; true criticism operates according to the stratagems of that which has been negated. The ethnographer as critic does well to realize that all criticisms are 'situated' within regimes of truth and zones of conflict out of which critics construct their criticism. Such an awareness helps to keep the ethnographer-as-critic honest and always open to self-criticism and helps to prevent her ideas from becoming transpersonal and transhistorical and vulnerable to an avant garde messianism.

Yet I want to extend Yarbrough's essentially conservative perspective on criticism by noting that, while it is true that the role of the critic is always paradoxically situated and universal, and while it only has the story of its own origins to share, it nevertheless has the capacity and the responsibility to disclose what lies behind the paradox of criticism. Modes of signification (what can be said) are always grounded materially in modes of production and in questions of human need and such a relationship is always occluded by the mystifications produced by ideology. Criticism does not coincide with a particular sign community or school of criticism but always emerges out of a struggle over the means of production, the politics of representation, and the interests that these social practices serve.

The type of criticism I have been describing in relation to the ethnographer-as-critic is suggested by Teresa Ebert's definition of critique. She writes:

> Critique, in other words, is that knowledge-practice that his-torically situates the conditions of possibility of what empirically exists under patriarchal-imperialist-capitalist labor relations and, more importantly, points to what is suppressed by the empirically existing: what *could be* (instead of what actually *is*). Critique indicates that what "is" is not necessarily the real/true but rather only the existing actuality which is transformable. The role of critique in postcolonialism and, what I call, resistance postmodern

feminism is exactly this: the production of historical knowledges that mark the transformability of existing social arrangements and the possibility of a different social organization—an organization free from exploitation. Quite simply then, critique is a mode of knowing that inquires into what is not said, into the silences and the suppressed or missing, in order to uncover the concealed operations of power and underlying socio-economic relations connecting the myriad details and seemingly disparate events and representations of our lives. It shows how the seemingly disconnected zones of culture—including the privileges of Western intellectuals and the suffering of subalterns—are in fact linked through the highly differentiated and dispersed operation of a systematic logic of exploitation and international division of labor informing all practices in societies globally under imperialist late-capitalism. In sum, materialist critique disrupts that which represents itself as what is, as natural, as inevitable, as the way things are, and exposes the way "what is" is historically and socially produced out of social contradictions and how it supports inequality. Critique enables us to not only *explain* how class, race, gender and imperialist oppression operate so we can change it, but also to collectively build the emancipatory subjectivities we need to carry out the revolutionary struggle. (1994, pp. 24-25)

Ebert finds evidence of such a notion of critique in the autobiographical history of Rigoberta Menchú, in terms of the writer's critique of the class and labor relations of colonialism. As ethnographers, we must be cautious not to overlook the relationship among relations of production and the politics of colonialism. We do not need to indulge ourselves in reporting or representing in a semiotic-chic manner, reassured by the authorial signatures of Foucault, Lacan, or Baudrillard, on the colonized or postcolonized other; rather, we need more concerted attempts at rupturing the circuits of economic exploitation with which we, as researchers, are often unwittingly complicitious.

Criticism must move beyond an epistemological maping of the world but towards its transformation. Arnold Krupat's concept of radical cosmopolitanism "doesn't quite ask people simply to discard ethnic and local attachments for more global ones, but, rather. . .to try to see how the local is *already* global, the ethnic and regional *already* shot through with other and distant perspectives" (pp. 244-245).

All ethnographic writing is situated in regimes of representation and discourses of disciplinary authority. While I agree with post-structuralist theorists who argue that language is constitutive of capitalist social relations and that the language of social theory can never capture fully or transparently the vagaries and indeterminacies of social life, I would caution ethnographers against reducing social life as well as the explanatory power of critical social theory to a mere "language effect" or the logic of textualization or to a form of rhetorical tropicity in which significations merely allegorize their referents. This does not mean that, as researchers, we cease to be rhetorical critics since the rhetorical self-reflexivity of ethnographers has certainly helped to politicize ethnography (Conquergood, 1991). Dwight Conquergood is correct in arguing for a rhetorical deconstruction of the fields of authority governing communication and ethnography. I am arguing that we not substitute our texualizations of social life for political intervention into the relations of exploitation which we uncover in our research. Consequently, I am calling for a rethinking of the role of the ethnographer along lines of a neo-Marxist politico-ethico intervention.

While new spaces of research can be mobilized within a postmodern logics of desire, we cannot simply dismantle by an act of will alone the material constraints that constrain our research. Consider, for instance, the international division of labor that makes it difficult for Western intellectuals to engage in theories global decolonization without being at the same time complicitious with Western international economic interests. Who are we when we invite the oppressed to speak for themselves? Where are we situated within this division of labor when, as economically collaborative Western intellectuals, we paternalistically encourage 'others' to define themselves. As Spivak, Ebert, and others have argued, Western intellectuals define the space for the subaltern's voice to be heard in a manner that helps to consolidate an imperialist based commercial liberalism (Ebert, 1994).

It should be remembered that when critical consciousness becomes criticism, it oscillates between a discourse of negativity and hope, between the relativization of radical doubt and a discourse of utopian dreaming: in short, between a language of subversion and one of invention. This back and forth, this *fort/da* of criticism is profoundly dialectical and as such needs to consider the way it unconsciously motivates an amnesia surrounding our construction of otherness. At the same time it needs to be clearer about the unstated political assumptions which guide it. As critical ethnographers, we must take human agency beyond the curator's display case where lost histories are contained, itemized, and made unimpeachable by the colonizer's pen and recover the meaning of identity as a form of cultural struggle, as a site of remapping and remaking historical agency within a praxis of liberation. In this way, ethography can serve both as a practical ethics and an ethics of practice that is never far removed from the frontiers of hope sought by those who still choose to struggle and to dream.

Notes

1. Some sections of this essay are expanded versions of McLaren 1991, 1994, 1995.

2. See McLaren 1987 and 1989.

3. See the review essay of these books in Marcus 1990.

References

Agger, B. 1989. *Socio(onto)logy*. Urbana: University of Illinois Press.

Anzaldúa, G. 1990. "Making Face, Making Soul: An Introduction." Pp. xv–xxviii in *Making Face, Making Sourl*, ed. Gloria Anzaldúa. San Francisco: Aunt Lute Foundation Books.

Bennett, K. P., and M. D. LeCompte. 1990. *How Schools Work*. White Plains, N.Y.: Longman.

Braidotti, Rosi. 1991. *Patterns of Dissonance: A Study of Women in Contemporary Philosophy*. New York: Routledge.

Britzman, D. 1991. *Practice makes Practice*. Albany: State University of New York Press.

Butler, J. 1990. *Gender Trouble*. London: Routledge.

Chambers, I. 1990. *Border Dialogues*. London: Routledge.

Clifford, J. 1987. "Of Other Peoples: Beyond the Salvage Paradigm." Pp. 121–30 in *Discussions in Contemporary Culture: Number One*, ed. Hal Foster. Seattle: Bay Press.

Clifford, J., and G. E. Marcus. 1986. *Writing Culture: The Poetics and Politics of Ethnography*. Berkeley and Los Angeles: University of California Press.

Clough, Patricia Ticineto. 1992. *The End(s) of Ethnography: From Realism to Social Criticism*. London: Sage Publications.

Comaroff, John, and Comaroff, Jean. 1992. *Ethnography and the Historical Imagination*. Boulder, Colorado and London, England: Westview Press.

Conquergood, Dwight. 1991. "Rethinking Ethnography: Towards a Critical Cultural Politics," *Communication Monographs*, vol. 58, pp. 179–194.

Ebert, Teresa L. 1994. "Subalternity and Feminism in the Moment of the (Post)Modern: The Materialist Re-Turn," *Alternative Orange*. Vol. 3, no. 3, Spring, pp. 22–27.

Feldman, A. 1991. *Formations of Violence: The Narrative of the Body and Political Terror in Northern Ireland*. Chicago: University of Chicago Press.

Foucault, M. 1980. "Truth and Power." Pp. 109–33 in *Power/knowledge: Selected Interviews and Other Writings, 1972–77*, ed. C. Gordon. New York: Pantheon.

Frank, A. W. 1990. "Bringing Bodies Back In: A Decade Review." *Theory, Culture, and Society* 7:131–62.

Giroux, H. A. 1988. *Schooling and the Struggle for Public Life*. Minneapolis: University of Minnesota Press.

———. 1990. "Postmodernism as Border Pedagogy: Redefining the Boundaries of Race and Ethnicity." Pp. 217–56 in *Postmodernism, Feminism, and Cultural Politics*, ed. H. A. Giroux. Albany: State University of New York Press.

Grossberg, L. 1988. *It's a Sin*. Sydney: Power Publications.

———. (forthcoming) *We gotta get out of this place*.

Hammer, R., and P. McLaren. 1991. "Reethinking the Dialectic: A Social Semiotic Perspective for Educators." *Educational Theory* 41, no. 1:23–46.

Harland, R. 1987. *Superstructuralism: The Philosophy of Structuralism and Poststructuralism*. London: Methuen.

hooks, b. 1993. "bell hooks Speaking about Paulo Freire: The Man—His Work." Pp. 146–54 in *Paulo Freire: A Critical Encounter*, ed. P. McLaren and P. Leonard. London: Routledge.

Jackson, M. 1985. *Path toward a Clearing: Radical Empiricism and Ethnographic Inquiry*. Bloomington: Indiana University Press.

John, M. E. 1989. Postcolonial Feminists in the Western Intellectual Field: Anthropologist and Native Informants? *Inscriptions* 5, 49–74.

Kincheloe, J. 1991. *Teachers as Researchers: Qualitative Inquiry as a Path to Empowerment*. London: Falmer.

Krupat, Arnold. 1991. *Ethnocriticism: Ethnography, History, Literature*. Berkeley and Lost Angeles. University of California Press.

Lather, P. 1986. "Research as Praxis." *Harvard Educational Review* 56: 257–77.

Levinas, E. 1981. *Otherwise Than Being or Beyond Essence*. Trans. A. Lingis. The Hague: Martinus Nijhoff.

Litchman, R. 1982. *The Production of Desire*. New York: Free Press.

Loriggio, F. 1990. "Anthropology, Literary Theory, and the Traditions of Modernism." Pp. 215–42 in *Modernist Anthropology: From Fieldwork to Text*, ed. M. Manganaro. Princeton: Princeton University Press.

MacCannell, D. 1994. *Empty Meeting Grounds*. London: Routledge.

Manganaro, M. 1990. "Textual Play, Power, and Cultural Critique: An Orientation to Modernist Anthropology." Pp. 3–47 in *Modernist Anthropology*, ed. M. Manganaro. Princeton: Princeton University Press.

Marcus, G. E. 1990. "Review of *Paths toward a clearing: radical empiricism, and ethnographic inquiry, Culture and truth: the remaking of social analysis*, and *Romantic motives: essays on anthropological sensibility*". *Anthropologica*, 32, 121–25.

Mascia-Lees, F. E., P. Sharpe and C. B. Cohen. 1989. "The Postmodern Turn in Anthropology: Cautions from a Feminist Perspective." *Signs* 15:7–33.

McLaren, P. 1995. *Critical Pedagogy and Predatory Culture*. London and New York: Routledge.

———. 1994. *Schooling as a Ritual Performance: Towards a Political Economy of Educational Symbols and Gestures*. London: Routledge and Kegan Paul.

———. 1989. "Schooling the Postmodern Body: Critical Pedagogy and the Politics of Engleshment." *Journal of Education* 170:53–83.

———. 1991. Field Relations and the Discourse of the Other. In W. B. Shaffir & R. A. Stebbins (Eds.), *Experiencing Fieldwork* (pp. 149–163). Newbury Park, CA: Sage.

Mihevc, J. 1989. "Interpreting the Debt Crisis." *The Ecumenist* 28:5–10.

Min-ha, T. T. 1989. *Woman, Native, Other: Writing Postcolonialism and Feminism*. Bloomington: Indiana University Press.

Min-ha, T. T. 1988. "Not You/Like You: Post-Colonial Women and the Interlocking Questions of Identity and Difference. *Inscriptions* 3/4:71–77.

———. 1987. "Of Other Peoples: Beyond the 'Savage' Paradigm." Pp. 138–41 in *Discussions in Contemporary Culture: Number One* ed. H. Foster. Seattle: Bay Press.

Parry, B. 1987. "Problems in Current Theories of Colonial Discourse." *The Oxford Literary Review* 9:27–58.

Patterson, D. 1990. "Laughter and the Alterity of Truth in Bakhtin's Aesthetics." *Social Discourse* 3:295–310.

Robbins, B. 1990. "Interdisciplinarity in Public" *Social Text* 8/9:103–18.

Rosaldo, R. 1989. *Culture and Truth: The Remaking of Social Analysis*. Boston: Beacon.

Simon, R., and D. Dippo. 1988. "On Critical Ethnography." *Anthropology and Education Quarterly* 17:195–202.

Sollers, W. 1986. *Beyond Ethnicity: Strategies of Diversity*. Bloomington, IN: Indiana University Press.

Spivak, G. 1989. "Who Claims Alaterity?" Pp. 262–92 in *Remaking History*, ed. B. Kruger and P. Mariani. Seattle: Bay Press.

———. 1990. *The Post-Colonial Critic*. London: Routledge.

Stacey, J. 1988. "Can There Be a Feminist Ethnography?" *Women's Studies International Forum* 11:21–27.

Stocking, G. W., Jr., 1985. "Romantic Motives: Essays on Anthropological Sensibility." *History of Anthropology* 6.

Torgovnick, M. 1990. *Gone Primitive: Savage Intellects, Modern Lives*. Chicago: University of Chicago Press.

Van Mannen, M. 1990. *Researching Lived Experience*. Albany: State University of New York Press.

Walkerdine, V. 1986. "Video Replay: Families, Films, and Fantasy." Pp. 167–99 in *Formations of Fantasy*, ed. V. Burgin, J. Donald, and C. Kaplan. London: Methuen.

Weedon, C. 1987. *Feminist Practice and Poststructuralist Theory*. London: Basil Blackwell.

West, C. 1990. "The New Cultural Politics of Difference." Pp. 19–36 in *Out There: Marginalization and Contemporary Culture*, ed. R. Ferguson, M. Gever, T. T. Minh-ha, and C. West. Cambridge: MIT Press.

Yarbrough, Stephen, R. 1992. *Deliberate Criticism: Toward A Postmodern Humanism*. Athens and London: The University of Georgia Press.

Young, I. M. 1990. *Justice and the Politics of Difference*. Princeton: Princeton University Press.

Young, R. 1990. *White Mythologies*. London: Routledge.

Afterword: Some Reflections on 'Empowerment'

The essays in this book provide an admirable index of current attempts to refashion educational research from a critical perspective, in ways that address challenges posed by new times to the task of determining what kinds of knowledge best serve human emancipation. In particular, they point a clearer path toward engaging educational research as a *practice* of emancipation, rather than merely an exercise in *theorizing* emancipation and emancipatory knowledge—although several of the authors here recognize limitations in efforts to date.

These essays place special emphasis on what Nicholas Burbules (Chap. 3 herein) calls research that *is* educational: research that is "less interested in the 'dissemination' of conclusions than with the shared edification of practice"; and, within this, as Peter McLaren puts it (see Chap. 15 herein), to engage researchers and researched in processes that respond directly to their understandings, situations, and concerns within cooperative, reciprocal, and mutually respectful relations.

The field of critical educational research as conceived in this book provides enormous scope for rich and varied inquiry. It also, however, harbors potential pitfalls for the unwary. One pitfall it is especially important to avoid involves the notion of *empowerment*, which, as Margaret LeCompte recognizes (see Chap. 5 herein), marks a central concern in many contemporary attempts at critical collaborative research. Certainly, if educational research is to have emancipatory force it must contribute to the empowerment of stakeholders whose emancipatory interest is compromised under existing educational arrangements. Furthermore, the relationship between emancipation and empowerment in and through educational research is complex and far from clear, and demands further investigation.

Writers laying claim to the status of critical educationists and researchers often invoke "empowerment" as some kind of educational magic bullet. It is as if merely inserting the term into educational discourse will point the way to meeting "critical" goals and overcoming existing barriers to "emancipation." In many cases little or no attempt is made to theorize *empowerment*. Indeed, it is often left undefined. Mere invocation is, seemingly, thought to suffice. Let me, in bringing this volume to a close, address this matter briefly as a signpost toward work I believe should be developed increasingly within critical educational research.

Roger Dale warns against draining vital concepts like empowerment of their original value by using them "to name the space where theoretical work is needed rather than to fill that space." Indeed, such "promiscuous use [of vital concepts] in exercises of theoretical painting by numbers" may appear to "preclude the need for more theoretical work" when, in fact, such work is sorely needed (Dale 1991, 417).

This work would need to take account of at least the following considerations.

1. Statements about "empowerment" are elliptical, in much the same way as MacCallum (1967) and Feinberg (1973) establish in the case of "freedom." Consequently, references to empowerment are often little more than slogans. Here, as with freedom and other relational social and political concepts, we do well to observe Maurice Cranston's advice to "call for the full version of all such abbreviated slogans" (1953, 12).

To paraphrase Feinberg, I would suggest that the full version of conceptually elliptical statements about empowerment will require attention to at least four variables. Adequate accounts will be required of (1) the *subject* of empowerment; (2) the power *structures* in relation to which, or in opposition to which, a person or group is becoming empowered; (3) the *processes* or "achievement" by which empowerment arguably occurs; and (4) the *ends* or *outcomes* of becoming thus empowered.

In other words, claims about empowerment must elucidate the values A through D in a schema of the form:

> *A* (the subject) is empowered in respect of *B* (some aspect of the discursive structuring of power) by/through *C* (a process or achievement) such that *D* (an end or outcome enabled by empowerment) may ensue.

2. Substantive claims about empowerment, therefore, presuppose some theory of power: for example, an account of how power is *produced* within discourse, and is relational and dynamic rather than some kind of "static possession," and so on (c.f. Luke 1993). The particular theory underlying substantive claims must be discernible.

3. Empowerment is a matter of degree, and in typical cases will comprise considerably less than the full demands of utopian

emancipation. Empowerment is not a "once for all" affair. This is shown very nicely by Peter O'Connor (1993) in his account of workplace literacy and basic education in Australia. O'Connor is well aware of class interests and economic imperatives at work behind current workplace literacy initiatives. Speaking as an advocate of worker-learner interests, O'Connor claims that workplace basic education has a modest but significant role to play in contemporary education, training, and economic developments. It has *some* "empowering" potential for worker-learners. To realize this potential, however, "workplace basic education should be presented realistically as an avenue for a great many people to enhance their present skill levels, employment and life opportunities. It is not a magic elixir to cure all, but rather is an integral component of a process of presenting people with more vocational and educational choices than they currently enjoy" (O'Connor 1993, 195).

Workplace literacy and basic education will not directly or in the short run transform the social relations of production under Australian capitalism. To pretend and claim otherwise would be naive or misleading. Equally unacceptable, however, is the failure O'Connor observes among many extant initiatives in Australia to implement important (democratic) principles of adult education. These initiatives are, instead, being driven by "narrowly conceived economic and industrial agendas and directives." In the event, "approaches aimed at meeting the needs of a range of workers based either on the broader developmental or individual 'empowerment' concepts or even [on a] more restrictive vocationalism are receiving very little attention in theory or practice" (1993, 199).

At the very least, an acceptable model of workplace literacy and basic education

would provide specific task-related learning with broader social and educational objectives as its context and basis. It would also include effective learning techniques and strategies to enable workers to study efficiently and independently. The structures of workplace basic education would need to incorporate workers in critical evaluation and decision-making. Structures would reflect input [into] and control over course design, content and curricula by workers in consultation with educationists. Further, it would involve utilizing the workplace venue [and] occupational settings, needs, and materials as the content and means for [delivering]

that education. The content and outcome of learning in the workplace must extend well beyond the restrictions of the workplace
and into the world of workers' daily lives. (Ibid. 196–197).

Without in any way being the last word on worker emancipation
mediated by critical educational research and practice, such an
envisaged model of provision could be recognized and accepted as
relatively empowering—assuming the requisite conceptual and
theoretical attention to the notion of empowerment.

4.   Empowerment is not only of, for, or by "the good guys." As James
      Gee makes perfectly clear, it is because existing discursive practices
      and arrangements empower elites that empowerment of marginal
      and otherwise subordinate groups becomes a guiding value for
      critical educational research and transformative praxis. Gee
      sketches the links between "power", "discourses", "dominance", and
      "empowerment" thus:

Discourses are intimately related to the distribution of social power
and hierarchical structure in society. Control over certain discourses can lead to the acquisition of social goods (money, power,
status) in a society. These discourses empower those groups who
have the fewest conflicts with their other discourses when they
use them.... [T]o take [an] example, the discourse of literary
criticism was a standard route to success as a professor of literature.
Since it conflicted less with the other discourses of white, middle-
class men than it did with those of women, men were empowered
by it. Women were not, as they were often at cross-purposes when
engaging in it. Let us call discourses that lead to social goods in
a society "dominant discourses" and let us refer to those groups
that have the fewest conflicts when using them as "dominant
groups" (Gee 1991, 5).

The dissonance between the primary discourses of marginal and
subordinate social groups and the dominant secondary discourse(s) of
school can be seen to account for much of the systematic patterning
of academic achievement and underachievement by class, race-ethnicity,
gender, and so on. Current arrangements empower and emancipate
(from certain impediments and disadvantages) dominant groups.
"Critically" informed approaches to empowerment seek to contest these
arrangements and their associated patterns of empowerment. The fact
that elites and subalterns alike can be empowered by (differing) social

arrangements highlights the importance of specifying the variables in the empowerment ellipsis.

Recent work by Concha Delgado-Gaitan (1990) provides an excellent example of critical collaborative research based on a soundly theorized account of empowerment. The political potential of the collaborative research approach, as well as an indication of the benefits to educational theory and practice deriving from careful attention to "empowerment", are readily apparent in her account.

Delgado-Gaitan's research addresses aspects of literacy and empowerment within a model of collaboration between researcher and researched (parents and school personnel), and from a broadly "critical" perspective that owes as much to Barr et al. (1984), Bronfenbrenner (1979), Cochran and Woolever (1983), and LeVine and White (1986), as it does to a tradition identified most closely with Paulo Freire.

In *Literacy for Empowerment*, Delgado-Gaitan reports an ethnographic study involving twenty children of Mexican emigré parents in a small southern Californian city (Portillo). The study was conceived in negotiation with the local school district, with a view to benefiting the school district as well as the academic community. Delgado-Gaitan was interested in classroom literacy. The school district was concerned about "the absence of Mexican parent involvement in the schools and a paucity of information about the family home culture" (Delgado-Gaitan 1990, 28). In the background, of course, lay the undeniable and universally recognized fact of disproportionate failure by Hispanic children within the U.S. school system.

The Portillo community, research design, and theoretical framework of literacy and empowerment are all described in detail. The ethnography itself focuses on classroom literacy activities involving the twenty second and third graders (divided into "advanced" and "novice" readers); literacy-related activities in the home, and parental involvement with their children's homework; attempts by the school to ensure home-school contact by soliciting parental involvement; and the process by which parents organized themselves to understand more about their children's schools and how to better assist their children's learning, and to establish parent-school relationships in which the school met its emigré parents on more reciprocal and better informed terms.

Of particular interest is Delgado-Gaitan's account of her initial resistance to using the notion of empowerment as an analytical and explanatory construct, and her reasons for subsequently using it. Initial resistance was based on the ambiguous connotations of "empowerment". It has been used to mean the act of showing people how to work within a system from the perspective of the people in power" (2). This connotation did not fit the facts in Portillo.

Among its other connotations is one Delgado-Gaitan associates with Freire's efforts, built around literacy learning, to assist "oppressed communities in Third World countries to become socially and politically conscious about their role and status in their society," and to address their subordination through transformative cultural action. It is this sense of empowerment Delgado-Gaitan believes applies to the participants in the Portillo research collaboration, notwithstanding the fact that the outcomes to date of this intervention fall well short of radical structural change.

The crucial feature of the study design was the active role played by parents and school personnel in analyzing the data collected in classrooms and homes. Parents, for example, often felt incapable of assisting their children with homework for want of a contextualized understanding of the tasks. In many cases their "help" was counter-productive. Moreover, they experienced alienation and frustration within the process by which the schools sought to involve them. The schools, at the same time, were unaware of the extent to which their well-intended efforts to involve parents were unsuccessful. Involving both groups in analyzing and interpreting the data prompted enhanced understandings and informed responses around the shared goal of improving the literacy acquisition of Mexican emigré children.

This feature of the study contributed to parents achieving a deeper awareness of their perceived condition of social isolation, and encouraged them to organize a parent leadership group, known as COPLA (165). Within COPLA the parents worked "to determine their own meaning and goals for their role in their children's education," as well as "to reverse the unidirectional communication [and exercise of power] between home and school. *As parents participated actively in the development of goals for learning to interact in their children's schooling, they empowered themselves, their children and the teacher*" (163, 165; emphasis added). The following statements encapsulate the notion of empowerment elaborated in the study, indicating the modest yet progressive attainments it denotes:

- "Empowerment theory. . .enables us to recognize that language, culture and class position need not constrain individuals or a group from actively participating in their social environment when controlling institutions (family and school) cooperate with each other to maximize the individual's influence over his/her own life" (2).

- "The [research] purpose is to understand how one group responds to a new culture and how the seeds of effort and commitment take hold in families as it is realized that children reap the benefits of parents' help. The study [reflects their] enormous hope and the potential...accomplishment that results from their commitment to organize for the purpose of mutual support" (4).
- "[The study] depicts the caring and hopes of a group of people in a difficult situation extending beyond perceived limitations to help achieve the institutional change necessary for their children to have the opportunities they should be afforded" (4).
- "[The study traces] how the Spanish-speaking parents assisted their children in the education process, and how these parents socialized each other to maximize their potential in dealing with the school" (4–5).

The extent and "depth" of empowerment evident in processes emerging from the research thus far are indeed modest and limited— as acknowledged by Delgado-Gaitan herself in noting that "the final chapter [of the research and wider political processes] is yet to be written" (169). At the same time, a coherent concept and theory of empowerment *is* developed in the study. The conceptual ellipsis is filled out; there is *at least* the basis of a theory of power grounded in discursive processes of meaning-making; and there is a self-conscious recognition of the responsibility of the critical educational researcher not merely to profess empowerment as an ideal, but to spell out what this entails theoretically and practically, and to ensure the research design is equal to its task.

The pay-off from Delgado-Gaitan's concern to address "empowerment" critically at the level of concept and theory, within a process of seeking to enhance the material empowerment of key players in the educational process, is the construction of a strong base for further political developments involving a dialectic of cooperation between community and school. No false promises have been made, and the ground won to date is secure. Moreover, the process set in train is one that can in time reveal, and reveal *critically*, the true limits to educational empowerment—as evidenced in long-term patterns of achievement among Hispanic children relative to dominant groups in Portillo—within structures and relations immune to change by the kinds of intervention enacted to date.

Genuine "limit situations" (Freire 1970) have still to emerge and be confronted. In the meantime, Delgado-Gaitan, the Mexican families, and the school personnel in the Portillo district are left with somewhere promising to go. How will the COPLA leadership group "execute their newly assumed responsibility?" How effective will they be "in motivating parents and educators to work together?" How will the parents who assumed leadership "transmit the knowledge as they socialize others into the school culture?" How will the school district respond to parents' efforts "to involve themselves in the schools?" "How will the new practices affect school and District policy on parent participation?"

> As these questions are answered through research, the families and the schools will have a stronger basis for communicating with each other and literacy can be better understood in relation to. . . home-school communication that. . .empowers those involved in the process. (169).

There is an important dynamic to be played out between research of the kind undertaken by Delgado-Gaitan, with its central focus on *empowerment* through nonhierarchical collaboration and participation, and the work of people represented in the present volume, which explicitly invokes a critical perspective in the pursuit of *emancipation*. As Carole Edelsky and Chris Boyd observe (1993), educational research grounded in nonhierarchical collaborative and participatory practices involving multiple stakeholders can be empowering *without necessarily being emancipatory*.

Edelsky and Boyd regret the extent to which educational research—including their own—fails to do anything significant about addressing the larger structural conditions of the lives of students and parents from low-status groups. Hence, collaborative participatory educational research projects often investigate literacy, for example, but much more rarely examine "why certain groups of people cannot use their literacy to change their status in the system" (Ibid: 11). The problem is that our research tends not to look at

> how systems are more than just accumulations of individuals, not to look at how individual biographies interact with societal structures, not to look at how inequalities are both accomplished and pre-established, and not to look at *how* the world is both "of our making and beyond our making". (11)

As such, our research may well be "nonhierarchical, participatory [and] empowering of individuals", yet lack genuine emancipatory force so far as low-status, low-power groups are concerned. The question is: what is required if educational research is to be "empowering *and* emancipatory"? (Ibid: 11, 18).

The invaluable and enduring contribution made by the authors in *Critical Theory and Educational Research* is that they keep this question in focus and provide essential theoretical and practical clues toward addressing it in praxis. Unless educational research is informed by the kinds of critical theoretical commitments and perspectives evidenced in this book, its emancipatory prospects will surely remain slim.

Colin Lankshear

References

Barr, D., M. Cochran, D. Riley and M. Whitman. 1984. "Family Empowerment: An Interview." *Human Ecology Forum* 14:4–13.

Bronfenbrenner, U. 1979. "Beyond the Deficit Model in Child and Family Policy." *Teachers College Record* 81:95–104.

Cochran, M. and F. Woolever. 1983. "Beyond the Deficit Model: The Empowerment of Parents with Information and Informal Supports." Pp. 225–45 in *Changing Families*, ed. I. E. Siegel and L. P. Laosa. New York: Plenum.

Cranston, M. 1953. *Freedom: A New Analysis*. London: Longmans, Green.

Dale, R. 1991. Review of *Education and State Formation: The Rise of Educational Systems in England, France, and the U.S.A.*, by Andy Green. *Journal of Education Policy* 6:417–420.

Delgado-Gaitan, C. 1990. *Literacy for Empowerment: The Role of Parents in Children's Education*. London: Falmer Press.

Edelsky, C. and C. Boyd. 1993. "Collaborative Research." Chapter 1 in *Delicate Balances: Collaborative Research in Language Education*, ed. S. Hudelson and J. Wells Lindfors. Urbana, Ill: ACTE, 1–20.

Feinberg, J. 1973. *Social Philosophy*. Englewood Cliffs, N.J.: Prentice-Hall.

Freire, P. 1970. *Pedagogy of the Oppressed*. New York: Continuum.

Gee, J. 1991. "What is Literacy?" Pp. 3–11 in *Rewriting Literacy*, ed. C. Mitchell and K. Weiler. South Hadley, Mass.: Bergin & Garvey.

LeVine, R. and M. White. 1986. *Human Conditions: The Cultural Basis of Educational Developments*. New York: Routledge & Kegan Paul.

Luke, A. 1993. "The Body Literate: Discourse and Inscription in Early Literacy Training." *Linguistics and Education,* 4:107–129.

MacCallum, G. 1967. "Negative and Positive Freedom." *Philosophical Review* 76:312–24.

O'Connor, P. 1993. "Workplace Literacy in Australia: Competing Agendas." Chapter 10 in *Knowledge, Culture and Power:International Perspectives on Literacy as Policy and Practice,* ed. P. Freebody and A. Welch. London: Falmer Press.

Contributors

Stephen J. Ball is Professor of Sociology of Education at King's College, London. He is the author of several books, including *The Micropolitics of the School* and *Politics and Policy-making in Education*. He is currently researching the impact of market forces in education and the health service in the United Kingdom. He is a regular visitor to the United States and has presented a number of papers at American Educational Research Association meetings.

Nicholas C. Burbules is Professor of Educational Policy Studies at the University of Illinois, Urbana-Champaign. He is the current editor of the journal *Educational Theory*. His main research and teaching interests are in philosophy of education and he has published articles in *Educational Theory, Harvard Educational Review,* and *Teachers College Record,* among other journals. Much of his recent work addresses the dynamics of communication in educational settings. His book, *Dialogue in Teaching: Theory and Practice,* was published by Teachers College Press in 1993.

Phil Carspecken is the author of *Community Schooling and the Nature of Power* and *Critical Qualitative Research: Philosophical Principles, Social Theory, and Methods.* He has coordinated the Cultural Studies Program Area of the College of Education at the University of Houston for several years. His research and scholarly work has focused on social theory and its applications to qualitative methodology and educational sociology. He is currently engaged with several new manuscripts on critical qualitative methodology.

Paulo Freire currently devotes most of his time to writing and lecturing, but still teaches occasionally at the Pontificia Universidade Católica de São Paulo, and at the Universidade de Campinas in the state of São Paulo. He has written many books and articles on pedagogy for liberation, his best-known works including *Pedagogy of the Oppressed, Education for Critical Consciousness, Pedagogy in Process* and *The Politics of Education.* His most recent books are *Educação na cidade* and *Pedagogia da esperanza.* Among many honors accorded him are the UNESCO Peace Prize in 1986 and the Organization of American States Simon Rodriguez prize in education in 1992.

Moacir Gadotti is one of the closest collaborators with Paulo Freire, having worked together with him for almost 20 years. Recently, he was Chief of Cabinet when Paulo Freire was Secretary of Education of the city of São Paulo. At present, he is Professor of Education at the University of São Paulo and Director of the Paulo Freire Institute.

James M. Giarelli is Associate Professor of Philosophy and Education in the Graduate School of Education, Rutgers University. He is the editor of *Philosophy of Education 1989* and has published widely in social philosophy, ethics, and education. He serves as an associate editor of *Educational Theory* and on the editorial board of *Studies in Philosophy and Education*. He is currently completing a book, *Education and Public Philosophy*, focusing on the progressive educational journal, *The Social Frontier*.

Henry A. Giroux is Waterbury Professor of Secondary Education Pennsylvania State University. He is the author of numerous books and articles in the fields of cultural studies, sociology of education, critical theory, and critical pedagogy. Giroux's works include *Critical Pedagogy, the State, and Cultural Struggle,* and *Between Borders*, both co-edited with Peter McLaren, *Postmodern Education* and *Education Still Under Siege*; coauthored with Stanley Aronowitz, and *Living Dangerously* and *Disturbing Pleasures*.

David M. Jones currently lectures in Eastern and Western Political Thought at the National University of Singapore. He received his doctorate in political philosophy from the London School of Economics and is completing a dissertation on a Foucauldian genealogy of the urban school teacher at King's College, University of London. He has contributed to *Foucault and Education* (1990), edited by Stephen J. Ball, and has published articles in the *History of Political Thought Journal* and the *Asian Journal of Social Science*. He is currently working on a jointly authored book on *Democracy and Identity in East Asia*.

Joe Kincheloe is Professor of Education at Pennsylvania State University. He is a student of social theory, research, social foundations, and educational reform. His latest books include *Teachers as Researchers: Qualitative Inquiry as a Path to Empowerment* (Falmer); *Thirteen Questions: Reframing Education's Conversation*, with Shirley Steinberg (Peter Lang); *Toward a Critical Politics of Teacher Thinking: Mapping the Postmodern* (Bergin and Garvey); and *Toil and Trouble: Good Work, Smart Workers, and the Integration of Academic and Vocational Education* (Peter Lang).

Wendy Kohli is an Associate Professor of Education at Louisiana State University in Baton Rouge. She is the editor of *Critical Conversations in Philosophy of Education*, forthcoming from Routledge, and is the author of numerous articles on critical educational theory and practice. She has traveled widely, lecturing frequently in the former Soviet Union and Eastern Europe.

Colin Lankshear is Associate Professor in the School of Language and Literacy Education at the Queensland University of Technology, Australia. His writing focuses on the politics of literacy. Over the past decade, he has been involved with a range of development and education projects in Nicaragua, including an ongoing investigation of the links between women's literacy and children's health. He is also active in the effort to raise funds to build wells in the poor Nicaraguan hamlets of San Francisco and Portillo. He is the author of *Literacy, Schooling, and Revolution*, and is coeditor with Peter McLaren of two books: *Critical Literacy: Politics, Praxis and the Postmodern* and *Politics of Liberation: Paths from Freire*.

Margaret D. LeCompte, who received her doctorate from the University of Chicago, is Associate Professor of Sociology of Education at the University of Colorado-Boulder. In addition to her academic career, she served for five years as Director of Research and Evaluation for the Houston, Texas, public school system. Her numerous articles and book chapters include studies of dropouts, school reform and organization, cultural diversity in schools, and classroom interaction and socialization. She also has written extensively on epistemological and methodological issues in qualitative and ethnographic research. Her books include a first (1984) and second (1993) edition of *Ethnography and Qualitative Design in Educational Research*, with Judith Preissle Goetz; *The Handbook of Qualitative Research in Education* (1992) with Wendy Millroy and Judith Preissle Goetz; *The Way Schools Work: A Sociological Analysis of Education* (1990), with Kathleen Bennett; and *Giving Up on School: Teacher Burnout and Student Dropout in America* (1991) with Gary Dworkin.

Yvonna S. Lincoln is Professor and Department Head of the Educational Administration Department at Texas A & M University. She also has served on the faculties of the University of Kansas and Vanderbilt University. She is the coauthor of *Effective Evaluation* (Jossey-Bass, 1981), *Naturalistic Inquiry* (Sage, 1985), and *Fourth Generation Evaluation* (Sage, 1989); the editor of *The Handbook of Qualitative Research* (Sage, in press); and the author of numerous chapters and articles concerning the paradigm revolution and new models of research in educational inquiry. She has served as president of the American Evaluation Association, vice-president of Division J of the American Educational Research Association, and is the recipient of several national awards for her work in paradigm-building, evaluation research, and the contributions to the conduct of educational research.

Peter L. McLaren is Associate Professor of Education at the University of California, Los Angeles. Formerly Renowned Scholar in Residence at Miami University, Ohio, where he served as director of the Center for Education and Cultural Studies, his current work focuses on the formation of cultural identity and the politics of student resistance in urban settings. He is the author of *Life in Schools* and *Schooling as a Ritual Performance* and coeditor, with Peter Leonard of *Paulo Freire: A Critical Encounter*, both award-winning books. He is also coeditor, with Christine Sleeter, of *Multiculturalism and Critical Pedagogy*. He is an Associate of the Paulo Freire Institute in Sao Paulo, is a member of the Chicano Faculty Advisory Committee, U.C.L.A., and is a consultant to the Frante Grande, Buenos Aires, Argentina. His work has been published in Spanish, Catalan, Polish, Portuguese, French, Hebrew, and German. *Critical Pedagogy and Predatory Culture* (1995) is his most recent book.

Thomas Popkewitz is Professor of Curriculum and Instruction at the University of Wisconsin-Madison. His work centers on a political sociology of educational reform, education sciences, and professionalization. His book, *Paradigm and Ideology in Educational Research* (1984), which focused on the relation of social and philosophical assumptions in educational research, was cited by the American Educational Studies Association as "one of the outstanding books in education in recent years." He recently completed a study of reform in the United States, *A Political Sociology of Educational Reform*, 1991, and an eight-country study of teacher education, *Changing Patterns of Regulation*, 1993. His current work includes studies of the changing social spaces of academic research, giving attention to the relations of the state, educational sciences, and reforms to professionalize teachers. His articles and books have been translated and published in Spanish, Hungarian, Norwegian, and Russian. He has been awarded numerous fellowships and received an honorary doctorate for his contribution to scholarship in studies of educational reform and research form Umea Universitet, Sweden, 1989.

Lynda Stone is Associate Professor of Philosophy and Education at the University of North Carolina at Chapel Hill. Educated at Stanford and formerly on the faculty of the University of Hawaii, her interests include philosophy of education and cultural studies, with special emphasis on social and feminist theory, curriculum, and teaching. She is editor of *The Education Feminism Reader* (Routledge, 1993). She is currently working through a project on postmodern teaching that combines qualitative interviews with modified philosophic analysis.

Ronald G. Sultana is a lecturer in Sociology in the Department of Foundations in Education (Faculty of Education) and the Department of Sociology (Faculty of Arts) at the University of Malta and directs the Comparative Education Program. His main research interests are in the political economy of education, social movements and transformation, and comparative education, especially with reference to the effect of globalization on educational policymaking. He has taught in schools at all levels and carried out research in universities in Malta, England, France, New Zealand, and in the United States where he was a Fulbright Visiting Scholar at Stanford University. He is the author of over forty articles published in such journals as *British Journal of Sociology of Education, International Studies in Sociology of Education, Qualitative Studies in Education*, and *Research Papers in Education*. He is the editor of *Themes in Education: A Maltese Reader* (Mireva, 1991), coeditor of *Maltese Society: A Sociological Inquiry* (Mireva, 1993), and author of *Education and National Development: Historical and Critical Perspectives on Vocational Schooling in Malta* (Mireva, 1992).

Carlos Alberto Torres is Professor and Assistant Dean for Student Affairs in the Graduate School of Education, University of California at Los Angeles. Extensively published in Portuguese, Spanish, and English, his most recent books include *The Politics of Nonformal Education in Latin America* (Praeger, 1990); *The Church, Society and Hegemony: A Critical Sociology of Religion in Latin America* (Praeger, 1992); *The State, Corporatist Politics and Educational Policy-Making in Mexico* (Praeger, 1990), with Daniel A. Morales-Gomez; and *Education, Policy, and Change* (Praeger, 1992). His forthcoming book with Raymond Morrow is titled *Social Theory and Education: A Critique of Theories of Social and Cultural Reproduction* and will be published by the State University of New York Press in 1994.

Kathleen Weiler teaches in the Education Department at Tufts University. Her major research interests include feminist pedagogy and the history of women teachers. She is the author of *Women Teaching for Change* (1988) and coeditor of *Rethinking Literacy* (1991), *What Schools Can Do: Critical Pedagogy and Practice* (1992) and *Feminism and Social Justice in Education* (1993). Her work has been supported by fellowships from the Spencer Foundation, the Bunting Institute, and the National Endowment for the Humanities.

Lois Weis is Professor of Sociology of Education at the State University of New York at Buffalo. She is the author and editor of numerous books and articles, most recently *Beyond Silent Voices: Class, Race, and Gender in United States Schools*, with Michelle Fine (State University of New York Press). She is currently working on a large-scale project with Michelle Fine on capturing the voices of young adults as they construct their lives in a rapidly changing economy and set of neighborhood structures. The project is funded by the Spencer Foundation and involves interviews with 150 low-income, working-class, Latino, African-American, Asian-American, and white men and women.

Name Index

Adorno, Theodor, 67n. 3, 224, 225, 230, 241
Agger, Ben, 24, 282; and methodological pluralism, 283
Alinsky, Saul, 91, 99
Althusser, Louis, 59
Anzaldùa, Gloria, 290
Apel, Karl-Otto, 61
Appiah, Kwame Anthony, 11
Apple, Michael, 123n, 149, 150, 152; in debate over clear language, 25
Austin, J. L.: speech act theory, 187

Bakhtin, Mikhail, 129, 142; on difference, 6-7
Ball, Stephen, 16-17
Barr, D., 305
Barrow, J., 172, 173
Bartky, Sandra Lee, 147, 158n. 14
Baudrillard, Jean, 295
Bauman, Zygmunt, 7
Bennett, Tony, 4
Bentham, Jeremy, 179
Bernstein, Richard, 2, 67n. 9
Berreman, Gerald, 106
Bhabha, Homi, 15
Bisseret, N., 119
Boas, Franz, 287
Bookchin, Murray, 224
Borsa, J., 28
Boru, K., 116-17
Bourdieu, Pierre, xiv, xv, xix, 149
Boyd, Chris, 308
Braidotti, Rosi, 277, 285
Brezhnev, Leonid, 223, 226
Bronfenbrenner, U., 305
Buck-Morss, Susan, 233, 236n. 15

Burbules, Nicholas, 17-18, 67n. 2, 122, 301
Butler, Judith, xix, 133, 141, 142

Cabral, Amilcar (revolutionary leader in Africa), 266
Canghoulem, Georges, 39-40
Carr, Wilfred, 85-86
Carspecken, Phil, 18
Cherryholmes, Cleo, xv; and critical pragmatic strategy, 154
Clark, John, xix
Clifford, James, 116; and "salvage ethnography," 287-88
Clough, Patricia Ticineto, 284
Cochran, M., 305
Comaroff, Jean: on ethnography, 277-78
Comaroff, John: on ethnography, 277-78
Conquergood, Dwight, 277, 296
Corey, Stephen, 71
Covas, Márion, 269
Cranston, Maurice, 302

Dale, Michael, 53
Dale, Roger, 302
Darcy de Oliveira, Miguel: and militant research, 241
Darcy de Oliveira, Rosiska: and militant reserach, 241
Davydov, Vasily, 235n. 11
deBeauvoir, Simone: The Second Sex, 131
Deleuze, Gilles, 12, 284; on Foucault, 42, 43-44, 50; reception among Russian scholars, 234

Subject Index

absolutism, 7
absence: politics of, 113; and
    qualitative research, 113–114. *See
    also* gaps; silences
Academy of Pedagogical Sciences
    (APS): role in Soviet educational
    research, 230–33; 235n. 9
action research, 241; contributions
    of post-structuralism to, 79–80;
    democratic, 71; roots of, 71–73;
    and teacher experience, 75–76;
    uncritical, 73–74, 81–85. *See also*
    collaborative research; critical
    action research; participatory
    action research
administration: authoritarian,
    264–65; Freire on, 266–67; Freire
    on his own, 268–69
administrators: role in defining
    research projects, 73
adult education: in Australia, 303;
    in Latin America, 237–41. *See also*
    literacy training; nonformal
    education; popular education
agenda: in critical collaborative
    research, 100, 102, 106–08; sample
    Foucauldian research agenda,
    48–50
agrarian reform: and participatory
    action research, 241–42
Alliance for Progress, 242
alterity, 281
anatomo-politics, 43
androcentrism, 287
anti-essentialism, 155
anti-intellectualism, 34; in
    arguments about language clarity,
    23; and plainspeak, 4

anti-Semitism: in Soviet education
    institution, 231
applied research: and collaborative
    research, 93
arch of social dreaming, 8, 14;
    defined, 115
archeology of knowledge. *See*
    Foucault, Michel
assessment, 180; self-assessment,
    181. *See also* examinations;
    teachers, evaluation
assistentialism, 260
audience, 33; in ideology-critique, 64
authoritarianism: in school
    administration, 264–65
autobiography: in action research,
    78. *See also* oral history
autocritique: failure of, 289

Barrow report, 173–74
basic education, 303. *See also*
    literacy training
Bentham's Panopticon, 43, 44
Berlin Wall: Freire on fall of, 261
binary oppositions, 8, 272; analysis
    of homologous strings of, 185–200
biography: in action research, 78.
    See also oral history
bio-politics, 44
biopower, 163, 168, 180; explained, 164
body, 279; educational science and
    ethics of, 50; metaphors of, 280;
    in social theory, 278–80
borders, 5
braindrain: from Russia to West,
    234n. 2
Brent, London Borough of, 173–77